PROLOGUE
TO
NUREMBERG

Contributions in Legal Studies
Series Editor: *Paul L. Murphy*

Popular Influence Upon Public Policy: Petitioning in
Eighteenth-Century Virginia
Raymond C. Bailey

Fathers to Daughters: The Legal Foundations of
Female Emancipation
Peggy A. Rabkin

In Honor of Justice Douglas: A Symposium on
Individual Freedom and the Government
Robert H. Keller, Jr., editor

A Constitutional History of Habeas Corpus
William F. Duker

The American Codification Movement: A Study
of Antebellum Legal Reform
Charles M. Cook

Crime and Punishment in Revolutionary Paris
Antoinette Wills

American Legal Culture, 1908-1940
John W. Johnson

Governmental Secrecy and the Founding Fathers: A Study in
Constitutional Controls
Daniel N. Hoffman

Torture and English Law: An Administrative and
Legal History from the Plantagenets to the Stuarts
James Heath

Essays on New York Colonial Legal History
Herbert S. Johnson

The Origins of the American Business Corporation, 1784-1855:
Broadening the Concept of Public Service During Industrialization
Ronald E. Seavoy

James F. Willis

PROLOGUE TO NUREMBERG

THE POLITICS AND DIPLOMACY OF PUNISHING WAR CRIMINALS OF THE FIRST WORLD WAR

Contributions in Legal Studies,
Number 20

GREENWOOD PRESS WESTPORT, CONNECTICUT • LONDON, ENGLAND

Library of Congress Cataloging in Publication Data

Willis, James F.
    Prologue to Nuremberg.

    (Contributions in legal studies, ISSN 0147-1074;
no. 20)
    Bibliography: p.
    Includes index.
    1. War crime trials.   2.   Leipzig Trials, 1921.
3.   War crimes.   I. Title.   II. Series.
JX5433.W54   341.6′9′02684321   81-1055
ISBN 0-313-21454-9 (lib. bdg.)   AACR2

Library of Congress Catalog Card Number: 81-1055
ISBN: 0-313-21454-9
ISSN: 0147-1074

First published in 1982

Greenwood Press
A division of Congressional Information Service, Inc.
88 Post Road West, Westport, Connecticut 06881

Printed in the United States of America

10 9 8 7 6 5 4 3 2 1

CONTENTS

ILLUSTRATIONS

PREFACE

Nuremberg, the city in which the International Military Tribunal arraigned the political and military leaders of Germany's Third Reich and convicted them of war crimes at the end of the Second World War, has come to symbolize the idea of a new order in international law and relations. In that order, all individuals, regardless of military rank or governmental position, are answerable to international law for their conduct in initiating and waging war. The controversial character of this idea and the drama of the Nuremberg trials and the other war crimes trials of that era have understandably received close scrutiny from historians, international lawyers, and other students of international affairs. Indeed, hundreds of books and articles have dealt with events and issues connected with the judgment at Nuremberg.

Yet the principal precedent for Nuremberg—the effort to punish the war criminals of the First World War—has attracted relatively little attention. Certainly, the fact that the first attempt at international war crimes punishment failed explains in part the sparse research on this topic. Perhaps, more importantly, some of the essential materials for its study remained unavailable until European archives were recently opened. Using that material, this book provides the first comprehensive examination of the subject.

The primary concerns in this book are the complex interrelationships between the politics and diplomacy of the First World War and the peace settlement and the development of new concepts of international war crimes punishment. This book also describes the failure to implement international war crimes trials and traces the influences of this experience of the First World War upon decisions to institute war crimes proceedings after the Second World War and upon proposals to establish a permanent international criminal court and to agree upon the law it would interpret.

This book deals sympathetically with the idea of international war crimes trials. I accept many of the assumptions that underpin the concept of international war crimes punishment, propositions that Michael Walzer referred to as the "legalist paradigm" of international relations.[1] It is not the purpose of this book, however, to engage in extensive argument regarding those propositions, which would more properly be the subject of another kind of study. A study of the effort to punish the war criminals of the First World War must inevitably concern itself with its failure and, thus, emphasize the problems and difficulties of international war crimes trials. But that emphasis does not lead necessarily to conclusions about inherent flaws in this means of dealing with the problems of war and war crimes. The new international order that so many individuals tried to plan during the First World War has, obviously, not become a reality. But the effort to punish the war criminals of the First World War may yet come to mark the beginning of a significant and lasting evolution in international law and relations.

I would like to express my thanks to the archivists and librarians at the Beaverbrook Library, Bodleian Library of Oxford University, British Museum, Koninklijk Bibliotheek at The Hague, Library of Congress, National Archives, Public Record Office, and the libraries of Duke, Georgetown, Princeton, Yale, and Southern Arkansas universities. I would particularly like to note the help of J. Wolftring and A. P. van Nienes of the Archieven van het Ministerie van Buitenlandse Zaken at The Hague and Mme. Enaux of the Archives des Affaires Étrangères, Ministère des Affaires Étrangères at Paris.

Grants from the Woodrow Wilson Foundation, Duke University, and Southern Arkansas University made possible the research that is the basis of this study. A grant-in-aid from the American Council of Learned Societies supported additional research and revision of the manuscript. I am grateful for this aid.

During my work, several scholars gave me assistance. I am especially indebted to Professor Robert B. Walz of Southern Arkansas University who served as a mentor from the beginning; Professor Richard L. Watson, Jr., of Duke University who provided instruction and warm encouragement; Professor David Sixbey of Southern Arkansas University who supplied useful criticism; and Professor Robert H. Ferrell of Indiana University who read the manuscript and made helpful suggestions. I owe the largest debt to Professor Calvin D. Davis of Duke University who guided the research and writing of this work from its inception to its completion. His patient direction and skillful criticism in matters of style and content contributed substantially to this study.

Special acknowledgment is also due to Henk Ypma for help in translating Dutch and German documents and to Linda Davidson for typing.

I am most grateful to my wife, Rebecca, for typing and for unceasing support and encouragement and to my parents, William and Louise Willis, whose constant approval sustained me.

Permission to quote from copyrighted material has been provided by the following: From "The Four Brothers" from *Cornhuskers* by Carl Sandburg, copyright 1918 by Holt, Rinehart and Winston, Inc.; copyright 1946 by Carl Sandburg. Reprinted by permission of Harcourt Brace Jovanovich, Inc.; the Carnegie Endowment for International Peace for *The Treaties of Peace, 1919-1923*; and the Controller of Her Majesty's Stationery Office, London, for E. L. Woodward et al., *Documents on British Foreign Policy, 1919-1939*. Quotations from crown-copyright records in the Public Record Office also appear by permission of the Controller of Her Majesty's Stationery Office.

PROLOGUE TO NUREMBERG

1

ORIGINS OF A WAR AIM

The idea of establishing an international court to judge national leaders and others accused of violating international law first received the serious attention of governments during the world war of 1914 to 1918. It was one of several new approaches to the problem of achieving a more peaceful world that emerged in response to the catastrophe of that war. The demand for trials by courts led to a seminal episode in the history of international war crimes punishments. Virtually without historical parallel, these proceedings might have produced a veritable revolution in international law and relations if they had not been largely stillborn.

It should not be surprising that, like many revolutionary developments, this one had incongruous origins in a complex interplay of disparate motives and influences. From the earliest days of the First World War, people in Allied countries urged that some enemy soldiers and leaders, especially Kaiser Wilhelm II of Germany, should be brought before international tribunals after the war and punished as war criminals. Initial demands for such prosecutions came out of indignation over the ruthless German invasion of neutral Belgium, an act that some people feared would destroy advances so recently made at the Hague Peace Conferences and elsewhere in the development of international law as a deterrent to international violence. Although they often violated international law themselves, Allied governments during the first year of the war encouraged, through propaganda about atrocities and other actions, vengeful hatred and desire for punishments of their enemies. The French government remained silent about postwar plans but prosecuted captured German soldiers for battlefield atrocities. The British government publicly announced intention of bringing guilty Germans to trial at the end of the war. Although war crimes trials had never been part of a major peace settlement, and no firm legal precedent existed, there was sentiment in Britain not only to crush German militarism but to seek new ways of organizing permanent peace in the world. Certainly, one of the most important factors stimulating the idea of international war crimes punishment was the dream of ending war and its cruelties forever.

1

In the years immediately before the outbreak of the First World War, the attitude of many people toward war had changed. A liberal peace movement of considerable influence flourished during the two decades before 1914. Peace societies were organized in all Western nations, and international groups devoted to peace, such as the Interparliamentary Union and the Universal Peace Congress, attracted support. Numerous books, particularly Ivan S. Bloch's *The Future of War*, persuaded a wide audience that war would soon become only a memory. Hoping to hasten the coming peace, Alfred Nobel established a prize for individuals who contributed to the ending of war. The peace movement spread the ancient idea that war, with all its destruction and suffering, was a monstrous evil; it proclaimed as well a modern idea, prominent since the Enlightenment of the eighteenth century, that men of reason could devise reforms to restrict or even abolish war. The solution to war championed most often by peace spokesmen was the strengthening of international law.

The dream of eventually eliminating war seemed in some respects realistic. Europe had lived in comparative peace for almost a century and had many common bonds of culture, religion, education, economics, and politics. Of course, occasional diplomatic and military confrontations occurred as the continent gradually became divided between two opposing alignments of states. Wars, too, occurred, most of them outside Europe, in this age of imperialism when governments clashed in the struggle for colonies or spheres of influence. The rulers of Europe—kings, ministers, generals, and others, proud of a warrior lineage—continued to play the great game of world politics in the traditional manner, viewing war as a function of statecraft, a ruler's rightful prerogative whenever *raison d'état* required. But these leaders were also influenced by the growing sentiment against war. Sometimes they made unusual gestures in support of peace. Tsar Nicholas II of Russia greatly raised the hopes of the peace movement when he took the lead in calling for disarmament and the convening of peace conferences at The Hague in 1899 and 1907.[1]

These meetings at The Hague appeared to mark a turning point in efforts to bring war under the rule of international law. These great conferences, with delegates of most of the world's governments in attendance, made little progress toward limiting armaments but produced numerous agreements about laws and regulations for making war. Governments never considered giving up the legal right to declare war upon occasions of their own choosing, but the establishment of a Permanent Court of Arbitration and a Convention for the Pacific Settlement of Disputes seemed to bring closer the time when governments would use judicial means to resolve differences rather than seek a decision by force of arms.

The greatest advances at the Hague Conferences were made in humanizing the conduct of war through the laws of war. Customs restricting unnecessary violence on the field of battle had existed for centuries, and much progress in codification of these rules had already occurred with the appearance of national military manuals, the first one having been issued by the government of the United States for guidance of the Union armies during the Civil War. The several Geneva Conferences, beginning in 1864, had adopted conventions on care of wounded and protection of medical facilities and personnel. Other meetings at Saint Petersburg and Brussels also had contributed to more precise formulation of restrictions in the conduct of war. At The Hague, for the first time, governments adopted comprehensive international agreements on the laws of war. The two Hague Conventions on the Laws and Customs of War on Land of 1899 and 1907 contained numerous provisions to forbid actions such as the bombardment of undefended towns, the use of poison and other weapons causing superfluous injuries, the declaration of no quarter, the improper use of a flag of truce, the destruction of enemy property, the abuse of authority over enemy civilians by an occupying army, the mistreatment of prisoners of war, and attacks on soldiers who had laid down their arms. Several special declarations were also adopted in 1899 and 1907 to ban dumdum bullets, to prohibit projectiles containing asphyxiating gases, and to forbid aerial bombs launched "from balloons or by other new methods of similar nature." The Convention on the Rights and Duties of Neutral Powers and Persons in War on Land of 1907 gave certain protections to neutrals, including a guarantee of the inviolability of the territory of a neutral state. Several restrictions were placed on naval warfare, which the London Conference of 1909 subsequently expanded into a code of maritime warfare. That code was, however, never ratified, and a few governments failed to adhere to the Hague conventions. Since many provisions merely restated long-established custom, some jurists considered them to be, nonetheless, legally binding.

Because of this defect and other problems of ambiguity and omission, no one regarded the Hague conventions as perfected. The doctrines of military necessity and reprisal, which permitted exceptions to strict observance of the laws of war to secure an object of war or to retaliate against an enemy, left room for interpretation and circumvention. Then there was the problem of enforcement. Article three of the Convention on the Laws and Customs of War on Land of 1907 made belligerent states responsible for acts of their armed forces and "liable to pay compensation" for violations. Punishment of individual soldiers, it was understood, would be left, as in the past, to military laws and courts of each government. No thought was given at The Hague to an international criminal court. The conference in 1907 did agree to an International Prize Court to ajudicate disputes arising over capture of merchant ships and cargoes in war at sea, but this tribunal was never actually established. In this instance, as in many other matters, governments were reluctant to consider restrictions of their sovereignty. This fundamental problem limited the extent and effectiveness of all reforms adopted at The Hague. These measures in reality led to few immediate changes in the conduct of relations between states or in the perceptions of leaders and soldiers of their responsibilities in matters of war and peace.

Many people believed that these achievements represented merely the first stage of a gradual evolution. Although arbitration had not been made obligatory, several governments employed it in dealing with relatively minor disputes in subsequent years. The merits of arbitration would eventually be proved, its supporters believed. The Third Hague Peace Conference, scheduled to meet in 1915, was expected to advance its use. There was confidence that if war should occur in the meantime the laws of war would have a restraining influence. Later Hague Conferences, reformers believed, would lessen the anarchy in world politics and establish a more peaceful international community where the rule of law would prevail.[2]

2

War suddenly broke out in Europe in August 1914. From the first, it was ruthlessly waged, and the Hague conventions were often flagrantly violated. A crisis in the Balkans, originally involving only Austria-Hungary and Serbia, developed into a general confrontation between the major alignments of states: the Central Powers, Germany and Austria-Hungary, lined up against the Allied Powers, Russia, France, and Great Britain. In one of the first actions of the war, Germany attacked Belgium, disregarding both a treaty guaranteeing that country's neutrality and the Hague convention on inviolability of neutral territory. At the same time, there were reports of German atrocities and violations of the laws of war in Belgium.

The war caused disillusionment; at the same time, it inspired determination to save mankind from other such catastrophes. With Western civilization seemingly crashing down, liberal reformers, like the British writer H. G. Wells, came to believe that this war must end war, and would, if it could be made the occasion for more thoroughgoing measures than those adopted at The Hague. What seemed to be required now, and what the breakdown presented an opportunity to achieve, was not an evolutionary but a revolutionary transformation of world politics.

From the earliest days of the war, numerous individuals and groups, especially in Britain, discussed new and radical schemes for reorganization of the international system. Permanent international institutions were needed, they agreed, through which the nations could establish the rule of law, prevent unwarranted use of force, and accommodate just demands for change. From such discussions came the idea for a League of Nations. Some of the men who first urged creation of a League, for example, G. Lowes Dickinson who coined the name, wanted to end the war immediately through a compromise peace. Other reformers believed the Germans must first be defeated before they could become fit members of new organizations to maintain world peace.[3]

From the advocates of a new world order came the concept of international punishment for war crimes. All of these proposals reflected varying views of the origins of war and of the nature of international violence. To those persons who thought that international conflict arose because of the aggressive and barbarous character of particular societies and leaders, rather than because of a defective structure of the system of sovereign states, it seemed that institutions were needed to deal with aggressors who wantonly assaulted innocent neighbors.[4] Among the institutions frequently proposed were international tribunals to judge guilty leaders and others, in much the same way that national communities dealt with ordinary criminals. The idea of a world community acting to bring guilty individuals to justice had wide appeal, perhaps, because it could serve the aims not only of those persons devoted to international reforms but also of those men concerned primarily with a victory for their own country.

There was little doubt in the Allied countries regarding the guilt of their enemies. The assassination by Serbian terrorists at Sarajevo of Archduke Franz Ferdinand, heir to the Austro-Hungarian monarchy, had not appeared to be an event that should have caused a general

European conflict—unless leaders bent on war wanted to use it as an excuse. In fact, as historians have subsequently shown, the Germans encouraged Austro-Hungarian officials to take strong measures against Serbia. When the leaders of Austria-Hungary did so, they produced a crisis they could not manage. There were attempts to reverse the course of events toward war, but they were too timid and too late to have any effect. The rulers of imperial Germany, including the kaiser and his chancellor, Theobald von Bethmann Hollweg, consciously risked, and may actually have sought, war. They wanted to end the diplomatic encirclement of the Allies, achieve hegemony over Europe, clear the way to world power, and, through such a triumph, renew popular support for the conservative order inside Germany. Defensive and aggressive motives were, no doubt, mixed, but it remains undeniable that the responsibility of German leaders for the outbreak of war was very large indeed. In Allied countries, the aggression of Germany was beyond dispute. Was not the Prussian militarist tradition in the ruling circles of Germany well known? Had not such military writers as General Friedrich von Bernhardi long urged war? Did Kaiser Wilhelm II not reject Tsar Nicholas II's proposal for arbitration? Was Germany, along with Austria-Hungary, not the first state to declare war and to attack not only enemy states but neutral Belgium as well?[5] Raymond Poincaré, president of the French Republic, expressed the attitude of Allied leaders and peoples when he declared that the Germans were guilty of a "brutal and premeditated aggression which is an insolent defiance of the law of nations."[6]

The clearest proof of German purposes, people thought, was the invasion of Belgium, a small nation that offered no threat to Germany. Chancellor Bethmann Hollweg admitted to the Reichstag that the invasion was a "breach of international law." His argument that the German army had to cross Belgian territory to defend itself in a two-front war against France and Russia, whose mobilization, he claimed, had made war inevitable, convinced few people in the Allied countries. Clearly, the assault upon Belgium had been cold-bloodedly planned long before, not actually to defend German soil but to conquer France.[7] The people of Britain supported their government's decision to oppose Germany in the Kaiser's War, as British journalists first called the conflict, largely because of sympathy for Belgium. The Belgians certainly needed protection from the kaiser, who proposed to his advisers the deportation of civilians in occupied Belgium and northern France so that land could be given to "deserving N.C.O.s" and other German soldiers.[8]

It was easy to blame Wilhelm II, with his bristling moustache, piercing eyes, stern poses, addiction to military attire, spiked helmet of the

German army, and huge, almost imposingly huge, field trench coat. The kaiser cut a fearsome figure in his military uniform, boasting of his authority as the supreme war lord of Germany. He was in many ways the perfect symbol of his nation—progressive and militaristic, brilliant and unstable. He had, in the years since accession to the Hohenzollern throne, gained a reputation for aggressive, but often maladroit, diplomacy.[9] His public image was not altogether undeserved, for in secret council with his military advisers he often spoke of war, declaring himself in one such meeting on December 8, 1912, in favor of immediate war with Russia, France, and Britain.[10] Compensating from birth for a withered left hand, he was also given to belligerent utterances in public, even praising the brutal use of military force. Telling his troops, at the outset of the Boxer Rebellion, to give no quarter to the Chinese, to fight like the avenging Huns of old under Attila,[11] the kaiser himself unwittingly provided the invidious epithet—"Huns"—with which the Allies would pillory his soldiers, as they crushed Belgium during the early weeks of the First World War.

The Germans seemed to Allied citizens to have discarded concern for humanity in Belgium. Pursuing quick victory in the West, the German army used brutal tactics. Strategy called for a rapid advance to encircle Paris and roll up French forces from the rear; no delay could be permitted in crossing Belgium. This military necessity caused harsh treatment of Belgian civilians. For civilians to defend home and country was a natural impulse, but the Germans argued correctly that the laws of war required all armed opponents to be members of an organized and identifiable military unit. If civilians were to enjoy immunity from attack, they must not offer resistance. The Germans did not treat captured Belgian civilian opponents as ordinary prisoners of war but as *franc-tireurs,* persons waging unlawful war against an occupying army, and often executed them. The German army not only shot *franc-tireurs* but took hundreds of innocent civilians as hostages, an ancient practice long discarded because of its questionable morality. Claiming that they were acting in reprisal for *franc-tireur* attacks, the Germans shot many hostages.[12]

Then there was the Sack of Louvain. No event of the first days of the war produced more indignation. When the Belgian army counterattacked on August 25, Germany forces fell back to Louvain. During the night, the Germans believed, mistakenly, that they came under civilian sniper fire. In retaliation during the next two days, German troops killed more than two hundred civilians and burned parts of the old medieval city, including the library of the University of Louvain that contained a collection of irreplaceable illuminated manuscripts.[13] British Prime Minister Herbert Asquith denounced the action as "the greatest crime against civilization and culture since the Thirty Years' War—the Sack of Louvain . . . a shameless holocaust . . . lit up by blind barbarian vengeance."[14]

This misconduct of German troops appeared so widespread, with pitiable Belgian refugees reporting new incidents almost daily, that many people came to believe the highest authorities must have ordered atrocities as a terroristic tactic. Many of the tales—the indiscriminate murder of women and children, the rape and mutilation of young girls, the impalement of babies on bayonettes—were subsequently proven to be fabrications of Allied propagandists. The truth, however, was bad enough, and the Germans did not make the best case for themselves. Some events during the invasion might have been truly justified by extenuating military circumstances. German Foreign Minister Gottlieb von Jagow, nonetheless, refused to seek a neutral, impartial investigation, because he was convinced that German soldiers had committed atrocities in Belgium.[15]

Allied citizens responded by calling for punishment of Germans responsible for the outrages, and they were especially loud in their demand for punishment of the kaiser. Some people looked to history for guidance. Remembering how Napoleon Bonaparte, the last ruler who tried to conquer all of Europe, had been dealt with in 1815, they argued that the kaiser deserved similar treatment. A Russian cossack leaving for the eastern front declared that his battlecry was "William to St. Helena!"[16] The prominent British writer Frederic Harrison urged his government to announce that "St. Helena or the Devil's Island" would become the kaiser's "prison and his grave."[17] Some people wanted another place for his incarceration. French citizens in Algeria petitioned "for the privilege of acting as gaolers" for German leaders.[18] This Napoleonic precedent, mentioned so frequently in the early days of the war, was a traditional form of punishment, seldom used, except in the case of Napoleon, since the days of ancient Rome when defeated leaders were often put to death. It represented a policy of exercising victors' rights over enemies, both to punish past misdeeds and to prevent renewed threats. It was an executive action, a matter of high policy; it did not employ judicial insitutions or generally explain policy in terms of criminal law, although the Congress of Vienna in 1815 had declared that Napoleon was an outlaw, "an enemy and a disturber of the tranquility of the world . . . liable to public vengeance."[19]

In dealing with the kaiser, some people in Britain proposed to establish a radically new precedent. They urged a trial of the kaiser for violating the treaty guaranteeing Belgian neutrality. Such an extraordinary measure, building in new ways upon the work of the Hague Conferences, they thought, might establish the idea that an unprovoked war of aggression was a crime against international law for which leaders might be held personally responsible. An anonymous writer in the *Edinburgh Review* declared in October 1914:

The thinkers of Europe must combine to find a sanction for the principles of international law; must make it clear that civilization does not ultimately rest upon Might but upon Right. . . . In particular the dignity and authority of international law must be asserted by the setting up of a special tribunal to deal with the men responsible for the violation of Belgian neutrality. The invasion of Belgium was not an "act of war" but a criminal act, and the nations of the world must devise means to bring the authors of such acts to trial and punishment.[20]

Such a trial could at last give legal meaning to the medieval Christian distinction between just and unjust wars that the father of international law, Hugo Grotius, and other jurists of early modern Europe had employed to condemn wars not fought in self-defense. It would require, however, the overthrow of a strong tradition in international law that upheld the right to make war as an essential characteristic of national sovereignty and that recognized the sovereign immunity of a head of state.[21]

If there were inadequate precedents for an extraordinary trial of the kaiser for initiating war against Belgium, many people thought the kaiser might still be brought to justice, along with his generals and ordinary soldiers, for violating the well-established laws of war during the occupation of Belgium. Allied citizens called upon their governments to insist upon such punishments in making peace. The Reverend Arnold Page, dean of Peterborough Cathedral in Britain, best expressed this viewpoint, declaring in mid-September:

We may be far still from the final abolition of war, but we should not be far from the end of atrocities in war if those responsible for them in whatever rank had the risk before their eyes that they might have to suffer just penalties as common felons.[22]

A remarkably wide variety of individuals, especially in Britain, but in France and Belgium as well, expressed themselves similarly, including the prewar French ambassador to Germany, Jules Cambon, who advised his government to collect evidence so that "at the end of the war proper retribution may be exacted, viz., the trial and punishment of the guilty."[23]

A few individuals urged pursuit of evenhanded justice. Santiago Pérez Triana, a Colombian delegate to the Second Hague Peace Conference, then living in Britain, called upon the Allies not only to make as a condition of peace the handing over for trial of all enemy "commanders and officers and any other functionaries" who committed or ordered atrocities, but to "bind themselves to mete the same treatment to any transgressors of their own, should any such arise in the course of the war." Along this path, Pérez Triana believed, lay the best opportunity to achieve real change and a lasting triumph for international law.[24]

3

The initial impetus for making war crimes trials a war aim came almost entirely from leaders of public opinion outside government circles who were angered by reports of the rape of Belgium. There is no evidence that Allied leaders paid any attention at first to proposals for a trial of the kaiser or his soldiers. Allied leaders expected to fight a brief and limited war, ending before Christmas in some great decisive battle. They were convinced that a German bid to overturn the balance of power and dominate Europe had to be turned back, and their principal war aim was to inflict such a military defeat upon German arms as to prevent that threat from arising again. Peace terms would be imposed to reduce German power through territorial or economic losses.[25] Such an overwhelming defeat might in fact lead to the downfall of Wilhelm II, much as Napoleon III of France had lost his throne in the Franco-Prussian War of 1870. But war crimes trials, particularly of national leaders, had too many radical implications to be attractive to other rulers of Europe. Allied governments soon adopted policies, however, often to achieve other objectives, that increased expectations that a peace settlement would include punishments.

When the war stalemated in the West after the battle of the Marne, Allied leaders rejected the idea of negotiated, compromise peace. Such a peace, they believed, could only lead to a new war in which the Germans would again strike, perhaps with more success, to gain supremacy. The Allies resolved instead to commit every available resource to break the deadlock. Influencing opinion in neutral countries that might join the war and maintaining civilian morale at home for a long war became as important as battlefield strategy.[26] Governments began extensive propaganda campaigns to sustain and spread a sense of outrage at German "frightfulness," as the British called it. All governments began to gather, often to manufacture, and publish reports of atrocities.[27] Few reports dealt as explicitly with punishments as the first Russian publication, which declared that "one of the clauses of the treaty of peace will bring before a tribunal the principal authors of the crimes," but this purpose was always strongly implied.[28]

These endless accounts of atrocities, the worst of them almost always distortions or outright fabrications, made the war seem a conflict between civilization and barbarism. They encouraged the growth of unreasoning, chauvinistic hatreds. In France the kaiser came to be portrayed as evil incarnate, "Guillaume le Ravageur," the object of universal execration.[29] In Britain the most successful leader of efforts to gain new army recruits, the notorious Horatio Bottomley, whose popularity with the masses was unequaled, invariably referred to Wilhelm II as the "Berlin Butcher."[30] Perfectly respectable Anglican rectors also identified the German emperor as the "Beast" or "Antichrist" and called for a "Holy War." Under the influence of the powerful emotions that such symbolism evoked, the war increasingly took on the character of a modern crusade, one of whose objectives many of these men of the cloth declared must be the righteous chastisement of the guilty.[31]

The most important way in which official action encouraged thoughts of postwar prosecutions was to bring captured German soldiers to trial during the early days of the war. Although belligerents had almost invariably in past centuries inserted in peace treaties an amnesty clause for violations of the laws of war, long-established custom permitted trials of captured enemy soldiers during hostilities.[32] Immediate deterrence of battlefield atrocities was usually the purpose of such action. While rather unusual, such trials represented no break with tradition. They could not fail to stimulate demands to punish malefactors who escaped capture.

The French government took steps to try enemy soldiers, because the Germans seemed to be continuing in France the deliberate use of terror that they had begun in Belgium.[33] Violations of the laws of war undoubtedly occurred, for some soldiers are ill-disciplined in every war. The kaiser himself may have had some responsibility for such war crimes. He told at least one assembly of troops going to battle in France "to take no prisoners." But his closest friends and advisers expressed dismay over his remarks,[34] and the German army as a general rule did accept surrender of enemy soldiers. Still stories of outrage—the destruction of the Cathedral at Rheims, tales of pillage and rape, accounts of murder of prisoners—dominated the news in France. The French government in late September ordered the collection of evidence and set up military courts. A *conseil de guerre* ("court-martial") handed down the first judgment on October 2, 1914, against three German prisoners of war who were sentenced to imprisonment for pillage.[35]

Such prosecutions continued sporadically for several months, but the trial that attracted the most public notice occurred in early October. It involved the sentencing of four soldiers of the Fifty-third German Infantry Brigade, commanded by General Karl Stenger, who was reported to have ordered his troops to give no quarter to French soldiers and to kill French civilians.[36]

Frenchmen heartily approved these trials and called for action against General Stenger and others after the war. Much public discussion of future trials occurred during the spring of 1915. Fernand Engerand, a member of the National Assembly, introduced legislation in January to facilitate postwar prosecutions, winning approval from the press.[37] Various Protestant church associations, the National Council of French Women, and the Société d'économie sociale expressed support.[38] Ordinary lawyers wrote articles explaining how best to accomplish legal arraignments.[39] A majority of the specialists in international law at meetings of the Société générale des prisons in May and June 1915 urged their government to make such proceedings a condition of peace.[40] None of these authorities mentioned precise precedents for such a policy. Apparently, the French did not remember a minor incident in the Franco-Prussian War in which the Germans had demanded that the defeated French army hand over an officer to stand trial before a German court-martial.[41]

Two famous French delegates to the Hague Peace Conferences cautioned against establishment of purely French or Allied trials of Germans. Louis Renault of the University of Paris, a renowned scholar of international law, warned that attempts to require surrender of offenders through a peace treaty might fail. He doubted that any "government, even if conquered, could consent to such a clause."[42] The Baron d'Estournelles de Constant, one of the most prominent personalities of the prewar peace movement, argued, too, that trials having the appearance of victor's justice should be avoided. He urged that work begun at The Hague be carried forward by establishing a high court to provide impartial judgment of individual crimes against international law. In this way, he declared, the war would not prove fruitless but would advance the cause of peace and justice.[43]

The Germans certainly did not passively accept French trials during the war. Like the Allies, the German government compiled reports of enemy atrocities[44] but did not at first prosecute captured prisoners for prior misdeeds, even when they had a strong case. Sensitive to possible subversion of military discipline if soldiers were encouraged to question the legality of orders under international law, German authorities wanted no inconvenient precedents. They took the position that jurisdiction over enemy soldiers began only from the time they became prisoners of war.[45] To retaliate, however, for French judgments against prominent officers, including the son of the Prince of Reuss, the Germans took reprisals against French prisoners.

A cycle of reprisal and counterreprisal began. The Germans incarcerated at Spandau prison in Berlin six French officers, including the son of

French Foreign Minister Théophile Delcassé, and held them as hostages pending release of Germans convicted of war crimes. The French in turn placed innocent German officers, including sons of important personages, in similar confinement. These measures continued throughout 1915, seemingly with no end in sight.[46]

Publicly, French leaders never responded in 1914-1915 to demands for postwar punishments. The record of evidence does not reveal the reason. Perhaps their experience with German reprisals produced caution. Of course, as long as French territory was occupied, other anxieties and concerns dominated the attention of the government and the public. It is possible that for this reason the issue of war crimes trials never generated as much discussion or controversy among French political parties as it did in Britain, and French leaders did not have to state their opinions. Perhaps, as Édouard Herriot claimed, the French people simply did not respond as emotionally as the British to stories of atrocities.[47]

4

Events in Britain, rather than developments in France, had the greatest influence in bringing an official commitment to the idea of seeking postwar punishments. The British press and public worked themselves into what the famous playwright George Bernard Shaw called a "blue funk," as they sought to respond to Teutonic "frightfulness."[48] An eagerness to believe the worst was perhaps more pronounced in Britain than in other Allied countries, for the British did not experience invasion and needed other reasons to fight. British leaders proved more receptive to demands to make war crimes trials a war aim, because German violations of international law most affecting Britain threatened to determine the outcome of the war itself.

What had begun as a traditional war between clashing armies in the field during the fall of 1914 became a total war six months later,[49] seemingly with almost no sanctuary or person safe from violent assault. Science and technology had provided new weapons—the zeppelin, the U-boat, and poison gas—whose use, the Germans believed, might break the military stalemate. The Germans were no more interested than the Allies in a compromise peace. Most German leaders were determined to impose, through annexations and economic arrangements, a unity upon Europe, a vast *Mitteleuropa*, which Germany would organize and dominate after winning the war.[50] These new weapons that held out the promise of victory could not be used effectively in many instances, however, within limits of the traditional laws of war. So important was the influence of purely military considerations in shaping German policies that the German government discounted the moral outrage these weapons would cause in both enemy and neutral countries. In this regard, as in the invasion of Belgium, the Germans arrogantly placed too much faith in the potency of sheer military force, failing to recognize that such power necessarily had limits.

The Germans first launched zeppelins against Britain in January 1915. Although the kaiser initially gave orders not to bomb innocent civilians, the restraints were soon relaxed to permit wider deployment of the aircraft. The attacks never had much military value, for crude bombing techniques rarely permitted accurate strikes. The raids did damage British morale, killing 208 civilians in 1915 and terrorizing the population. Aerial assaults on cities, striking directly and openly at noncombatants, were virtually unprecedented, and they were clear violations of a Hague declaration. The Germans justified the raids as reprisals in answer to the British navy's illegal "hunger" blockade, which, they said, caused starvation among civilians. The Germans also claimed that munition plants and similar installations in cities were legitimate targets. If bombs went astray, killing civilians, the blame lay with the enemy for placing military objectives in the midst of population centers.[51]

The British were fiercely indignant. Lord John Fisher, the erratic first sea lord, wanted to shoot German prisoners of war, but other officials quickly squelched that idea.[52] There was much discussion of punishing zeppelin crews. Sir Arthur Conan Doyle, the author, demanded execution of captured airmen whose bombs had killed women and children. This idea received wide approval.[53] Most British leaders and people supported retaliation in kind. Late in the war, Allied bombers became capable of flying far inside Germany, and the Allies then bombed German cities.[54] There was a reluctance in Allied countries to champion a standard of international law in the case of aerial bombing that would deny future military advantages.

Like the Germans, British leaders accepted the imperative of victory at all costs and adopted policies in violation of international law. The British exercised greater restraint early in the war than did the Germans. Whether from moral or utilitarian concerns, the British rejected several measures that would have constituted gross violations of international law, including the sinking, without search, of all ships near the Dogger Banks, the seizure of neutral Dutch coastal islands, and the destruction of German crops by incendiary bombs or blight.[55] The British did extend the scope of naval blockade beyond previous limits, clearly in violation of international law. But they carried out these actions only gradually and often showed deference to neutral opinions and pressures. It is probable that in the long run British officials bore large responsibility for the deaths of thousands of German civilians as a result of illness brought on by malnourishment,[56] but in the short run the British blockade killed no one, while a German reprisal—the U-boat war—took the lives of innocent people.

If the Germans had possessed sufficient submarines to destroy the enemy merchant marine, greater justification of military necessity for their use might have been claimed. The U-boat campaign would have ended the war much sooner by knocking Britain out of it. But when Berlin proclaimed a war zone in February 1915 around the British Isles, in which submarines might sink enemy merchant vessels without warning and without safeguarding the lives of crew or passengers, the Germans had only twenty-one U-boats and could not seriously endanger the sea lanes. German leaders hoped in 1915 not to sink large numbers of ships but to frighten Allied seamen from sailing. The aim of the U-boat war was terrorist, with no immediate, achievable military objective. Because of its size and fragility, the submarine could not easily observe the rule of international law requiring commerce destroyers to protect enemy crews and passengers. Many citizens of neutral nations as well as belligerent personnel lost their lives from its attacks.[57]

Of all new weapons, the U-boat provoked the greatest horror and outrage and received the strongest condemnation in Britain. The British understood how potentially dangerous it was to their island empire, whose very existence depended upon control of the seas. Winston Churchill, first lord of the admiralty, and other British officials had declared, before the war, that no civilized navy would use a submarine in this way,[58] and they determined to adopt every possible measure against the U-boat.

Churchill, believing the submarine attacks illegal, decided to treat captured U-boat crews as accused war criminals. After British destroyers had sunk the U-8 and the U-12, capturing thirty-nine enemy sailors, the Board of Admiralty announced on March 8, 1915, that these prisoners would be specially confined in naval detention barracks rather than in the usual camps for prisoners of war. Possible charges might be lodged against them for attacking unarmed merchant vessels, but the Admiralty planned no immediate trials, because sufficient evidence "was not obtainable until the conclusion of peace."[59]

Churchill's action, of course, provoked renewed public discussion of postwar punishments. Popular reaction to the Admiralty action was divided. Prestigious opinion makers such as the *Times* and the *Nation* fully backed special detention and the threat to conduct trials.[60] Many prominent persons approved, including T. E. Holland, Chichele professor emeritus of international law at Oxford University.[61] Other individuals found the idea of trials repulsive and raised legal questions. Lady Maud

Selbourne, a daughter of Lord Salisbury, the former prime minister, deplored the desire for "vengeance."[62] Several eminent lawyers pointed out potential problems of jurisdiction.[63] Sir Graham Bower told the Grotius Society, an organization devoted to the study of international law, that a defense of obedience to superior orders, recently recognized in the British *Manual of Military Law*, would likely lead to acquittal of enemy sailors. Such a development would be in the best interest of Britain, he believed, for it would avoid precedents disadvantageous to British naval discipline.[64]

Many people criticized Admiralty policy after the Germans on March 20 threatened to retaliate against British prisoners.[65] There were divisions within the government. The Admiralty wanted to respond defiantly, drafting a message to the Germans condemning U-boat "offences against the law of nations" and warning that "cases will be fully investigated after the War is over, and no effort will be spared to bring home to the proper quarter the responsibility" for these acts. The Foreign Office toned down the draft, omitting much that the Admiralty wanted to say. Foreign Minister Sir Edward Grey himself disapproved the passage about postwar punishments.[66] The official reply to Germany, as revised by Grey, merely defended special detention of U-boat crews.[67]

The Germans subsequently placed thirty-nine officers from distinguished British families, including a close relative of Grey and numerous scions of the British aristocracy, in military and ordinary criminal prisons.[68] These hostages were encouraged to write home. Captain Ronald Stewart-Menzies wrote an old family friend, Lord Stamfordham, secretary to King George V, that he and ten other officers were held in the Fortress of Cologne and "treated in every way like criminals."[69] British-born wives of German nobility contacted friends in Britain, urging action to relieve the suffering of these officers.[70]

At once, there was pressure on the Admiralty to change policy. King George vehemently criticized Churchill, whom he already regarded as "irresponsible and unreliable." Lord Stamfordham conveyed the king's dismay to Churchill. The first lord was unmoved.[71] Churchill resisted efforts of the Foreign Office to comply with a German request for inspection of the conditions of imprisonment of the U-boat crews by neutral American diplomats.[72] Dissatisfied with Churchill's responses, the king protested to Prime Minister Asquith against continuation of special detention.[73]

The prime minister, at first, stood by Churchill. He agreed to American inspection but refused to abandon the policy of imprisoning U-boat crews. Probably as a result of this controversy, Asquith brought the matter to the Cabinet's attention for the first time. He informed the king on April 27 that the "general opinion of the Cabinet was still in favor of differential treatment."[74]

Asquith, however, came under increasing pressure to clarify his government's position on war crimes trials. During February and March, reports appeared of widespread brutality in German prisoner of war camps, causing anxiety in Britain. In mid-April the Germans began a new and terrible kind of warfare with a gas attack during the battle of Ypres. Some members of the Cabinet wanted to react strongly. Lord Kitchener, secretary of state for war, and the most respected and popular leader in the country, angrily presented evidence of "horrible and disgusting things" to the Cabinet. He asked for a "statement to the effect that the war would not cease until the men who had done these things were handed over to the British Government to deal with." Most members of the Cabinet undoubtedly knew that the British government in 1902 in a most unusual action had compelled the defeated Boers to agree in the Treaty of Vereeniging to exclude from amnesty certain persons accused of violating the laws of war and had subsequently condemned a Boer officer to death. But they must have doubted the Germans could be dealt with in the same way. A majority of the Cabinet refused Kitchener's proposal, according to David Lloyd George, chancellor of the exchequer, because they feared the war might be prolonged as much as five years. They thought Germany would "do anything rather than be humiliated to that extent."[75]

Nonetheless, political pressure to do something mounted, particularly from critics in Parliament. The opposition Conservative party was increasingly dissatisfied with the conduct of the war and took every opportunity to attack what they saw as Asquith's weak and ineffectual leadership. Conservative critics feared Asquith was not prosecuting the war vigorously enough, and they wanted to stiffen national resolve to destroy German power once and for all.[76] The question of punishments became one issue, among many others, in this growing controversy.

Some opponents in parliamentary debates criticized Asquith for negligence in protecting British prisoners from German abuse. One critic, Lord Robert Cecil, later one of the planners of the League of Nations, early advocated international war crimes trials and strongly pressed Asquith to threaten future prosecution of those who mistreated British prisoners of war, "whether he be Kaiser or any subordinate of his."[77] Other Conservative leaders singled out Churchill, whom they especially disliked, for criticism, because imprisonment of U-boat crews had led to reprisals against British officers. Several members of the House of Lords, whose sons or grandsons were among the thirty-nine officers, pled for a change in policy, pointedly asking if Churchill had the full support of the Cabinet. A Conservative leader, Lord Curzon, bluntly accused the first lord of having acted precipitately and independently of the Cabinet.[78] Another opposition leader, Austen Chamberlain, along with Lord Robert Cecil, offered Asquith a way out. They urged him to abandon measures against U-boat crews, for the present, to give relief to the British officers. At the same time, he should announce that post-war trials of war criminals was "an essential part of the policy of the Government."[79]

Asquith tried to deflect these attacks with assurances that he, too, was determined to bring the guilty to account. He said nothing about altering policy toward U-boat crews. But twice, on April 27 and May 5, in major debates regarding ill-treatment of British prisoners, Asquith told the House of Commons that his government was keeping careful records so that "when the proper hour comes the technical difficulties may be as few as possible and the means of convicting and punishing the offenders, whatever the appropriate mode of punishment may turn out to be, may be put in force."[80]

Asquith's statements prompted responses across the spectrum of British political opinion. The conservative *Times* "welcomed" his pledge of punishments.[81] A liberal journal, the *New Statesman*, praised the pledge's moderation, noting that Asquith was committed "if and so far as we win; but it binds him so definitely in that event as to leave German authorities under no illusions." The *New Statesman* thought the threat should cover crimes such as the Sack of Louvain. It feared the laws of war might be "buried beyond hope of resurrection" unless guilty individuals were "unambiguously punished."[82] One Labour member of Parliament protested that Asquith's declaration doomed all hope of a compromise peace.[83] Other men, especially conservative critics, thought the prime minister had not gone far enough. Some leaders of liberal opinion agreed. Austin Harrison, editor of the *English Review*, called for a specific declaration that the "Allied Powers will hold crowned heads, the Princes, Generals, Ministers, and higher officials responsible, who will be tried accordingly." Harrison declared: "We sent Napoleon to St. Helena. If the Germans kill these prisoners, we must send the Kaiser and his confederates to their deaths."[84]

This harsh sentiment secured almost universal assent in Britain a few days later when a U-boat sank the famous liner *Lusitania*, killing 1,198 civilians.[85] No event of the war aroused greater anger. Lord Robert Cecil and Lord Charles Beresford, recently retired commander of the Channel Fleet, appearing together at Chelsea Town Hall on May 14, stirred crowds to wild enthusiasm by calling for an official announcement regarding the "personal responsibility of the German Emperor and others in authority in Germany for any outrages perpetrated." Cecil said he "hoped people would not forget punishment at the end of the war" and urged citizens to "compel whatever Government might be in power to enforce this at any rate as one of the conditions of any peace we made."[86]

Soon the Conservatives had an opportunity to implement their ideas when they joined a new coalition government of national unity. To save his faltering government, under attack in mid-May over alleged shortages in munitions and difficulties in the Dardanelles campaign, Asquith negotiated with the opposition. At the insistence of the Conservatives, he dropped Churchill from the Admiralty and shuffled other offices to make room for several opposition leaders who agreed to serve in a coalition with the Liberals.[87] Cecil entered the Foreign Office as an assistant to Grey. There he immediately began work on the question of punishment. The reconstructed Cabinet also determined on a new policy on June 4.[88] Afterwards, the new first lord of the admiralty, the Conservative elder statesman Sir Arthur Balfour, announced that henceforth all U-boat crews would receive treatment "absolutely identical" to that of other prisoners of war. At the same time, as Cecil urged, Balfour declared that violations of international law could not be dealt with "in isolation, and that the general question of personal responsibility shall be reserved until the end of the war."[89]

Obviously, the end to political struggles over control of government and policy had permitted public rhetoric to cool. Balfour's announcement was no ringing pronouncement. It was in fact a withdrawal from positions taken by Churchill and Asquith. Churchill was undoubtedly removed from the Admiralty for larger reasons of policy, particularly because he was blamed for the fiasco at the Dardanelles, where the British were unable to mount a successful attack against the Turks of the Ottoman Empire, who had joined Germany in the war. His departure presented an opportunity to back down from the policy of special detention of U-boat crews. But retreat was not matched with a definite threat of postwar proceedings. Perhaps, once the critics began to share the responsibilities of power, they no longer felt the need to stiffen Asquith's resolve and preferred not to limit the options of a government they had now joined. The idea of war crimes trials, however, had not been abandoned. Several British leaders, particularly Sir Edward Grey, were already thinking of a League of Nations to prevent future aggressions, once the "Prussian militarists" were defeated. Lord Robert Cecil believed the organization of permanent peace required not only the League but international tribunals to punish the guilty.

Cecil began preparations for the day when war criminals would be arraigned. He had discovered that, contrary to Asquith's assurances, no careful record of atrocities against British prisoners was being kept.

Cecil brought together a small committee and legal staff to collect evidence. The Government Committee on the Treatment by the Enemy of British Prisoners, under supervision of Sir Robert Younger, a judge of the Chancery Division, gathered information and periodically issued public reports, which circulated as propaganda pamphlets. The organization also supplied the Cabinet with confidential materials.[90] When the war ended, the files of this committee provided the basis for deciding which German prison camp personnel the British would insist upon prosecuting.

Even such tentative official preparations for postwar trials was one indication, among many, that the First World War had taken on a revolutionary character. Many of the belligerents, especially the Germans, had adopted such extensive aims of territorial, economic, and other changes that their achievement would overturn, not restore, the traditional balance of power in Europe. From various sources and motives in some Allied countries, an extraordinary claim of another kind against the traditional order was advanced to hold enemy leaders and soldiers criminally responsible before tribunals for violations of international law. This idea had revolutionary implications. The proposal to establish international war crimes trials to enforce restrictions on the initiation and conduct of war would require radical alteration of the world's political and legal order. To do so unilaterally and only against enemies would require a victory of overwhelming proportions. The evolution of this war aim was, of course, always dependent upon such military considerations.

2

AN ALLIED WAR AIM

The support of Allied governments during the course of the First World War for postwar prosecutions was inconstant. Many people who believed such proceedings would be a significant international reform urged close and continuing cooperation in formulating plans for trials. But Allied governments did not attempt to develop an overall, common policy. They acted together on this matter only once. The Allies did issue a joint declaration in 1915 threatening to punish Turkish officials responsible for the massacre of Armenians in the Ottoman Empire. But the Russians and the French in 1916 refused to agree to a British proposal for a joint declaration regarding German violations of the laws of war. Clearly, such trials were dependent upon a crushing defeat of the enemy. Opinions frequently differed about that possibility and about the goals that would justify such a victory. Many persons remained more interested in the material objectives of war—territorial gains, economic benefits, military advantages—than in schemes of international reform. Russian and French leaders generally were prepared to make punishments a part of a program of total victory only if the principal purpose was to achieve other goals. Some British leaders agreed. Other officials in Britain, who thought it important to eliminate militarist influences in German politics, occasionally were ready to accord war crimes trials a primary place among war aims. But even in Britain official commitment to this objective fluctuated throughout the war as attitudes changed concerning the need and opportunity to achieve total victory.

1

Long before the First World War the massacre of Armenians in the Ottoman Empire had gained the attention of Europe. The Armenians, a Christian minority, followed the example of other peoples in agitating for national independence from the empire during the nineteenth century. Armenian unrest resulted in tragedy on many occasions. During the 1890s, Sultan Abdul Hamid incited Moslem religious fanatics to massacre Armenians. At that time, liberal and Christian protest forced intervention of the great powers of Europe to stop the slaughter.[1]

A "Young Turk" revolution in 1908 overthrew Abdul Hamid and inspired hope of a changed policy, but these new leaders took the opportunity presented by the First World War to resolve the Armenian problem in the most horrible fashion.[2] The Armenians became the first victims of twentieth-century genocide. Long before Adolf Hitler decreed the "final solution" of the Jewish question, the Young Turks adopted measures that led to the virtual extermination of the Armenians.

It must be conceded that the leaders of the Young Turks—the ruling triumvirate, Enver Bey, Talaat Pasha, and Djemal Pasha—had some justification for moving against the Armenians. When the Ottoman Empire joined Germany in November 1914, many Armenians hoped for an Allied victory, for they believed this outcome would offer them an opportunity for independence. Some Armenians went further, particularly in the Transcaucasus, and collaborated with advancing Russian armies. It was evident, however, that the punishment the Turks meted out to the Armenians was completely out of proportion to the offense. Subversion by some Armenians gave the Young Turks an excuse to carry out a nationalistic program designed to rid their country once and for all of a troublesome minority problem.[3]

From April to October 1915, the roads of Asia Minor were crowded with Armenian exiles, hurried along to their deaths. The Ottoman government ordered the deportation of nearly all Armenians, not merely those living near the battlefront. Women and children as well as men were marched off to the Syrian desert, and there were widespread massacres. Whether Young Turk leaders actually ordered the massacres or merely permitted them to occur remains a matter in dispute. In any case, estimates of the number of people who died from the massacres and the hardships of deportation range from two hundred thousand to one million.[4] Allied propagandists, such as Arnold Toynbee, prepared reports to spread news of this atrocity around the world.[5] After the war, revisionist studies often deprecated stories of German brutality, but western opinion about Young Turk responsibility for the fate of the Armenians did not change. Fifty years afterwards, Toynbee, then a world famous historian, recalled: "My study of the genocide that had been committed in Turkey in 1915 brought home to me the reality of Original Sin."[6]

Allied propagandists often wrongly blamed the Germans for Turkish actions.[7] Many Germans were shocked and attempted to restrain the Young Turks. The German ambassador to Constantinople, Baron Hans von Wagenheim, reported to Berlin that the Turks intended "to exterminate the Armenian race," and he made representations to Ottoman rulers. General Otto Liman von Sanders personally prevented deportations at Smyrna, an area under his army command. The German government, however, set first priority on preserving its military alliance with the Turks, and its efforts to encourage moderation were for the most part calculated not to offend the Young Turks.[8]

The Allies could respond without restraint, for they had decided to destroy the Ottoman Empire. Each of the major Allies had territorial ambitions in the Middle East, and in the spring of 1915 they signed the first of the secret treaties agreeing to dismember and to divide most of the Ottoman Empire among themselves.[9] Perhaps since this action committed the Allies to a policy of total victory, they did not hesitate to pledge punishment of Ottoman leaders involved in the Armenian massacres. While recognizing the political context of this action, one should not, however, doubt the moral outrage felt by many Allied leaders and peoples at the massacre of Armenians.

The Russian government initiated the threat against Turkish leaders. Foreign Minister Sergei Sazanov in April 1915 asked London and Paris to join in a protest against the deportations. He also proposed that the three governments declare that all of those responsible, even members of the Turkish Cabinet itself, would be held liable to personal punishment.[10] There was sincere indignation in Russia over barbarous aspects of the war. Tsar Nicholas II, for example, had ordered in February that German airmen who bombed unfortified towns should be treated "as criminals without benefit of the privileges extended to prisoners of war."[11] There were also motives beyond a concern for morality. Sazanov admitted to two principal reasons for seeking the declaration. He hoped a threat would dissuade the Turks from total extermination of the Armenians. In addition, he believed the gesture would raise Armenian morale, particularly the morale of Armenians fighting in Russian armies.[12] One might speculate that the Russians saw an opportunity to guarantee further against a negotiated peace that could block realization of Russian territorial ambitions at Constantinople and elsewhere.[13] Perhaps another factor, far more sinister, was at work. Toynbee claimed, a half century later, that the Tsarist regime cynically used the Armenian massacres to divert attention from barbarities committed by Russian troops against Jews in Poland during a disorderly retreat when Germany made a major breakthrough on the eastern front in the spring of 1915.[14]

The French government quickly supported Sazanov's proposal. Foreign Minister Delcassé completely approved and promised to work for British acceptance of the measure.[15] No doubt the French wanted to accommodate the Russians whenever possible in recognition of the burden they were bearing, for during the first half of 1915 the Russians rather than the French faced the main German offensive.[16]

The British Foreign Office, however, was reluctant to endorse the threat. Sir Edward Grey suggested that the Allied governments await the results of a request by the Katholicos, head of the Armenian Christian church, for diplomatic intervention by the United States and Italy.[17] Sir Arthur Nicolson, permanent undersecretary of state for foreign affairs, told the Russian ambassador at London that some reports indicated that Turkish action was not unprovoked.[18] Somewhat later the ambassador reported that Grey had "expressed doubts about the material efficacy of the publication of threats which could make only a small impression on Turkey."[19]

Grey changed his mind for several reasons. He knew the importance the Russians attached to raising the morale of Armenians in their armies. He saw the positive results of a unilateral British threat against Turkish leaders in early May. The Turks were holding some fifty British and French hostages at unfortified towns in Gallipoli to deter further Allied naval bombardments of these places. The British warned that Ottoman authorities would be held "personally responsible" for injuries suffered by Allied citizens. The combined representation of the American, German, and Austrian ambassadors was probably responsible for freeing the hostages, but Grey may have believed otherwise.[20] Grey may have changed his mind in response to mounting public anger in Britain about Armenian massacres, and he probably wanted to remain faithful to the British tradition of protecting Christian minorities in the Ottoman Empire.[21] Grey no doubt saw the threat of punishments as a continuation of nineteenth-century policies against Turkish atrocities. He was not learned in international law and probably never conceived of this measure as recognizing a new crime in international law. In any case, Grey eventually approved a joint Allied statement.[22]

The declaration was issued simultaneously on May 24 in London, Paris, and Petrograd. It accused the Ottoman leaders of deliberately exterminating the Armenians and specified the location where mass murders had occurred. It warned:

In view of these crimes of Turkey against humanity and civilization, the Allied governments announce publicly to the Sublime Porte that they will hold personally responsible [for] these crimes all members of the Ottoman Government and those of their agents who are implicated in such massacres.[23]

The American ambassador, Henry Morgenthau, had the task of delivering what he called "this somewhat embarrassing message" to the grand
vizier, Prince Said Halim, on June 3.[24] This declaration did not refer
to violations of international law but to crimes against civilization and
humanity. The records do not reveal whether Allied governments at
the time thought of using forms of law to prosecute Turkish leaders,
for in fact the Allies made no preparations to carry out their threat.
The phrase "crimes against humanity," however, would acquire meaning
by the end of the war as a new category of crime—the crime of exterminating an entire people.

The declaration had no effect in 1915. The Turks refused to change
policy. Prince Said Halim expressed resentment at foreign interference
in the "sovereign rights of the Turkish Government over their Armenian
subjects." He said that the Ottoman Empire merely exercised the right
of self-defense against Armenian revolutionaries acting in support of
the Allies, and the Allies, therefore, must hold themselves accountable
for the fate of the Armenians.[25] Twice more, during the fall of 1915, the
British government in parliamentary debates repeated its pledge to
punish Turkish leaders.[26] But the tragic journey of the Armenian refugees
continued through the sands of the Syrian desert.

2

Despite the failure of threats to deter either the Turks or the Germans,
the British government continued to issue more warnings than did
other Allied governments. Almost every new report of atrocities set
off another series of demands from the public for the trial of war criminals, and the government often responded. No outrage during the last
half of 1915 prompted more calls for punishment than the execution
of Nurse Edith Cavell.

Scholarly studies have rated the shooting of Nurse Cavell the "second-
ranking atrocity story of the war." She became, like the *Lusitania*, a
symbol of "Prussian savagery" and helped sustain the passion for war.[27]
The embittered British seemed to consider the fact that Miss Cavell had
violated German military law an irrelevant point. The head of a school
for training nurses in Brussels, Cavell participated in a widespread
scheme to hide Allied soldiers and to aid their escape from occupation
authorities during the fall of 1914. According to German military law,
this action was a capital offense. Cavell was arrested in August 1915,
tried by a German court-martial in October, and after she openly
confessed her activities, was sentenced to death. Despite vigorous
efforts by American and Spanish diplomats in Brussels to arrange for
clemency, German military authorities were inflexible.[28] They refused

to permit an appeal to Berlin, where the kaiser could be expected to commute the sentence. At seven o'clock on the morning of October 12, a firing squad executed Nurse Cavell. The execution was a typical German error, an example of a lack of sensitivity to world opinion that so plagued the kaiser's regime. Even those sympathetic to the German cause called it an "incredible stupidity."[29] It led to another Allied propaganda triumph and renewed demands for postwar punishments.[30]

News of the "murder of Nurse Cavell" came to Britain simultaneously with a zeppelin bombing raid against London that killed 127 civilians on October 13, and there was a paroxysm of popular hatred.[31] To blunt the many appeals for terror bombing of German cities, the dean of Canterbury, Henry Wace, urged the government to make "an indispensable condition of peace" the surrender of responsible German officials "for public execution."[32] Others added to a growing list of alleged war criminals the name of General Moritz Ferdinand von Bissing, military governor of Belgium, whom they mistakenly believed responsible for Cavell's death. The arch conservative *National Review* included among its war aims the public hanging of von Bissing "prior to any peace pourparlers."[33] Sir John Macdonell, Quain professor of comparative law at University College, London, explained how postwar punishments might be accomplished legally through clauses in a peace treaty.[34] Macdonell was later chosen to head Britain's war crimes commission, established just before the war ended, and he then secured inclusion of his proposal in the peace settlements of the First World War.

The British government repeated its warning of future punishments in response to the Cavell death, but the threat made little impression in Germany. Lord Robert Cecil told the House of Commons in October that Asquith's previous pledges applied "with two-fold force in the case of the savage murder under legal forms of a noble woman."[35] A German newspaper editor professed amusement at the "foolish boasts" of Cecil. Amazement was expressed that at a time when Allied armies were "in a worse way than ever, he [Cecil] has the impudence to look to punishments of German officers and officials which could not take place without Germany being entirely smashed."[36]

The Germans also believed Allied professions of outrage over violations of international law were disingenuous. In fact, various events had occurred during 1915 that tarnished Allied claims of moral superiority. The *Baralong* incident, a British war crime, incensed the Germans, for the sailors of this Q-ship had not only sunk the U-27 but mercilessly shot surviving members of the U-boat crew.[37] The unhealthy conditions of Serbian prisoner of war camps were notorious, and captured Austro-

Hungarian soldiers died by the thousands during the first year of the war.[38] Finally, French and British forces, seeking to prevent the complete defeat of Serbia, peacefully but illegally landed troops at Salonika in October, violating Greek neutrality. Later, the Allies threatened to intervene with force in Greece. These threats secured the triumph of Greek leaders who then brought that country into the war on the side of the Allies.[39] The Germans thought this action differed little from their own occupation of Belgium. The Germans saw Allied threats to punish war criminals as merely a hypocritical way of justifying the ambition to conquer Germany.

It was, of course, true that such trials depended upon total victory. Allied pledges of war crimes punishment waxed and waned throughout the war as hopes and prospects of victory fluctuated. During the first half of 1916, the British government discouraged talk of future trials as the Allies came near defeat. Despite complaints from members of Parliament, Lord Newton, who had replaced Lord Robert Cecil as head of the Prisoners of War Department in the Foreign Office, refused to complain about German care of prisoners.[40] This unusual moderation was not due to secret information indicating improvements for the prisoners. To the contrary, confidential reports of the "Younger Committee" to the Cabinet told of increasing deficiencies in German feeding of prisoners.[41] Within the Prisoners of War Department, Newton's assistant, Robert Vansittart, was eager to issue new threats of future punishment,[42] but his superiors did not share this view. Probably, their hesitancy was due to the real danger that the Allies might lose the war. In late 1915, Bulgaria had entered the war on the side of Germany, and despite the fact that Italy had joined the Allies, the war did not go well. During the first six months of 1916, the Germans launched a major assault at Verdun that bled France to the point of exhaustion.[43] Another reason for British reticence was a desire to arrange prisoner exchanges. Negotiation rather than intimidation began to appear to many officials as the best means of improving the lot of British prisoners.[44]

British moderation disappeared, however, in late summer when anticipation of victory rose as Rumania joined the Allies and as the British began their great offensive on the Somme. During this period of confidence, the British government began for the first time to set forth in specific detail its war aims. Almost without exception, the war aims, including the restoration of Belgium, the return of Alsace-Lorraine to France, and other territorial adjustments to weaken the Central Powers, envisioned a decisive defeat of Germany. Some officials, like Arthur Balfour, thought such terms sufficient and doubted the advisability of interfering in the internal political affairs of Germany.[45] Other British leaders, however, agreed with the analysis made the previous year by Lord Haldane, who argued that peace would not be secure without the "dethronement" of Germany's leaders and military hierarchy.[46] Lloyd George, who took over the War Office after Kitchener's death, was wildly enthusiastic about delivering a "Knock-Out Blow."[47] With such optimism, the British approached their Allies about making war crimes punishment, including a trial of the kaiser, a joint war aim. Such a policy would, of course, have the effect of reforming Germany's political system, discrediting the militarists whom most British leaders blamed for the war and its horrors.

3

The occasion for this British proposal was the execution of Captain Charles Fryatt. As commander of an unarmed cross-channel steamer, he had been captured in June. The Germans discovered that he had attempted to ram a submarine the previous year, and they charged him with being a *franc-tireur* of the sea, convicted him in a court-martial, and shot him on July 27.[48] Fryatt's execution was partly in retaliation for what the Germans considered criminal attacks on U-boats. The Germans, outraged in the fall of 1915 by the *Baralong* incident, had protested unsuccessfully to London and had warned that they would deal with illegal attacks on U-boats. The Germans contended that if U-boats were to observe rules providing for safety of crews and passengers before sinking merchant vessels, then merchant ships must not attack U-boats. But the British armed their merchantmen and ordered them to resist U-boats. Even in an unarmed ship, Fryatt had been under orders to try to ram U-boats. The Germans in prosecuting Fryatt undercut Britain in the unarmed-armed ship controversy with neutrals and struck at the heart of British defenses against the undersea war. If the German position was accepted, it would justify a policy of sinking without warning, and it would permit the trial of other captured merchant mariners. That possibility, the Germans hoped, would frighten merchant seamen and diminish resistance to U-boats.[49] Since a failure to defeat the submarine might lose the war itself, the British obviously could not allow the execution of Fryatt to go unchallenged.

The British public reacted angrily to news of Fryatt's death. The indignation was aimed directly at the kaiser, for many persons believed that only the highest authority could have sanctioned such an unusual court-martial. The shipping community quickly put pressure on the government. At Liverpool on July 30 a "League of Britons" was formed with each member pledging that in the next election he would reject any government that failed to make war crimes trials an indispensable condition of peace.[50] Merchant marine organizations sent petitions and letters to officials urging plans to shoot the kaiser and the members of the Fryatt court-martial. Sir Horace Rumbold of the Foreign Office said such sentiment "reflects the views of most of us."[51]

Prime Minister Asquith's response was swift. He told the House of Commons on July 31:

Yes, Sir, I deeply regret to say that it appears to be true that Captain Fryatt has been murdered by the Germans. His Majesty's Government have heard with the utmost indignation this atrocious crime against the law of nations and the usages of war. Coming as it does contemporaneously with the lawless cruelties to the population of Lille and other occupied districts of France, it shows that the German High Command have, under the stress of military defeat, renewed their policy of terrorism. It is impossible to guess to what further atrocities they may proceed. His Majesty's Government therefore desire to repeat emphatically that they are resolved that such crimes shall not, if they can help it, go unpunished. When the time arrives they are determined to bring to justice the criminals, whoever they may be and whatever their station. In such cases as this the man who authorizes the system under which such crimes are committed may well be the most guilty of all.[52]

Public reaction to Asquith's declaration was generally favorable. British newspapers almost without exception supported the prime minister.[53]

Many liberal reformers urged the British government to act jointly with the Allies to establish a permanent international tribunal. There was much discussion of the need to devise a truly international court, free of immediate Allied control to avoid appearances of seeking vengeance, and to reach agreements with neutral states to prevent accused war criminals from obtaining refuge after the war. The Nation questioned the wisdom of aiming so directly at the kaiser but believed in "the constitution of a Court, associated, maybe, with The Hague jurisdiction" to try the real culprits.[54] Dr. Hugh H. Bellot, who became secretary of the British government's war crimes commission in 1918, proposed convening a special postwar conference to establish a "Hague Court of Criminal Appeal," so that international criminal proceedings could become a permanent part of international relations. As secretary of the Grotius Society, he called upon the other major international law organizations, such as the American Society of International Law and the Société Française de droit international, to begin work on an agenda for such a meeting.[55]

After Asquith's announcement, British leaders considered how best to implement the policy and what other measures might be adopted to deter German misconduct. Balfour told the War Committee of the Cabinet on August 1 that upon hearing of Fryatt's execution, he was "inclined for the moment to take out a German officer, selected by lot, and shoot him." Grey and Cecil opposed any action that would strike at innocent prisoners and warned of German retaliation. Grey declared that "they wanted to get at the guilty people, and they could not do that until the end of the war." Lord Curzon, the lord privy seal, proposed confiscating all German property in Britain, and the hard-headed businessman from Glasgow, Andrew Bonar Law, leader of the Conservative party, found this idea acceptable. He said Britain might also deny the Germans trading privileges after the war or even the privilege of residence in Britain, a suggestion enthusiastically championed by the minister of munitions, Edwin Montagu, who urged immediate legislative action. Grey and Cecil and the new chancellor of the exchequer, Reginald McKenna, opposed economic retaliation because of possible damage to British economic interests and because, said Cecil, such measures "did not secure the punishment for the real culprits." Lloyd George doubted the efficacy of any direct reprisals against either property or persons. He said a "terrible reckoning" after the war was best. Asquith responded that "they had said all that already," and he ordered inquiries about the amount of German property in Britain and consultations with the Allies about a joint declaration.[56]

Grey in early August instructed British ambassadors at Paris and Petrograd to inquire whether those governments would join in an Allied declaration "to bring home to the Germans that their barbarous acts will not go unpunished."[57] Some officials in the Foreign Office were reluctant to associate Britain with the Allies because their care of German prisoners seemed inadequate. Cecil agreed that the Russians and French should not be included in any negotiations about treatment of prisoners. "But that has nothing to do," he said, "with a declaration that after the war we will try the Kaiser & his principal advisers for outrages & murder."[58]

The British believed the moment opportune for approaching France. Indignation in that country in the summer of 1916 was at a high pitch. Since April the Germans had forcibly deported at least twenty thousand, and perhaps as many as fifty thousand, men, women, and children from the cities of Lille, Roubaix, and Tourcoing. These people were taken to agricultural districts and made to work in the fields. The Germans claimed the measure was necessitated by widespread unemployment and starvation caused by the British blockade. The French heard stories of families torn apart, young girls raped, and mothers forced into prostitution. After unofficial American protests, the Germans eventually permitted some five thousand women and children to return home, but this concession did not lessen reports about the "enslavement" of their fellow citizens that poured from French propagandists.[59]

French leaders showed more interest throughout the war in economic reparations than in individual punishments, and they were unresponsive when the British asked them to participate in a joint declaration. Grey noted in mid-August that consultation with France and Russia had "led to no result." Those two powers subscribed to an announcement "in principle," but no proper formula could be worked out. The French wanted adoption of a uniform system of reprisals among the Allies against German prisoners, an idea the British found morally repugnant. Besides, they feared reprisals would provoke retaliation.[60] The French may have deliberately proposed harsh measures in the hope that the British would reject them, eliminating the possibility of a joint declaration. The French were then negotiating an agreement with Germany about prisoner of war treatment, which such a pronouncement could abort. Intervention by the king of Spain had secured the release from Spandau of Lieutenant Delcassé and other French officers during the summer of 1916. This mediation also helped the two sides reach an accord that went into effect on September 1, suspending "all judicial pronouncements against prisoners of war" until the end of the war.[61] These arrangements were not, however, publicly acknowledged.

Many Frenchmen meanwhile were insisting upon an official pledge of future prosecutions. One senator in June had introduced a measure in the National Assembly to permit French legal authorities to receive formal complaints of German crimes in occupied areas, and Fernand Engerand continued efforts in the Chamber of Deputies to secure passage of similar legislation.[62] News of Asquith's declaration sparked a larger and more widespread agitation. Many prominent political figures, including Charles Benoist, Georges Berthoulat, Maurice Barrès, and Joseph Reinach, praised the British prime minister and urged an Allied agreement not to conclude peace until Germany had surrendered guilty individuals. The president of La Ligue des droits de l'homme (The League of the Rights of Man), Ferdinand Buisson, called for establishment of a special "High International Court." Jacques Dumas, like Bellot of Britain, hoped the Allies would create a permanent international criminal jurisdiction.[63] If the Allies could not achieve these goals, said Paul Pic, professor of international law at the University of Lyon, they should still plan to conduct trials *par contumace* ("in the defendant's absence"), a respected judicial procedure in French law, which would avoid the many political, diplomatic, and legal difficulties standing in the way of postwar prosecutions.[64]

Eventually, Premier Aristide Briand was compelled to give a grudging and indirect approval to Asquith's declaration. Leo Bouyssou, a deputy from the occupied region, harassed Briand continually about what he called Asquith's announcement of "a new principle of international law." Bouyssou accused Briand of indifference toward the recent victims of deportation.[65] Finally, Briand told the Chamber of Deputies on September 14 that "the hour of reparations approaches" and "pending the moment when these criminal acts can receive their sanction it is fitting to report them to the civilized world." This statement was as near as he came to supporting Asquith. Briand immediately went on to warn the deputies against "a careless excess of optimism," which ideas of punishments implied. "It would be fatal to us," said Briand, "if we slackened our activity under pretext that victory cannot escape us."[66] Seared by the experience of Verdun, Briand believed British predictions of victory unrealistic. He did not want to raise false hopes by promising to try German war criminals. He gave Asquith no commitments when they met in late September and briefly discussed the "possibility of international sanctions."[67] Briand generally was interested only in the return of Alsace-Lorraine and reparations for damages in occupied areas.[68]

Russians also disapproved of Asquith's declarations. One Russian journalist suspected the British of trying to commit the Allies to unreasonable terms. He said that Asquith was "planning a tribunal such as sentenced to death Mary Queen of Scots and Joan of Arc." He charged that the British, who had advanced only a few hundred yards in two years on the western front, intended for the Russian army to capture the kaiser or carry on the struggle long beyond a time when an honorable and advantageous peace could be secured.[69] In Russia that demoralization had already appeared that would lead to revolution and defeat.

Setbacks on the battlefield soon caused the British to soften threats of war crimes punishments. The Somme offensive proved disastrous. On the first day of the battle, British forces suffered sixty thousand casualties, the greatest loss sustained in a single day by any army in the First World War. When the battle ended in November, almost a half million British soldiers lay dead or wounded. Lloyd George told an associate: "We are going to lose this war." Lloyd George regained his confidence when he replaced Asquith as prime minister in December. He rejected Lord Lansdowne's proposals for a negotiated peace and American offers of mediation,[70] but he issued no new threats about war crimes trials.

Even when the Germans adopted one of the most infamous policies of the war, the Allies did not threaten punishments. Beginning Octo-

ber 26, 1916, occupation authorities in Belgium began deporting civilians to Germany to use in a forced-labor program. During the next
three months, some 66,000 Belgians were arbitrarily conscripted and
transported to Germany under the harshest conditions; as a result,
1,250 of the workers lost their lives. The Germans claimed that this
measure was meant to relieve unemployment, but the real reason was
to help industry meet the High Command's orders for increased war
production. Germany seemed bent on using occupied areas as a slave
labor market, for more than one hundred thousand workers from Poland
were also conscripted. There were worldwide protests. Some German
officials were shocked, too. Only the kaiser's insistence kept Governor-
General von Bissing, who thought the action violated Hague conventions, from resigning. Pressure from neutral governments finally led
in February 1917 to an end of the deportations of Belgians, most of
whom were repatriated.[71]

The British government in 1917 virtually abandoned hope of postwar trials. In January the Germans announced that in reprisal for
Allied misuse of hospital ships to carry troops and munitions, henceforth, U-boats would sink hospital ships without warning.[72] Faced once
more with the question of reprisals, British leaders refused to adopt a
warning of future punishments. A small committee whose principal
members were Lord Curzon, Balfour, and Cecil told the War Cabinet:
"This was considered impracticable. Threats to this effect have already
been made in the case of other atrocities; but it is doubtful to what extent we may be able to put them into execution."[73] Rather than make
new threats, the British for the first time entered into negotiations with
Germany at The Hague about treatment of prisoners of war.[74]

Little more was heard in Allied countries either about prosecution
of war criminals. In France, Tancrède Martel, an international lawyer,
published a book in which he listed specific indictments against 762
individuals, including the highest leaders, from all enemy nations, but
his effort for a time attracted little attention.[75] When several French
senators in late March urged prosecution of Germans for war crimes
in the occupied regions, René Viviani, the minister of justice, cut them
off, saying, "it is necessary to conquer" before speaking of punishments.[76]

Even when Allied governments were hopeful of victory during the
first two years of the war, their warnings of future punishments served
largely as a means of waging war—moral war—against the enemy.
Few officials seem to have paid much attention to the ideas of reformers
such as Bellot, who saw international war crimes trials as one way to
achieve a true world community. Allied leaders consulted no eminent

jurists and appointed no committees to deliberate on the steps required to carry out postwar prosecutions. The failure to examine carefully the implications of this measure and to make extensive preparations subsequently proved a serious mistake. At the time, even those statesmen most interested in holding war crimes trials focused almost entirely upon the first and most necessary step—winning the war.

The year 1917 was the low point of the war for the Allies and, understandably, there was less thought of prosecuting enemies. The Russian Revolution began in March, and in November Lenin and his Bolsheviks seized power and withdrew from the war. The Allies were left to face the full brunt of German power. In the spring of 1917, German U-boats were sinking merchant ships at such a rate that utter defeat appeared probable to the Admiralty, for they knew that economic strangulation would force Britain from the war. Unable to stand the endless and senseless slaughter in the trenches, French soldiers mutinied in May. This military demoralization was checked, but France had been permanently crippled. Italian defensive positions collapsed at Caporetto in October, and Italy could have been forced out of the war, but the Germans failed to exploit this disaster to the fullest extent. Serious domestic opposition to continuing the war arose in Britain in the fall of 1917. There was much consideration, and some diplomatic maneuvering, in all Allied governments regarding possible peace negotiations with Austria-Hungary, the Ottoman Empire, and even with Germany. The only bright point in a dark scene was the entry of the United States into the conflict.[77] During 1917 it was the American people who took up the cry for war crimes punishment.

3

AMERICA AND THE KAISER

The American people had long wished to avoid war, but once they were in it, they demanded the crushing of Germany and the dictating of peace in Berlin. They took up the idea of prosecuting war criminals with enthusiasm. Americans, for many reasons, including, one must suspect, a historic enmity toward kings, were particularly insistent upon punishing Kaiser Wilhelm II. Most Americans interpreted President Woodrow Wilson's call for a war to make the world safe for democracy as a call for the overthrow of the kaiser himself. Since a democratic revolution in Russia had overturned the tsarist regime, many individuals in the Allied countries, under the influence of Wilson's inspiring rhetoric, also came to see the war as a struggle in which democratic peoples would make an example of the autocratic overlords of Germany. Wilson who at times spoke privately of the need for punishments did not, however, make that objective one of his war aims. Uppermost in his mind was the future organization of permanent peace, not the punishment of individuals for past transgressions. Ignoring popular sentiment in the United States, Wilson in fact eventually became an obstacle to Allied plans to hold war crimes trials.

1

American public opinion early became receptive to demands for war crimes punishment. Even during the period of neutrality from 1914 to 1917, the thinking of many Americans on this issue grew to resemble the attitudes of the Allied peoples. In 1914 the kaiser appeared as the chief villain in cartoons and editorials in American newspapers, for many editors blamed Wilhelm II for Germany's declarations of war.[1] Other important leaders of public opinion had similar views. Although Austria-Hungary had "initiated the war on the surface," said ex-President William Howard Taft, "William was behind it all the time."[2] The horrible conflict was the "work of *one man*," declared Joseph Hodges Choate, former ambassador to Great Britain, and he expressed the hope that the war would "put an end to this *Imperial Dynasty* and give the people of Germany a chance."[3] Men such as Taft and Choate spoke for a much larger group of Americans who were, from the beginning of the war, pro-Ally. These people had close political, cultural, and economic ties to Britain, and they naturally echoed British views about the war. Even among people not sympathetic to Britain, German violations of international law created hostility toward the kaiser's regime. Allied propagandists made the United States the target of intense campaigns. One propaganda report in particular— the Bryce Report—concerning atrocities in Belgium became especially influential because of the prestige of its principal author, Viscount James Bryce, a liberal intellectual who had been British ambassador to the United States.[4] Many citizens, including ex-President Theodore Roosevelt, vigorously urged official American protests against German violations of the Hague conventions.[5] President Wilson refused, however, for he feared such a step would impair his usefulness as a peace-maker.[6]

The thoughts of many Americans turned to war crimes punishment when submarines attacked merchant vessels in 1915 and killed citizens of the United States. After the *Lusitania* disaster, in which 128 Americans died, Theodore Roosevelt expressed a common attitude, condemning U-boat warfare as "piracy on a vaster scale of murder than old-time pirates ever practiced."[7] The editor of the Nashville *News Leader* asserted that the "Kaiser himself, the Crown Prince, the high admirals, the general staff, and the army commanders" were the "real criminals." Humanity, he declared, would not be satisfied until such men "stand in the common dock of international crime and receive the sentence which they deserve for the murder of non-combatants, the ravishing of women, and the mutilation of children."[8]

The annual meeting of the American Society of International Law in December 1915 heard Theodore S. Woolsey, former professor of international law at Yale University, suggest an innovative idea regarding trials of war criminals. He urged that offenders be turned over to "neutral hands. That is, that an international court . . . previously agreed to in treaty form" should "judge and affix the penalty to crimes" with sentences carried out by "that belligerent which happened to have the body of the delinquent in its power." Woolsey feared that "unless something like this ideal is realized, we may well despair of the future of international law as relating to war."[9]

President Wilson protested vigorously against "illegal and inhuman acts" of the U-boats and called upon Germany and Austria-Hungary to abandon this form of warfare and punish submariners who had violated the "law and principles of humanity." Wilson's strong defense of the principle of freedom of the seas, so vital to American commerce, forced the Germans on several occasions to moderate the conduct of submarine warfare.[10] But submarines were inherently subject to errors, because U-boat captains, while submerged, had difficulty determining the character of potential targets.

The torpedoing of the *Sussex* in 1916 was a mistake so exasperating to President Wilson that in private he spoke of the need for individual penalties. Frustrated in all of his mediation efforts and seemingly trapped in a series of cyclical collisions with the Germans over use of the U-boat, Wilson's patience wore thin. His close adviser on foreign affairs, Colonel Edward M. House, wrote on May 3 that he

found him set in his determination to make Germany recede from her position regarding submarines. He spoke with much feeling concerning Germany's responsibility for this world-wide calamity, and thought those guilty should have personal punishment.[11]

Colonel House was even more disgusted with the Germans than Wilson, and he thought he knew which German was most to blame for submarine warfare, Grand Admiral Alfred von Tirpitz. House said "if he got his deserts he would be hanged at the end of a yardarm like any pirate of old."[12]

Such indignation, however, never governed the making of American policy. The president unceasingly worked for a moderate, negotiated peace. Wilson reluctantly sent Germany an official protest against the deportation of the Belgians carried off to work in German factories in 1916. Wilson preferred, however, to subordinate concern for war crimes to the goal of a mediated peace.[13] Twice he sent House on peace missions to Europe, and he made public efforts to mediate the conflict. Addressing the Senate of the United States on January 22, 1917, the president appealed for "peace without victory" and pledged that the United States would participate in a new world order to preserve the peace of all nations in the future. His efforts were unavailing. Leaders in Berlin decided to seek total victory through an all-out U-boat campaign, sinking neutral as well as enemy vessels, in complete disregard of international law. This action forced Wilson to take the United States into the war against Germany in April 1917.[14]

2

After the United States went to war, many Americans came to believe in a punitive peace and personal punishment for the kaiser. As
newspaper editors examined American aims immediately after the entry
into the war, many interpreted the president's statement to Congress
that the "world must be made safe for democracy" to mean that the
kaiser must be overthrown.[15] Governmental propaganda agencies and
private rumor spread numerous atrocity stories.[16] Soon reminders were
everywhere that the purpose of the war was to punish the kaiser.
Cartoons showed a fighting Uncle Sam dragging the Hohenzollern
monarch away from a devastated town and preparing to string him
up to a convenient tree limb.[17] A Liberty Loan Drive advertisement
asked, "What Shall Be Done With the Kaiser?" and answered, "Shall
he not be made an example for all other ambitious rulers for all time?
No punishment is adequate."[18] Soldiers on troop trains drew crude
stick-man portraits of "Kaiser Bill" swinging from a gallows.[19] Even
the popular poet Carl Sandburg joined the attack. In "Four Brothers:
Notes for War Songs (November, 1917)," he found words for the
inarticulate chalk art of soldiers.

> They are hunting death,
> Death for the one-armed mastoid Kaiser.
> They are after a Hohenzollern head;
> There is no man-hunt of men remembered like this.
> The four big brothers are out to kill.
> France, Russia, Britain, America—
> The four republics are sworn brothers to kill the Kaiser.
> Yes this is the great man-hunt;
> And the sun has never seen til now
> Such a line of toothed and tusked man-killers,
> In the blue of the upper sky,
> In the green of the undersea,
> In the red of the winter dawns,
> Eating to kill,
> Sleeping to kill,
> Asked by their mothers to kill,
> Wished by four-fifths of the world to kill—
> To cut the Kaiser's throat,
> To hack the Kaiser's head,
> To hang the Kaiser on a high-horizon gibbet.[20]

Clergymen gave their sanction to this goal. They encouraged their
congregations to hate the kaiser. Many ministers saw the war as Arma-
geddon and Wilhelm II as the biblical Beast of the last days.[21] A Broad-

way show and a movie appealed to contrasting aspects of the anti-kaiser mania. A Schubert musical revue, opening in December 1917, produced a popular hit when Ed Wynn sang the comical song, "We're Going to Hang the Kaiser Under the Linden Tree" (a pun on the name of the Berlin boulevard, Unter den Linden, on which stood the Imperial Palace).[22] The film, "The Kaiser, the Beast of Berlin," on the other hand, depicted gruesome atrocities in Belgium, and its concluding scene showed Allied generals in conquered Berlin handing over a captive kaiser to King Albert of Belgium for imprisonment in Louvain.[23] Under the influence of these popular images, some citizens personally contacted governmental officials to urge that punishment of war crimes should be a war aim.[24]

American leaders generally resisted such a policy. When planning for peace was assigned to the Inquiry, its secretary, Walter Lippmann, did recommend preparation of material on the "procedure for determining violation of the laws which may give rise to claims for punishment of guilty persons. . . ," but he thought that the State Department rather than the Inquiry should study such questions of international law.[25] Secretary of State Robert Lansing ignored Lippmann's suggestion when he fixed the agenda for his advisers on international law.[26] Lansing opposed war crimes punishment. In conflicts between international law and national interests, he placed highest priority on national interests. Less than three weeks after the *Lusitania* sank, when many Americans were still raging against the Germans, Lansing privately wrote a memorandum on "Cruel and Inhuman Acts of War." In it he argued that "the practical standard of conduct is not moral or humane ideas but the necessity of the act in protecting national existence or in bringing the war to a successful conclusion."[27] Shortly afterwards, Colonel House observed that "Lansing exhibited one curious state of mind. He believes that almost any form of atrocity is permissible provided a nation's safety is involved." When House inquired, "who would determine this question," Lansing answered, "the military authorities of the nation committing the atrocities."[28] Lansing feared that punishment of war crimes could establish precedents dangerous to the defense of the United States in later crises. In addition, he believed punishment contrary to the immediate national interest of America, for such a step could hinder resistance to bolshevism. To friends who urged him to work for the kaiser's abdication and punishment, he warned that any breakdown of authority in Germany must be avoided to prevent the spread of bolshevism.[29]

House was reluctant to adopt a policy aimed at overthrowing and bringing the kaiser to trial and punishment, an attitude he pressed

upon the British. Shortly after the United States entered the conflict, the War Cabinet sent a special mission to Washington. Headed
by Arthur Balfour, who had taken over the post of foreign secretary
in Lloyd George's government, the mission was largely concerned
with technical, economic, and military cooperation. But Balfour did
reveal many Allied war aims to Wilson and House, including territorial changes that had already been the subjects of numerous secret
treaties. American leaders were not happy with such imperialistic
plans and refused any commitment to them. On war crimes trials,
House noted that in talks on May 13 Balfour "agreed to the proposal
that there should be no insistence that the makers of the war should
be punished before a settlement had been even tentatively discussed."[30]
At the same time, House and Balfour also agreed, however, that no
peace should ever be concluded with representatives of the German
military clique.[31]

Wilson's attitude toward punishing the German nation or the kaiser
was ambiguous throughout the war. His most carefully considered
statement of war aims—the Fourteen Points—did not include measures
of retribution. The proposed territorial changes based upon the principle of self-determination did include the return of Alsace-Lorraine
to France, and demands were made for reparations for damages inflicted upon Belgium and northern France. These points implied a
certain kind of punishment of Germany, and their achievement seemed
unlikely unless Germany was severely defeated. But the Fourteen
Points were essentially moderate, promising fair treatment of all countries and, most importantly, calling for a League of Nations to guarantee
the security of all nations.[32] No possible interpretation of the Fourteen Points will yield even the vaguest hint of war crimes punishment.
Wilson found atrocity stories distasteful and unnecessarily inflam-
matory,[33] and he rarely mentioned outrages in his public addresses.
Yet Wilson contributed substantially to directing public wrath toward
German leaders and the kaiser. Wilson accepted and encouraged the
prevailing view that the war was a conflict between autocracy and
democracy. He came to believe that the future peace of the world
depended upon vesting ultimate control of foreign policies in the hands
of the peoples of nations, naturally more peace loving than tradi-
tionally militaristic and imperialistic aristocracies.[34] In his wartime
speeches, he attacked Germany's "military masters," predicted the
"liberation" of the German people, and called for the "destruction of
every arbitrary power anywhere that can separately, secretly, and of
its single choice disturb the peace of the world." He rejected Vatican mediation of the war on the grounds that the word of Germany's

rulers could not be trusted sufficiently to negotiate with them. He repeatedly expressed friendly feelings toward the German people.

Wilson's war rhetoric was a tactic both to stimulate support for the war and to promote moderation by carefully distinguishing between the relatively blameless German people and their government. In offering moderate peace terms to the German people, he came close to calling for the overthrow of the kaiser's government.[35] The former ambassador to Turkey, Henry Morgenthau, gave such an interpretation of Wilson's statements to the American public. In an article entitled "Emperor William Must Go, Says Morgenthau," he declared that there could be "no end of the war" as long as the kaiser remained in power. The struggle was "one between the spirit of autocracy as represented by Emperor William and the spirit of democracy, justice, and right as typified by Woodrow Wilson." Just as Alexander II had freed the serfs of Russia and Lincoln, the slaves of America, "so Woodrow Wilson has the task of freeing the German people from the thralldom of the Hohenzollerns."[36]

Some Germans thought that one of Wilson's objectives was to secure the kaiser's abdication and trial. Wilhelm II himself complained in February 1918 to subordinates that the president had "proclaimed the removal of the Hohenzollerns as a war aim."[37] One member of the Reichstag believed Wilson's terms would include "a request . . . for the Kaiser and the Government to be brought before a war court, and for peace to be concluded at Berlin."[38]

Privately, Wilson probably did entertain such ideas. When news came of Allied successes on the western front in the late summer of 1918, there was anticipation of victory at the White House. The British liaison officer to Colonel House, Sir William Wiseman, said that the president's "personal hatred of the Kaiser, whom he has never seen," was "most amusing. The elected autocrat can see no good in the hereditary tyrant."[39] General Maurice Janin of France, who stopped in Washington on his way to assume command of Czechoslovak troops in Siberia, said that Wilson told him in mid-September that "Germany's war leaders would have to be tried in a court of justice after their defeat."[40]

When the possibility of conquering Germany became apparent in the fall of 1918, Wilson's fellow citizens took up the idea of war crimes punishment with far greater seriousness than he did. Charles H. Livermore of the World Peace Foundation drew up a list of eleven "outlaws of civilization" and insisted the peace terms include their surrender for "condign punishment." On Livermore's list were the kaiser; the crown prince; von Tirpitz; and Germany's principal military commanders, Field Marshal Paul von Hindenburg and General Erich Ludendorff; the Turkish leaders, Enver Pasha, Talaat Pasha, and Djemal Pasha; King

Ferdinand of Bulgaria; Count Stephen Tiza, former Hungarian prime minister; and Heinrich von Tschirschky, former German ambassador at Vienna.[41] Livermore was merely the most prominent and articulate of numerous persons who wrote similar letters to the editors of the *New York Times*.[42] A survey of editorials in the American press showed wide advocacy of the kaiser's abdication and exile to Saint Helena.[43] The former ambassador to Germany, James Gerard, after finishing a speaking tour around the country, said that the American people were "for more than a dictated peace. They are for the personal punishment of those responsible for this war and the horrors of it. Nothing less will satisfy them."[44]

The demand for a harsh peace, including war crimes punishments, became a domestic political issue in the United States as the war drew to an end. Mid-term congressional elections were due in November, and Wilson's Republican opponents tried to exploit fears that he would treat Germany too leniently. Roosevelt and Senator Henry Cabot Lodge of Massachusetts severely criticized Wilson for not waging the war to a "dictated peace" of "unconditional surrender."[45] Senator William E. Borah of Idaho wrote a special article entitled "No Peace With the Hohenzollerns" in which he urged sending the kaiser to Saint Helena as the "first step for permanent peace."[46] The *Outlook*, a journal with progressive Republican ties, began demanding individual penalties in late August.[47] Three weeks before the election, the Republican Club of New York City passed a resolution prepared by Nicholas Murray Butler, president of Columbia University, and other leaders that called for bringing "public criminals . . . to the bar of international justice . . . to answer personally for their crimes."[48]

This furor probably influenced Wilson to some extent when he began armistice negotiations with the new German chancellor, Prince Max of Baden, on October 6. He told a Cabinet member that public opinion "was as much a fact as a mountain and must be considered." He himself did not want an excessively punitive peace settlement, and he complained about the spirit of vengeance that had seized the American people.[49] Yet the tone of Wilson's communications with Prince Max was undeniably exacting. His diplomatic rhetoric may have been designed in part to appease angry Americans who were preparing to vote in the forthcoming elections.[50]

German misconduct during the armistice negotiations made Wilson momentarily consider adopting war crimes punishment. He received reports of deliberate, wanton destruction during German withdrawals from northern France and Belgium. Submarine attacks continued. The Japanese liner *Hirano Maru* was sunk on October 4 with 292 persons killed. The Irish mail steamer *Leinster* went down on October 10 with a reported loss of more than four hundred people.[51] After a conversation with the president on October 13, Sir Eric Geddes, first lord of the admiralty, reported to London that Wilson was "inclined to take Germany to task for recent atrocities such as the sinking of the 'Leinster' . . . ," and he added that the president might "also take up questions of personal guilt for such murders as Fryatt and Cavell."[52] Wilson did put Germany on notice. He threatened Prince Max with "no armistice so long as the armed forces of Germany continue the illegal and inhuman practices which they still persist in,"[53] but Wilson did not demand punishments for prior misdeeds.

Wilson, nonetheless, gave the appearance of wanting to depose the kaiser. His inquiries to Prince Max about German democratization grew stronger. In his third and final armistice note of October 23, the president declared that recent German constitutional changes were inadequate. He warned that if the American government had "to deal with the military masters and the monarchial autocrats . . . now, or . . . later . . . it must demand, not peace negotiations, but surrender."[54] Wilhelm II told an aide: "Read it! It aims directly at the overthrow of my house, at the complete overthrow of monarchy."[55]

Wilson probably did not aim at that objective. He told some Cabinet members on October 21 that the feverish hankering for "blood" and for imprisoning the kaiser on Saint Helena was "ridiculous." He expressed fear of bolshevism spreading to Germany and asked: "Had you rather have the Kaiser or the Bolsheviks?" He asserted that the German ruler "was needed to keep it down—to keep some order."[56] One might speculate that Wilson wanted to impress upon the Germans his desire for a constitutional monarchy, resembling, perhaps, the British system.

The Germans, however, were convinced that Wilson wanted abdication as a condition of peace. Foreign Minister Dr. Wilhelm Solf believed that the president wished to secure the kaiser's removal as a symbolic act to check Allied and American critics and to encourage their acceptance of moderate peace terms. Acting upon this analysis, Prince Max unsuccessfully tried to persuade Wilhelm II to retire voluntarily.[57] Revolution achieved what Prince Max could not. Resentment toward the monarchy grew as defeat impended. After naval and military mutinies and outbreaks of proletarian violence, German Socialist leaders forced Prince Max to turn power over to them. In an increasingly confused situation, a republic was proclaimed on November 9, and the next day Wilhelm II fled from his army headquarters at Spa in Belgium to the Netherlands. The new government agreed to an armistice on November 11, and the fighting stopped.[58]

3

The end of the war and the kaiser's abdication did not end American interest in punishing war criminals. If anything, it grew more intense. Armistice celebrations were marked by both joy and hate. No parade in New York City was complete without an effigy of "Kaiser Bill" hanging by the neck from a pole or at rest in a coffin. One group of men even tried to hold a mock trial with the assistance of a night court judge. James Gerard brought the happy day to a close with a speech between acts at the Hippodrome in which he called for Wilhelm II's "extradition" from the Netherlands, so that he could be tried in Britain on a charge of murder for ordering the sinking of the *Lusitania*.[59] In the days that followed, many other persons and groups, including the governors of several states, took up the demand for a trial of German leaders.[60] Well-known Americans, such as Frederick Penrose, former ambassador to Vienna; James M. Beck, former attorney general; and John Hays Hammond, the famous engineer, publicly announced their support for trying the kaiser.[61] Authorities on the laws of war, among them Major General William Crozier, American delegate to the First Hague Peace Conference, and Asa Bird Gardiner, former professor of law at West Point, advocated war crimes trials in articles explaining the legal issues to the American public.[62] Americans were reminded that a principal precedent for such proceedings had been established when the government of the United States had hanged a Confederate officer, Captain Henry Wirz, following the end of the Civil War, for having murdered Union soldiers at the infamous prisoner of war camp at Andersonville, Georgia.[63] Privately, Theodore Roosevelt and his former secretary of war and state, Elihu Root, expressed approval of such measures. Many individuals making these demands were conservative opponents of President Wilson, and their demands for war crimes trials, apart from sincere concern about justice, complemented their desire for a harsh, punitive peace settlement.[64] They remained suspicious of the liberal, internationalist program of the president. But radical, liberal opinion also saw merit in individual penalties. The *Dial* believed that useful psychological results might be obtained. One great barrier to a moderate, internationalist peace was mass hatred of Germany. This obstacle might be removed "by signal penalties inflicted on those who can be held personally responsible for the war," deliberately making the kaiser and others serve as "scapegoats" upon whom the masses could discharge their pent-up hatred.[65]

Wilson's attitude and policy in the immediate postwar period remained ambiguous, as his responses to Allied overtures illustrated. The Allies at British insistence had decided to press for war crimes punishment at the peace conference. In December 1918 Allied leaders approached Wilson about trying the kaiser.[66] Colonel House told a British diplomat that Allied views about the need to do this "coincided entirely with his own." House claimed to have "already expressed them to the President" and was "sure that he expressed no dissent."[67] House was probably attempting to be agreeable to everyone concerned, as was his practice, for he advised Wilson to wait until arriving in Europe to discuss the matter, a course of action that the president followed.[68] Wilson was dubious of any indictment assigning sole guilt for the war to Wilhelm II. While on the *George Washington*, en route to Europe, Wilson told reporters:

I am not wholly convinced that the Kaiser was personally responsible for the war or the prosecution of it. There are many evidences that he was coerced to an extent, that the war was the product of the system of the Great General Staff by which he was surrounded. . . . The Kaiser was probably a victim of circumstance and environment. In a case of this sort you can't with certainty put your finger on the guilty party.[69]

Wilson, however, had become concerned that the kaiser might threaten the future peace. He expressed some anxiety about the "many serious disadvantages in having the Kaiser so near his former Kingdom and so near also to the centers of intrigue." He said that he was "at a loss to suggest what course ought to be taken," but he thought the Netherlands would "find him an exceedingly inconvenient and even dangerous guest."[70] Because of this consideration, Wilson probably decided to cooperate with the Allies to the extent of removing the kaiser from the Netherlands and punishing him, as Napoleon had been punished, by exile at some spot far from Europe. Wilson's response to his welcome in France on December 14 was an address containing a passage affirming the "necessity" of measures not only to "rebuke such acts of terror and spoilation, but make men everywhere aware that they cannot be ventured upon without the certainty of just punishment." The *New York Times* interpreted this statement in a headline to mean: "He Declares For Exemplary Punishment of War-Makers."[71] His personal secretary, Joseph Tumulty, who had remained in Washington to keep Wilson abreast of events and public opinion in America, informed the president that the "most popular note in this country in your speech" was the reference to personal punishments.[72]

Wilson's plans for peace focused, however, almost entirely upon creation of a League of Nations, not upon international war crimes trials. Many Americans probably found the internationalism of a trial of the kaiser for violations of international law as appealing as the idea of a League. Many undoubtedly thought these two innovative approaches to international relations complemented each other. Wilson would not have disagreed, for he, too, thought that the rule of law should ultimately govern relations between states and that all men should be obliged to obey it.[73] Wilson, however, was opposed to the vengeful sentiment that underlay much of the demand for punishments. He knew that since few precedents existed, particularly for dealing with the kaiser, any Allied effort to set up an international tribunal must have the appearance of victors' justice. Above all else, Wilson wanted, as a firm foundation for the League, a peace of impartial justice. He feared that extraordinary war crimes trials might impair rather than contribute to the establishment of lasting peace.

4

THE BRITISH ELECTION

The decision to hold war crimes trials after the First World War has always been closely associated with demagogic pledges to "hang the kaiser" made in the British election of December 1918, but the final formulation of this war aim resulted from more complex causes than an episode in an election. Postwar British politics undoubtedly played a large role. But, as pointed out in previous chapters, this idea took shape early in the war. Moreover, the announcement by the Germans of intent to try Rumanian war criminals in the spring of 1918 did not escape the notice of the Allies. When victory at last seemed likely, Allied statesmen, reacting to intense public pressure, renewed earlier pledges to punish war criminals. They did so to varying degrees a month before the conflict ended. The French issued a warning to Germany. The British made serious preparations to try war criminals, although not without some hesitancy, for some men, among them Lord Milner, feared the policy would prolong the war unnecessarily. Many British politicians anticipated the popularity of this issue with the voters: this was especially true of the punishment of the kaiser. Lloyd George clearly had votes in mind when he arranged for French and Italian leaders to approve, in the midst of his electoral campaign, a resolution for the trial of the kaiser. Nothing appeared to be more popular among British voters, and almost without exception successful candidates bowed to the will of their constituencies. Other Allied peoples urged their leaders to support British proposals, and most quickly did so. Some men embraced the project in total cynicism; others sincerely believed the measure was just and would erect new protections against aggression and barbarity; still others hoped it would serve some immediate political or diplomatic purpose.

1

If one can judge by the peace imposed upon Rumania in 1918, had the Germans won the war in the West, they might have tried Allied war criminals.[1] The High Command wanted to depose King Ferdinand, whose attack against the Central Powers in 1916 broke an alliance with Germany. Austro-Hungarian opposition prevented this "punishment."[2] The Germans complained about the conduct of other Rumanians who were accused of mistreating prisoners of war and interned German civilians.[3] In the harsh treaty imposed upon Rumania in May 1918, the Germans reserved the right to keep imprisoned until a general peace settlement certain men guilty of violating the laws of war. General Ludendorff declared that the Rumanians themselves "were to institute proceedings against Bratianu & Co., the instigators of the war."[4] Georg Ledebour, a leading Independent Socialist, warned the Reichstag that "punishing Rumanian war criminals would justify a similar demand of the Entente."[5] Almost no one heeded him because Germany, having beaten Russia and Rumania, appeared likely to emerge victorious in the West.

After initial successes, however, the last great German offensive on the western front failed in the summer of 1918. Ludendorff had exhausted his armies and faced an enemy reinvigorated almost daily by arrivals of American soldiers. The coordinated thrusts of Marshal Ferdinand Foch, recently appointed Supreme Allied Commander, soon cracked German defenses. After the first disaster on August 8, which Ludendorff called the "black day of German history," the end came quickly for Germany as well as for her allies, Austria-Hungary, Bulgaria, and Turkey.[6]

Sensing impending victory, the French and British governments determined to make war crimes trials a part of the peace settlement. The development of this decision can be traced in greater detail in Britain than in France, because a more complete record of official deliberations has been preserved in Britain. It is clear, however, that in both countries leaders acted hesitantly. The war ended through a negotiated armistice, not through the total destruction of the armed forces and the complete occupation of enemy countries, and Allied officials at first remained uncertain about the terms of peace they could expect to impose. At the same time, the climate of public opinion among the Allied peoples virtually compelled adoption of this policy.

As German armies retreated, they engaged in widespread destruction in northern France, and many Frenchmen renewed the demand for punishments. *Le Temps* asserted on August 25 that *les coupables* ("the guilty"), including Wilhelm II, must stand trial.[7] Many people believed that German leaders ordered devastation to cripple postwar economic competition and thought a threat to lay waste once inside Germany would be a more effective deterrent than a declaration on individual punishments. Much French attention focused upon the punitive idea of securing economic reparations in the peace settlement.[8] The French government in early

September requested Allied support for a "solemn declaration by the Allies forecasting . . . punishment . . . and due reparation."[9] The British War Cabinet and President Wilson feared the French wanted to take reprisals in Germany rather than hold trials and so refused.[10] Premier Georges Clemenceau clarified his intent on September 17 when he told the French Senate that nothing "could justify an amnesty for so many crimes."[11]

The French proposal prompted Sir F. E. Smith, British attorney-general, to urge Lloyd George to take action. Smith had long advocated war crimes trials. In an address to the New York State Bar Association in January 1918, he had displeased President Wilson by questioning the viability of a League of Nations and by arguing that prosecution of guilty individuals would prove more effective in preserving the future peace.[12] A close associate of Lloyd George, Smith probably knew of plans to hold an election before the end of 1918,[13] and he must have known that in his own constituency in Liverpool many men had pledged to vote against any government unwilling to make individual penalties a condition of peace. He assured a Liverpool audience in mid-September that he stood for such a measure.[14] Smith and Solicitor-General Gordon Hewart pointed out to Lloyd George on September 30 the recent French proposal, and they reminded the prime minister of earlier British pledges. They said the time had come to prepare for trials of specific enemy individuals. They urged appointment of a "strong Committee of Jurists and others" to assist in this work.[15] Lloyd George, however, took no immediate action on this proposal.

Germany asked for an armistice on October 4, thus admitting defeat, and on the same day the French government unilaterally issued a threat:

Conduct which is equally contrary to international law and the fundamental principles of all human civilization will not go unpunished. . . . The authors and directors of these crimes will be held responsible morally, judicially, and financially. They will seek in vain to escape the inexorable expiation which awaits them.[16]

Minister of Foreign Affairs Stephen Pinchon repeated these words on October 15 before the French Senate. That body at once voted its unanimous approval. The press gave the idea lively support.[17]

In Britain demands for war crimes trials increased along with calls for unconditional surrender. Many people opposed an armistice, fearing a German trick to gain time for regrouping. Francis Gribble, a journalist, expressed this view when he said that the Allies must fight on until Germany agreed to surrender accused criminals. He appealed for a "Bloody Assize" in which "the Kaiser himself must be regarded as the principal offender."[18]

Reports of the mistreatment of British prisoners of war produced the most sustained public pressure for a renewed official commitment to bring war criminals to justice. The Germans had refused to ratify a comprehensive agreement on the treatment of prisoners concluded at The Hague in July 1918,[19] and many people, hearing of reports of brutalities in work camps near the front lines, feared German defeats would result in even greater deterioration in the care of prisoners.[20] As in 1915, the treatment of prisoners now became a political issue, and critics used it to attack the government. A hysterical witch-hunt for pro-Germans among British leaders had gained momentum since the Pemberton Billing libel case in June, and Lord Newton became one of its principal targets because of his alleged lax administration of the Prisoners of War Department in the Foreign Office.[21] Lord Northcliffe's newspapers, the *Times* and the *Daily Mail*, began a campaign that combined attacks against "Hunnish" cruelties and official "indifference, or neglect, or mismanagement." As a remedy, the *Times* prescribed "blunt and immediate notice" threatening penalties for camp guards and others.[22] The more sensational *Daily Mail* demanded an unconditional surrender in which Germany would be forced to hand over "for trial by the Allies the great criminals of the war," including "Wilhelm II, the author of the war and of the order to murder prisoners," and five hundred other persons who had "conspicuously violated the laws of war and The Hague conventions."[23] Prominent leaders of public opinion, including Arthur Conan Doyle; Frederic Harrison; Lord Midleton, a former secretary of state for war; Lord Wrenbury, one of Britain's most renowned judges; and many others, wanted immediate issuance of a "blacklist" of the accused.[24]

The government tried to appease its critics. Lord Newton's organization was superseded by an Inter-Departmental Committee on Prisoners of War. To indicate special concern, the head of the Home Office, Sir George Cave, was appointed chairman of the new body.[25] Cave quickly carried the popular demand for war crimes punishment into the highest councils. Cave told the Inter-Departmental Committee that Germany's measures against Rumanians would serve as an "excellent precedent" for similar British action. Cave secured approval for a public announcement of reprisals and future penalties for individuals who mistreated prisoners.[26] He took this recommendation to the War Cabinet on October 11.

The War Cabinet declined to go as far as Cave proposed. Many ministers hesitated to take action that might disrupt armistice negotiations. In unattributed remarks, one minister asserted that "no nation, unless it was beaten to the dust, would accept such terms." Therefore, "as a matter of principle, threats should not be made which in practice could not be enforced." Possibly because of a fear of bolshevism, which was fast replacing fear of Prussianism, or perhaps because of simple war weariness, many British leaders did not want to fight the war to a total victory and a dictated peace in Berlin. The War Cabinet did decide, however, to announce publicly that British leaders "would take all steps in their power to insist that the persons responsible for these outrages should be punished for their misdeeds."[27] The Inter-Departmental Committee on October 14 released the text of this warning to the press.[28]

The debate in the House of Lords on October 16 made clear that critics found the declaration inadequate,[29] and the next day the War Cabinet made secret contingency plans for war crimes trials. The ministers approved the Smith-Hewart proposal and authorized the attorney-general to establish a committee to collect evidence and to make recommendations about the establishment of tribunals. The War Cabinet ordered that its action "should not be made public."[30]

British leaders still differed about what conditions they could safely impose without unnecessarily prolonging the war. Lord Curzon urged on October 15 that the Allies include among the terms of the armistice "the trial and punishment of the principal criminals, possibly including the Kaiser, unless he abdicated."[31] Arthur Balfour and Austen Chamberlain, on the other hand, after reading Wilson's second armistice note, expressed fear that the president meant to continue the war to "get rid of the Hohenzollerns." Lloyd George agreed that Britain would not fight on for that objective.[32] Lord Milner, probably remembering the difficulties he had encountered in imposing war crimes trials upon the Boers in 1902, made his anxieties known publicly. He appealed to the British people on October 17 to "think more of victory and less of vengeance." Thus "the punishment of the men who made the war and were responsible for its crimes, the question of reparation . . . , even territorial readjustments" were "all secondary to the one object of rendering Prussianism impotent for evil."[33] Other ministers openly disagreed with Milner. Lord Finlay, the lord chancellor, told an Inter-Allied Parliamentary Committee meeting on October 26 that Britain had "two aims in this war. One of them was the punishment of those who could be proved guilty of outrages," and "the other was reparation for the wrongs that had been done." Prosecution of "offenders would not be mere vengeance; it would be the vindication of international morality."[34]

Anger over treatment of prisoners erupted in the House of Commons on October 29, and opinion strongly favored preparations for holding trials. Reporters said that they "had never seen such a bitter and strong feeling pervade" the House. "No attacks of such bitterness" had "been made on any Minister since the war began" as those against Lord Newton.[35] Conservative and Liberal back-benchers joined together to criticize governmental weakness. The day before the debate, the Liberal and the Unionist (Conservative) War Committees, the policymaking bodies of the political parties, had resolved that "as a condition of peace," Britain should "insist upon the surrender, trial, conviction, and punishment of all persons responsible for cruelties perpetrated upon our prisoners."[36] Almost all speakers in the House supported those resolutions as the only satisfactory action the government could take to atone for past failures to protect prisoners.[37] Much of the press agreed.[38]

The War Cabinet made Lloyd George aware of this insistent public pressure while he was in Paris conferring with Colonel House and Clemenceau about armistice terms. The War Cabinet agreed on October 31 to urge Lloyd George to include terms in the armistice for punishment of war criminals.[39] Lloyd George was not prepared to risk imperiling an armistice over this issue, but he did try to make certain that nothing would appear in the agreement that would preclude later action. When House and Clemenceau innocently proposed a clause on October 31 for the "protection of people and property" in the Austrian armistice, Lloyd George "objected, claiming . . . it might be inferred that certain German officers should not be punished for some of the atrocious acts committed during the war." House said that after considerable debate Lloyd George was permitted to prevail "in the interest of harmony."[40] Reporting to the Imperial War Cabinet on these negotiations, Lloyd George said, "the question of the punishment of individuals guilty of war crimes was left over to the Peace Conference."[41]

After Lord Northcliffe indiscreetly published on November 4 a semi-official set of war aims that contained a moderate proposal for war crimes punishment,[42] British leaders, increasingly certain of the collapse of the Central Powers, at last disclosed their plans. Sir George Cave told the Commons the next day that Britain had requested French aid in capturing the Bulgarian commandant of the Philippopolis prisoner camp and that other guilty men in Germany and elsewhere would become the object of similar efforts.[43] Sir F. E. Smith revealed on November 7 the membership and purpose of the committee he had just appointed.[44]

This Committee of Enquiry into Breaches of the Laws of War, the attorney-general declared, had already begun work. Smith had named its members on November 1, and among them were some of Britain's finest lawyers. The chairman was Sir John Macdonell, and the vice-chairman was J. H. Morgan. The most distinguished participant was Sir Frederick Pollock, whose legal scholarship had exercised profound influence in all common law countries. Another member of considerable reputation was A. Pearce Higgins, soon to succeed to the Whewell chair of international law at Cambridge University. Other members were leaders of the bar and included Sir Ernest Pollock, Sir Alfred Hopkinson, C. A. Russell, C. F. Gill, and H. F. Manistry. The War Office, Admiralty, and several other departments also had representation.[45]

At their first meeting on November 6, the attorney-general explained to the members of the Committee of Enquiry their unprecedented task, but he also limited their investigations. He told them that they should not determine whether anyone was to be tried "for the highest of all the crimes against civilization. The enquiry into the origins of the War" could not "usefully be undertaken." This issue raised policy questions that only Allied leaders could decide. Rather, they should concentrate upon "fixing and assigning responsibility for specific breaches of International Law" by enemy soldiers and sailors. They should also draft a constitution for a proper tribunal to try these crimes.[46] Shortly after the armistice was signed on November 11, the Committee of Enquiry's charter was expanded to include the question of trying the kaiser for starting the war. The subject of the kaiser's trial came to dominate all public debate in Britain in the days immediately following the end of the conflict.

2

As in America, many people in Britain had no pity for the defeated and exiled Wilhelm II. Civilians and soldiers joyfully scourged effigies of the kaiser during armistice celebrations in London and in army camps in France.[47] Calling for the trial and punishment of the kaiser were leaders such as Lord Morris, former prime minister of Newfoundland; the Reverend Alfred Gough, prebendary of St. Paul's Cathedral; the Reverend Arthur Guttery, president of the National Council of Free Churches; Acting Prime Minister Sir Thomas White of Canada; and Prime Minister William Massey of New Zealand.[48]

Men of all political persuasions agreed in wanting to secure just retribution and to deter future aggression but differed about other reasons for prosecuting the kaiser. The *New Statesman*, like most liberal opinion makers, wanted a moderate peace settlement of reconciliation, including amnesty for soldiers who merely obeyed orders, with punishment reserved for commanders, "whether the Kaiser, or Ludendorff, or some lesser man," who initiated criminal acts. Such a policy might usefully deflect the hatred of the masses away from the entire German people. Even in the kaiser's case, however, "shame" was a more appropriate sentence than "hanging or shooting," for the Allies should not "erect a gallows just outside the gates of the new world."[49] Conservative opinion worried about the appeal of bolshevism, which seemed poised to sweep away the established order everywhere in Europe. The *Spectator* argued against being "too pedantic or too fastidious or too timid" about punishing the kaiser and warned that revolutionary unrest made his trial imperative to guard "admired monarchies" and "democratic nations" against criticism.[50] Some conservatives, thus, hoped an international trial of the kaiser would draw attention of the masses away from domestic problems and demands for internal change.

Only hours after the signing of the armistice, British leaders began to think about the issue of the kaiser when they thought about the forthcoming parliamentary elections. Lloyd George, Churchill, who had become minister of munitions, and F. E. Smith toasted victory that evening at an intimate dinner at Ten Downing Street. Chief of the Imperial General Staff Sir Henry Wilson, who also attended, said that the statesmen "discussed many things, but principally the coming General Election. Lloyd George wants to shoot the Kaiser. F. E. agrees. Winston does not."[51]

Lord Curzon took the initiative. Acting unofficially and on his own, he asked Clemenceau on November 13 what he thought about a trial of the kaiser. The premier said "he had not seriously considered" the possibility. Curzon proposed as a "first step to a League of Nations" the establishment of "an international tribunal of jurists of the highest eminence," perhaps, including representatives from neutral countries, to render judgment. He admitted that he knew little about international law and said that he was not at all certain the Netherlands would surrender the kaiser because of that country's long history of granting asylum to political refugees. But, for purposes of condemnation, he thought the Allies might hold a trial, even if the German ruler was not present. After securing Clemenceau's support, Curzon pressed the project upon Lloyd George. The aristocratic Curzon, however, was no killer of kings. He told Lloyd George: "Execution, imprisonment, these are not, or may not be, necessary. But continued life . . . , under the weight of such a sentence as has never before been given in the history of mankind, would be a penance worse than death."[52]

Lacking Curzon's reticence about physically punishing the kaiser, Lloyd George enthusiastically took up the idea of a trial. Lloyd George had long expressed an interest in making a war of aggression a crime. He had told a meeting of the National Council of Evangelical Free Churches in August 1918 that British war aims included "above all, making sure that war shall henceforth be treated as a crime, punishable by the law of nations."[53] Apparently, he saw an opportunity to achieve this objective by trying the kaiser. Lord Haldane, who disapproved, said, not altogether correctly, that "the trouble with Lloyd George is that he thinks in images, not in concepts."[54] Certainly, the prospect of seeing Wilhelm II actually stand in the dock fascinated Lloyd George far more than other British leaders. Apparently, it somehow stirred his Welsh radicalism.[55]

Lloyd George and Curzon on November 20 sought approval from a reluctant Imperial War Cabinet. Some ministers thought Curzon was confused about his objectives, since he did not necessarily want to punish the kaiser or even have him appear before a tribunal.[56] Lloyd George left no doubt about what he had in mind, saying: "I do not know why we should prescribe limits of punishment at the present stage. . . . Kings have been tried and executed for offences which are not comparable." The prime minister wanted a real trial of the kaiser and of the crown prince who had followed his father into exile. Lloyd George was "perfectly certain that under pressure Holland would give up these two criminals." He thought "Germany ought to be invited to join" in the prosecution. Discounting all legal objections to such proceedings, he argued that "we are making international law." He for one wanted to establish a new precedent by placing the kaiser on trial for "plunging this world into war."[57]

This line of reasoning failed to persuade most members of the Imperial War Cabinet, which included British Cabinet members and ministers from the British Empire. Prime Minister William Hughes of Australia said: "You cannot indict a man for making war." War had been the prerogative of every sovereign. "If you say that it is a good thing that he should die, let us say so," said Hughes, not because the kaiser waged war, which he had a perfect right to do, but because "we have a perfect right to kill him" now that he has lost. Churchill agreed with Hughes and cautioned that an impartial tribunal might not find the kaiser guilty of starting the war, for there was "a great deal to be said about Russia in this matter, if you unfolded the question." Lord Reading, soon to become lord chief justice, foresaw "very great difficulties" in convicting the kaiser for waging a war of aggression, and General Jan Smuts of South Africa agreed. Sir Robert Borden, prime minister of Canada, thought it would be better to exile the kaiser without a trial as was done with Napoleon. Balfour warned that "difficulties would be prodigious" in securing the kaiser from the Netherlands. Other than Curzon and Lloyd George, no one appeared eager to try the kaiser, but only Austen Chamberlain openly opposed the prime minister. "Let us beware that we do not create a Hohenzollern legend like the Napoleonic legend," he said.[58] Although Milner and Andrew Bonar Law were also opposed, they said nothing.[59] No member of the Imperial War Cabinet raised the point, but the reluctance of some ministers may have been due to a recognition of the potential embarrassment for the British royal family of a trial of Queen Victoria's German grandson. King George V approved of trying some men accused of misdeeds, for example, General Liman von Sanders,[60] but proceeding against his cousin, Wilhelm II, was going too far, and the king had privately expressed his opposition to some members of the Imperial War Cabinet.[61]

Eager to secure approval of his fellow ministers, Lloyd George grew "very insistent," as one observer noted,[62] alternately exhorting and ridiculing his associates. He declared that their "hesitancy" was a "cardinal mistake." He told Churchill he had heard the argument against the guilt of Wilhelm II from "pacifists," but he knew of no one else who "doubted that we could go before any decent tribunal with a clear conscience." If the Imperial War Cabinet decided against a trial, said Lloyd George, he would accept the decision, but he would do so "under strong protest." Before making a final determination, the Imperial War Cabinet agreed to seek legal advice from the law officers of the crown.[63]

The attorney-general, making it clear that he favored trying the kaiser, referred the question to the Committee of Enquiry.[64] Its Sub-Committee on Law, composed of Morgan, Macdonell, Higgins, Sir Frederick Pollock, and several other members, recommended proceeding against Wilhelm II. The lawyers declared that "vindication of the principles of International Law" would otherwise remain "incomplete." Such action would serve as a "deterrent and warning to rulers and highly placed officials" in the future. Furthermore, prosecution of lesser figures "might be seriously prejudiced, if they could plead the superior orders of a sovereign against whom no steps had been taken." The lawyers cautioned that the international tribunal established to hear the cases against the kaiser or other individuals should contain only Allied judges, for neutrals would probably "contend that outrages were equally committed by both belligerents." The lawyers concluded that the kaiser as head of the German armed forces could be charged with ordering or sanctioning violations of the laws of war as contained in the Hague conventions of 1899, and they suggested fifteen categories of applicable offenses, including unrestricted submarine warfare, execution of hostages, and ill-treatment of prisoners of war. Despite dissent, a majority of the lawyers by a vote of four to three also recommended indicting the kaiser for "having provoked or brought about an aggressive and unjust war."[65] The internal deliberations of this group were not recorded, and it is therefore not possible to analyze the arguments they used in reaching these conclusions, particularly the extraordinary recommendation to charge the kaiser with the crime of aggression.

Lloyd George easily won the approval of the Imperial War Cabinet on November 28 for a trial of the kaiser. Lloyd George claimed that the attorney-general converted the ministers with a spell-binding presentation. F. E. Smith was among the finest extemporaneous speakers of his era, and he spoke that day without notes for forty-five minutes in delivering the conclusions of the Committee of Enquiry and the similar opinions of himself and the solicitor-general.[66] No minister raised serious objections. Chamberlain and Churchill who might have opposed were not present. The Cabinet gave unanimous consent for a trial of the kaiser. As events would subsequently show, however, the British government was not truly united on this matter, and Lloyd George's later efforts to implement the policy were sometimes sabotaged by other British officials. Several ministers had merely acquiesced in the decision of November 28.[67]

It was clear from Smith's arguments, as well as from the report of his legal advisers, that British policy would fall short of the ideals of impartial international justice that Baron d'Estournelles and others had called for during the war. There was to be no possibility of raising the issue of Allied war crimes; since judges from neutral countries might ask inconvenient questions, they would not be used. Smith did want to establish a precedent in international law, but it was one peculiarly advantageous to British interests. He stressed the need to ensure that submarine warfare became recognized as an international crime. Smith himself remained dubious of indicting the kaiser for beginning the war, not because of legal difficulties but because of possible embarrassment to the Allies if the diplomatic record was subjected to close scrutiny. Smith was much interested in the trial of the kaiser as an election issue. As the meeting of the Imperial War Cabinet ended, he asked if he had "liberty to say anything" about the decision, since he would go before his "constituency very soon."[68]

3

The most popular slogans in the election of 1918—"hanging the kaiser" and making Germany pay "til the pips squeak"—created a lasting image of demagoguery. Lloyd George's historical reputation was irreparably marred by his exploitation of issues such as trying the kaiser, exacting full war indemnities, and excluding resident or immigrant enemy aliens. Promising, without many qualifications, to achieve these goals and refusing the "coupon" (a statement of support) to most Liberals, the prime minister carried the coalition of his personal Liberal adherents and the Conservative party to an overwhelming triumph, destroying in the process the Liberal party. Lloyd George, nonetheless, did not manufacture these issues, and he appeared to believe fully in the necessity of the kaiser's trial, even if his sincerity about reparations and exclusion of aliens was questionable. In any case, the aroused electorate probably would have compelled any leadership to adopt such a program. Lloyd George was not alone, for many Asquithian Liberal and Labour candidates also supported these aims.

Before the prime minister or any other candidate made a campaign pledge, many voters had decided that the kaiser's punishment was the election's key issue. Between November 12 and December 27, ninety-two towns and villages sent resolutions to the War Office demanding "immediate steps" to force the Netherlands to surrender Wilhelm II.[69] Following a canvass of his typically working-class district at Shoreditch on November 27, Dr. Christopher Addison's strongest impression was "the absolute determination of the people that the Kaiser and others responsible for the war must be brought to trial."[70] Two days later the *Times'* parliamentary correspondent reported: "The test for the simple elector is clearly the position of the Kaiser."[71] The historian Trevor Wilson concluded that "one might almost imagine" that "the election was arranged to determine what should be done with the Kaiser."[72]

Some liberal and socialist intellectuals condemned a trial of the kaiser, as the *Nation* said, because it was "a red-herring" that reactionaries used to divert attention from social reconstruction and Wilson's Fourteen Points.[73] George Bernard Shaw publicly ridiculed the "childish nonsense," and Beatrice Webb privately deplored Lloyd George's "low moral and intellectual values."[74] Similarly, C. P. Scott's *Manchester Guardian* stood firmly against the kaiser's trial as an irrelevant distraction.[75]

Nevertheless, the stance of most Labour and Asquithian Liberal candidates was similar to that of the coalition's.[76] At first, Herbert Asquith himself called for calm impartiality, so that "not only the form but the spirit of justice" prevailed.[77] He faced an opponent, Pritchard Morgan, who colorfully claimed that he would give the kaiser "a place in the sun and let him frizzle for the rest of his life."[78] By balloting day, December 14, Asquith took a less aloof tone, saying "no punishment can be too severe," but he lost his seat in the House of Commons.[79] Candidates who did not give way to the "hanging craze" received rough receptions. The Reverend Herbert Morgan, standing for Labour at Neath, spoke of the "poor old Kaiser" in exile. The *Times* reported: "Booing, hissing, and general uproar followed . . . , and the meeting ended abruptly in disorder."[80]

Few coalition speakers had such problems with audiences. George N. Barnes, the Labour leader who supported Lloyd George, coined the election's slogan when he announced on November 30: "I have heard the Kaiser mentioned. Well, I am for hanging the Kaiser."[81] Only slightly less dramatic, Sir Auckland Geddes declared that "such men as the Kaiser, Enver Pasha," and the Bulgarian and Austrian rulers should be so charged that "if they were found guilty, their lives would be forfeit."[82] Most coalition leaders used more moderate language, but virtually all promised complete support for war crimes trials.[83] Sir F. E. Smith had to say very little at Liverpool, a reporter declared, because his official advice to the

Imperial War Cabinet was well known and "would ensure his election, for here, as everywhere, the punishment of the guilty" was "uppermost in the public mind."[84]

Some men, personally opposed to the idea, nonetheless, loyally supported Lloyd George and bowed to their constituents' desires. Churchill, anticipating the decision of the Imperial War Cabinet, said on November 26 that German malefactors must be "punished as criminals, however highly placed." He later explained that because of the "deep-seated demand from all classes and all parties in the city Dundee that the Kaiser should be hanged" he was "constrained to support his being brought to trial."[85]

Lloyd George always claimed that he spoke moderately during the election and vigorously denied that he ever advocated "hanging the Kaiser" in his speeches, a charge that plagued him for years afterwards.[86] His principal address on the issue at Newcastle-on-Tyne on November 29 set the tone of his campaign. He said: "It must be a just peace, a sternly just peace (loud cheers), a relentlessly just peace (renewed cheers)." Banging the table before him, he shouted that Britain would never again receive aliens who abused her hospitality. "Germany must pay the costs of the war up to the limit of her capacity to do so." As for war crimes,

Is no one to be made responsible for this horror? (Loud cheers.) If a man takes another's life the law seizes upon him, and demands life for life. Somebody—it is not for me to say, but that will be a question for investigation—Somebody has been responsible for this war that has taken the lives of millions of the best young men in Europe. Is no one to be made responsible for that? (Voices, "Yes.")

All I can say is that if that is the case there is one justice for the poor wretched criminal, and another for Kings and Emperors. (Cheers). . . .

I do not want when the war is over to pursue any policy of vengeance, but we have got so to act that men in future who feel tempted to follow the example of the rulers who plunged the world into this war will know what is waiting them at the end of it. (Cheers)

Concluding, he announced the decision of the Imperial War Cabinet, supported by "some of the greatest jurists," that "the Kaiser was guilty of an indictable offence for which he ought to be held responsible. (Cheers)"[87]

The legal community was not as unanimous as Lloyd George implied. Albert V. Dicey, the great scholar of common law history, and Lord Bryce analyzed the question privately. Dicey and Bryce agreed that since there was no precedent a judicial prosecution of the kaiser would be little more than a "sham trial." They believed, however, that Wilhelm II should suffer Napoleon's fate for the "grave moral offence" of violating the neutrality of Belgium. Bryce was willing to deal more summarily with Turkish leaders. He said that "Enver and Talaat, the two chief villains, ought to be hanged if they can be caught."[88] Sir Herbert Stephen, whose views Dicey commended, was the chief public advocate against an ex post facto "mockery" of a trial.[89] A scholar of international law, Coleman Phillipson, asserted, however, that "every ultimate precedent was itself at one time a novelty without exact parallel." The occasion was important enough to create a "new rule" that might serve as "an eminently desirable precedent" for succeeding generations who might face "an ambitious, arrogant, and unconscionable aggressor." Morality came before the law, and under "the unwritten law of humanity and civilization" the "Kaiser and his satellites may lawfully be called to account before a specially erected tribunal of Allied judges."[90]

4

Lloyd George quickly sought support from other Allied leaders for war crimes trials. He arranged for an Inter-Allied Conference to meet in London, but he found other leaders less enthusiastic than he was. Clemenceau was quite willing to go to London to help Lloyd George, but his interest in the kaiser's trial did not match that of the British prime minister's. He gave Colonel House "his solemn word of honor that he would discuss no question of importance" while in London. He said that Lloyd George wanted him to come "simply for electioneering purposes."[91] When he returned from Britain, he told House that he was "in favor of it [the kaiser's trial] in a mild way."[92]

Before Clemenceau left for London, the French government had taken some steps on war crimes punishment independently of the British. Fernand Ignace, undersecretary of state for military justice, ordered the renewed court-martial of German prisoners of war who were accused of violating the laws of war; he also instructed military judges to sentence some Germans in absentia.[93] The Ministry of Foreign Affairs amended an earlier outline of subjects it wanted the peace conference to consider to include war crimes trials.[94] Clemenceau also asked the Faculty of Law of the University of Paris for advice about the feasibility of extraditing Wilhelm II from the Netherlands.[95]

Clemenceau was under less public pressure than Lloyd George. He faced no election, and the French people seemed less aroused than the British about punishments. An enterprising American reporter did elicit a favorable response to penalizing the kaiser from some French soldiers, but other Frenchmen regarded the idea of sending Wilhelm II to Saint Helena as an insult to Napoleon and the French nation.[96] One Madame Prieur, widow of a Sussex victim, tried to lodge a complaint of murder against Wilhelm II with French legal authorities.[97] Several members of the

Chamber of Deputies introduced a resolution requesting that France conclude an agreement with the Allies to try all former enemy rulers responsible for the war.[98] *Le Matin* and *Le Temps* called upon the Dutch to
expel their refugee as an undesirable guest, so that the Allies could seize
him.[99] But many newspapers, including Clemenceau's *Homme Libre*,
carried mostly British items on war crimes punishment. They were more
concerned about reparations.[100]

At the Inter-Allied Conference on December 2, Lloyd George, Clemenceau, and Premier Vittorio Orlando of Italy quickly agreed upon a
trial of the kaiser and brushed aside the opposition of Balfour and Baron
Sidney Sonnino, the Italian foreign minister. Completely against the
project, Sonnino questioned whether individual leaders should be held
responsible for the corporate action of a nation. He doubted the "desirability of making a scape-goat. Was not St. Helena useful to the Bonapartists?"
He believed the Netherlands would refuse to surrender the kaiser because
of its tradition of protecting political refugees. Balfour unsuccessfully
attempted to persuade Lloyd George to forget about a trial and to settle
for "administrative action" against the kaiser.[101] Outside the meeting, when
asked, Marshal Foch told Lloyd George that war crimes trials were "without
doubt inappropriate." He too was ignored.[102]

Except for occasional interjections, Lloyd George let Clemenceau deliver
the counterarguments. Clemenceau said he supported a trial because he
was uncertain about immediately establishing a League of Nations, but he
thought the Allies could make "immense progress" by punishing "the man
who was guilty of a great historic crime like the declaration of war in
August, 1914." He was certain that the Allies could get the kaiser from
the Netherlands. Lloyd George added that the Allies could deprive the
Dutch of supplies, including food, and exclude them from the League of
Nations. Clemenceau discounted fears of martyring Wilhelm II. Lloyd
George warned of the real danger: the kaiser in the Netherlands was far
closer to Germany than Napoleon in Saint Helena had been to France.
Orlando obligingly acquiesced. He thought the matter was "exclusively
one of sentiment; it had nothing to do with interests," and he, therefore,
felt free to differ with Sonnino. The method of dealing with the kaiser "was
a question of detail" about which he deferred to his colleagues. He said that
they "could not calculate for centuries ahead" about how history would
judge the proceedings. They "had to deal with a very strong sentiment in
all countries at the present time."[103]

Allied leaders also discussed the trial of individuals other than the
kaiser. Lloyd George suggested trying the crown prince and General
Erich von Falkenhayn. Clemenceau readily agreed that the crown prince
should be tried but did not want to prosecute "great soldiers, who had

merely obeyed orders." He did not want to try more than "seven or eight persons." Balfour offered Talaat as a suitable choice because, although he had "committed no definite legal offence," he was responsible for massacring the Armenians. Clemenceau objected to "mixing" Turks "with the ex-Kaiser. He thought for the moment people were not particularly interested in Talaat."[104] Allied leaders came to no definite conclusion about other prosecutions. They tried to secure the immediate concurrence of President Wilson[105] but learned that he had not yet decided what should be done with Wilhelm II.

Victorious, the Allies determined at last to prosecute enemy war criminals. Public opinion, particularly in Britain, compelled the Allies to make this effort. Largely at Lloyd George's insistence, the kaiser was to be brought before an international tribunal rather than dealt with as Napoleon had been. But many Allied leaders only reluctantly endorsed this measure, and some came to oppose the plans of the British prime minister. Disagreement and delay subsequently undermined the undertaking, which otherwise might have succeeded.

5

THE PARIS PEACE CONFERENCE

Efforts at providing for punishment of war crimes floundered at the Paris Peace Conference of 1919. Translating policy into law, even domestically, is often difficult; on the international scene, where unanimity is more important, it is often impossible. International prosecution for war crimes was largely an uncharted area of international law in 1919. Had there been harmony among the Allies on goals, some disagreement on legal implementation might have been expected. There were, however, crucial differences of opinion on both the objectives of peace and proper functions of international law in international relations. After a long struggle, American statesmen reluctantly agreed to the demand for punishment but secured elimination of much of the proposed legal framework. This unsatisfactory compromise weakened the undertaking and left in doubt the cooperation of the American government in future actions on war crimes. No effective solution for arranging the surrender of the kaiser by the Netherlands was devised at Paris. If quick action had been taken, the Allies probably could have persuaded the Dutch to hand over Wilhelm II. But Allied disunity caused delay and led to Dutch resistance. The vigor of German opposition was also revealed at the peace conference. Although they were compelled to accept clauses in the Versailles treaty for a trial of the kaiser and other accused persons, it was certain that German recalcitrance would continue. The treaty was a landmark in the international law of war crimes punishment, but it was a flawed landmark. Events at Paris did not encourage hope of practical achievements.

1

Allied leaders paid little attention initially to the problem of getting the Dutch to hand over the kaiser, possibly because they learned he was

not particularly welcome in the Netherlands. Dutch officials had been surprised by the sudden appearance of the kaiser and the crown prince at the
Dutch frontier at the end of the war. Queen Wilhelmina and Foreign
Minister Herman A. van Karnebeek were sympathetic toward the kaiser,
but other Dutch leaders feared complications, even Allied retaliation, if
the Germans were granted asylum. Neither the kaiser nor his son was
warmly received, but the Dutch were intensely proud of their country's
tradition as a haven for political refugees and decided they must not
tarnish it. They accepted Wilhelm II "provisionally" and persuaded a
private citizen, Count Gontard Bentinck, to house him at a country estate
at Amerongen rather than offer the queen's official hospitality.[1] The
crown prince was sent to live in a tiny, abandoned parsonage with no
modern conveniences on the desolate island of Wieringen in the Zuyder
Zee. The Dutch exercised close supervision over both men to prevent
intrigues.[2]

The Allies vigorously criticized the Dutch. They suspected at first that
the kaiser had been invited to the Netherlands because Queen Wilhelmina's
adjutant-general had visited German headquarters at Spa in early
November.[3] They doubted that the kaiser had really given up his throne
and feared he might attempt to regain power in Germany.[4] Dutch diplomats
reported that public opinion in Allied countries would force those
governments to take action to secure the kaiser. The Dutch minister in
London, René de Marees van Swinderen, sent alarming cables to The
Hague regarding the British election. He warned that even British mod-
erates were determined to punish the kaiser. He said that former Foreign
Minister Sir Edward Grey, now Lord Grey of Fallodon, told him that
Wilhelm II should be sent to the Falkland Islands and that the Dutch could
not be permitted to stand in the way.[5] Such reports greatly worried
Dutch leaders.

Publicly, the Dutch defended the right of asylum and tried to reas-
sure the Allies. Prime Minister Charles J. M. Ruijus de Beerenbrouck
and Foreign Minister van Karnebeek declared that the Dutch government
played no role in the kaiser's arrival. They said he was an undesirable
guest who nonetheless had to be admitted to uphold a national tradition. They discouraged extradition demands, pointing out that such requests would probably not meet the standards of treaties governing
extradition, for extraditable offenses were generally limited to violations
of national criminal law. These treaties made no provisions for the kind
of offenses with which the Allies might charge the kaiser.[6]

Privately, the Dutch did not take so strong a stand. They indicated that
they might surrender the kaiser. Two powerful figures of industry and
politics, Ernst Heldring and Hendrikus Colijn, played significant roles
in secret overtures to the Allies. At a meeting of an Advisory Council

in early December, van Karnebeek agreed to a proposal to send Colijn to confer "tête à tête" with British officials whom Colijn had come to know intimately from wartime blockade negotiations.[7] At the same time, Ruijs de Beerenbrouck signalled a willingness to cooperate with the Allies. He told the States General that, although the Netherlands could not comply with an extradition request, the existing arrangement remained "a provisional one," and he was prepared to discuss with foreign governments a permanent domicile for the kaiser "provided that the Netherlands could participate in such deliberations" with the assurance of obtaining a solution "compatible with . . . honor and dignity."[8]

In both London and Paris, Dutch emissaries made the prime minister's statement clear. After a conversation with de Marees van Swinderen on December 14, Arthur Balfour recorded that the Dutch minister

made it quite clear to me that, though Holland in obedience to immemorial tradition, did not feel able to refuse at least a temporary asylum to the Kaiser, the Dutch Government would not decline to discuss with other Powers questions that might be raised with regard to his possible extradition.[9]

Colijn's message was even more explicit, for he offered a concrete proposal. Sir Laming Worthington-Evans, minister of blockade, circulated a memorandum to the War Cabinet relating what Colijn had said in their meeting of December 16:

He felt sure that if the legal question of the right of asylum was not raised, and the Allies requested the Dutch Government to appoint a representative to a Commission of, say, four nominated by the Allies, to enquire whether any legal questions did in fact arise, it could be arranged beforehand, if necessary, that the Commission should report no such legal questions arose, whereupon he felt sure the Dutch Government would be prepared to hand over the Kaiser.[10]

Colijn repeated a similar declaration to Sir William Tyrrell, head of the Political Intelligence Department in the Foreign Office.[11] Meanwhile, Heldring had taken an identical message to Paris.[12]

At the same time that the Dutch approached the Allies, they also tried to get the kaiser to leave the Netherlands. The Council of Ministers decided to inform the kaiser that although asylum was not being officially denied to him, his continued presence in the country was "undesirable."[13] Van Karnebeek expected that this action might cause the kaiser to commit suicide.[14] The kaiser did not take the hint.

The Allies failed to take advantage of Dutch overtures. Lloyd George was ill-served by some of his fellow ministers and subordinates who began to undermine his plans to punish the kaiser. They ignored the Dutch and repudiated Lloyd George's policy. Balfour made no response at all when de Marees van Swinderen told him extradition was open to discussion.[15] At the same time, the permanent undersecretary of the Foreign Office, Lord Hardinge, told the Dutch minister that he was not upset with the Netherlands: "Not a bit, I even much prefer to see the Kaiser staying in Holland than any where else."[16] Later the Dutch minister reported that one man highly placed in the Foreign Office had characterized the kaiser's trial as "perfectly idiotic."[17]

Lloyd George was serious about wanting to punish the kaiser, but he, too, weakened his chance of success. Occupied with other problems of peacemaking, he may have been unaware of the circuitous Dutch overtures. If he knew of them, he may have been indifferent, believing the Dutch would have to cooperate whenever the Allies desired. Lloyd George's single most important error was disregarding President Wilson's readiness to dispose of the problem of the kaiser in the first days of the Paris Peace Conference.

When Allied leaders met in early January to establish an agenda for the conference, Lloyd George proposed referring the issue of the "responsibility of the authors of the war" to a special commission. Wilson replied that "this question need not be referred to a Committee, since it could be settled forthwith by themselves."[18] One must assume that Wilson, knowing Lloyd George's determination in this matter, was prepared to outlaw and exile Wilhelm II following the Napoleonic precedent. If this approach had been adopted at this time, the Dutch would probably have gone along. Lloyd George, however, wanted to erect an international tribunal to try the kaiser for initiating a war of aggression, thus establishing a new kind of responsibility in international law. This idea, so much more complex than merely exiling the kaiser, had to be turned over to legal experts for special study. The disagreements that subsequently appeared in debates at Paris led the Dutch to reconsider their initial inclination to cooperate with the Allies.

2

At the insistence of Lloyd George and Georges Clemenceau, the issue of war crimes was the first item on the agenda when the conference officially convened on January 18, 1919.[19] A Commission on the Responsibility of the Authors of the War and the Enforcement of Penalties was established to study questions concerning the origins of the war and culpability for it, offenses against the laws and customs of war in its conduct, and the constitution of a tribunal to try the accused.[20] Then for two months, the matter was obscured from public view while the commission deliberated in secret.

The Commission on Responsibility was a group of distinguished inter-national lawyers. It was composed of fifteen men, two from each of the five major Allies and one each from five lesser powers. It numbered among its members two future judges of the Permanent Court of International Justice,[21] three members of the Institut de droit international,[22] and several editors of the world's three most important journals of international law.[23] Six men dominated its meetings. Foremost was the chairman, the American secretary of state, Robert Lansing, who before 1914 had one of the largest private practices in international law in the United States and had partic-ipated in more international arbitrations than any other American.[24] His associate, Dr. James Brown Scott, was recognized as a leading scholar of international law. A delegate to the Second Hague Peace Conference of 1907, he had an intimate knowledge of the laws and customs of war.[25] Their principal counterparts did not have an equal reputation in the field of international law. France was represented almost entirely by Fernand Larnaude, dean of the Faculty of Law at the University of Paris, for his colleague, Andre Tardieu, was busy elsewhere. Britain's principal spokes-man was Sir Ernest Pollock, the new solicitor-general. Two delegates from the smaller states who took a very active part were men of eminence in international law. Édouard Rolin-Jaequemyns of Belgium had been the reporter of the commission on the laws and customs of war at the First Hague Peace Conference of 1899.[26] Nicolas Politis, foreign minister of Greece, had been a professor of international law at several French uni-versities before the war.[27] Representatives from Italy, Japan, Poland, Yugoslavia, and Rumania made few contributions to the discussions.

The meetings of the Commission on Responsibility immediately became the scene of prolonged and sometimes stormy conflict between the Ameri-cans and the Europeans. Scott later recalled: "Feelings ran about as high as feelings can run. It ran especially high in the British membership and it ran extremely high in the French membership. It ran so high that relations were somewhat suspended."[28] Lansing, as noted earlier, opposed international punishment of war crimes, believing observance of the laws of war should be left to the discretion of military authorities of each state. Understandably, he did not generally admit this viewpoint in public. Rather, he stressed the lack of precedent, opposed all innovations, and thus rejected virtually every important proposal offered by the Europeans. Lansing, who believed the scheme to try the kaiser was solely the result of Lloyd George's election campaign, had little respect for the British and French members of the commission and sometimes did not conceal his distaste for men whose "intellect," he said privately, was "prostituted to political ends."[29] He thought that the "British Delegates were not very sincere in their desire to try the Kaiser, etc., but merely felt that they had to urge this measure because of a political pledge."[30] He used every tactic he could think of to frustrate their efforts. Although Colonel House remained silent, Lansing had the support of the other American peace commissioners, Henry White and General Tasker Bliss.[31] President Wilson "approved entirely of my attitude," said Lansing, "only he is even more radically opposed than I am to that folly."[32]

Unlike other delegations, even the French, British representatives came to Paris ready for quick action on war crimes. The attorney-general's Committee of Enquiry worked steadily, turning out reports that included everything from Sir Frederick Pollock's opinion of a plea of superior orders to briefs of *prima facie* cases against specific enemy individuals.[33] The British wanted to take custody of such individuals as soon as possible. At the first meeting of the commission, the new attorney-general, Sir Gordon Hewart, suggested that the Supreme War Council insert a clause in one of the periodic renewals of the armistice with Germany that would compel surrender of persons named by the Allies. Larnaude endorsed the idea but admitted that the French had not yet decided which individuals were wanted. Lansing ignored both men by raising another subject.[34] Aware that there was "misgiving" in Britain that suspected "some influence at work seeking to damp down the whole business,"[35] Pollock renewed the proposal at the commission's second meeting, urging the need to prevent the escape of those believed guilty of war crimes and the destruction of incriminating documents. Lansing ruled Pollock's motion out-of-order, because it "exceeded the province of the Commission" and declared that, consequently, as chairman, he would not bring the resolution before the Supreme War Council. Such transparent evasion undoubtedly contributed to ill feelings. For the record, Pollock secured a near unanimous vote for such an armistice clause, with only Lansing and Scott opposed,[36] and undertook to have the matter brought before Allied leaders by another route. He had Balfour take the proposition to the Council of Ten on February 10, but Balfour halfheartedly supported his own motion, and Lloyd George was not present to press for action. President Wilson summarily dismissed the scheme. He said difficulties in securing war criminals would be no greater after the peace was signed than before.[37]

On the same day, Larnaude was no more successful in seeking support for war crimes punishment in the Commission on the League of Nations, on which he also sat. The French draft of a League Covenant included international criminal jurisdiction for an International Court of the League. Larnaude called for a decision on whether the League would "take upon itself to judge and punish those who have been to blame." He was dissuaded from pressing that task upon the League that would include neutrals probably unwilling to approve.[38]

The French plan for war crimes punishment would have come closest to carrying out the ideas of those men who during the war had urged establishment of international tribunals as a fundamental international reform. In this instance, as with French proposals to set up armed forces under an international staff to enforce the principle of collective security, other members of the Commission on the League of Nations were opposed. Neither Woodrow Wilson nor Lord Robert Cecil, the two dominant figures of these sessions, supported the French. They did not believe their nations should make the kind of open-ended commitments that these proposals seemed to require. They thought the French merely wanted to use the League as a victor's condominium against Germany. Both American and British delegates at Paris generally feared that the French were seeking to break up the German state or to keep it permanently subjugated, as indeed some French officials were. Such suspicions unfortunately prevented serious consideration of the merits of French ideas about international reforms.[39]

Despite a lack of American cooperation, European governments took unilateral, and often arbitrary, measures to gain custody of a large number of accused enemy individuals while the peace conference temporized. Belgian and French military forces arrested many persons during the initial occupation of the Rhineland, despite rulings of the Inter-Allied Armistice Commission against such actions.[40] The British captured one U-boat commander who was returning to Germany from internment in Spain and held him in the Tower of London.[41] At Constantinople the British arrested scores of Turks, several Germans, and one Bulgarian and took them to Malta where they imprisoned them.[42] Some of these men were held without trial for as long as two years. Others were released quickly. A few were actually tried. The most famous conviction was that of the Röchling brothers, members of an important Saarland industrialist family who had benefitted from the wartime seizure by the German army of machinery and raw material from French factories and mines. Robert Röchling, arrested in early 1919, was tried in December by a French court-martial at Amiens, and his brother, Hermann, was tried *in absentia;* both were condemned to ten years' imprisonment and fined ten million francs for confiscations and theft of private property. An appeals court eventually reversed the conviction of Robert and freed him, after he had spent some twenty-two months in a French prison.[43] Hermann, it might be noted, was sentenced after the Second World War by a French tribunal to seven years' imprisonment as a Nazi industrialist found guilty of war crimes and crimes against the peace.[44]

After the Commission on Responsibility's opening clashes, it divided its work among three subcommittees. These groups made substantial progress for a time by concentrating upon less contentious subjects. The first subcommittee on criminal acts, presided over by Prime Minister William F. Massey of New Zealand, collected and collated allegations concerning atrocities.[45] It concluded that Germany, Austria-Hungary,

Bulgaria, and Turkey waged war "by barbarous or illegitimate methods" and prepared a list of thirty-two categories of war crimes with a thirty-page annex cataloging alleged incidents, some very specific, many rather general and sometimes vague. Urged to finish quickly, the subcommittee's evidence was unsatisfactory, resting mostly upon documents such as the Bryce Report and similar sources. It recommended that the peace conference create a more permanent body for additional investigation and more complete compilation of enemy outrages.

The first subcommittee also hurriedly composed a part of what later became the most controversial legacy of the peace conference—the war guilt of Germany. The subcommittee did not make, and could not have made under the circumstances, an extensive, new inquiry. It did not have access to governmental archives. Relying almost entirely upon the various official publications of diplomatic notes exchanged during July 1914, the evidence available to the subcommittee did not justify its strong conclusions. It asserted that the "war was premeditated," indeed, was "nothing but a plot engineered by heads of four states against the independence of Serbia and the peace of Europe." The assassination of Sarajevo was used as "a pretext to initiate war." After a "decisive consultation" at Potsdam on July 5, Germany had "deliberately worked to defeat conciliatory efforts by the Entente." Therefore, responsibility for the war "rests first on Germany and Austria, secondly on Turkey and Bulgaria."[46] The Allies did not include this accusation in the peace treaty. The famous war-guilt clause, article 231, came from a separate and unrelated technical compromise in the Commission on Reparations, which devised the statement to justify a financial claim for all damages caused the Allies by Germany's aggression. With article 231 directly following the treaty's war crimes clauses (articles 227 to 230), the Germans assumed, erroneously, that the commission's report was the basis for article 231.[47]

The second subcommittee on responsibility for the war took up the legal consequences of war guilt.[48] It considered whether launching a war of aggression was an international crime and whether a nation's leadership could be held personally culpable. Larnaude and Albert de Lapradelle, the commission's secretary-general, had coauthored a pamphlet at Clemenceau's request, suggesting that the peace conference should impose penal responsibility upon Wilhelm II for starting an "unjust war."[49] The resurrection of the natural law concept of just and unjust wars from an earlier tradition in international law did not appeal to other members of the subcommittee trained in the positivist school of international law dominant in the nineteenth century. They looked to treaty and state practice as virtually the sole source of international law rather than normative theories derived from concepts of natural law. Larnaude had barely begun to explain his ideas to the subcommittee when Scott interrupted with a curt lecture on the contemporary state of international law that clearly recognized any sovereign state's unrestricted right to make war, an act of state for which an individual leader might be called to moral, not legal, account. Although Pollock quickly agreed,[50] British delegates were by no means in agreement on this point. Lloyd George and his private secretary, Philip Kerr, tried unsuccessfully to convince Pollock to secure a recommendation for prosecuting the kaiser for starting the war. Pollock's failure to do so was a "great pity," said Kerr.[51] Lloyd George later told Wilson and Clemenceau:

Personally, I regret this decision; but I accept it. In my view, if the important personages who unleash such calamities could be rendered responsible for this, the greatest of all crimes, there would be less danger of war in the future.[52]

The subcommittee concluded that due to the "purely optional character of the institutions at The Hague for the maintenance of peace" a "war of aggression may not be considered an act directly contrary to positive law." In addition, the subcommittee declared, no criminal charge could be made against German leaders for breaking the treaty that guaranteed the neutrality of Belgium. To placate Lloyd George and others, the subcommittee concluded that the peace conference, lacking legal precedents, could rightly "adopt special measures" and even "create a special organ in order to deal as they deserve with the authors of such acts." The subcommittee recommended that "for the future penal sanctions should be provided for such grave outrages against the elementary principles of international law."[53]

The third subcommittee on responsibility for violations of the laws and customs of war quickly deadlocked in a bitter struggle between Lansing and Pollock.[54] Obviously intending to delay decision, Lansing announced at the first meeting that all other questions must be deferred, pending preparation of a comparative compilation of the military codes of the laws of war of all belligerent nations, a project everyone knew could take weeks.[55] When Rolin-Jaequemyns proposed at the next session that the Allies use Germany's code to prosecute war criminals, Lansing baldly ruled such a decision beyond the competence of the subcommittee.[56] Throughout, Lansing stemmed efforts by Pollock and Larnaude to discuss creation of an international tribunal. Rolin-Jaequemyns lamented on February 25 that the group had wasted an hour and a half on a simple question. Pollock, not willing to accept further delay, *demanded* an immediate vote on whether the subcommittee would recommend establishment of an international tribunal. Lansing had to comply, and he lost.[57]

Thereafter, he capitulated completely and allowed the Europeans to draft the subcommittee's report without further obstruction.

When the full commission reassembled on March 12 to approve its final report, Lansing renewed his objections and in the next several sessions made counterproposals so contrary to the thinking of the other members that they recognized that he was trying to prevent decision. He urged as a substitute for trying the kaiser an annex to the peace treaty denouncing as "infamous" his many crimes and demanding "the judgment of the ages against Wilhelm of Hohenzollern." Lansing further proposed the establishment of an International Commission of Inquiry to investigate German archives. This commission would report on November 11, 1919, on the extent of the kaiser's responsibility for the war and violations of the laws of war.[58] Lansing for the first time frankly told his colleagues that he was unalterably opposed to any judicial prosecution of the kaiser. Larnaude sharply criticized Lansing, telling him that he had withheld his opinion too long. Lansing was not moved by this comment. He told the group that:

The essence of sovereignty was the absence of responsibility. When the people confided it to a monarch or other head of State, it was legally speaking to them only that he was responsible, although there might be a moral obligation to mankind. Legally, however, there was no super-sovereignty.[59]

Lansing was entirely consistent with his views on international relations and international law. Basic to his conception of international law was the sovereign nation-state, bound ultimately by no rules except those to which it explicitly consented and always free to resort to whatever means its leaders judged necessary to protect and advance its welfare. In the final analysis, Lansing believed that force, not law, governed international relations, and that to pretend or act otherwise was visionary. He did not want to create misleading precedents. For much the same nationalistic reasons that he opposed war crimes trials, Lansing also disagreed with the idea of establishing a League of Nations capable of infringing upon national sovereignty.[60] Nicolas Politis could not dissuade Lansing despite his persuasive argument that the kaiser was no longer a head of state and that his own people would by treaty give consent to his trial. Larnaude said bluntly: "The Kaiser must not be allowed to escape by any finespun theories."[61]

On March 15 Lansing made a new proposal, a veiled threat, that he believed struck the commission like a "high explosive." He said he would agree to all European plans if his government was granted freedom to withdraw its judges from any trial in which it did not want to participate.

By prior arrangement, he was called away from the meeting before there was time for discussion, leaving the weekend for commission members to contemplate the disastrous public effect that might result if, during the kaiser's trial, American judges dramatically walked out.[62] Lansing was probably bluffing. In any case, Wilson did not want the Europeans to agree. That same day, Wilson told Lansing that he wanted "a minority report rejecting High Tribunal and opposing trial of Kaiser."[63] Lansing so informed the commission on March 17, and both sides set to work on final reports, the European delegates ranged against the Americans and the Japanese, whose imperial government did not want to call into question the inviolability of any monarchs.[64]

The majority and dissenting reports agreed in several respects. The Americans, adding newly secured documents that had just been revealed in Germany, affirmed that the Central Powers had instigated the war and that Germany had deliberately violated the neutrality of Belgium, but that neither deed was a crime under international law. The Americans also expressed hope that, despite the difficulty of defining aggression, penal sanction might be devised in the future to punish an aggressor. Finally, the Americans recognized that all persons, except heads of state, who had violated the laws and customs of war could be made liable, through provisions in the peace treaty, to punishment by various Allied national military tribunals. In cases involving a crime against more than one ally, these national tribunals could be merged into one mixed court.[65]

The Americans disagreed with the Europeans on four major points. The Europeans proposed creation of an international court composed of Allied judges to try all persons, including heads of state, accused of ordering, or of failing to prevent, violations of the laws and customs of war and the laws of humanity. The Europeans set forth in great detail the composition and law for such a tribunal but also admitted a need for national military tribunals to try lesser cases. The Americans rejected as unprecedented: (1) an international court, (2) the trial of a head of state, (3) the doctrine of negative criminality, and (4) the laws of humanity. To assure prosecution of such atrocities as the Armenian massacres and other outrages not clearly prohibited by the laws of war, the Europeans, anticipating the idea of crimes against humanity and genocide, wanted reference to the laws of humanity that were mentioned in the preamble to the Hague convention of 1907 as supplementing the laws of war. The Americans, however, declared that such an undefined standard as laws of humanity was arbitrary, because it varied "with individual consciences." The Europeans claimed that judgment of failure to prevent war crimes was necessary, for, otherwise, the principle of command irresponsibility could be used to justify unlimited barbarity.

The Americans, however, while not rejecting negative criminality completely, said that the applicable criteria must be not the knowledge of or the ability to prevent a crime but the clear duty and authority of a commander to act in particular circumstances. The Europeans believed that the occasion and opportunity to advance international law justified the creation of an international court to try the kaiser. If this were done, they argued, heads of state in the future would be more aware of personal and legal obligations that transcended the rights of the nation-state. The kaiser would be tried for violating the laws and customs of war and the laws of humanity to which he, as commander of German military forces, was as responsible as the lowliest soldier. He was not protected by the customary immunity of heads of state, because that principle was a mere "practical expedience in municipal law," and in any case, the German government itself would consent to the trial. The Americans did not agree. Citing the opinion of Chief Justice John Marshall in *Schooner Exchange* v. *McFaddon and Others* (1812), they proclaimed once again a sovereign's immunity from a foreign state's jurisdiction, for to do otherwise was to deny "the very conception of sovereignty." The Americans recognized the right of the Allies to impose "political sanctions" on the kaiser but not legal penalties, which would assume a "degree of responsibility hitherto unknown to municipal or international law, for which no precedents are to be found in the modern practice of nations." In judging lesser figures, the Americans wanted to "use the machinery at hand," national military tribunals, for which there was law and procedure, rather than an international court, for which there was "no precedent, precept, practice, or procedure." A precedent existed for use of national military tribunals—the trial of Henry Wirz after the American Civil War. Nothing else was needed. To create completely new institutions would be "*ex post facto* in nature" and contrary to the Constitution of the United States as well as the "law and practice of civilized communities."[66]

The Americans, on the whole, made a strong case but not without some misrepresentations. They did not mention that Marshall had discussed sovereign immunity as an international comity existing in peacetime and explicitly refrained from considering the issues raised when a sovereign entered another state's territory or jurisdiction without its consent as, for example, by means of invasion. They also did not point out that the ex-president of the Confederacy, Jefferson Davis, had been charged, although never brought to trial, with conspiracy to violate the laws of war. It must be said that because there was no firm legal ground of any kind the Europeans made as good a case as the Americans. Many reputable scholars in the United States, such as Quincy Wright and James W. Garner, believed a way could be found to try the kaiser legally.[67] The primary strength of Lansing and Scott's position rested upon the presumption, and little else, that because nothing had been done in the past, nothing should be done. The conclusion is inescapable that disagreement about a trial of Wilhelm II resulted as much from political as from legal differences.

Lansing and Pollock told their respective leaders as much when submitting their final reports. Pollock informed Lloyd George that the Americans remained "reluctant to create the possibility of their President ever being incriminated."[68] Lansing advised Wilson that the British and French were determined to try the kaiser, "the former because of promises on the hustings, the latter because the French members of the Commission had previously written a monograph in favor of his trial and punishment." What both wanted, said Lansing, was "international Lynch Law." He warned Wilson, quite correctly, that popular sentiment in the United States supported "the judicial trial and punishment of the Kaiser."[69] Even the Springfield *Republican*, Wilson's favorite newspaper, advocated establishment of a new precedent to create a basis for future proceedings.[70] Wilson had to stand alone against his associates on the Council of Four who had pledged that Germans would be prosecuted.

3

The discussions in the Council of Four about war crimes trials occurred during the nadir of the peace conference. Wilson, locked in struggle with Lloyd George and Clemenceau over several crucial issues, considered withdrawing and returning home. The Italians and Japanese were poised to present imperialist challenges to the principle of self-determination. Russia, the Balkans, and the Near East were in chaos.[71] The question of sentencing war criminals, even the kaiser, must have seemed small when compared with these threats to Wilson's dreams for a new world order. Wilson was ambivalent about a punitive policy toward Germany. Like Lansing, he wanted to conciliate German democracy, not drive it in desperation toward bolshevism, but he wanted as well to prevent any resurgence of German militarism. At the same time, his moralism demanded repentance for the old regime's misdeeds. His views on international law were less rigid than Lansing's, more concerned with the dynamic spirit than the letter of the law. He was certainly not opposed in principle, as was Lansing, to the idea of international war crimes trials. He expected the League of Nations to bring many changes in international law. Finally, Wilson had to worry about the reactions of Lloyd George and Clemenceau.[72]

Discouraged and ill, Wilson on April 1 tried to dissuade Lloyd George from pressing for a trial of the kaiser. He warned of the danger of making Wilhelm II a martyr. But Lloyd George thought that possibility was remote.[73] The next day, Wilson continued to oppose individual punishments. The whole idea ran counter to his sense of justice. He asserted that the kaiser's guilt remained unclear, for some accounts "picture him signing orders with regret." Wilson doubted whether the Allies had any right to be both judge and prosecutor. It might also create a "dangerous precedent," because not all future victors would dispense impartial justice. A leader's acts had always been "solely a collective responsibility" and to make them an individual crime, after the fact, was "inequitable." He cautioned: "We must not allow History to reproach us with having judged before establishing the juridical basis for the sentence." He had recently reread documents on the war of 1870 and had concluded "that the behavior of the Germans at that time resembles what we condemn them for today." He warned against verdicts "rendered in an atmosphere of passion." He explained: "You think me unfeeling. But I constantly struggle against emotion, and I have to exert pressure on myself to maintain my reliability of judgment." Clemenceau said little but could not resist a rejoinder to this remark: "Nothing is accomplished without emotion. Was Jesus Christ not carried away by passion the day he chased the money changers from the Temple?" Lloyd George stressed again and again the League of Nations, appealing to Wilson's hopes for a strong international organization. He declared:

If the League of Nations is to have some chance of success, it must not appear as just a word on a scrap of paper. It must have the power from this moment to punish crimes against international law. The violation of treaties is precisely the sort of crime to be of direct concern to the League of Nations.

Wilson ended the discussion on a characteristic note: "I agree with you about the crimes committed, but I want us to act in a manner to satisfy our own consciences."[74]

For the next several days, Wilson lay ill in bed, where he must have weighed his conscience against the imperative need for Lloyd George's support to avoid an aborted peace conference. He must have known that Lloyd George had to secure the trial of the kaiser. There is much evidence to suggest that Lloyd George sincerely believed in the necessity of warning future aggressors; he also clearly wanted to prevent restoration of Wilhelm II and the resurgence of German militarism. Apart from his conscience, which was irregularly active on many matters, at that moment, he was under severe pressure from Parliament to fulfill his election pledges.[75] He could not have repudiated the idea of war crimes trials even if he had wanted to do so. Wilson could not hope to stay in Paris without Lloyd George's support and beat back assaults on his conception of a just and durable peace. The president needed Lloyd George on two issues requiring immediate resolution: French demands for annexation of the Saar and an amendment to the League Covenant recognizing the Monroe Doctrine. Of the two, the Monroe Doctrine issue was more important, for without it, Wilson believed, he could not persuade the Senate of the United States to ratify the Versailles treaty and thereby approve American participation in the League. Wilson learned on April 7 that Lloyd George threatened to reject the Monroe Doctrine amendment unless the United States scaled down its naval building program, a program aimed at parity with Britain. Wilson capitulated on that point and, at the same time, took a tough stance of his own, dramatically recalling his ship, the *George Washington*, to Brest, a clear signal that he would leave the conference unless the Europeans made concessions.[76]

Did Wilson also concede war crimes trials as added inducement to secure British support for the Monroe Doctrine amendment? The close conjunction of decisions makes such a thesis not unreasonable. Wilson compromised on the kaiser's trial on April 8, and on the evening of April 10, the British helped him override French opposition to the amendment. Moreover, on the afternoon of April 9, the Saar impasse was broken when Lloyd George enthusiastically championed Wilson's compromise proposal, something he had not done before.[77]

Wilson on April 8 made a brief effort at dissuasion, and he convinced a dubious Orlando against trying the kaiser. But Lloyd George bluntly told the president: "This question, with that of reparations, is the one that interests English opinion to the highest degree, and we could not sign a peace treaty that left it without solution." Lloyd George said that the method was "of small importance" to him "provided that the man be punished and put where he can do no further harm; we must prevent the intrigues which might make him once more dangerously powerful, and at the same time make an example of him."[78] Clemenceau, who was certainly aware that French opinion had of late become almost as strong on this issue as the British,[79] said that the kaiser must not go free, for that was "something our peoples would never understand." Wilson replied that he could "only do what I consider to be just, whether public sentiment be for or against the verdict of my conscience." Lloyd George proposed bringing the kaiser to judgment "solely for the violation" of the treaty guaranteeing the neutrality of Belgium, saying:

War between nations is justifiable in conformity with the precedents. But an aggression without provocation, without any grievance against the country attacked, committed because it was convenient to cross her territory and in spite of a solemn engagement treated like a scrap of paper, is an indisputable crime.

Wilson's conscience found this indictment persuasive:

It is certainly a crime, but for which no sanction has been provided, because there is no legal precedent for it. We are founding today the regime of the League of Nations from which will emerge the new rules and the new formulas of international law. But today we are obligated to create the principle and the punishment.[80]

That same evening, after consulting Lansing, Wilson closely followed his recommendations in drafting two clauses on war crimes and trials, recommendations that Lansing must have known would undermine the proposed prosecution of the kaiser.[81] The next morning, the European leaders, without much discussion, approved these proposals. Somewhat later, the Japanese gave their assent. The first clause provided for trial before Allied national or mixed military tribunals of persons accused of violating the laws and customs of war. Thus Wilson preserved the essence of the American legal position, excluding an international tribunal, the laws of humanity, and negative criminality. The second clause provided that the Allies would request the Netherlands to surrender the kaiser so that he could appear before a "special tribunal" of five judges from the major powers. The charge against him would "not be defined as an offence against criminal law, but a supreme offence against international morality and the sanctity of treaties." The judges in rendering a verdict were to be "guided by the highest motives of international policy."[82] These provisions with slight amendments became articles 227 to 230 of the Versailles treaty. The Council of Four later ruled that peace treaties with the other defeated nations—Austria, Hungary, Bulgaria, and Turkey—must include similar, although not identical, war crimes clauses. These are discussed separately in Chapter 9.

This compromise, in retrospect, appears incongruous. It did not serve the purposes of either Lloyd George or Wilson. The prime minister wanted to establish a new precedent in international law. He wanted to establish the principle that national leaders might be held criminally responsible for their actions, especially for waging a war of aggression. Yet he accepted a formulation that did not use the word *aggression* and specifically denied that the kaiser was charged with a crime. Wilson, on the other hand, doubted Wilhelm II's personal responsibility and wanted above all else to ensure justice to the kaiser. Yet the president settled upon the kind of proceedings least likely to be conducted fairly. Charging the kaiser with an offense against international morality before a tribunal guided by motives of high policy would deprive him of whatever protection a process grounded in law might provide. It opened the trial of the kaiser to charges of victor's justice to an even greater degree than a prosecution resting upon, at least, some principles of law, to which the kaiser might also appeal in his defense.

The objectives of both Lloyd George and Wilson would have been better served if they had followed the recommendation of the majority report of the Commission on Responsibility to try the kaiser for violations of the laws of war. Such a trial would have established a new precedent in international law regarding the responsibility of national leaders. The charges would not, however, have been of an ex post facto character, for the Hague conventions contained relatively clear standards for the conduct of war. The kaiser would have been afforded well-established protections for defendants in criminal proceedings before military tribunals.

It is not clear why Lloyd George and Wilson failed to accept the recommendation of the Commission on Responsibility. The record of their discussions suggests that they had not studied carefully the reports of the commission and relied instead upon a hastily conceived improvisation to settle the matter. Arthur S. Link, the principal biographer of Wilson, suggested that the president may have cynically settled upon this compromise, because he believed it would never be carried out anyway.[83] Lloyd George certainly remained committed to a trial of the kaiser but was more interested in the actual punishment of Wilhelm II than in the method of accomplishing that end. It is clear that Lansing, through his recommendations to Wilson, managed in the end to triumph in his opposition to international war crimes punishments.

Opposition persisted among other Allied statesmen who unsuccessfully sought modifications in the war crimes clauses agreed to by the Council of Four. Several embarrassing episodes resulted. The Council of Four had agreed that Belgium should provide the prosecutor for the kaiser, but on April 16 Premier Paul Hymans announced that in deference to the monarchial principle Belgium must decline. Belgium's absence from the trial of the man charged with violation of its neutrality would prove most awkward, many people thought. But Wilson said he did not believe this "obstacle unsurmountable," because Belgium "could not refuse to be a witness."[84] Lloyd George had to quiet the objections of two powerful members of his own delegation, Jan Smuts and Louis Botha of South Africa, who remembered the delay in arriving at peace in 1902 when they had resisted British demands for punishment of Boer war criminals. Smuts and Botha insisted upon restricting surrender of alleged German war criminals to a few persons actually named in the peace treaty. Threatening to protest publicly, these men temporarily prevented a plenary session of the peace conference from giving final approval to the war crimes clauses.[85] When informed of this dissent, Wilson said he "had always felt that this was the weak spot in the Treaty of Peace"[86] but none-theless defended the punitive aspects of the peace settlement, telling Smuts that they were necessary because of the "very great offence against civilization" the Germans had committed.[87]

Lloyd George refused all efforts to retreat on war crimes punishment. Rather, he strengthened the clauses, for he secured elimination of the statement that the kaiser was not charged with a criminal offense and addition of a statement that German proceedings would not bar Allied prosecution of the same crime.[88] He also tried unsuccessfully to get Wilson to agree to the holding of important German prisoners of war as hostages to ensure surrender of the accused criminals,[89] for it had become a certainty that the new German government would not willingly cooperate.

4

The Germans were almost unanimously opposed to articles 227 to 231. Radical left-wing proletarian groups called for summary justice against the officer class and leaders of the old regime and would have eagerly handed over such persons to the Allies.[90] The Social Democrats and bourgeoisie parties who controlled the government, however, had no such desire. Their protection against revolutionary upheaval rested in large measure upon the tenuous backing of the army. For that reason alone, they believed, agreeing to surrender accused military personnel was impossible. In addition, no modern nation had ever been forced to hand over soldiers, who in many instances had merely followed orders in defense of their country. The whole idea was repugnant to anyone with nationalist feelings. Moreover, because the new leaders who had been ruling Germany since the armistice had vigorously defended their country's actions during the war, they could hardly accept the verdict of war guilt.[91]

German leaders were uncertain and divided about how to persuade the Allies to abandon articles 227 to 231. Before going to the peace conference, they took a number of steps to justify rejecting those clauses. They proposed creation of a neutral commission "to probe responsibilities for the war," but the Allies rebuffed this proposal, declaring that German guilt "had already been established."[92] One member of the Cabinet, Matthias Erzberger, leader of the Catholic Center party, suggested setting up a state tribunal to examine and sharply condemn the actions of Germany's former leaders. If such proceedings were going on during the peace negotiations, Erzberger believed, the Allies would be sympathetically impressed. The ministers prepared legislation for a state tribunal and for a parliamentary investigation commission but did not act immediately to establish either body.[93] Other ministers, particularly Foreign Minister Count Ulrich von Brockdorff-Rantzau, thought it unwise to concede guilt, for the Allies would undoubtedly use such an admission to help justify a harsh peace. These ministers preferred to challenge Allied views.[94] Preparations were made to secure documents from Austro-Hungarian archives, showing that Austrian officials had misled Bethmann Hollweg in July 1914.[95] The General Staff drew up a memorandum claiming military necessity as a reason for the destruction of French and Belgian industry.[96] The government appointed a Commission for the Investigation of Accusations of Violations of International Law in the Treatment of Prisoners of War in Germany. Later expanded to inquire into other charges, this group, under the direction of Professor Walther Schücking, began in December 1918 to refute one by one specific allegations of war crimes, a project that continued for several years.[97]

When the German peace delegation was handed the treaty at Versailles on May 7, the anniversary of the sinking of the *Lusitania*, Count Brockdorff-Rantzau made the first of many defiant protests against war guilt and accusations of war crimes. "Such a confession in my mouth," he said, "would be a lie." In "the manner of waging war, Germany was not the only one that erred." At least, Germany's excesses had been committed in the passion of war, but the appalling continuation of the Allied blockade after the armistice had killed hundreds of thousands of noncombatants. This had been done, he charged, "coolly and deliberately after our opponents had won a certain and assured victory. Remember that," he told the assembled Allied leaders, "when you speak of guilt and atonement." He renewed the request for an "impartial inquiry, a neutral commission before which all the principals in the tragedy are allowed to speak, and to which all archives are open."[98]

When the terms of the treaty reached Germany, there were mass demonstrations against their acceptance in many cities. The harsh territorial, military, and financial settlements were denounced. Much attention focused upon articles 227-231. At a special session of the National Assembly at Berlin on May 12, Chancellor Philipp Scheidemann said the hand that signed such a peace would "wither," and, supported by all parties except the Independent Socialists, he declared that Germany would never agree to the conditions.[99]

At Versailles the German peace delegation, with whom the Allies would not negotiate face to face, was limited to written remonstrances. The Germans requested immediate, unconditional repatriation of prisoners of war.[100] The Allies refused and announced that many prisoners would be retained after the peace to stand trial.[101] The Germans retorted that accusations of war crimes should be referred to a neutral commission to which they could bring numerous instances of Allied atrocities.[102] The

Germans centered much of their attack upon article 231. Four scholars led by the great sociologist Max Weber were brought to Paris to draft a repudiation of war guilt. The Allies denied them a copy of the report of the Commission on Responsibility. They could only rely upon news accounts in preparing their reply, and they drew up a point-by-point correction of the commission's errors.[103] The most serious, they charged, was the "silence concerning the general Russian mobilization." If Paris and London had worked for peace in Saint Petersburg, they said, as earnestly as Berlin had in Vienna, this "fatal step" might "have been averted." The true premeditation that caused the war was Russia's long quest for the Bosporus.[104] In their comprehensive counterproposal of May 29, the Germans declared that "honor" made articles 227 to 231 unacceptable. The Germans would abide by preliminary rulings of an international tribunal of neutrals regarding accused war criminals, reserving the right to impose the actual punishments, if the Allies would also permit such a court to render verdicts against their citizens. Concluding, the Germans condemned the recent arrests in occupied areas.[105]

The Allies yielded nothing to German "honor." Lloyd George asked Philip Kerr to draft a harsh ultimatum for the Council of Four. Wilson said that Kerr's note "would not prove satisfactory to the future historian,"[106] but, he said, the German challenge to the war-guilt clause must be refuted. The Allies castigated Germany for the "greatest crime against humanity" ever committed. The "outbreak of the war was deliberately plotted and executed by those who wielded the supreme power in Vienna, Budapest, and Berlin." Germany had conducted the war in a "savage and inhuman manner." The Allies could not leave punishment of criminals in the hands of "their accomplices." The Allies preferred to "stand by the verdict of history as to the impartiality and justice with which the accused will be tried." The Allies gave the Germans seven days in which to sign the treaty or suffer invasion.[107]

The Germans searched frantically for some means to escape their dilemma. Max Weber was so concerned about the moral impact of articles 227 to 231 that he urged military and political leaders responsible for war policies to surrender voluntarily so that the nation would not have to accept these clauses. He believed that such a heroic gesture on their part would restore German morale and rally the people. He approached General Ludendorff with his scheme.[108] The general, who, disguised by false beard and dark blue glasses, had fled to Sweden after the armistice because he feared revolutionary justice,[109] rejected Weber's idea. Denouncing the German people as ingrates, Ludendorff refused to do anything to save German democracy from this humiliation.[110]

The so-called *Schmachparagraphen* ("shame paragraphs") made signing the treaty a matter of honor, not utility, destroyed one Cabinet, caused dangerous military unrest, and almost led Germany to repudiate the entire peace settlement.[111] That Germany did not do so was due largely to the machinations of Erzberger.[112] Chancellor Scheidemann and most other ministers opposed acceptance on June 18. Scheidemann said they must tell the Allies: "Do not think we can be your bum-bailiffs and hang-men among our own people."[113] The next day Defense Minister Gustav Noske met with some thirty army officers, many of whom wanted to overthrow the government and fight to the end. Field Marshal von Hinden-burg and his chief assistant, General Wilhelm Groener, however, con-vinced the officers to accept the peace on condition that articles 227 to 231 were removed. They told Noske that, otherwise, they must withdraw support from the government.[114] The Cabinet fell, but Erzberger, with great difficulty, managed to construct a new coalition in the National Assembly. He secured support only after he was able to tell leaders of various political factions that French agents had assured him that the Allies would not insist upon articles 227 to 231.[115] After the new Cabinet was formed, the Germans informed the Allies on June 22 that the treaty would be signed "without, however, recognizing thereby that the German people was the author of the war, and without undertaking any responsi-bility for delivering persons in accordance with Articles 227 to 230."[116]

The French promises had not been authorized; the Council of Four rejected the German offer. At the last minute, the Vatican, which was to intervene many times in connection with this issue in coming months, unsuccessfully appealed to the British to give way.[117] Wilson said that he "would gladly accede to the Germans' request, but felt himself bound by his agreement with his associates."[118] Clemenceau and Lloyd George re-mained obdurate. A new ultimatum was dispatched, requiring uncon-ditional acceptance of the treaty and pointing out that Allied troops would march into Germany in less than twenty-four hours.[119]

The Germans wanted desperately to avoid this decision. After an all-night session of the Cabinet, President Friedrich Ebert telephoned Hinden-burg and Groener, less than three hours before the ultimatum's expiration, to ask if military resistance was feasible. Groener said no; the treaty must be signed. He advised a special appeal to the army to continue support of the government. A few minutes before the deadline on June 23 the German government capitulated unconditionally.[120]

For the first time, a major international peace treaty had established the principle in international law that war crimes punishment was a proper conclusion of peace, that the termination of war did not bring a general amnesty as a matter of course. The culpable acts for which men might be held personally responsible did not include initiation of aggressive war, but, nonetheless, the penalty clauses were clear evidence of changes in moral, political, and legal attitudes toward international violence. But for

American opposition, the Europeans probably would have provided for an international tribunal to judge war criminals, and Lloyd George might even have secured a special accusation against the kaiser for the crime of aggression.

Problems still would have remained. The arrangements made at Paris provided for one-sided justice. That alone called into question their value for the future development of international law and the attainment of a more peaceful world. In the discussions of the peace conference, there was little consideration of international war crimes punishment as a permanent international reform. The French suggestion to establish an international criminal court associated with the League of Nations was scarcely given a hearing. The German offer to submit cases of accused war criminals to preliminary judgment of an international court of neutral jurists, if the Allies would do the same, was not considered at all. Understandably, in the immediate postwar period when hostile feelings toward the Germans still ran high, the admission that there had been violations of international law on all sides probably could not have been obtained. Instead, Allied leaders, who did not fully agree on war crimes punishments, attempted to implement a victor's justice with which neither the neutral Netherlands nor the defeated Germany was willing to cooperate. If there had been a thorough debate of the problem of war crimes committed by the Allies as well as the crimes of the Germans, it is possible that the peace conference could have made provisions for punishment of war crimes a permanent part of international relations.

WILFUL MURDER.

THE KAISER. "TO THE DAY——"   DEATH. "——OF RECKONING!"

Figure 1. *Punch* Sketch, May 19, 1915. Source: Library of Congress. Reprinted by permission of *Punch*.

ON THE BLACK LIST.

KAISER (*as Executioner*). "I'M GOING TO HANG YOU."

PUNCH. "OH, YOU ARE, ARE YOU? WELL, YOU DON'T SEEM TO KNOW HOW THE SCENE ENDS. IT'S THE HANGMAN THAT GETS HANGED."

The *Deutsche Tageszeitung*, remarking on "the black and distorted souls of decadent peoples," issues a warning to *Punch* and others. "Their performances," it says, "are diligently noted, so that when the day of reckoning arrives we shall know with whom we have to deal and how to deal with them most effectually."

Figure 2. *Punch* Sketch, June 16, 1915. Source: Library of Congress. Reprinted by permission of *Punch*.

CAIN.

MORE THAN FOURTEEN THOUSAND BRITISH NON-COMBATANTS—MEN, WOMEN AND CHILDREN—HAVE BEEN MURDERED BY THE KAISER'S COMMAND.

Figure 3. *Punch* Sketch, February 13, 1918. Source: Library of Congress. Reprinted by permission of *Punch*.

WANTED.

WILLIAM THE GALLANT (*to Holland*). "COURAGE! I WILL NEVER DESERT YOU."

Figure 4. *Punch* Sketch, December 11, 1918. Source: Library of Congress. Reprinted by permission of *Punch*.

"WANTED."

Holland. "SO YOU SAY YOU'D LIKE ME TO SURRENDER THE EX-KAISER?"
Entente Policeman. "WELL, MA'AM, I DIDN'T GO SO FAR AS THAT. I ONLY *ASKED* YOU FOR HIM."

Figure 5. *Punch* Sketch, January 21, 1920. Source: Library of Congress. Reprinted by permission of *Punch*.

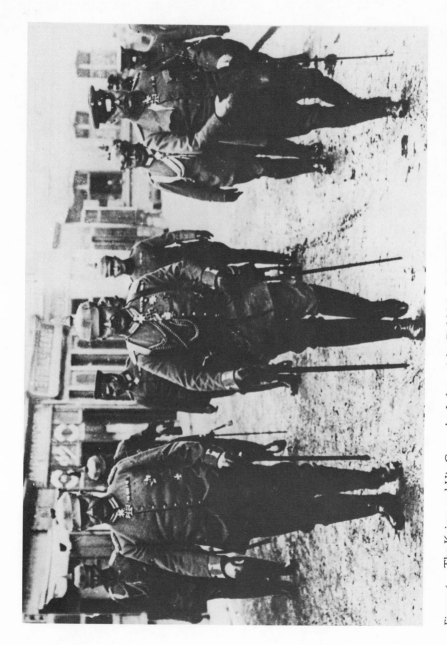

Figure 6. The Kaiser and His Generals. *Left to right:* Field Marshal Paul von Hindenburg, Kaiser Wilhelm II, and General Erich Ludendorff. Source: National Archives.

Figure 7. Allied Leaders at a Meeting of the Council of Four. *Left to right:* Vittorio Orlando, David Lloyd George, Georges Clemenceau, and Woodrow Wilson. Source: National Archives.

Figure 8. Delegates at a Meeting of the Commission on the Responsibility of the Authors of the War and the Enforcement of Penalties. *Right front of table,* Édouard Rolin-Jacquemyns; *third from right,* William F. Massey; *fourth from right,* Robert Lansing; *fifth from right,* James Brown Scott; *seventh from right,* Fernand Larnaude; *third from left front of table,* Nicolas Politis. Sir Ernest Pollock is not pictured. Source: The Bettmann Archive. Reprinted by permission.

Figure 9.   Reichsgericht Building at Leipzig. Source: National Archives.

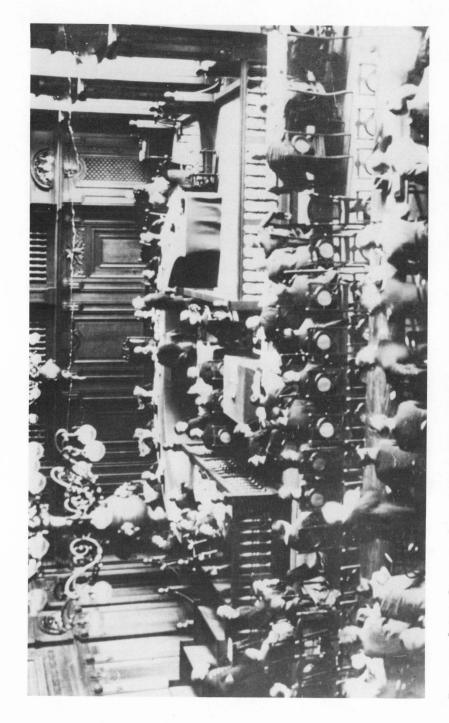

Figure 10. Leipzig Courtroom during First War Crimes Trial. Source: Ullstein Bilderdienst. Reprinted by permission.

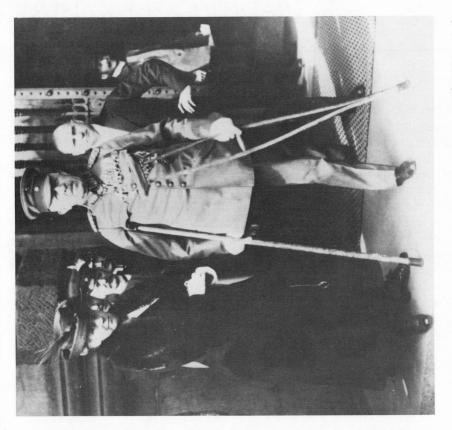

Figure 11. General Karl Stenger Leaving Court. Source: The New York Times. Reprinted by permission.

6

EXTRADITING THE KAISER

Even if the Allies had agreed on punishment for Wilhelm II, it is unlikely that the ex-kaiser would ever have appeared before a tribunal. Recognizing his peril, the kaiser prepared to disappear into hiding and even considered suicide. In the end, he did not have to resort to such desperate measures. The government of the Netherlands learned from various sources that the Allies lacked determination and concluded that it could safely reject any request for the surrender of the kaiser. Lloyd George remained committed to the idea of a trial for Wilhelm II, but other British officials, respecting the wishes of their royal family, virtually forced him to abandon efforts to bring the kaiser before a court. Lloyd George eventually was willing to settle for internment of Wilhelm II on an island under Allied supervision, much in the way Britain had confined Napoleon to Saint Helena, but failed to secure even that solution. The Dutch remained true to their tradition of providing refuge for the vanquished and would not agree to such an arrangement. Dutch intransigence was made possible, in part, because British diplomats unsympathetic with Lloyd George's wishes sabotaged his efforts. Other Allied governments also let the Dutch know that the scheme did not have their approval. Italian and French leaders would not even help force the exile of the kaiser to the Dutch East Indies. Instead, the Allies accepted Dutch internment of the kaiser in the Netherlands with assurances that he would not be permitted to carry on political intrigues.

1

While his fate was being debated at Paris, the kaiser anxiously anticipated the worst. At Amerongen, he felt like a prisoner awaiting sentence. Although his host, Count Bentinck, was friendly and hospitable, Wilhelm II, along with a few aides, and his wife, who had joined him in exile, was otherwise besieged. Threatening mail came from all over the world, and hordes of journalists lurked outside the walls of the estate.[1] Guards patrolled as much to prevent the kaiser from leaving as to keep out un- wanted visitors. The Dutch government censored his correspondence, would not allow him to purchase a home, and permitted excursions outside the grounds of the estate only when accompanied by a Dutch official. The kaiser grew despondent and told his aide, Captain Sigurd von Ilsemann: "Every criminal has the right to asylum. But it is not allowed me." War guilt and extradition worried him constantly. He studied various published collections of documents on the outbreak of the war and began writing a defense of his own actions. But he was haunted by thoughts that the Allies would eventually get him.[2]

When the Dutch government indicated that his presence was undesir- able, he turned to his own resources to escape the Allies. Working secretly with the German minister to the Netherlands, Friedrich Rosen, the kaiser's aides tried to make arrangements for his protection. But Rosen told them that Berlin would not permit the kaiser to return to Germany and would imprison him if he appeared. Sweden, Spain, and Switzerland were approached unsuccessfully about asylum.[3] One of his aides in com- plete despair proposed surrendering voluntarily to America or Britain, although never to France. The kaiser categorically rejected the idea. He said:

I do not want to be dragged like the basest criminal through the streets of Paris or London where I will be spit upon and so that those bastards can cut off my head. Because there is no doubt about that: once I am in their hands they will kill me. This dishonor and shame I cannot bring myself, my house, and Germany; this triumph the enemies shall not have.[4]

The kaiser decided he would have to disappear into hiding. With the help of the German minister, who acted without Berlin's knowledge, arrangements were made for a false passport and a car and an escape route to Germany where friends would secretly house him. Von Ilsemann was to accompany the kaiser, who planned to disguise himself in a cap, dyed hair, turned-down moustache, and glasses.[5] He also began to grow a beard, which many people later said made him unrecognizable as the old kaiser.[6] Concerned about his readily identifiable crippled arm, he decided to wear a long covering sleeve that he could stuff in his pocket. To protect his host against blame, he kept these preparations a secret from Count Bentinck.

The kaiser did not believe his chances of escape were very good, and he dwelt upon suicide as a better alternative, much to his wife's distress. On one occasion, the kaiser told his aides: "It would be better if one of you would shoot me." Later, when he talked of taking poison, the anxious empress said: "Wilhelm then I will go with you into the hereafter."[7] The empress eventually broke down completely. The strain of these days aggravated her heart condition and contributed to her early death.[8]

Several old friends and subordinates in Germany deserted the kaiser. They privately urged him to agree voluntarily to a trial to prove that the Allies had caused the war and to secure moderate peace terms for his defeated country. The kaiser refused and declared:

The proposition is false. A court which is impartial does not exist at present in Europe. Against a single person (here the German Emperor) such a procedure cannot be initiated. It must be directed against all sovereigns and statesmen who partook in the war, that is, against Poincaré, the Kings of Italy, England, Rumania, Bulgaria, the Serbs, the Sultan, and so forth. The proceedings would mean a dishonoring of the principle of monarchy. . . . I do not have any guilt and I do not recognize any court having jurisdiction over me. I always have to play the sacrificial lamb. I will not think of it.[9]

As a precaution, the kaiser nonetheless accepted the services of an international lawyer, Dr. Johannes Kriege, who also worked in the German Foreign Office. Kriege began commuting from Berlin to Amerongen to provide legal advice about extradition and war crimes trials.[10]

Eventually, Minister Rosen persuaded the kaiser and his aides to remain in the Netherlands as long as possible. He said they could always flee later, if the Dutch showed signs of cooperating with the Allies. He convinced the kaiser to feign illness to gain time and sympathy. Rosen arranged for a doctor from Amsterdam to examine Wilhelm II periodically and to issue reports of declining health, which did appear regularly for a time in the world press. Von Ilsemann said: "How terrible is this comedy game for the poor Kaiser!"[11]

Early in 1919, the kaiser briefly faced danger from a group of American soldiers who tried to spirit him off to Paris. Colonel Luke Lea, former United States senator and publisher of the Nashville *Tennessean*, suspected that the British did not really intend to "hang the Kaiser" and thought that if the kaiser were brought to Paris public opinion would force action. "The capture, trial, and punishment of the Kaiser," he said, "was to the American doughboy the object which inspired him" to fight. Lea undoubtedly wanted to be remembered as the man who achieved the soldier's fantasy, the man who bagged "Kaiser Bill." Lea led six soldiers to Amerongen just after New Year's Day. They planned to seize the kaiser by surprise and roar off to Paris, daring the Dutch to shoot while the kaiser was held prisoner in their car. Near Amerongen, however, they came upon a washed-out bridge and saw that capture was inevitable at that point in a return trip. What had begun as a serious undertaking consequently turned into a semicomic confrontation. The Americans determined to persuade the kaiser to go with them voluntarily to face his accusers manfully. They continued on to the Bentinck estate on the night of January 5, bluffed their way inside the house, and demanded to see Wilhelm II. After a two-hour standoff, during which the kaiser refused to meet with the Americans, Dutch troops surrounded the estate with spotlights and machine guns, forcing Colonel Lea and his men to depart.[12] Subsequently, Allied governments had no more success in getting the kaiser out of the Netherlands than did the venturesome American soldiers.

2

During the Paris Peace Conference, there was, however, little concern about getting the Netherlands to hand over the kaiser. Journalists and individuals who did not understand international law spoke of extradition, but the statesmen on the Council of Four when framing article 227 recognized, as Wilson said, that they had "no legal means of forcing Holland to deliver up the Kaiser." Extradition, properly used, was a technical legal term and a process strictly governed by international treaties that specified the crimes for which persons might be transferred from one nation's jurisdiction to another's, and international law had little to say about political crimes. No extradition treaty covered the charge against Wilhelm II, "a supreme offence against international morality and the sanctity of treaties," which was, if anything, a political offense. Gaining custody of the kaiser, Allied leaders knew, would require an exercise of power, not law, and they expected opposition because of the Dutch tradition of providing refuge for political exiles. Lloyd George argued that the Allies could "say to Holland that, if she refuses, she will not be received into the League of Nations."[13] When this problem was taken up by the Council of Four again on June 25-26, Wilson, who believed the Netherlands "morally obliged to surrender the Kaiser," wanted to "make it as easy for her as possible." Lloyd George was unconcerned about Dutch sensibilities. The Four did not discuss alternatives if the Dutch should refuse, for they assumed that the Netherlands, however reluctantly, must give way. They agreed that the best method was a joint demand upon ratification of the Versailles treaty for delivery of the kaiser, and they directed Lansing to draft such a note.[14]

In the meantime, they had received reports[15] that the kaiser and crown prince might try to return to Germany to stir up "mischief." The Council of Four sent a severe warning on June 27 to The Hague that the Dutch should prevent an escape. "To permit it would be an international crime, which would not be forgiven those who have contributed to it by their carelessness or their connivance." The Allies offered to take immediate custody of Wilhelm II if the Dutch government felt the "responsibilities heavier than any which it is prepared to bear."[16] They discovered that dealing with the Netherlands would not be an easy task. In an equally stiff rejoinder the "painfully surprised" Dutch claimed to have fulfilled their international obligations and indirectly rejected the implication that they were the kaiser's jailers.[17]

A British diplomat at The Hague, Arnold Robertson, said the warning had made the problem "considerably more difficult," a judgment in which an American colleague, Frank Gunther, concurred. Gunther complained that it had made no allowance "for the psychology of the Dutch." Robertson believed the Dutch would like to get rid of the kaiser, but "if we threaten or try to coerce them, they will shelter themselves behind the wall of their conception of International Law, and we shall not be able to budge them, unless we don 'shining armour' and shake a 'mailed fist' at them."[18] Gunther cautioned that "this matter cannot be handled too delicately or intelligently if we really wish to pull it off."[19]

Gunther had raised an intriguing question: Did the Allies really want to get the kaiser? Was article 227 a "hollow sham" whose provisions the Allies never intended to carry out? Many persons, then and later, suspected Allied leaders of just such a cynical maneuver to extricate themselves from a venture forced on them by public opinion.[20] This reasoning may explain the behavior of some leaders, but Lloyd George's sincerity cannot be doubted.

So intent was he upon trying the kaiser that Lloyd George overreached himself. After repeated requests, he finally got Georges Clemenceau and President Wilson to acquiesce in his plan of holding the trial in Britain.[21] When he presented the Versailles treaty to the House of Commons on July 3, he announced that the international tribunal would "sit in London for the trial of the person supremely responsible for this War."[22] Of Lloyd George's many declarations that day, it "was cheered most of all."[23] It also provoked a stormy public debate. Many persons who had called for the kaiser's punishment, such as Lord Beresford, now believed Lloyd George had gone too far.[24] The *Nation* spoke for much liberal opinion when it condemned Lloyd George for giving a good idea a "morbid theatrical turn," for his plan raised visions of the Tower of London and gawky holiday crowds.[25] The conservative *Times* and *Spectator* supported Lloyd George, but they were less enthusiastic than before.[26] Even the usually sensational *Daily Mail* was restrained.[27] When the House of Commons debated the treaty on July 21, critics appeared among those individuals formerly in favor of trying the kaiser.[28] What troubled most persons, said A. G. Gardiner, editor of the *Daily News,* was the "act of extraordinary thoughtlessness" in having the trial of the kaiser "within musket-shot of Buckingham Palace," for he was, after all, the grandson of Queen Victoria and the cousin of King George V.[29]

Probably, the harshest critic of Lloyd George's announcement was King George, who was working against the trial. Sir Maurice Hankey, secretary of the Cabinet, reported that upon meeting the king in August, he "burst out into a violent tirade against trying the Kaiser in England, a subject on which he was moved to vehement eloquence" for half an hour.[30] The king spoke to Lord Curzon, who had become foreign minister, and to Lloyd George as well.

Out of consideration for the royal family, Curzon deserted Lloyd George. He wrote the prime minister a long letter on July 7, which Lord Beaverbrook called a "hysterical composition," raising every imaginable objection.[31] Curzon, like everyone else, had not heard of the choice of London until Lloyd George's speech, for the prime minister had consulted none of his colleagues about the matter.[32] Curzon told Lloyd George he "had never contemplated, and am a good deal staggered at, the idea of the trial taking place in England." The king would be placed "in a very delicate and invidious position." A trial in London "amid the jeers and insults of the crowd" would be "disgraceful." Lodging such witnesses as the kaiser's ministers and generals would create enormous problems in logistics and protection. If Britain executed the inevitable verdict, Germany would become an enemy "till the end of time." An acquittal, on the other hand, would leave Britain all the "blame and ridicule of the fiasco." France, Belgium, and Italy were no more suitable than Britain, Curzon concluded, and then, almost plaintively, he asked: "Is it altogether impossible that the Kaiser should be tried at The Hague?"[33]

Lord Curzon had been one of the few members of the Cabinet originally supporting the kaiser's trial, and the prime minister realized the implications of his new foreign secretary's virtual repudiation. He gave Curzon "a stinging rebuke," said Lord Beaverbrook, "an insulting reply which would have driven most Ministers to hand in their resignations forthwith."[34] Lloyd George said he had already heard all of Curzon's arguments "from the King—every one of them," and they were really against any trial at all. He said, however, he did not want to believe that the king had made the "suggestion that the Cabinet should be invited to throw over its principal delegate to the Peace Conference in an important decision which he had taken on their behalf." He told Curzon that to retreat now would make everyone concerned look "extremely foolish." Britain was the only country in which such proceedings could be conducted fairly. The Netherlands would never permit a court to assemble on its territory. London, Lloyd George conceded, was undesirable, but Hampton Court would meet all necessities as to space, crowd control, and protection. Many lesser Germans would be brought to Britain in any case for trial by national military tribunals. "Is it suggested that we should abandon these prosecutions and let these ruffians go, merely because there is a society objection to the trial of the Kaiser?"[35]

When the Cabinet discussed the issue on July 23, Lloyd George was more conciliatory. He "agreed that London was not a very suitable place, and it had been his intention, in his speech on the subject, to say that it would take place in *England.*" Officially, the Cabinet supported the prime minister and discussed the "relative advantages" of Hampton Court, Dover Castle, and the Channel Islands but made no final decision.[36] Lloyd George liked the idea of holding the trial at Dover, for, said Hankey, on channel crossings, he "was wont to gaze at the solid mass of Dover Castle perched on the white cliffs of old England and to murmur—'That's the place for the Kaiser's trial!' " As late as December, he was still talking about trying Wilhelm II at Dover.[37]

Nonetheless, one cannot avoid the conclusion that by silent understanding the trial of the kaiser was no longer a part of British policy after August. Despite a memorandum from Hankey pointing out the need for selection of a British judge, place of trial, and other arrangements, the Cabinet never again took up these problems. A minor official in the procurator general's office collected memoirs and documentary material to "give effect to article 227," but there were no significant preparations for a trial.[38] In January 1920 when the demand for surrender of the kaiser was finally made, neither the British nor any other Allied government would have been ready to institute proceedings if the Dutch had handed him over.

The Dutch never seriously considered surrendering the kaiser for trial after June 1919, for they recognized the disagreements among Allied governments. Some hints of these differences were public, and some, in the words of Churchill, were due to "the subterranean intrigues of old world secret diplomacy."[39] Belgium had dissociated itself from the project at the peace conference and refused to take part in any demands for the kaiser.[40] The Belgians could have had considerable influence with the Dutch, for the two countries were engaged in difficult negotiations over revision of boundaries and use of the Scheldt River, and the Dutch feared these problems would be used to force concessions on a trial of the kaiser.[41] The positions of Tokyo and Washington were well known from their dissent at the peace conference. The Americans subtly indicated to the Dutch their continuing opposition. Secretary of State Lansing told

Gunther on July 21 that his "non-committal attitude in this matter of the case against the Emperor and Crown Prince is approved." However, Lansing cautioned Gunther to say nothing "which, if made known to our associates, would tend to question our good faith."[42] Later, of course, failure of the Senate to ratify the Versailles treaty meant that the United States would play no role in its execution. The Italian Parliament in approving the treaty singled out article 227, questioned its legality, and the new foreign minister, Tommasco Tittoni, told Allied leaders in Paris in August that he thought it inadvisable to pursue the kaiser.[43] A Dutch envoy at the Vatican reported that the Italian government had decided not to participate in an extradition demand.[44] In official French circles, there was little desire to pursue the kaiser, although the Chamber of Deputies in approving the Versailles treaty vigorously applauded article 227.[45] The French ambassador to Britain, Paul Cambon, warned against "its practicality and wisdom" and deplored the "histrionics" of those who persisted.[46] His brother, Jules Cambon, actually asked the Dutch minister at London to use his influence at The Hague to prevent Wilhelm II's surrender.[47] Sir Eyre Crowe said that Clemenceau told him on October 3 that "it was practically certain" that the Netherlands would not hand over the kaiser, and "he apparently contemplated this contingency with equanimity." Clemenceau believed a trial *par contumace* was "an excellent way out of the difficulty" and would "probably have all the effect really desired."[48]

Neutrals also influenced the Dutch. The press in neutral countries was virtually unanimous in opposing the kaiser's trial.[49] The kings of Spain and Sweden privately encouraged the Dutch to resist.[50] The Vatican was especially active. Papal Foreign Secretary Cardinal Gasparri appealed to Balfour, Curzon, and the presidents of France, Italy, and the United States, calling attention to the danger of embittering national hatreds and undermining constituted authority everywhere.[51] To the Dutch ministry, which relied heavily upon Dutch Catholic support, Pope Benedict XV sent a personal message, declaring that "civilized peoples will applaud" a refusal to hand over the kaiser to his enemies. Confidentially, he told the Dutch that authoritative persons in Italy and Britain held similar sentiments.[52] The Vatican may also have known that Cardinal Felix von Hartmann of Cologne was attempting to arrange a compromise in which the kaiser would submit to the judgment of the pope and neutral monarchs, including Queen Wilhelmina.[53] Queen Wilhelmina was interested in protecting the kaiser, but her personal role in shaping Dutch policy is unclear.[54]

Germany, still a powerful neighbor whom the Dutch did not want to offend, generally opposed surrender of the kaiser. The Independent Socialists favored a trial, but they were a small minority. The German government rejected any thought of cooperation in the prosecution.[55] The Foreign Ministry closely watched all matters concerning the kaiser and was well-informed, especially by the Vatican, regarding Allied disunity.[56] German leaders did not intervene in the affair diplomatically but warned publicly of the danger that a trial would make Wilhelm II a martyr and cause a monarchist-militarist reaction in Germany.[57] Journalists kept the German public informed and generally emphasized the illegality of Allied plans to try the kaiser.[58] Some Germans thought the kaiser should nonetheless offer himself voluntarily to save his reputation and to prevent a trial of his generals. When the crown prince publicly offered to be tried in place of other German soldiers, his father furiously rejected the idea that he follow his son's example.[59] Many Germans, following the lead of monarchist political circles and military associations, remained loyal to their former monarch and agitated against surrender. Some observers feared these monarchists might try to engineer a return of the kaiser to Germany and a coup against the government.[60]

For a time after the signing of the peace treaty, it was fashionable to volunteer oneself as a sacrificial defendant in place of the kaiser. Hundreds of commoners and ex-royalty alike sent telegrams to Britain making such offers.[61] The most serious bid to stand judgment in place of Wilhelm II came from former Chancellor Bethmann Hollweg. German diplomats brought his offer to Allied leaders when they came to Versailles to sign the peace treaty. Bethmann Hollweg asked the Council of Four to try him, since he, not the German monarch, was constitutionally responsible for all state actions. Bethmann Hollweg was prepared to offer a vigorous defense against charges that German leaders had deliberately sought war in 1914. The Council of Four rejected his interpretation of the German constitution and did not answer him.[62] Subsequently, both Field Marshal von Hindenburg and General von Falkenhayn, as former chiefs of the General Staff, also indicated to the Allies their readiness to accept responsibility for the conduct of the war during their time of command, so that the kaiser might not be held accountable for military policies.[63]

In view of all the opposition to a trial of the kaiser, it is understandable that Curzon could not convince the Dutch minister at London on July 16 that the coming demand for extradition was serious business. René de Marees van Swinderen told Curzon that the British foreign minister was the only person "who had defended the policy of the trial, which he now believed to be condemned by an almost unanimous public opinion." The Dutch minister said that "several persons of the highest eminence had implored him to use his influence with his own Government to induce them to refuse the surrender. . . ."[64] De Marees van Swinderen informed The Hague that he believed Curzon also would be pleased at a Dutch refusal but did "not dare say so."[65]

Throughout the fall of 1919, the Allies received reports that the Dutch would not hand over the kaiser, although diplomats at The Hague said Allied unity and participation by the League of Nations might possibly change Dutch policy.[66] To avoid confrontation with the Dutch, some men argued that a direct summons should be sent to the kaiser to appear before the tribunal. The news in August that the Dutch had permitted the kaiser to purchase Castle Doorn, however, indicated that he expected a long residence in the Netherlands.[67] For a short time in December, Dutch public opinion wavered. Publication of Wilhelm II's marginalia (the so-called Kautsky revelations) on diplomatic despatches raised questions about the innocence of the kaiser's role in July 1914. A few members of the Dutch Parliament demanded his expulsion. But the government did not respond.[68]

3

When Allied leaders met on January 15, 1920, to prepare the formal demand for delivery of the kaiser, they expected a Dutch refusal. They discarded the note that Lansing had drafted at the peace conference in favor of a stronger, insulting French creation, calculated to appeal to public opinion. The lord chancellor, Lord Birkenhead (formerly Sir F. E. Smith), who had advised Lloyd George on the kaiser's trial from the beginning, went to Paris at the behest of the prime minister to sit through what they both knew was a futile exercise. Birkenhead, giving British approval to the note, said: "It did not appear necessary to say much more at this stage, but when the reply of the Netherlands Government was received, a good deal more might have to be said."[69] The despatch was sent on January 16 by Clemenceau as one of his last official acts, and he took much satisfaction, and found considerable humor, in this public humiliation of the once proud House of Hohenzollern.[70]

To make clear to the Dutch the *pro forma* nature of the demand, Premier Francesco Nitti of Italy told the Dutch minister in Paris on January 19 that he would not insist upon extradition of the ex-kaiser. Nitti said what the Allies really wanted was to prevent the kaiser from living close to the German border where he might plot a return to power. Nitti claimed that Lloyd George agreed.[71] French Foreign Minister Stephen Pinchon had given the Dutch minister similar assurances.[72] The Dutch legation in London reported the "strong impression" that high political circles looked forward to a refusal despite the desire of the British masses who still expected a trial.[73]

The Dutch declined on January 23 to hand over the kaiser, pointing out that the Netherlands had not signed and was not bound by the treaty of

Versailles. In the future, if the League created an international jurisdiction to judge crimes committed in war, the Netherlands would "associate itself with this new regime." At present, however, the Dutch government's duty was to abide by Dutch law and the national tradition as a "land of refuge for the vanquished in international conflicts."[74]

A real crisis with the Dutch could have occurred in negotiations surrounding a demand for internment of the kaiser outside Europe. Lloyd George and Lord Birkenhead agreed on January 27 upon a course of action designed to salvage British policy. Returning to the precedent of Napoleon on Saint Helena, they decided to tell the Dutch that leaving the kaiser so near Germany was an intolerable menace. To ensure the future peace of Europe, the kaiser would have to be held by the Allies at a safe distance, probably in the Falkland Islands. If the Dutch refused to hand over the kaiser, they would be denied entry into the League of Nations, and the Allies would sever diplomatic relations with the Netherlands. Lloyd George took under consideration severe economic measures that might be taken.[75] Lord Hardinge, permanent undersecretary of state for foreign affairs, was entrusted with implementing these ideas.

Hardinge, who had previously made indiscreet remarks to Dutch diplomats criticizing the kaiser's trial, cooperated with his protégé, Sir Ronald Graham, recently appointed minister to The Hague, in sabotaging the new policy.[76] Hardinge in transmitting the prime minister's instructions left the way open for Graham to use delaying tactics.[77] Graham asked for new instructions. He said that the Dutch would not consider Allied internment "as any concession at all. They would prefer a trial to internment without a trial, and they are perfectly aware that latter course would save Allies from embarrassment which they have no desire to spare them." Graham believed, however, that exile in the Dutch East Indies could be secured "without pressure or menace."[78] Before receiving new instructions, Graham in what he termed an "unofficial" visit with Herman van Karnebeek on February 2 proceeded to give away the entire British position. He warned that there would be threats of severe reprisals, and van Karnebeek seemed surprised and agitated. Graham did not mention Allied internment because, he said: "Such an offer might be extorted from him, but is not likely to be spontaneous." Graham, of course, was ignoring Lloyd George's intentions. "We eventually touched upon the idea of internment in the Dutch Indies," said Graham, but van Karnebeek refused to commit himself one way or the other. Graham, reporting of his efforts, admitted he had "to some extent exceeded the instructions" but amazingly claimed that he had "in no sense committed His Majesty's Government to anything" or "implied that there was any weakening in their resolution."[79] After seeing Graham ignore instructions on several occasions, the French minister, Charles Benoist, said that Graham upon receiving news of the retreat of Allied leaders would exult: "You see, he would declare with a mild seriousness, we would be in for it if we had made our *démarche* yesterday."[80]

Perhaps, Graham's actions mattered little. On February 5 the British Cabinet failed to approve Lloyd George's new policy. The records of the meeting do not provide any details of the discussion leading to this decision. The Cabinet agreed to seek an offer by the Netherlands "to intern the Kaiser safely in distant possessions, such as the Netherlands East Indies."[81] Moreover, the French and Italians wanted no part of Lloyd George's reprisals against the Netherlands. The *Journal des Débates* published on February 5 an exact account of Lloyd George's instructions to Graham and asserted that they represented purely British, not Allied, plans.[82] Van Karnebeek took considerable interest in this article, which he believed "an indiscretion of the French government which apparently was intended to leave responsibility for the future threat completely in the hands of England."[83] The new French premier and foreign minister, Alexandre Millerand, did not permit Benoist to support the British policy.[84] Premier Nitti assured the Dutch minister in Rome that "the Allies would not carry out their threat, especially because they had their hands so full in other parts of Europe that they would not want to create still more entanglements."[85] The Dutch apparently also got unofficial assurances from the American government that it would not look favorably on coercion.[86]

The Dutch government, therefore, decided to stand firm. The Council of Ministers on February 5 approved that stance and authorized van Karnebeek, if necessary, to request the Allies to permit the Netherlands to break relations first, if it came to that.[87] Van Karnebeek informed Graham of this determined attitude but said that the Dutch recognized the need to prevent the kaiser from engaging in intrigue and would take appropriate action. He noted that the East Indies would be considered, but there were "grave difficulties" about that solution, for the kaiser could not be deported involuntarily under Dutch law, and there was risk that his presence might cause "dangerous complications" in the restless East Indies. Furthermore, the health of the empress would not permit such a journey. Van Karnebeek expressed hope that the kaiser would eventually go to Chile or Peru. He warned that threats would make it more difficult to meet the legitimate wishes of the Allies.[88]

A second formal demand for the kaiser was long delayed, but when Allied leaders finally approved the action on February 12-14, the British thought it would result in the kaiser's internment in the East Indies. After lecturing the Dutch on their failure to appreciate the great international obligation to punish war crimes, the Allies on February 14 renewed their demand for surrender of the kaiser for trial. The Allies told the Dutch that at the very least they expected "measures of effective precaution taken either in place or in maintaining the ex-Emperor far away from the scene of his crimes" to prevent the kaiser from seeking his restoration in Germany.[89]

The French had drafted this note, and they had outwitted the British. Curzon told Graham the demand gave the Dutch an opportunity to make "on their own account the suggestion of internment elsewhere. A place in Holland would not prove acceptable. Some remote Dutch colony will be required."[90] In that case, Graham replied, the Allies should have "omitted the words 'soit sur place' " from the final paragraph of the note, for the Dutch would regard the words "as a direct invitation" for internment at Castle Doorn.[91] Graham tried to correct the error through a Dutch intermediary, but van Karnebeek produced a copy of the despatch "with the words soit sur place underlined in red." He asked: "Does this phrase mean anything, or does it not? If it does, it can only mean Amerongen or Doorn. The British Minister is simply trying to bluff us and to go one better than his Government." Graham reported that only united diplomatic action would change the Dutch attitude.[92]

Lloyd George unsuccessfully tried to secure such support from Nitti and Millerand in London on February 24. Lloyd George asked repeatedly for clarification of French and Italian policies. "If they were indifferent, he would like to be told so at once." He personally thought that leaving the kaiser in the Netherlands was a great risk, but Britain "could not go further in such a question than France." He considered it "essential not to create the impression in Germany that the Treaty of Versailles merely constituted a gigantic bluff." He wanted to know "whether the French and Italian Governments were going to insist on the Kaiser being cleared out of Holland or not." When Millerand and Nitti baldly claimed they had not understood the second Allied note as requiring internment in a colony, Lloyd George invited them to examine the minutes of their previous meeting. Nitti and Millerand finally agreed to demand overseas internment of the kaiser but only on condition that no threats would be employed against the Dutch.[93] The records do not reveal the reasons for French and Italian policies. Millerand and Nitti probably thought the effort to move the kaiser would not be worth the difficulty.

For the first time, then, the Allies unanimously undertook a joint démarche at The Hague on February 26.[94] The effort was so mild and so late in the day that it had little effect. Van Karnebeek was "visibly impressed" and promised to give "careful consideration" to internment overseas, said Graham, but since the queen, the Council of Ministers, and parliamentary leaders had already approved a reply to the second Allied note, the representations had no influence.[95]

The Dutch on March 5 provided vague promises of precautions in regard to the kaiser but did not go far enough for the British.[96] Upon receiving the communique from de Marees van Swinderen, Lloyd George said he hoped its contents would not lead to any "unpleasantness." The Dutch minister predicted trouble ahead.[97] On March 5 Allied leaders agreed to another joint *démarche* opposing internment of the kaiser at Castle Doorn, barely twenty-five miles from the German border.[98] Curzon told Graham that he and his colleagues were to tell the Dutch that Doorn was "wholly unacceptable."[99]

The second joint *démarche* on March 8 was as futile as the first. In a "very stiff" interview, van Karnebeek told the Allied diplomats that the Dutch "would not tolerate anything that might be regarded as foreign dictation or interference in a matter involving the exercise of their sovereign rights."[100] Graham believed the Dutch response was "due in great measure to a seemingly ineradicable conviction that our representations contain a large element of bluff."[101] Even in this matter of Doorn, the French deserted the British. Millerand told French diplomats at The Hague to remain passive in any joint *démarche*.[102]

Hearing on March 11 that Queen Wilhelmina would soon issue a decree interning the kaiser, Sir Ronald Graham did not oppose the decision but merely made inquiries. As a slight concession, the Dutch promised him the decree would not specifically mention Doorn.[103] Complaining about the role played by his envoy at The Hague, Curzon said that Graham "himself suggested the Colonies and said deliberately that we could get that solution. Then he fell back on some other part of Holland than Doorn. Now he is all for Doorn. Next it will be Amerongen—and finally Berlin."[104] Millerand, on the other hand, was pleased with the internment, which he said was "timely and urgent."[105]

On March 16 Queen Wilhelmina interned the kaiser in the province of Utrecht as an "alien dangerous to the public tranquility." Van Karnebeek said that the unprecedented measure was "unique in the history of Holland" and showed how far the Dutch had gone to meet Allied demands. He also assured the Allies that the kaiser had promised to abstain from political activity and had agreed to censorship of his correspondence.[106]

There was momentary concern about a move to restore Wilhelm II during the Kapp *Putsch* in Germany in early March, but this anxiety had faded by the time the Allies began talking about an appropriate response to the internment order.[107] Curzon told Allied leaders on March 18 that matters had now "reached a very critical stage." Were they going to accept the "third successive defeat of the Allies?" he asked. Curzon said that he "felt deeply humiliated by the course the negotiations had taken," but he offered no new proposals. Allied leaders agreed, of course, to Paul Cambon's suggestion that the "best thing to do was for the Allies to cover their retreat in as dignified a manner as possible."[108] The British tried to secure a strongly worded reprimand, but Millerand, anxious not to offend public opinion in the Netherlands, persuaded them to adopt a more moderate tone.[109]

There was a mixed reaction among peoples of the Allied countries. Many people were relieved, and there was considerable admiration for the Dutch, but dissatisfaction remained. Many people in Britain and France thought justice had not been served.[110] A poll of American lawyers showed that the desire to bring the kaiser to trial ran deep.[111] Many people expected that the Allies would conduct proceedings in the kaiser's absence, a proposal that Millerand did make to the British,[112] but Lloyd George had had enough. He dismissed the idea as "rather futile."[113]

The Allies watched the kaiser closely for a time. When the empress died in 1921, they insisted that he not attend her funeral in Potsdam.[114] Soon thereafter, he passed into obscurity and ceased to be a subject of controversy. As a result of the German government's efforts to discredit the war-guilt clause of the Versailles treaty, German archives were opened to scholars, and many historians in the interwar era cast doubt upon the idea that German leaders had been solely responsible for the First World War. Even Lloyd George later altered his opinion of the war's origins, writing that the kaiser "never had the remotest idea that he was plunging—or being plunged—into a European war." What Wilhelm II had wanted in 1914 was "a cheap diplomatic triumph."[115] The kaiser was consequently able to spend his later years as a respectable country gentleman, sawing wood daily for exercise and writing daily, too, while astride his special saddle-seated chair. He turned out several books defending his actions in the war.[116] He was acquitted in the only trial he ever received that came in an imaginative account, George Sylvester Viereck's *The Kaiser on Trial*, one of the innumerable studies in the debate on war guilt in the interwar era.[117] As a detached observer, Wilhelm II saw history come full circle. Before he died in 1941, he declined a British offer of refuge when the Germans invaded the Netherlands during the Second World War, and he followed closely Adolf Hitler's conquest of France.[118]

The Allied experience with the Dutch demonstrated, like the negotiations at the peace conference, some of the pitfalls of international punishments. Conceivably, if the Allies had been united, they could have compelled the Netherlands to surrender the kaiser. Undoubtedly, strong measures would have been required. The war-weary people of the Allied nations probably would not have approved such action so long after the war had ended. Certainly, most Allied leaders had become convinced that a trial of the kaiser was no longer worth the effort. In a world in which neutrality and political refuge remained acceptable, profound problems in gaining custody of accused war criminals also remained.

7

A COMPROMISE

Allied leaders felt compelled to abandon the idea of actually forcing Germany to surrender accused individuals for trial. They became convinced that an attempt to implement articles 228 to 230 would provoke civil war in Germany or a new war between Germany and the Allies. The resulting chaos might even lead to the triumph of bolshevism in Germany. The French were ready to strike a practical bargain, giving up war crimes trials for material concessions, but the British preferred a compromise that would still uphold the principle of punishment. British and French leaders had difficulty, however, extricating themselves from this project because of domestic pressures. To resolve this dilemma, Allied governments demanded the surrender of 854 Germans, including heroes such as Hindenburg, and immediately conceded to the Germans the right to try the accused.

1

During the summer and fall of 1919, the Germans nervously prepared for the Allied demand for surrender of war criminals. In early July, the government set up the Hauptstelle für Verteidigung Deutscher vor Feindlicher Gerichten (General Committee for the Defense of Germans before Enemy Courts). Publicly, this organization was not connected with the government. But it was in fact staffed by detached army and navy officers and headed by an official of the Foreign Ministry who kept in close touch with his superiors. The Hauptstelle sought to create united opposition among the German press and public to articles 228 to 230 of the Versailles treaty. It also gave legal and other assistance to accused individuals who might have to stand trial, if resistance to the Allies failed.[1] Through informants in the British legation at The Hague and the French embassy at Madrid, the Germans learned the names of many persons that appeared on lists of war criminals circulating among Allied diplomats.[2]

Those individuals who anticipated finding their names on the official Allied list reacted in various ways. A young naval officer, Captain Erich Raeder, whose name appeared on the list of war criminals in 1920 and who would subsequently stand convicted at Nuremberg as one of the major war criminals of the Second World War, took no precautions himself in 1919, but he was aware of plans to provide hiding places in Germany and abroad for some officers.[3] Some individuals hired Swiss lawyers,[4] and others sought legal aid from official German sources. General Sauberzweig, who had refused to stay the execution of Nurse Cavell, applied for the assistance of a special legal defense unit set up by the army, before "going away for some time, on account of severe heart trouble."[5] Baron von der Lancken, also blamed for the death of Cavell, got the Vatican and friendly neutral diplomats to intercede on his behalf with the British.[6] Walther Rathenau, accused throughout the war of authoring plans to destroy French and Belgian industry to cripple postwar competition, vigorously denied the charge in letters to Colonel House and others and appealed to them to keep his name off any extradition list.[7] Hindenburg responded passively, declaring that "if our foes want to stand an old man like me, who has but done his duty, up against a wall, they may have me."[8] Former Crown Prince Rupprecht of Bavaria, who wanted to avoid renewed war or civil disorder inside Germany, publicly announced his readiness to submit voluntarily to Allied judgment.[9] He was virtually the only individual to make such an offer; many military men made plans to resist to the end.[10]

Surrendering war criminals was one of several peace terms affecting the army that so alienated some officers, such as General Walther von Lüttwitz, that they plotted with antidemocratic elements to overthrow the government. Many Germans hoped to use the issue of fulfillment of the harsh treaty as a means of peacefully discrediting the Weimar Republic. Lüttwitz and others planned to destroy the regime by military coup, if it should comply with Allied demands to turn over war criminals or reduce the armed forces to one hundred thousand men, as the disarmament clauses required. These conspirators thought the ideal occasion for a coup would occur if the government tried to hand over officers accused of war crimes.[11]

For six months, the war crimes problem threatened the stability of the Weimar Republic and constantly agitated German politics. Contrary to a pledge in June 1919 not to question the patriotism of those who agreed to the Versailles treaty, conservative and nationalist parties attempted to discredit the ruling coalition. Much criticism centered on acceptance of articles 228 to 231. During debates in the National Assembly on ratification of the treaty, the extreme Right again protested these points.[12] This attack marked the start of a campaign against the Weimar Republic that grew ever more savage in the following months, since all national disasters and defeats since 1918 were blamed on the new regime.[13]

Responsibility for the war and war crimes was, however, a two-edged issue that Matthias Erzberger, the dominant figure in the government, was not above using to intimidate opponents. Erzberger secretly asked the French in late June for the names of persons the Allies would demand so that he could lay the groundwork for their delivery.[14] A month later, he lashed out at the Right, revealing the insincerity with which the Vatican peace proposals had been handled in 1917. He called for establishment of a state tribunal to investigate the origins of the war and its conduct. In bitter debates, he warned critics to be careful lest their attacks force the government to reveal other confidential materials that might adversely affect the fate of certain individuals.[15]

Erzberger's challenge was taken up by a former imperial minister, Karl Helfferich, who became the intellectual leader of the foes of the Republic. Helfferich hated Erzberger inordinately and blamed him for German acceptance of the armistice and the *Diktat* of Versailles. He accused Erzberger of making "a low-down denunciation of my person [as a war criminal] to the Entente." Helfferich set out to destroy Erzberger and the Republic through vilification.[16]

If Erzberger perhaps briefly considered using war guilt and war crimes to attack the old regime and opponents of the Republic, other ministers did not. Supporters of the Republic, including the Social Democrats, were not prepared to seize this opportunity.[17] They believed they needed the help of the army and officer corps to prevent a Communist revolution. Moreover, most of Germany's new leaders had enthusiastically supported measures, such as unrestricted submarine warfare, which the Allies wanted to condemn as criminal. Whatever plans Erzberger may have had went quickly awry. A German tribunal, such as he urged, could also be employed to justify refusing Allied trials, and most ministers preferred to use it for that purpose. Dr. Eduard David, minister of the interior, told the National Assembly that "Germany must have such an institution to offset the Entente's proposed court."[18] The National Assembly agreed to set up a special parliamentary commission, rather than a state tribunal, to investigate, but it was given no power to impose penalties.

This commission, the Committee of Inquiry into the Causes of Germany's Defeat, began hearings in late 1919, but they benefitted the opposition more than the government. Helfferich, Ludendorff, and Hindenburg put supporters of the Republic on the defensive. In a carefully prepared speech Hindenburg proclaimed the "stab in the back" myth, placing the blame for the army's defeat on traitors at home who had toppled the monarchy. The first fruit of the proceedings, paradoxically, was to label Germany's new leaders as the "November criminals," a smear that, repeated over and over again, undermined the legitimacy of the Weimar Republic.[19]

2

Allied awareness of the German government's domestic weakness did more than anything else to cause a retreat from full enforcement of the treaty's war crimes clauses. The Allies feared that the collapse of moderate forces would leave the way open for a monarchist restoration or a Communist revolution. The Allies were particularly anxious not to provoke a takeover by the Bolsheviks. The French government, especially, wanted to make concessions and hoped to gain, in return, more practical and material benefits from a grateful Germany.

Georges Clemenceau responded positively to an appeal on August 1 by Erzberger to postpone execution of the "delivery clause." Erzberger warned that the German government could "only maintain itself by leaning on the military element"; otherwise the government would be "overthrown and the country given over to communism."[20] Clemenceau was willing to waive articles 228 to 230 in return for "compensation." At a Heads of Delegations meeting in Paris, Clemenceau secured Arthur Balfour's agreement to a request that Marshal Foch report on appropriate "military compensations,"[21] but after Philip Kerr told Lloyd George about this "dodge of Clemenceau's," Balfour had to reverse himself.[22] Nonetheless, Foch told Erzberger on August 8 that France would forgo war crimes trials in return for certain secret financial concessions. The marshal said that he found the idea of trials "odious and contrary to his military conception of honor." Foch told Erzberger that the French attached "no value" to the practical implementation of this part of the peace treaty, which was "placed there purely because of the demand of England." He thought the "provision can be explained only with reference to the narrow puritanical British mentality, which wishes *replacer le bon Dieu* in the punishment of the guilty."[23] Erzberger later tried to negotiate a similar secret financial deal with Belgium,[24] but he was never able to complete the bargain with the Belgians or the French. These discussions undoubtedly sufficed to convince the Germans that the penalty clauses could be evaded.

After Balfour reversed himself on compensation, he and Clemenceau turned their attention to Britain's principal concern—the future stability of the German government. They sought the views of their military representatives in Berlin on Erzberger's assessment. The French military control mission declared Erzberger's arguments "well-founded" and urged limiting any trial to a few men who had exceeded orders in committing atrocities.[25] The British mission did not agree. A spokesman for the British mission asserted that Erzberger was "overstating his case" and that the German government would not necessarily fall without army support.[26]

Clemenceau therefore recommended on August 11 a gradual approach, limiting the demand, at least initially, "to a few symbolic persons." He believed the Germans would probably not resist such a request. He said he had a list of more than a thousand names but preferred to "execute the Treaty bit by bit." Italian Foreign Minister Tittoni quickly agreed.[27] From London Lloyd George sent his "strong opinion" that the Allies should seek the surrender of "the most important and notorious offenders and let the rest go." The law officers hoped to keep the British demand to fifty or sixty of the "worst offenders," and he urged the French to do likewise.[28] President Wilson also sent approval.[29] When Lloyd George and Clemenceau met face-to-face on September 15, they reaffirmed this policy. Lloyd George said he "only wanted to make an example. To try very large numbers would be to create great difficulties for the German Government, which he believed to be better than either a Bolshevist Government or a Militarist Government."[30]

This decision was easier to make than to implement. Allied leaders found themselves trapped by public opinion. The French press favored strict application of the war crimes clauses of the peace treaty.[31] Clemenceau observed in early October that "there was intense feeling on this subject in France and no Government especially on the eve of a general election [November 1919] could oppose the popular demand for bringing the offenders to trial." For that reason, the French list had to include the names of men such as the German crown prince and Crown Prince Rupprecht of Bavaria on charges of seizing private property during the occupation.[32] Clemenceau admitted "frankly that it was such a serious political question in France he could not stand up against it."[33] British difficulties were not quite so great, but neither government made more than modest efforts to limit the number of persons whom they would demand. A Commission on the Organization of Mixed Tribunals began work on November 18. This body, presided over by Édouard Ignace, French undersecretary of state for military justice, drafted proposals for the composition and procedure of mixed military tribunals and drew up a list of war criminals, largely by combining unexamined national lists. The commission made little effort to reduce the list.[34]

When Allied leaders reviewed the results in early December there was serious disagreement. Shocked, Lloyd George said he was "startled" at the total of 1580 German offenders and was "taken aback by the idea of more than 1500 separate trials." Clemenceau differed. He said he "had considered this question carefully, and had reached the conclusion that it was almost impossible to reduce the list." British members of the commission defended French and Belgian demands, much to Lloyd George's dismay. They did not seem concerned about actually trying anyone, a policy obviously in accord with French thinking. Sir Ernest Pollock said that even if the Allies did not succeed in extraditing anyone the "summary of the charges preferred would remain for all time a record of German brutality." Lloyd George was determined to bring some men to trial and insisted upon further efforts to cut the list.[35]

The Germans, aware of the vacillations of the Allies, increased their demands for concessions. When German officials came to Paris to arrange implementation of the treaty, Baron Kurt von Lersner spent much of his time talking with Allied statesmen about the war crimes issue.[36] He put forward the basic German position on November 5. No German government could survive a surrender of its citizens to a foreign tribunal, he said, and because no Allied government could renounce the penalty clauses completely, Germany should be permitted to try in its own courts all alleged war criminals.[37] To prove good faith, the German National Assembly passed a law on December 13 giving exclusive jurisdiction in such cases to the Reichsgericht (Germany's supreme court) at Leipzig.[38] The Allies at first rebuffed von Lersner and required the Germans to sign a protocol repudiating for purposes of war crimes trials article 112 of the Weimar constitution, which prohibited the extradition of German citizens to a foreign criminal jurisdiction.[39] Von Lersner, however, received a sympathetic response from the American delegation, which the Germans, crediting the Americans with more influence than they had, believed was a good sign.[40] The Germans also placed much faith in the efforts of the Vatican to persuade the Allies to compromise.[41]

The Germans made a special effort to convince the British government to give up its war crimes project. A key role in this effort was played by one of those shadowy figures of British diplomacy, Lieutenant-Colonel William Stewart Roddie, a military intelligence officer with personal access to men in high places. Prince Münster, whose wife was a member of the British aristocracy, arranged for Roddie to meet several important German officials at a dinner party in Berlin in early December. Defense Minister Noske, who served as spokesman for the group, urged Roddie to take a message back to London. Noske said:

Europe always wanted a democratic Germany, and now—to have to see the end of it—to have to face revolution and riot, bloodshed and butchery once again—and then Bolshevism—O my God, where are we being driven to? Where is the way out? If we refuse to hand these officers over, the *Entente* will act, and the Government will have to go. . . . God in heaven, make these people see us as we are! We are down—down, and almost out. Our cards are all on the table. England has clever men: why won't they believe us? . . . Leave me the means of maintaining order. Don't ask for these officers.[42]

Convinced of the accuracy of Noske's plea, Roddie immediately returned to London to inform his superiors. He spoke to Churchill at the War Office, and a close friend, Sir Almeric Fitzroy, clerk of the Privy Council, took Roddie to see Balfour. Impressed, Balfour brought the matter before the Cabinet. The Cabinet, after learning of Roddie's assessment, agreed that there was "real danger" of causing the fall of the German government. The Cabinet decided to send Lord Birkenhead to Paris with Lloyd George to press the view that the list of war criminals must be limited to "flagrant cases."[43]

British attempts to force a reduction failed. When Birkenhead arrived in Paris, he found that the list had been pared to 1,043 but that Poland had belatedly submitted a list of 361 names, a double embarrassment since serious legal objections could be made to any Polish demand. Poland had not existed as a state during the war, and there was therefore considerable doubt about its right to try German war criminals.[44] Birkenhead proposed an arbitrary reduction of the list to five hundred names, but French and Belgian representatives on the Commission on Organization of Mixed Tribunals resisted.[45] They compromised on January 13, 1920, on an approximate figure of 890. They also gave final approval to a statute for the mixed tribunals.[46]

When Allied leaders met on January 15, the British continued to urge additional deletions. The treaty had come into force the week before, and action was urgent because a list had to be presented to Germany within one month. Undoubtedly, said Birkenhead, all of the original three thousand names were "justly included," but the question was "one of high policy." The British wanted to vindicate the "moral law of the world" by punishing some guilty individuals, no matter how few. He thought that Germany "might be willing to hand over 100." Lloyd George declared that the numbers must be "considerably reduced. If even twenty were shot it would be an example," he said. He told Clemenceau that they "were asking for more than any Government could be expected to comply with." Clemenceau admitted the truth of what Lloyd George said, but domestic pressures did not permit further compromise. He said: "The difficulty was to give a reply when women came up from the provinces and told him that their daughters had been carried off by the Germans and that they had their names and yet they were not included on this list."[47] It was a particularly difficult time for Clemenceau to have to deal with such a politically sensitive issue, for the election of the French president was only days away, and he was a candidate. Clemenceau agreed to further conferences between Birkenhead and Ignace,[48] but they accomplished little. When they presented the complete list to Allied leaders on January 20, it was still too large. The numbers were as follows: Britain—95, France—334, Italy—29, Belgium—334, Poland—51, Rumania—41, and Yugoslavia—4. The total was 854 because a few individual names appeared on more than one list. Clemenceau, Lloyd George, and Nitti approved this number, believing they could not enforce such a demand.[49]

There were increasingly serious reports about the situation in Germany. French representatives in Berlin told Paris that the Right was using the issue to excite public opinion to such a degree that a "new civil war" was possible.[50] Execution of articles 228 to 230 would cause the "most dangerous" crisis in Germany since the end of the war.[51] Colonel Roddie, after another meeting with German leaders, sent a new warning, this time to Lord Stamfordham, the king's secretary, who passed it on to Lloyd George. Roddie declared that *the thing is impossible,*" and if it is tried "the Russian Bolsheviks will find a welcome and a warm fireside in Germany."[52] The new British *chargé* in Berlin, Lord Kilmarnock, said that Noske "practically presented me with an ultimatum." Noske claimed that if the German police tried to make any arrests "they would be killed in the attempt, and his own life would not be worth a moment's purchase." Kilmarnock endorsed Noske's statements with only slight reservations and urged the Allies to compromise.[53] The danger to German leaders from the extreme Right was dramatically illustrated on January 26 when an ultra-nationalist ex-army officer wounded Erzberger.[54] Von Lersner, with some exaggeration, told Allied statesmen in Paris that the attempted assassination of Erzberger "was due to fact that he is looked upon as being German representative who advocated agreeing to surrender" of war criminals.[55]

Convinced that he could not secure further reduction from the French and that Germany could not comply, Lloyd George turned to the German offer to hold trials. Lloyd George told Clemenceau's successor, the new French premier, Alexandre Millerand, on January 30 that he was thinking about the "possibility of the prisoners being tried before a German tribunal in occupied territory with Allied prosecutors and assessors, or similar safeguards for the execution of justice."[56] Millerand was willing to consider this proposal but not before making the demand for surrender of the accused as treaty terms required. He wanted to avoid any "sign of weakness," and, like Clemenceau, he felt constrained by domestic pressures.[57]

3

Millerand's insistence led to a crisis. When the list was presented to von Lersner on February 3, he refused to transmit it to Germany and left Paris the next day. Many people feared that his defiance fore-shadowed an official German refusal to comply with the Versailles treaty,[58] a development that seemed possible considering the list, which, as one journalist noted, contained the names of the "pillars of Prussianism as well as the heroes of Germany."[59] The famous scientist Fritz Haber, for example, who had received a Nobel prize in chemistry in November 1919, was included on the roster of war criminals. He had developed poison gas for the German army and had personally supervised its first use in battle in 1915.[60] Many of the persons listed were famous military and political figures. Charged with offenses against international law were over eighty generals, admirals, princes, and statesmen. Among the individuals demanded by France were the crown prince and his brothers; Crown Prince Rupprecht of Bavaria; the grand duke of Hesse; the duke of Mecklenburg; Field Marshal von Hindenburg; General Ludendorff; and Generals von Moltke, von Bülow, von Kluck, Stenger, and many more. Belgium asked for Bethmann Hollweg; Hindenburg; and Generals von Falkenhausen, von Boehm, von Bonin, von Domming, and others. Rumania and Yugoslavia wanted Field Marshal August von Mackensen. Britain demanded Admirals von Tirpitz, von Capelle, Bachmann, Scheer, Hipper, von Müller, von Ingenöhl, Schroeder, and Behncke. Poland and Italy asked for a number of generals. The list also included hundreds of lesser known officers, soldiers, and sailors, and one woman, Elsa Scheiner, who had guarded imprisoned French women during the war.[61]

Von Lersner had copied the list before returning it, and it was im-mediately published in Germany. There were explosive results. Lord Kilmarnock sent London a series of warnings that spoke of a "great sensation," an "extremely serious situation," a "crisis of extreme gravity," and a "catastrophe."[62] He said that all parties, except the Communists, were united in opposition. The inclusion of Hindenburg, particularly, "provided a rallying cry to unite the people in a way which nothing else could have done. If Germany can be said to possess a soul, that soul has been touched."[63] In their deliberations about how to proceed, German ministers counted heavily on an "unbroken inner front," and almost no political faction broke ranks.[64] Even the *Freiheit*, the newspaper of the Independent Socialists, reappearing after a month's suppression, opposed extradition.[65] A large number of generals and admirals, including von Tirpitz, Ludendorff, von Falkenhayn, Scheer, and von Kluck, issued a declaration announcing that they would never stand before a foreign tribunal, because "it would not be compatible with our soldier's honor and our sense of personal dignity"; they stood ready, however, to submit to the Reichsgericht's judgment.[66] French representatives in Berlin reported that the issue had "placed a marvelous weapon in the hands of the reactionaries."[67] The violent Pan-German journalist Count Ernst von Reventlow called for resurrection of the doctrine of "domestic enemy" and declared that "all who may proceed against such foes at home should know in advance that they will remain unpunished."[68] The army prepared to oppose surrender of the accused. The army immediately ceased all cooperation with Allied disarmament control missions.[69] The chief of the army command, General Hans von Seeckt, prepared to cooperate with Lüttwitz and other conspirators to overthrow the government, if necessary, rather than turn over fellow officers.[70] He called his staff together on February 9 to inform them that if the German government did not refuse Allied demands the army would resort to force. Seeckt presented a strategy for taking up defensive positions behind the Weser or Elbe and concluding an alliance with the Soviet Red Army with which they could then march westward.[71]

There was consternation in the British government over German reaction. Lloyd George asked the French to delay transmitting the list officially to Berlin[72] and on February 5 convened his Cabinet in emergency session. When the group met, there was no copy of the official list available for their discussions. Lloyd George at once sent a man to fly to Paris to get a copy of the list and to return that same day.[73] When the official list arrived, the Cabinet was surprised to discover that the French and Belgians had asked for Hindenburg and so many other prominent figures. A special War Crimes Committee of the Cabinet met most of the afternoon with Lord Birkenhead to decide how to get their Allies to agree to revise the list. Just why the British did not know in advance the names of individuals demanded by their Allies is not clear. The committee authorized Birkenhead to go to Paris and offer to eliminate von Tirpitz and other admirals if the French and Belgians would drop Hindenburg and the generals. The Admiralty, which had prepared the list of German naval personnel, believed unrestricted U-boat warfare justified asking for German admirals but thought their Allies' demand for the generals was excessive, an example, perhaps, of national myopia.[74]

In Washington, Secretary of State Lansing was appalled. He instructed American diplomats in Berlin to make clear that the United States was in "no way backing" the Allies.[75] He tried to get President Wilson on February 7 to intervene with a "strong protest." American leaders, however, had lost touch with the Allies after the Senate had repudiated the treaty and Wilson fell ill. Lansing did not understand the problem. He told the president that he feared Birkenhead's presence in Paris added "to the gravity of the situation," for "in order to gratify his inordinate vanity" as the originator of the idea of war crimes trials, he might "insist on pressing for the immediate delivery of prescribed Germans regardless of consequences."[76] Wilson was just as confused as Lansing. He told the secretary that he did not want American representatives to take part, but he wanted to let the Germans know "that we stand inexorably with our associates in insisting that every item in the treaty be complied with in letter and in spirit." He wondered if Lansing could "think of some way to accomplish this" objective.[77] Lansing did not, for that same day Wilson forced him to resign for other reasons, and the United States played no role whatsoever in resolving the crisis.

When Birkenhead met with Allied leaders on February 6, he found them strongly opposed to the idea of deleting more names. At once he tried another tack—he urged acceptance of the German offer to hold trials. He said "that in the history of war, so far as I am aware, no such demand has ever been made." He admitted that he was "not unaware" that "it might reasonably be said to us that these observations are made at a somewhat late period in the history of the matter." Time, itself, however, had "produced, both in our country and in Germany, changes of which we feel bound to take cognizance."[78]

The following morning, when Birkenhead and other Allied leaders met again, they discovered that the German government had disavowed von Lersner's actions. As a result, matters were less urgent. They agreed to postpone final decision until Lloyd George could meet with Millerand and Nitti in London the following week. Birkenhead did acquiesce in a French demand to forward the list at once to Berlin and to send a covering letter that noted that the Allies were considering the German offer to hold trials.

Millerand explained to Birkenhead the policy he wanted to adopt. He preferred to allow Germany to default on articles 228 to 230, for the Allies could then "delay" evacuation of occupied territories and "contemplate economic measures." The Allies could try the accused *in absentia*, and such trials would have a proper moral effect.[79] The French press had already begun a campaign urging exploitation of the situation to strengthen French security.[80]

The British would not support the French policy. The British Cabinet on February 9 considered various alternatives to strict application of articles 228 to 230. They generally agreed that the best idea was an international court with German and neutral judges to sit in the occupied zone.[81] When Lloyd George met Millerand and Nitti on February 12, he rejected the French designs. He said that "political and criminal questions should not be mixed up." It "came as a great surprise to the British Government to find such names as those of Marshal Hindenburg, Bethmann Hollweg, and Ludendorff on the list." Surrendering such personages was "something which no nation could agree to, however crushed and defeated it might be." It was as if Germany had asked for Marshal Joffre or Marshal Foch or Lord Kitchener. When Germany refused, what would the Allies do? "Would Italy, Great Britain, or France go to war in order to force the surrender of Hindenburg? It was incredible."

Millerand, however, would not delete any names, including Hindenburg, for that would be "absolutely incompatible with the dignity of the Allies" and would have "an extraordinarily bad effect in the ten devastated departments of France." Millerand said that he feared the Germans, through "trickery and bluff," would entangle the Allies in interminable negotiations. If the Allies retreated, he warned, "the result might be a breakdown of the whole Treaty." Lloyd George told Millerand that they could not cling to a literal interpretation of the treaty, because "public sentiment had undergone a change, and there was a general desire to return to the ordinary business of life." The "last thing" the Allies "wanted was to destroy the present Government, and to have it succeeded by a Spartacist or militarist Government, which would inevitably be the case."[82]

Finally, Millerand gave in. The Germans and not the Allies would conduct trials. Allied leaders agreed to demand that Germany try a selected number of cases to uphold moral principle and treaty rights. They appointed an Inter-Allied Mixed Commission to choose cases for presentation to Germany. Lloyd George objected to continuing any members of the old committee on the new one, especially Ignace, because this problem was "not a question of law, but an important question of politics." They agreed to appoint Jules Cambon chairman.[83] Germany was officially informed of the new Allied policy on February 17.[84]

Despite the large role of public opinion in making war crimes punishment a condition of the peace settlement, the retreat aroused little public protest, except in France. There was much criticism in the Chamber of Deputies. There, several speakers warned that the compromise would lead to other concessions threatening French security. They also declared that the French people would not be satisfied until the guilty had been judged.[85] In Britain there was very little criticism. Almost everyone seemed to agree that compromise was the only practical solution.[86] Austin Harrison said that time had changed much, including the right of the British to condemn the Germans. He thought the British should be "peculiarly careful" now that they had Ireland on their "conscience—and it is—and the abomination of Amritsar to atone for."[87] According to a survey, most American editors continued support for surrender of Germans. But very few took issue with the Allied reversal in policy.[88] Most Americans were more interested in economic problems and the "Red Scare," then reaching its most virulent phase.

Among individuals who had conceived of international war crimes punishment as an important international reform, there was disappointment. The influential American peace spokesman Theodore Marburg believed that nothing was "more important than to carry out the provisions of the treaty which call for the trial of German offenders." It was an objective, he said, that "should be pursued at any cost and through years if necessary." He hoped some new arrangement providing for neutral and League participation could be agreed upon.[89] Allied governments never took any serious action along those lines.

Failure to secure surrender of German war criminals, in retrospect, does not seem surprising. The reasons for the lack of success are clear: the unprecedented character of the project, the large number of individuals demanded, the long delay from the end of the war to the implementation of the peace terms, the disagreements among the Allies, the weakness of the Weimar Republic, the unwillingness to take forceful measures, and the fear of bolshevism. Behind all of these factors was a fundamental obstacle, German nationalism. Germans momentarily forgot their many antagonisms as they united to oppose Allied demands. The Germans were particularly sensitive about dishonoring the officer corps because the military tradition had such an intimate connection with the unification of Germany in the nineteenth century. In the trauma of defeat, German nationalists, to protect the image of the army, had already convinced themselves of the truth of two myths: Germany bore no responsibility for the war, and the army had been "stabbed in the back."[90] Understandably opposed to victor's justice, the Germans, with nationalistic feelings uniquely grounded in militarism, also accepted a third myth: Allied accusations of war crimes were almost all false, and the German military did not truly deserve any kind of censure.

8

LEIPZIG

The German war crimes trials at Leipzig proved unsatisfactory to the Allies, and the measures the French took against the Germans in retaliation disturbed Franco-German relations throughout the 1920s. The Allies believed, with good reason, that the Germans did not fully carry out their pledge to punish their own war criminals. There was a long delay before they began proceedings. The Reichsgericht handed down few convictions. Those found guilty received light sentences, and the two most notorious war criminals soon escaped from prison and disappeared. Subsequently, in secret session, the Reichsgericht reversed itself and found even those two men innocent. The British preferred to allow the issue to fade away, for they adopted a policy of reconciliation with Germany. The French and Belgians did not.

Upon the insistence of the French, the Allies in 1922 repudiated the compromise arrangement for German trials and reserved all formal rights under articles 228, 229, and 230 of the Versailles treaty. The French and Belgians subsequently tried hundreds of accused Germans *par contumace* and attempted to use the war crimes issue as a diplomatic weapon to force compliance with other provisions of the treaty, particularly the articles on reparations. The French and Belgians stopped their trials only after the Locarno treaty of 1925 improved relations with Germany. The French, nonetheless, continued a discriminatory policy toward Germans who had been convicted, denying them entry into France until 1929. Many Germans bitterly resented the humiliation of having their soldiers branded as war criminals and did everything possible to erase what they saw as a stain on their national honor.

1

Many matters intervened to delay the German war crimes trials. Although the German government moved promptly in February 1920 to secure additional legislation to facilitate prosecutions,[1] domestic turmoil sidetracked the National Assembly for some weeks. In the Kapp *Putsch* in mid-March, General Lüttwitz and others, having lost the ideal issue of a surrender of officers to the Allies, mounted an unsuccessful coup over the government's compliance with disarmament provisions of the peace treaty.[2] The revolt itself failed to secure much support. But the desire to resist the Allies was widespread.

Only with difficulty was the government able to persuade the National Assembly to approve war crimes trials. Conservative and nationalist members of the assembly believed that such proceedings would be an unacceptable national humiliation. They attacked the government for not insisting that the Allies also try their own guilty soldiers. To lessen opposition, Chancellor Hermann Müller approved creation of a secret fund to pay expenses of the defendants to be tried before the Reichsgericht at Leipzig.[3] Publicly, he revealed that his government had compiled a 381-page list of Allied war criminals that might be published at an appropriate time.[4] Other official spokesmen argued that German trials were necessary not so much to meet Allied demands as to vindicate the honor of the German army.[5]

In the election of June 1920, German voters repudiated the parties of the original Weimar coalition and thereby rejected cooperation with the Allies. Conservative forces made substantial gains by blaming the government for domestic economic ills and abject submission to the Allies. One historian attributed this electoral success in part to the "strong emotional factor" of pledges made by the conservatives to protect Kaiser Wilhelm II and others against renewed threats of Allied prosecution.[6] The new Cabinet, headed by Chancellor Konstantin Fehrenbach, was a coalition of leaders of bourgeoisie parties and could retain power only by resisting implementation of the Versailles treaty.[7] These men were not eager to begin war crimes trials.

There was much sentiment to condemn Allied war crimes rather than deal with Allied accusations against Germans. During the fall of 1920, a retired army officer, Major Otto von Stülpnagel, in *Die Wahrheit über die Deutschen Kriegsverbrechen* (The Truth About German War Crimes), surveyed Allied violations of international law.[8] This book quickly went through several editions. It inspired widespread demands for the publication of the German list of enemy war criminals. Gustav Stresemann was one of several prominent opposition leaders who urged such action.[9] Numerous organizations, such as Rette die Ehre (Vindication of Honor), were formed to agitate for this policy and against prosecution of alleged German offenders.[10] Some persons hoped von Stülpnagel's book would influence opinion in Allied countries. Prince Max of Baden sent copies to individuals in Britain who he hoped would be persuaded to work against the Versailles treaty.[11] The Fehrenbach government did not issue a list of enemy war criminals. But it did not move quickly against the accused in Germany.

Allied difficulties in choosing the names of a select number of German war criminals caused some delay. The Allies excluded certain individuals and categories of cases whose indictment was deemed politically objectionable or legally untenable. Heinrich Sahm's name was expunged completely, even from the original list of war criminals, to avoid embarrassing the League of Nations. Charged by the Polish government with deporting Poles to work in German war factories, Sahm had become lord mayor of the free city of Danzig under League supervision, and Sir Eric Drummond of the League secretariat complained to the British Foreign Office that labeling Sahm a war criminal would destroy his usefulness.[12] To make sure that the French would not place the names of famous generals on the select list, the British Cabinet, overriding objections of the Admiralty, determined not to include names of German admirals on the select list. This policy meant abandoning prosecution of the admiral who had authorized the court-martial and execution of Captain Fryatt.[13] The law officers had already determined that they could not sustain indictments against those responsible for Nurse Cavell's death, for she had been dealt with fairly, if harshly.[14] Thus no one was to be punished for two of the outrages that had most angered the British public during the war. Serious disputes arose within the British government over proceeding against German aviators. The Air Council and Churchill, who had become secretary of state for air, had opposed plans of the law officers to try German airmen for bombing London and other cities. General Hugh M. Trenchard, chief of the air staff, wanted to protect the Royal Air Force against any untoward precedents and threatened to testify in defense of German airmen. After the Allies agreed to German trials, the Air Council prevailed, and the select list was drawn up without any names of German airmen.[15] Such problems held up the work of the Inter-Allied Commission responsible for preparing the select list, and it was not ready until March 31, 1920. The Allies determined that the Germans should prosecute forty-five individuals, dividing that number in the following manner: Britain—7, France—11, Italy—5, Belgium—15, Poland—3, Rumania—3, Yugoslavia—1.[16]

Allied disagreement about participation in the German prosecutions caused further delay in forwarding the select list to Germany. French Premier Millerand objected to sending Allied witnesses to Leipzig to testify. He feared hostile confrontations and incidents. Besides, he did not believe German justice could be relied upon, and he wanted the Germans to have complete responsibility for any failure. He proposed that the

Allies institute trials *par contumace*. Lloyd George suspected that Millerand desired that the Germans not proceed with prosecutions, for this would lend justification to an occupation of the Ruhr Valley. At the San Remo Conference in late April, Millerand strongly urged such an occupation as punishment for Germany's failure to meet reparation obligations. Lloyd George argued the need to send Allied witnesses to German trials to ensure convictions. At the insistence of Lloyd George, Millerand agreed to permit, but not compel, attendance of Allied observers.[17] He and Lloyd George gave final approval to the select list that, together with the stipulations regarding witnesses and observers, was finally sent to Berlin on May 7, 1920.[18]

The French refused to abandon their own prosecutions. Despite rulings of the Inter-Allied Armistice Commission against the practice, the French and Belgians persisted as late as March 1920 in arresting Germans in the occupation zone.[19] They had imprisoned approximately fifty-five individuals accused of war crimes,[20] and trial and sentencing of these persons, which had begun in 1919, continued into the spring of 1920.[21] The Germans repeatedly demanded release of prisoners held by the Allies and promised to try them in German courts.[22] The British who had also imprisoned some Germans responded positively and returned twelve men charged with violations of the laws of war to Germany. The Foreign Office, overriding opposition from the Admiralty and law officers, secured release of the last two Germans in September 1920. The British paroled the men on condition that they promise to return to stand trial in Britain if German prosecutions proved unsatisfactory.[23] After the German prosecutor *nol-prossed* his case in 1926, the British released one of their former prisoners from his pledge.[24] In contrast to the British policy, the French and Belgians ignored German protest; apparently, they did not free German prisoners until they completed their sentences or secured reversal of their convictions.

After receiving the select list of war criminals, the Germans did not immediately indict the accused. Officials in the Ministry of Justice determined that the Allies had not sent sufficient evidence to begin proceedings in even a single case,[25] and the German government asked the Allies for additional evidence and names of witnesses. When Allied and German leaders negotiated in July at Spa face-to-face for the first time since the war, Lloyd George angrily asked for an explanation of German failure to start war crimes trials. The German minister of justice, Richard Heinze, defiantly criticized the "insufficient proof" offered by the Allies.[26] To avoid further mutual recriminations, the problem was referred to legal experts. After agreeing that the German request for more evidence was "reasonable," the negotiators devised a method to expedite delivery of this material.[27] Allied and German leaders approved an arrangement providing for direct communication outside diplomatic channels between the prosecutor's office in Leipzig and the legal departments of Allied governments.[28]

Legal difficulties and political obstructions prevented commencement of trials for another nine months. Once the matter clearly came within the province of judicial processes, Allied and German authorities encountered many impediments in preparing cases. The incidents had occurred several years before, and investigators often found that accused individuals and witnesses had died or disappeared. Material evidence was almost impossible to obtain.[29] The British worked more diligently than the other Allies but were unable to submit new evidence and lists of witnesses until late October.[30] The French, Belgians, and Italians did not do so until much later.[31] Apparently, the governments of Poland, Rumania, and Yugoslavia never bothered to do anything. Other problems that took time to negotiate were provisions for expenses of Allied witnesses and their safety. Because some witnesses refused to travel to Leipzig, arrangements had to be made for formal interrogatory hearings to secure their testimony. In February 1921 German legal representatives went to London and Brussels to reach agreement on scheduling these proceedings,[32] and in April counsel for the defendants and the German government attended hearings in London.[33]

Allied officials believed the Germans were deliberately procrastinating. Sir Eyre Crowe doubted that there was "any chance of justice being done by the German Court."[34] Allied suspicion of German bad faith was, perhaps, excessive. The Fehrenbach government did not move with dispatch, but it did take care to prevent the trials from becoming anti-Allied propaganda shows. The German Cabinet on January 26, 1921, rejected a defendant's request for access to official documents concerning Allied atrocities. The ministers agreed to release this material only upon demand of the Reichsgericht itself and, then, to make public only a small number of documents.[35]

To prove German sincerity, the Reichsgericht took up the first war crimes case in early January 1921. This prosecution was not one the Allies had demanded but one the Germans had decided to pursue on their own. Three former privates, workmen in civilian life, who had been accused of robbing a Belgian innkeeper in October 1918, were sentenced to prison terms ranging from two to five years. Later, a soldier charged with a similar offense received two years' imprisonment. The Germans probably held these trials to test procedures and to resolve legal difficulties before moving to the trials of individuals accused by the Allies. One important difference was later quite apparent. The Reichsgericht imposed far heavier sentences upon the soldiers charged by German authorities than upon Germans accused by the Allies.[36]

Dissatisfied with the slow progress on war crimes punishment and with the defiant German attitude concerning reparations and disarmament, the Allies took stern measures to compel compliance with the Versailles treaty. The Allies summoned the Germans to the London Conference in March 1921 to receive an ultimatum. Speaking for his associates, Lloyd George charged the Germans with defaulting on reparations, disarmament, and war crimes punishment and gave them three days to make clear their readiness to comply with the treaty or to face sanctions.[37] When the Germans temporized, Belgian and French troops occupied several towns at the entrance of the Ruhr Valley, and the Allies announced on May 5 that occupation of the Ruhr would begin the following week. The Fehrenbach Cabinet resigned, and a new government was formed under Chancellor Josef Wirth, committed to a policy of fulfillment of the treaty.[38] Within three weeks, the war crimes trials began, but the results did not prove agreeable to the Allies.

2

The Leipzig trials were conducted before the Penal Senate of the Reichsgericht, which met in the Kaiserhalle of the supreme court building, a long assembly room dominated by life-size, full-length portraits of Frederick the Great and Kaiser Wilhelm I.[39] These paintings were a reminder that Weimar Germany had not repudiated the imperial past, that it continued to honor a tradition in which the military held special privileges.

Germans generally took a negative view of the trials. Most German press coverage, except for the *Vossische Zeitung*'s strictly factual account of each day's proceedings, was hostile and emphasized the arguments of the defense. Even journalists of the Left deplored the prosecution of ordinary soldiers who were described more as victims than as criminals of the old regime.[40] The Deutschen Offizierbundes (German Officers League) and other groups staged demonstrations, and in the Reichstag, the leader of the Nationalist party, Count Kuns von Westarp, denounced the trials as "the greatest indignity a people could be subjected to."[41] Retired officers wrote articles justifying the offenses with which the accused had been charged.[42] Other writers explained how much worse Allied violations of international law had been.[43] One pamphlet on Allied war crimes, August Gallinger's *Die Gegenrechnung* (The Countercharge), went through three editions before the summer ended.[44] The Wirth government came under intense pressure to name the Allied war criminals, but it refused. It was determined not to provoke the Allies unnecessarily and, thus, jeopardize favorable settlement of the reparations question.[45]

The prosecutors and judges at Leipzig were reluctant to punish fellow Germans. The *oberreichsanwalt* ("solicitor-general"), Dr. Ludwig Ebermayer, who directed the prosecution, later referred to his participation as the "most painful and sad aspect" of his entire career.[46] In accordance with continental judicial practice, Ebermayer's role was decidedly overshadowed by that of the president of the court, Dr. Karl Ludwig Friedrich Schmidt, who did most of the questioning of witnesses. Whatever their private feelings, almost all observers agreed that Schmidt and the other judges were eminently fair in procedural matters. Schmidt announced his intention to uphold the ideals of impartial justice. He declared that his primary purpose was to keep politics, "whether from left or right, or foreign" sources, out of the proceedings. But the sentences the judges imposed on the guilty were notably lenient.[47]

The trials attracted much attention from the world press. Journalists representing some eighty newspapers from all over the world went to Leipzig to provide detailed coverage of this unprecedented event. Frequently, they had to scramble to gain access, for the courtroom was almost always packed with German spectators.[48] All participants sat at one end of the room on a raised dais. The seven judges and two prosecutors, dressed in magenta robes, velvet caps, and large, white bow ties, sat around a horseshoe shaped table covered with green baize. To the right was a separate stall for the accused and his defense counsel. To the left were separate tables for Allied observers. Witnesses were called to testify, standing within the horseshoe table. Paneled in oak with adornments of dull gold and stained glass windows, the rest of the room, which one journalist described as "more than slightly reminiscent of the theatre at Monte Carlo," was filled with rows of chairs for the audience. The hearings began at nine o'clock in the morning, recessed at two o'clock, resumed from four to seven or eight o'clock in the evening, and often continued six days a week. Despite poor acoustics, spectators at times filled the room to suffocation. They followed the testimony intently and, during hearings of the French and Belgian cases, vented hostility openly. Crowds frequently gathered outside the building to rail at Allied representatives and witnesses.[49]

The Reichsgericht began the trials on May 23, first hearing the cases submitted by the British. The British had carefully chosen these cases, accusing only low-ranking officers and soldiers directly involved in criminal acts and against whom there was strong evidence from both German and Allied sources. Sir Ernest Pollock led the British mission to Leipzig, a group of some seventy witnesses and observers. Pollock took every precaution to see that his party did not offend German dignity; he declined a German offer to act officially as co-plaintiff but communicated informally with the court and prosecutors, resolving potential problems before they led to embarrassing incidents. The sympathetic Pollock contributed substantially to the calm handling of the British cases.[50] Of the original seven individuals named by the British, the Germans decided to prosecute four. The other three men had died or disappeared.[51]

The Reichsgericht readily convicted three of the men accused by the British, all of whom were charged with mistreating prisoners of war. Both German and Allied witnesses testified that Sergeant Karl Heinen, Captain Emil Müller, and Private Robert Neumann beat prisoners with fists and rifle butts and otherwise acted with brutality. In some instances, the prisoners, it was admitted, had malingered at work or refused to obey orders. The military assessor of the court, General von Fransecky of the German Defense Ministry, embarrassed other German officials when he passionately defended the actions of the accused as necessary to discipline. Schmidt interrupted him several times to contradict these assertions. Dr. Ebermayer recommended several years' imprisonment for each of the accused. But the court refused to impose long sentences. Despite proof of the death of several prisoners, the court found no evidence that the defendants had actually killed them and consequently sentenced Heinen to ten months', Müller to six months', and Neumann to six months' imprisonment.[52] The judgments contained some extraordinary statements, for the court wanted to avoid impugning the honor of the German military. Delivering the verdict against Müller, Schmidt declared that Müller did not act "dishonourably, that is to say, his honour both as a citizen and as an officer remains untarnished," although his "conduct has sometimes been unworthy of a human being."[53] British observers noted that Captain Müller received a lesser punishment for crimes that did not differ substantially from those of Sergeant Heinen.[54]

From the British viewpoint, the last British case had a deplorable outcome, for it was an indirect justification of U-boat warfare. The Germans deliberately *nol-prossed* this case in open hearings on June 4. The court called no witnesses, and the whole process took less than two hours. The *oberreichsanwalt* recommended that the court acquit Lieutenant Karl Neumann and clear his name publicly. The British had accused Neumann, commander of the U-67, of torpedoing without warning a hospital ship, *Dover Castle*, in 1917. Neumann appeared in court to admit this action and to claim superior orders as his sole defense. The German Admiralty had ordered hospital ships sunk in specified zones, claiming that it was to take reprisals against Allied transport of soldiers and munitions on hospital ships, abuses of traditional immunity for such ships. The Reichsgericht accepted without question the legality of instructions to U-boat commanders and consequently upheld Neumann's plea of the necessity of obeying orders that he believed legal. Schmidt declared: "It is irrelevant whether the objective result was legal or illegal."[55]

As the British mission was departing Leipzig after this concluding trial, the Germans, as if to make up for the *Dover Castle* decision, told the British that prosecution would begin in mid-July in a case in which there was unquestionably a criminal attack against a hospital ship. Although the Germans were taking the initiative in this case, they invited the British to supply witnesses and to return to Leipzig as observers.[56]

The Reichsgericht took up a Belgian case immediately after the British left Leipzig and, following a short break, heard the French cases. From almost every viewpoint, these proceedings were disastrous. German Foreign Office officials complained that the Belgians and the French "never tried to make the trials a success." Belgian observers refused to shake hands with the Germans, and the conduct of the leader of the French mission, Paul Matter, *avocat général près le cour de cassation* ("attorney general of the Supreme Court of Appeal"), was described as "impossible" and "humiliating." Witnesses from those countries "breathed hatred."[57] On the other hand, courtroom audiences applauded counsels for the defense when they bitterly denounced Belgium and France; crowds in the streets cheered defendants and jeered French witnesses as they left the court.[58] The Belgians and French made the mistake of accusing high-ranking officers without substantiating their evidence with German sources. Consequently, out of six individuals tried in these cases, only one man was found guilty. Far from resolving the issue of war crimes punishment, the Leipzig trials created additional resentment between Germany and Belgium and France.

The Reichsgericht outraged the Belgians by acquitting Max Ramdohr on June 11. Ramdohr, who headed the secret military police at Grammont during the war, was accused of torturing children in 1917. In an effort to suppress sabotage of railway lines carrying troop trains, Ramdohr arrested several boys, ranging in age from nine to twelve years old, and had kept them imprisoned for two months before bringing them to trial. These young boys, some still not old enough to give testimony on oath, told the court of Ramdohr's brutal extraction of confessions. They claimed that during interrogation he had held their heads in buckets of water for long periods and that he had beaten them. The *oberreichsanwalt* asked for a sentence of two years' imprisonment against Ramdohr, but the court discounted the statements of the Belgian witnesses as the wildly imaginative stories of impressionable adolescents. Since there was no corroboration of their allegations from Germans, the Reichsgericht found Ramdohr not guilty. Ramdohr, the son of a Leipzig physician, had much local support, and courtroom spectators enthusiastically applauded the verdict.[59]

The Belgians promptly repudiated the Leipzig trials. The Belgian mission left Leipzig at once and reported to its government that the Reichsgericht's decision was "a travesty of justice." The Belgian government protested officially to Berlin and gave notice that it would no longer participate in the proceedings. The Belgians withdrew evidence previously submitted to authorities at Leipzig, evidence that apparently concerned the execution of hostages in the fall of 1914. The Belgians made clear their desire to revert to full enforcement of articles 228 to 230 of the Versailles treaty.[60]

A similar outcome occurred when the Reichsgericht dealt with the French cases from June 29 to July 9. The French were anxious to secure a conviction of General Karl Stenger and his subordinate officers. His alleged order to his troops to give no quarter to French soldiers in August 1914 had greatly excited French public opinion and had been one of the principal incidents provoking the demand for punishments during the early days of the war. After more than six years, the French believed they were about to settle with Stenger. The Germans had decided to try in one case both Stenger and one of his officers, Major Benno Crusius, who readily admitted shooting or ordering the murder of French prisoners.

The French could not have chosen a case more disagreeable to the Germans, for General Stenger was a war hero of an almost classic type. Although retired, he appeared in court in his field grey uniform, wearing the highest German war decoration, the blue Maltese Cross of the order *Pour le Mérite*. He stood on crutches, for a French artillery shell had blown away his left leg. The case further distressed the Germans because, contrary to traditional concepts of military loyalty, the retired Major Crusius to save himself testified against his former commander.

The tense courtroom atmosphere revealed that this was a case in which the honor of the German army was at stake. No one denied that German troops had murdered wounded French soldiers and prisoners of war. French Alsatian witnesses who had served in Stenger's brigade recounted shocking incidents that German soldiers corroborated. When an Alsatian, however, claimed to have heard Stenger give the order to shoot prisoners, the general jumped up, interrupting the proceedings, and shouted: "It is all a swindle! The witness is a lying Alsatian!" The spectators acclaimed Stenger, and violence hovered over the hearings. Members of Stenger's party assaulted an American film crew employed by the French when they tried to photograph the general outside the courtroom.[61]

Major Crusius confessed to his own participation in the murder of prisoners, basing his defense upon diminished mental capacity and the superior orders of Stenger. Stenger categorically denied ordering prisoners shot but admitted saying on two occasions that French soldiers who feigned wounds or death and then treacherously fired upon Germans from the rear must be killed. Several of Stenger's former subordinates confirmed his account. In an impassioned final statement, Stenger bitterly complained that for more than six years the world press had labeled him a war criminal. He swore before God that he had never issued any orders contrary to international law. He declared: "I did nothing in the war except my duty and obligation to the leaders of the German Fatherland, to my Kaiser, the Supreme War Lord, and in the interest of the lives of my fighting German soldiers." When Stenger sat down after this address to the court, spectators responded with wild applause and shouts of bravo.[62]

The verdict of the Reichsgericht outraged the French. The *oberreichsanwalt* recommended imprisonment of Major Crusius for two and one-half years but expressed no opinion regarding a judgment against Stenger. Schmidt delivered the court's opinion on July 6 acquitting Stenger and sentencing Crusius to two years' imprisonment. As Stenger left the supreme court building, a large crowd jubilantly presented him with flowers. The crowd taunted and spat upon members of the French mission.[63] The French government decided to recall these observers in protest.

Subsequent judgments in the French cases provoked equal indignation in France. On July 7 the Reichsgericht quickly found Lieutenant Adolf Laule not guilty of murdering a French soldier.[64] The trial of Generals Hans von Schack and Benno Kruska, which began on July 8, also angered the French. Charging the two officers with criminal negligence in failing to suppress a typhus epidemic in a prison camp they commanded in 1915, where more than a thousand prisoners had died, the French claimed the generals had not provided adequate sanitary facilities or medical care. The abrupt departure of the French mission cut short the trial. Without warning, the French left Leipzig during the midday recess on orders from Paris.[65] Since there were no French witnesses remaining to testify against the two generals, the Reichsgericht acquitted von Schack and Kruska the next day. In announcing that decision, Schmidt criticized French legal authorities. He declared that rather than discovering the criminals referred to in the French accusations the Reichsgericht had found only brave German soldiers who had served their country faithfully.[66]

Aristide Briand, who had replaced Millerand as French premier, wanted to pursue an essentially moderate policy toward Germany[67] but also wanted to avoid attacks from more intractable French leaders, such as ex-President Raymond Poincaré who demanded immediate retaliation. To appease critics, Briand dramatically explained to the Chamber of Deputies the recall of the French mission and denounced the "parody of justice" at Leipzig.[68] The French mission in its official report condemned the judges of the Reichsgericht, especially Schmidt, and recommended ending all cooperation with the futile proceedings, which were bound to result in one acquittal after another.[69] Briand reproached London for the friendly gestures of the British at Leipzig and requested consultation on joint Allied measures against Germany for the "scandalous" verdicts.[70] Neutral observers at Leipzig believed the French overreacted. A Dutch judge who had watched the Stenger trial wrote that the court acted in a "perfectly correct manner" and that the "fairly general disapproval of the judgment is misplaced."[71] British officials agreed and refused the French request to end British participation.[72]

Rather, the British mission went once more to Leipzig on July 9 to hear the most significant decision of the war crimes trials, the opinion in the *Llandovery Castle* case. The British had accused Helmut Patzig, commander of U-86, of sinking this hospital ship and, afterwards, of firing on survivors in lifeboats. Patzig, however, could not be prosecuted, for he lived in Danzig outside German jurisdiction. On their own initiative, the Germans indicted two of Patzig's subordinates, Lieutenants Ludwig Dithmar and John Boldt, hardened veterans who had served in the infamous freebooter Ehrhardt Brigade after the war.[73]

There was much opposition in Germany to the prosecution of these men. Prominent military figures criticized the proceedings, and the Deutschen Offizierbundes staged numerous protests in the weeks before the trial began.[74] Admiral Adolf von Trotha, former chief of staff of the navy, testified in their behalf. He claimed all responsibility for acts that in normal times appeared inhumane. He expressed confidence that Dithmar and Boldt, like members of all U-boat crews, had observed requirements of international law.[75] The *oberreichsanwalt* virtually apologized for having to bring charges. Ebermayer told the court: "In my forty years as public prosecutor and judge my office has never been so difficult, as today, when I must proceed against two German officers, who fought bravely and faithfully for their Fatherland. . . ."[76]

The facts of the grim story were, however, indisputable, as Ebermayer recognized. Crew members of the U-86 and several British survivors related essentially the same horrible details. The U-86 torpedoed the *Llandovery Castle* one hundred miles off the Irish coast on the night of June 27, 1918, well outside the zone in which the German Admiralty had ordered hospital ships sunk. The vessel went down in ten minutes, drowning most of a medical staff of 80 men, 14 nurses, and a crew of 164; no wounded soldiers died, for the ship was returning from Canada without patients. Patzig knew when he fired the torpedoes that his target was a hospital ship, for the vessel was lighted and marked, and he knew he was exceeding orders. But, at the time, he professed to believe that the ship was carrying American airmen and thus violating international law. Afterwards, Patzig took the U-86 to the surface to question persons in three lifeboats that had survived the sinking. When his suspicions about American airmen proved untrue, Patzig ordered deck crews to blow the lifeboats out of the water. One lifeboat escaped in the darkness. Recognizing the criminal character of these actions, Patzig falsified his logbook and swore his crew to secrecy. Dithmar and Boldt refused to break their oath to Patzig and steadfastly refused to testify. Boldt did make an indignant speech, defending Patzig as a great commander and declaring that Britain would never have won the war if Germany had possessed more men of Patzig's caliber.

The Reichsgericht handed down its judgment on July 16. The court accepted the plea of the counsel for Dithmar and Boldt that Patzig's orders absolved them of responsibility for the initial attack on the hospital ship but rejected such a defense for firing on lifeboats. The court pointed out that German military law did not excuse subordinates who exceeded orders or who carried out orders that they knew were illegal. Although there was sufficient doubt about the knowledge of Dithmar and Boldt concerning the legality of torpedoing the *Llandovery Castle,* the court concluded that they obviously knew that killing defenseless persons in lifeboats was forbidden. The court declared that they could have dissuaded Patzig from making that attack, with no danger to themselves, by threatening to report him to the Admiralty upon returning to Germany. Deciding that the officers acted on impulse rather than with premeditation, the Reichsgericht convicted them of manslaughter and imposed prison terms of four years on each man. Dithmar was dismissed from the navy, and Boldt, who had retired, was forbidden to wear his uniform ever again.[77]

This decision established a precedent in international war crimes prosecution, even though it was based upon German civil and military penal law, and during prosecutions after the Second World War lawyers often found one passage of the Reichsgericht's judgment especially pertinent, for it clearly placed international law above national law:

The firing on the boats was an offence against the law of nations. In war the killing of unarmed enemies is not allowed . . . , similarly in war at sea, the killing of shipwrecked people, who have taken refuge in lifeboats, is forbidden. . . . The killing of enemies in war is in accordance with the will of the State that makes war (whose laws as to the legality or illegality on the question of killing are decisive), only in so far as such killing is in accordance with the conditions and limitations imposed by the Law of Nations.[78]

Reaction in Germany to this decision was mixed. Liberal circles took pride in the impartiality of the Reichsgericht and thought the judgment had "for all time brought honor" upon German justice.[79] Nationalist and military figures argued that the court had made a terrible mistake. The judges had shown that they did not understand the proper relationship between international law and war at sea. Vice-Admiral Andreas D. Michelsen, former commander of the U-boat service during the war, gathered and published voluminous materials to demonstrate the innocence of Dithmar and Boldt.[80] Admiral Paul Behncke, chief of naval administration in 1921, secretly told fellow naval officers that he intended "to bring about every possible obtainable mitigation" for the two men.[81]

3

Although the French and Belgians were outraged over the results of the Leipzig trials, the British viewed the proceedings with some satisfaction. The *Times* called them a "scandalous failure of justice," but other newspapers and journals thought that the principle of punishment had been observed, despite the light sentences.[82] Several members of Parliament fumed over the "farce," but most politicians had lost interest. The House of Commons by a large majority decisively defeated a motion to hold a special debate on the trials.[83] In Britain it was becoming fashionable to be ashamed of the Carthaginian peace, as John Maynard Keynes called it in his influential diatribe, *Economic Consequences of the Peace*. Of all aspects of the peace, none seemed harsher, and consequently a matter of reproach, than the provisions for war crimes trials. The British gratefully accepted the opinion of the law officers who pronounced themselves satisfied. Sir Ernest Pollock told the Cabinet, and later the House of Commons, that the Reichsgericht "acted impartially" and that the "moral effect of the condemnation" outweighed the leniency of the sentences.[84]

The British thought it was time to allow war crimes punishment to pass into oblivion and to restore normal relations with the Germans. British leaders believed it unwise to make further trouble for the government of Chancellor Wirth, for he seemed committed to a policy of carrying out other provisions of the Versailles treaty, as much as possible. The British government suspected the French had an ulterior motive in their protests; they feared the French might seek to use Germany's failure to try war criminals properly to justify extending the occupation.[85] The British came to believe the French were as much a cause of tensions in Europe as the Germans.[86]

Reluctantly, the British continued to cooperate with German legal authorities for several months after the Leipzig trials. Another interrogatory hearing was held in London in late August to supply the Germans with testimony against Captain Wilhelm Werner, commander of the U-55.[87] He reportedly sank the hospital ship *Torrington* on April 8, 1917, and, afterwards, murdered thirty-four survivors by submerging while they clung to the deck of his submarine. Werner had disappeared, but the Germans wanted to assemble evidence in case he was found. Most British statesmen wanted to allow prosecutions to lapse, even against a man like Werner. British military intelligence told the Foreign Office that Werner was living in Rotterdam under an assumed name, but one official wrote on the report that "everybody concerned—most of all the Attorney-General—is only too anxious to let the whole war criminals question sleep. It only brings us trouble both with the French & with the Germans."[88]

The Wirth government also hoped the issue of punishing war criminals would fade. The new minister of justice, Gustav Radbruch, who said British disinterest was "distinctly recognizable," dealt deliberately with the matter in a "dilatory fashion."[89] The Cabinet, resisting continuing pressure to issue a list of Allied war criminals, remained determined to take no provocative action while Foreign Minister Walther Rathenau made progress in resolving other difficulties with the Allies.[90]

Hoping to avoid disturbing his policy of conciliation toward Germany, Premier Briand also procrastinated, but French public opinion would not permit him to drop the issue. Briand told Allied leaders on August 12 that the "best solution in a matter so delicate" was to "refer the question to a committee of specialists, high legal authorities. . . . Time would thus be gained and public opinion would have the opportunity to calm down." Curzon readily agreed to this suggestion.[91] The Allies allowed months to pass before this committee met. Eventually, Briand could no longer resist popular pressures. In December 1921 La Ligue pour perpétuer le souvenir des crimes allemands (The League to Perpetuate the Memory of German Crimes), among whose members were many prominent intellectuals and politicians, presented Briand a petition with two million signatures, a demand for action. Briand told French ambassadors in London and Rome to request an urgent convening of the committee.[92]

The Inter-Allied Commission on the Leipzig Trials, after two days of discussions in Paris on January 6-7, 1922, arrived at an awkward conclusion. The delegates condemned the proceedings in Germany as "highly unsatisfactory." They recommended that the Allies cease participation and begin enforcing articles 228 to 230 of the Versailles treaty requiring surrender of the accused to Allied tribunals.[93]

Admittedly, the Germans had provided provocation through their remiss handling of several convicted war criminals. To some Germans, the war criminals were national heroes, victims of Allied revenge and Weimar betrayal; Dithmar and Boldt were almost popular heroes. A number of members of the old Ehrhardt Brigade had founded the Organization Council (also called Organization C or O.C.), a group of political assassins. These people set out to free former comrades. After several efforts, Organization C succeeded in arranging the prison escape of Dithmar and Boldt.[94] The Allies did not know about Organization C and suspected the German government of complicity. The lenient treatment of other war criminals seemed to confirm German bad faith. Captain Müller served three months and was then released on parole after a doctor claimed he was on the verge of insanity. Sergeant Heinen served five months and was paroled at his employer's request. Heinen needed his job so he could support his wife and nine children. Actions that appeared merciful to the Germans were condemned in official British and French protests to Berlin. Allied representations secured the return to prison of Müller and Heinen, but German authorities never found Dithmar and Boldt.[95]

A new French government wanted to take stronger action than did the British. Replacing Briand in January 1922, Poincaré believed he had to deal with the Germans uncompromisingly on every issue, or the peace settlement would collapse. He viewed most problems from the standpoint of the security of France that he thought could be assured only by keeping Germany weak. Poincaré favored any policy that contributed to that end, and a German default on war crimes could be used to justify material sanctions.[96] Poincaré felt betrayed by conciliatory British attitudes toward Germany. He decided that France must act alone, if necessary, to secure German compliance with every provision of the peace treaty.

Chancellor Wirth in response to the declaration of the Inter-Allied Commission announced to the Reichstag that his government would never comply with demands for the surrender of the accused.[97] Demonstrations were held all over Germany once again in a show of unity.[98] It perhaps should be noted that the paths of Adolf Hitler and Hermann Goering first converged when Goering watched Hitler's posturing at one of these protest meetings.[99] Chancellor Wirth regarded the "situation as serious"[100] during the spring of 1922 and decided to renew prosecutions at Leipzig against individuals whom the Allies had named in the select list of war criminals. By taking such action, he hoped to prevent new Allied demands. Dr. Oskar Michelsohn was brought before the Reichsgericht in late June. The French had accused him of contributing through deliberate neglect to the deaths of more than seven hundred Allied prisoners who had been patients in a hospital that he directed during the war. Fourteen French witnesses were scheduled to testify against Michelsohn, but Paris ignored notice of the resumption of proceedings. Consequently, after hearing from German defense witnesses, the Reichsgericht acquitted Michelsohn on July 3.[101]

Poincaré did not want German war crimes trials, and he pressed the

British to join France in acting upon the recommendations of the Inter-Allied Commission. Poincaré, like Briand, felt the pressure of French public opinion. La Ligue pour perpétuer le souvenir des crimes allemands demanded action in a petition with ten million signatures and the support of fifty-eight diverse organizations such as Union française and Société nationale l'encouragement à l'agriculture.[102] Poincaré wanted to end the German trials to place Germany clearly in default of the Versailles treaty, for then he could approach the Allies about sanctions under article 428 of the treaty permitting an extension of the occupation.[103] When the French proposed this policy, at a meeting of the Conference of Ambassadors on July 26, 1922, the British resolutely opposed any explicit recognition of a German default or any application of sanctions. As a compromise, the British and the Italians agreed to a joint Allied note to Germany criticizing the trials and declaring that, henceforth, no sentences imposed at Leipzig would be considered valid and that the Allies were reserving full rights under articles 228 to 230. The Italians accepted this note, pleased perhaps that it would preclude prosecution of the cases previously submitted to Germany by Italy. As a concession to Poincaré, the British and Italians agreed to include a statement reserving freedom to prosecute accused war criminals *par contumace*. Germany was informed of this new Allied policy on August 23.[104] Thereafter, the British and Italians took no further action on war crimes, but the French and Belgians had already instituted new measures.

The French began an extensive program of court-martialing German war criminals *par contumace*. Such trials had been held from time to time since the end of the war. Poincaré expanded the proceedings by ordering the Ministries of War and Justice on April 18, 1922, to prosecute the 2,000 Germans named in the original French list, not merely the 334 on the list of February 3, 1920.[105] A commission headed by Paul Matter was established to oversee these prosecutions. The *conseil de guerre* of the First, Sixth, and Twentieth Army Corps at Lille, Nancy, and Chalons sur Marne carried out these trials. By December 1924 more than twelve hundred Germans had been condemned.[106] In some instances, the French were cautious. Poincaré suspended some prosecutions against notable public figures, such as Prince Rupprecht of Bavaria, Hindenburg, and Ludendorff, to avoid unwanted reactions in Germany.[107] The Belgians undertook only a limited number of prosecutions and tried approximately eighty cases.[108] Pleasing public opinion was the primary purpose of these trials, but soon war crimes punishment once again became a diplomatic weapon to use against Germany.

The Germans had not lived up to their obligation to pay reparations, and in early January 1923 Poincaré moved to enforce full compliance with the Versailles treaty. France and Belgium both sent troops into the Ruhr Valley. The Germans responded with passive resistance, and the result was a stalemate for months. Germany sank into economic and political chaos, a situation retrieved only when Gustav Stresemann came to power and resumed a policy of conciliation toward the Allies.[109]

During the Ruhr occupation, Poincaré twice tried to resurrect the war crimes issue. The French handed the German Foreign Office thirty-six requests in July for legal assistance in gathering evidence for use in the French trials *par contumace*. When the Germans failed to take action, the French ambassador presented an ultimatum declaring that refusal would be a default in the execution of the Versailles treaty. Stresemann feared the French intended to build another case for additional sanctions, and he moved to comply with the demand. Stresemann on December 17, 1923, secured the consent of the Cabinet to provide such evidence if French applications conformed to proper legal procedures.[110] Poincaré then sought the surrender of the crown prince as a war criminal. To appease nationalist critics, when he abandoned passive resistance to the Ruhr occupation, Stresemann had arranged for the crown prince to return to Germany from exile in the Netherlands. The British and French unsuccessfully tried to persuade the Dutch government to prevent the crown prince from leaving, and they vigorously protested to Berlin, charging that the German government had taken a step that might endanger peace.[111] Poincaré proposed to the British a joint Allied declaration demanding that Germany hand over the crown prince for trial and punishment or face sanctions. The British Cabinet bluntly refused.[112] Strongly opposed to Poincaré's harsh policies toward Germany, the British had refused support for his occupation of the Ruhr and did not want to raise the issue of war crimes again. Lord Curzon predicted that Germany would decline to hand over the crown prince and that Poincaré would ask for joint implementation of sanctions. Britain, Curzon was certain, should not become a partner in Poincaré's deplorable treatment of Germany. Confronted with British opposition, the French abandoned the idea of asking for the crown prince's surrender. Poincaré was seeking extrication from the impasse of the Ruhr occupation, whose economic repercussions had injured France, and further talk of the crown prince could only add to his difficulties.[113]

The French retreated on war crimes punishments when Poincaré fell from power in June 1924. He was replaced by a *cartel des gauches*, a coalition of center and socialist parties, led first by Édouard Herriot and later by Aristide Briand. This new leadership abandoned Poincaré's uncompromising stance toward Germany.[114] Herriot did not stop the trials *par contumace*, but on June 13 he cautioned the Ministries of Justice

and War to proceed carefully and to exercise the "greatest discretion . . .
vis-à-vis the press."[115] Herriot wanted to avoid disturbing progress toward
the normalization of relations with Germany, which the London Conference brought much closer in August with the adoption of the Dawes
Plan settling the long standing conflict over reparations.[116]

The issue of war crimes, however, continued on occasion to disrupt
Franco-German relations. A disturbing incident occurred in November
when General von Nathusius, who had been condemned *par contumace*,
visited the grave of his father-in-law in Alsace-Lorraine. The seventy-year-
old von Nathusius was arrested and taken to Lille, where he was retried
on November 20 and sentenced to a year's imprisonment for wartime
pillage. After vigorous official protests and a thunderous German press
reaction, Stresemann and Herriot arranged a compromise. Herriot, who
regarded the incident as a "thoroughly troublesome" distraction, proposed
a pardon for von Nathusius in exchange for clemency for several French
citizens in German prisons. Stresemann agreed to take "parallel" action
regarding the French prisoners if von Nathusius were pardoned unconditionally. This bargain was not made public. Von Nathusius received
a hero's welcome when he returned to Germany after spending several
weeks in a French jail.[117]

The French government decided upon clemency in this case in part
to avoid upsetting negotiations for a Franco-German commercial treaty
then in progress. Warned by the von Nathusius affair, the Germans
demanded guarantees of immunity for all technical advisers sent to Paris
to aid in the discussions. The French at first refused. One official said
that it "was truly impossible to give a safe-conduct to an individual
who was under sentence of condemnation, for if the German government
must reckon with its nationalists, we must equally reckon with our public
opinion." Eventually, the two governments reached a compromise. The
Germans agreed not to include Hermann Röchling, whom the French had
convicted *par contumace* of war crimes, among the industrialists in its
delegation, and Herriot instructed the Ministries of War and Justice to
arrest no German delegates.[118]

Hoping to avoid further incidents, Herriot instituted several new
measures. He issued secret orders to customs officials and the police that
henceforth any condemned German entering France was not to be arrested
but "returned discreetly" to German territory. All French consuls in
Germany in April 1925 were given a list of Germans convicted *par contumace*, a document of some 130 pages, and told not to issue visas to any
German whose name appeared on the list. The two governments agreed
to keep this French concession a secret.[119] The French trials *par contumace*
continued, sentencing Lieutenant General Ernst Kabisch, for example,

to life imprisonment in October.[120] But such judgments came less frequently than before. The election of Hindenburg as president of Germany briefly stirred French public opinion, for he was still considered one of the great criminals of the war.[121] Movement toward improved relations was, however, too powerful to be diverted significantly by this event.

Signature of the Locarno pact in late 1925, guaranteeing the borders between France, Belgium, and Germany and assuring Germany entry into the League of Nations, began a new period in postwar relations,[122] and the war crimes issue, like all other subjects of contention, was permitted to slip into the background. The Belgian government took the initiative to end the problem of war crimes trials, informing Berlin on October 29 that trials *par contumace* would cease.[123] Briand took the same step a short time later. Still wary of public opinion, Briand persuaded other French political leaders to permit the trials to lapse quietly in early 1926 rather than to end proceedings officially.[124] The French did not, however, abandon the policy of denying visas to condemned Germans until 1929. Many influential Germans suffered embarrassment and humiliation as a result of this procedure. Two particularly disturbing incidents involved the head of the national museum in Berlin, Dr. Theodore Demmler, and Count Max Montgelas, a former general who had become a historian of the war-guilt question.[125] After Briand again became premier, he ended the policy of denying visas in October 1929 and ordered instead police surveillance of all condemned Germans who visited France.[126] With this action, official French interest in war crimes punishment ended.

German concern with articles 228 to 231 of the Versailles treaty did not cease until the end of the Second World War. A desire to repudiate these humiliating clauses persisted in Germany throughout the interwar era. As Lord Kilmarnock said in 1920, the "soul of Germany" had been assaulted by efforts to punish German war criminals. Many Germans resented even more the accusation that Germany had been the aggressor in the First World War, and they attempted to erase these stains on national honor. The German government, particularly during Stresemann's six years as foreign minister, repeatedly and unsuccessfully tried to raise the issue of war guilt with the Allies.[127] Statesmen and politicians at every opportunity reaffirmed faith in German innocence in the outbreak of the First World War, and Germany was the first nation to publish a major part of its diplomatic correspondence of the prewar period, an attempt to prove that Germany had not sought war. The German government established a division of war guilt in the Foreign Office, the Schuldreferat, and even published a monthly periodical, *Die Kriegsschuldfrage*, to influence opinion at home and abroad. The Schuldreferat tried to prevent publication of materials that cast doubt upon the official posture of innocence or that would otherwise cause difficulty for German foreign policy. It opposed, for example, inclusion of documents in *Die Grosse Politik* showing that the Germans had demanded the French surrender an officer for court-martial in 1871, because this revelation would undermine opposition to article 228 of the Versailles treaty.[128] Long after revisionist historians in Allied countries had essentially accepted German arguments, the Germans continued attacks on the war-guilt clause. This behavior, some historians suggest, was due to a deep psychological need to deny responsibility for the national disaster of the First World War.

The Germans acted as diligently to refute accusations of war crimes. Stresemann on several occasions during the mid-1920s protested to British and French leaders, telling them that good relations with Germany depended in part upon an end to rhetorical references to German crimes in their speeches.[129] In the summer of 1927, the Reichstag Commission of Inquiry on Violations of International Law published findings of the study it had been conducting since 1919. Strongly influenced by the Schuldreferat, it exonerated in almost every instance the German government and particular individuals. To reach such conclusions, it resorted in some cases to strained interpretations of the laws of war.[130] The Belgians, then dedicating memorials to civilians whom the Germans had executed in 1914, vigorously condemned the study. Briefly, the two governments discussed establishment of an international inquiry into German actions during the invasion of Belgium, but they soon abandoned this idea.[131] The Germans were satisfied with the vindication provided by the Reichsgericht.

After the Allies had officially repudiated the Leipzig trials in 1922, the Reichsgericht proceeded to *nol-pros* cases with regularity. By late 1925, some 861 out of 901 allegations had been disposed of in this manner.[132] The accused individuals did not appear at these hearings, which apparently amounted to little more than a formality. A closed session of the Reichsgericht reviewed the convictions of Dithmar and Boldt in 1928 and on the basis of new testimony annulled its earlier decision and declared the two men innocent. This decision was never publicly revealed. A few months after Adolf Hitler and the Nazis came to power, the prosecutor's office at Leipzig on June 7, 1933, formally quashed all war crimes proceedings.[133]

Complaints about Allied efforts to bring alleged German war criminals to trial at the end of the First World War continued to the end of the Second World War. Even some members of the German resistance to Hitler during the war regretfully recalled the earlier demands for surrender of German statesmen and army commanders and expressed the hope that such dishonorable peace terms would not be instituted again.[134]

German war crimes trials were obviously not a success. Political and diplomatic considerations encroached upon impartial justice. Neither the Allies nor the Germans dealt with the problem of war criminals in a commendable fashion. But whatever the measure of Allied vindictiveness, German reverence for military honor prevented a proper handling of the issue. At Leipzig the Germans had difficulty distinguishing the acts of individuals from the military tradition for which they felt a special respect. Arising from nationalistic sentiments, this reaction was not confined to Germany. The Allies encountered similar obstacles in trying to punish war criminals of other defeated countries.

9

OTHER WAR CRIMINALS

The Allies, particularly the British, devoted much effort to punishing Turkish war criminals, but paid little attention to bringing individuals from Austria, Hungary, or Bulgaria to trial. The major Allied governments discouraged their small Balkan allies from pursuing such prosecutions. The Bulgarian government, however, conducted several war crimes trials. Motivated more by internal politics than Allied demands, the Bulgarians tried, among others, the ministers of state who had led Bulgaria into the war.

Allied efforts to bring Turkish war criminals to justice came near success, only to collapse ignominiously. Ample opportunity existed to begin proceedings. To appease the Allies, authorities in Turkey court-martialed some individuals, and the British imprisoned more than one hundred Turks accused of war crimes at Malta for two years but never brought any of them to trial. For legal and political reasons, the Allies allowed opportunities to drift away. More concerned with peacemaking in Europe, the Allies disagreed over how severely to treat the Turks, and by the time the Allies had turned their full attention to the problems of Asia Minor, the sultan's government at Constantinople, which had been submissive in regard to punishments, no longer ruled much of Turkey. The Nationalist Revolution was rising to power under the leadership of Mustapha Kemal Pasha. He established a new government and forced the Allies to abandon efforts at prosecuting war criminals.

1

The major Allied governments did not pursue Austrian or Hungarian war criminals for several reasons. In contrast to attitudes toward Kaiser Wilhelm II and the Hohenzollerns, virtually no one believed that ex-

Emperor Karl of Austria-Hungary deserved punishment. The most implacable antagonist of the kaiser, Lloyd George, in fact initiated action to save Karl from prosecution. He urged the Council of Ten at the Paris Peace Conference on March 10, 1919, to grant the Habsburg ruler immunity. Lloyd George asserted that there was no reason to place Karl on trial because Austro-Hungarian responsibility for the war lay with the dead Franz Josef, not Karl, who upon succeeding to the throne in 1916 had begun the secret Sixtus negotiations and "had done his best, though rather clumsily, to bring about peace." Other Allied leaders readily agreed to a proposal to promise Switzerland, which had agreed to grant Karl asylum, that the Allies would not demand his surrender for trial, a decision later reaffirmed by the Council of Four.[1] Subsequently, after Karl twice returned to Hungary in 1921 in unsuccessful attempts to regain his throne, the Allies did treat Karl as Napoleon had been dealt with, keeping him in permanent exile, under Portuguese authority, on the island of Madeira. But this action had nothing to do with war crimes punishment.[2]

Allied leaders thought the forces of Austria-Hungary had a relatively clean war record, and the Italians, who had been the principal Western opponent of Austria-Hungary, took little interest in punishing war criminals. The conduct of the Austro-Hungarian armies in fighting the Russians was ignored, for, of course, the Bolshevik government in Russia was not represented at the peace conference. The Commission on Responsibility in drawing up a comprehensive list of enemy atrocities leveled fewest important charges against Austro-Hungarian military forces.[3] Although Premier Orlando told the Council of Four that "there was a terrible record of crimes against some Austrians," the Italian foreign minister, Sonnino, said that "the question was less serious than in the case of Germany."[4]

Dealing with the issue of Austro-Hungarian misdeeds on its merits, however, was never considered as important as its relationship to the German peace settlement. Uppermost was the need to give the Germans as little reason as possible to complain of discrimination. Allied leaders decided, therefore, that penalty clauses in the Austrian and Hungarian treaties should conform to those in the Versailles treaty.[5]

It proved impossible to copy those provisions without modification. Austro-Hungarian military forces had been composed of many men who lived in territory taken over by Rumania, Czechoslovakia, Poland, Yugoslavia, and even Italy, after the disintegration of Austria-Hungary. Requiring these new states to surrender newly acquired citizens as war criminals was not deemed feasible. President Wilson said that the Allies could not "compel the Czech-Slovak Government to surrender people accused of crimes."[6]

The Austrian delegation to the peace conference tried to exploit this awkward matter. As an illustration of the anomalous situations likely to arise, the Austrians asked: what if two officers of the same regiment of the Austro-Hungarian army—one an Austrian-German, the other a Czech—were accused of the same crime? The Austrian would have to be surrendered, while the Czech would not. Another reason for not punishing soldiers of Austria-Hungary, said the Austrians, was that the laws of war had not applied in the struggle between the old empire and the successor states, for those new states had been merely rebellious areas during the war, not belligerents entitled to protection of the laws of war.[7]

The Allies determined nonetheless to provide for trials. In the end, the penalty clauses of the Austrian treaty of Saint Germain-en-Laye (September 10, 1919) and the Hungarian treaty of Trianon (June 4, 1920) contained a compromise solution for the complications resulting from the empire's disintegration. Article 176 of the treaty of Saint Germain and article 160 of the treaty of Trianon obliged states that had acquired territory from the empire to take "all measures necessary to ensure the prosecution and punishment of such persons" accused of war crimes as resided within their new borders. With this exception and the omission of any trial of Emperor Karl, the penalty clauses of the Austrian and Hungarian treaties duplicated those of the German settlement.[8]

These provisions were never implemented. Austria did establish a Commission of Inquiry into Military Breaches of Duty in the spring of 1920, which court-martialed two officers charged with ordering the murder of Serbian and Russian prisoners of war, but the two men—one General Ljubičič and one General von Lütgendorff—were acquitted. If the Austrians held these trials to appease the Allies, it was unnecessary, as was the agitation of some Austrian officers against the delivery of soldiers to foreign tribunals,[9] for when the major Allies abandoned the idea of trying Germans, they easily extended this concession in greater measure to Austria and Hungary, overriding the opposition of the Balkan powers. The Allies merely observed the formality of delivering official requests to Austria and Hungary to hand over war criminals.[10] There is no evidence of any response by Austria or Hungary to these demands, nor of steps taken by the successor states to punish former soldiers of the Austro-Hungarian Empire residing within their borders.

2

At the Paris Peace Conference, those governments most concerned with Bulgarian atrocities—Yugoslavia (formerly Serbia), Rumania, and Greece—sought ways to escape responsibility for holding war crimes trials. Although the Yugoslav delegation at first proposed demanding the immediate surrender of the twenty-five worst offenders before signing any peace treaty with Bulgaria,[11] Premier Nikola Pashitch agreed on June 26, 1919, to join with Eleutherios Venizelos of Greece and Ion Bratianu of Rumania in advancing draft penalty clauses that would place much of the burden for trying Bulgarians upon the major Allied governments. Ignoring the fact that the Council of Four had already rejected the concept of an international court, the Balkan leaders urged the establishment of a High Tribunal composed of seven judges, one each from Britain, France, Italy, and Belgium, as well as three members from their own countries, to try ordinary war criminals. No special provision was made for a trial of ex-Tsar Ferdinand of Bulgaria. When Nicolas Politis, the Greek foreign minister, submitted these draft articles to the Commission on Responsibility, he said that no mention was made of Ferdinand, because it was feared that there was not enough evidence to ensure a conviction; he thought it was best "to pass over this matter in silence."

Politis, who piloted the measure through the commission, strongly favored establishment of an international criminal court as a permanent international reform. Having failed to secure establishment of an international tribunal in the Versailles treaty, he thought, perhaps, that this Balkan proposal would make up for that missed opportunity. Since Robert Lansing was no longer present to oppose such an idea, Politis was able to persuade most members of the commission of its merits.[12]

The Commission on Responsibility approved the Balkan proposal, but major Allied leaders refused to depart from the precedents laid down in the Versailles treaty. At a Heads of Delegations meeting on July 25, Georges Clemenceau persuaded Arthur Balfour and Tommasco Tittoni that the commission's decision should be reversed.[13] Allied leaders also summarily rebuffed Bulgarian offers. Premier Theodore Theodorff pledged to the peace conference on September 19 that Bulgaria would "punish the authors of those excesses pitilessly," but the Allied leaders may have had reason to doubt his sincerity when they heard him call for a tribunal that would not include Greek, Rumanian, and Yugoslav judges. The Allied leaders rejected his requests. The Bulgarians were forced to sign the treaty of Neuilly-sur-Seine on November 27, 1919, with articles 118 to 120 copied virtually unchanged from articles 228 to 230 of the Versailles treaty.[14]

In the fall of 1920, the major Allies, again following the pattern set with Germany, urged the Balkan states to let the Bulgarians try accused war criminals. The Balkan governments drew up lists of accused persons and formally demanded surrender of Bulgarians on September 9. But the number of persons called for had been reduced as much as possible.

The major Allied governments did not demand the surrender of anyone,[15] partly because the British Commission of Enquiry concluded that the Bulgarians had given their soldiers "preferential treatment."[16] The British released Captain Georges Nicoloff, former commandant of the prisoner of war camp at Philippopolis, who had been held at Malta since January 1919,[17] and Lord Curzon sought "favourable consideration" for the request of the Bulgarians to try their own citizens in lieu of Allied trials.[18] At a War Criminals Committee meeting in Paris on November 10, 1920, the Greeks and Rumanians renounced their right to hold trials provided that Bulgaria assume that task. The Yugoslav government refused to give up its right to prosecute Bulgarians, for the Yugoslav public retained strong memories of the harsh Bulgarian occupation.[19]

Both to appease Yugoslavia and to eliminate political opponents, the radical Agrarian regime of Alexander Stamboliski carried out the Bulgarian promise to hold war crimes trials.[20] The wartime Cabinet of Vasil Radoslavov and other former high officials, some two hundred persons in all, had been arrested on November 4, 1919, but Radoslavov and ex-Tsar Ferdinand, both of whom had fled to Berlin at war's end, remained free because the Germans refused to extradite them.[21] The Sobranje (Bulgarian legislature) in late March 1921 enacted into law an extraordinary indictment against the former ministers for the actions that had brought about national disaster. Among the charges were the illegal and secret diplomatic preparation for war, the unconstitutional declaration of war, and the unlawful waging of war. One specific accusation—"allowing atrocities committed in occupied territory to go unpunished"—was quite clearly related to the concept of war crimes.[22] The tribunal specially created to hear the case was composed of six judges drawn from the regular judiciary, including the presiding judge of Bulgaria's highest court, and twelve people's judges, described by a reporter as "hard-faced Balkan peasants with only one collar among the lot."[23]

The trial of the Radoslavov Cabinet continued for almost two years. Eleven men were arraigned on October 11, 1921, including General Nikola Jekov, commander of Bulgaria's army during the war, who had voluntarily returned from Berlin to stand beside his former colleagues. The proceedings dragged on so interminably, one journalist reported, that even the daily parade through the streets of Sofia of the defendants marching from jail to courtroom became such a common sight "that scarcely anyone turns his head to look at the prisoners who were once the rulers of the country." After hearing more than a million words of testimony, the court finally handed down verdicts on March 31, 1923, ranging from life imprisonment for six persons, including Radoslavov who was sentenced *in absentia*, to ten years for General Jekov.[24] A British diplomat, Sir Herbert Dering, expressed the most common Western opinion when he said that the case seemed "to savour more of revenge on the part of the present Agrarian Government in power than of abstract justice."[25]

Besides trying former ministers for war guilt, Stamboliski also arranged more conventional war crimes trials of lesser figures to pacify Yugoslavia. He wanted to conciliate that country, for it was vital to his dream of organizing a "Green International" party and a South Slav federation, uniting the Balkans in the interests of the peasantry.[26] By the time the two countries resumed diplomatic relations in October 1920, the Bulgarian government claimed to have court-martialed 534 persons for offenses against the laws of war,[27] but the Yugoslav government did not believe the Bulgarians and refused to repatriate about a dozen Bulgarian soldiers who had been sentenced to death for war crimes. It gave the men a reprieve only after the British intervened and only on the condition that Bulgarian trials proceed forthwith.[28] Stamboliski promptly had various persons arrested, some of them quite prominent, such as the head of the occupation government at Nish, whose detention in May 1921, a British observer said, was "a sop to appease Serbian opinion." Eventually, one man, a Major Kulchin, was executed for having massacred civilians during the capture of Nish.[29]

The Agrarians overreached themselves when they extended judicial scrutiny to the war guilt of almost all former Bulgarian ministers. The so-called bourgeoisie bloc parties had in 1922 mounted a growing campaign against the reform program of Stamboliski and appeared to be preparing for a coup d'etat. As a countermeasure, the government arrested on September 22 many opposition leaders who had served in past administrations. The Sobranje authorized a national referendum to determine if the Cabinets of Ivan Geshov and Stoyan Danev should be prosecuted for waging the Second Balkan War of 1913 and if the Cabinet of Alexander Malinov should be tried for not ending the war soon enough in 1918. The electorate on November 19 by a three to one margin voted its approval, and in March 1923 the Sobranje created another special court to try thirteen officials from these ministries. This court never met, because the Agrarian regime was overthrown in June, and Stamboliski was murdered.[30]

3

The principal Allied powers were much more interested in the war crimes of Turks than in those of Bulgarians. Prospects for bringing Turkish war criminals to justice seemed at first most promising. Soon after the armistice of Mudros in October 1918, Sultan Mehemet VI pledged to court-martial persons responsible for the Armenian massacres and other atrocities. The Committee of Union and Progress was suppressed, and many Young Turk leaders fled into hiding. Despite the gathering of evidence by ten regional teams and a large number of arrests, there were long delays in prosecution.[31]

The British, more interested in the matter than the other Allies, pressed the Turks to act more vigorously and undertook unilateral measures of their own. Their greatest concern was to punish officials responsible for mistreating British prisoners of war. The attorney-general's Committee of Enquiry determined that Turkish neglect and brutality had led to the deaths of half of the thirteen thousand soldiers captured at Kut-el-Amara and recommended that twenty-seven persons be charged with violations of the laws and customs of war. The Committee of Enquiry did not investigate the Armenian massacres, believing that these incidents lay beyond the British jurisdiction and should be left to the Paris Peace Conference.[32] The Foreign Office, however, made no distinctions when it instructed Admiral Somerset Calthorpe, the British high commissioner, to demand that the sultan surrender certain individuals accused of atrocities.[33] The War Cabinet went further in mid-January 1919 when it authorized Calthorpe to "arrest Enver, Talaat, and their leading confederates, if he could do so," even without the Turkish government's consent.[34] British authorities seized several persons and interned them at Malta.[35] Among these individuals were two men of high rank, Generals Liman von Sanders and Ali Ihsan Pasha. King George V took a personal interest in the case of the German general, Liman von Sanders, and cabled Constantinople on January 10: "His Majesty trusts that no mercy or pity will be shown him, and that everything possible will be done to bring him to justice."[36] It proved difficult, however, to substantiate charges against him in regards to the Armenian massacres, and he was released in August.[37] The Turkish officer, Ali Ihsan Pasha, arrested on similar charges, was not freed for more than two years.[38]

Soon Turkish efforts became more energetic with the appointment of a new grand vizier, Damad Ferid, the sultan's brother-in-law. More than any other Turkish leader, he sought to restore the sultan's power and Turkey's status by single-minded cooperation with the Allies.[39] Under his administration, the principal military tribunal, presided over by General Mustapha Nazim Pasha, began prosecutions in earnest. The severity of its first verdict impressed all observers. In April it convicted Kemal Bey and Major Tevfik Bey, former officials in the Yozgat Sanjak, of ordering the robbery and murder of Armenians. Tevfik was sentenced to fifteen years at hard labor, and Kemal Bey was hanged four days later. This execution caused a disturbing popular reaction. Elements hostile to Damad

Ferid made Kemal Bey a national martyr and turned his funeral into a patriotic protest against abject submission to the Allies.[40] To appease his critics, Damad Ferid sought an alternative course of action. He proposed to various neutral governments the creation of a court composed of two representatives each from Switzerland, Denmark, Spain, Sweden, and the Netherlands, but nothing came of this move.[41]

He went ahead, therefore, with preparations for a grand inquest against Turkey's wartime rulers. The trial of some twenty Young Turk leaders began on April 27 in the Great Hall of the Ministry of Justice at Constantinople. Most of the more important figures, including Talaat, Enver, Djemal, Dr. Behaeddin Shakir Bey, director of the deportation squads, Dr. Nazim, and Aziz Bey, head of public security, had fled to Germany at the war's end and had to be tried *in absentia*. Several high officials had been arrested, however, and appeared before the court in person. Among them were the former grand vizier, Prince Said Halim Pasha; two former ministers of foreign affairs, Halil Bey and Ahmed Nessimi Bey; a former minister of justice, Ibrahim Bey; a former seikh-ul-Islam, Musa Kiazim Effendi; and Atif Bey, Midhat Shukri, and Mehmen Zia Guekalp, all important members of the central committee of the Committee of Union and Progress.[42] These proceedings seemed full of promise; yet the trial accomplished little.

Most of the responsibility for the failure rested with the Allies. Damad Ferid's policy of cooperation received a severe setback when the Council of Four permitted Greece to occupy Smyrna on May 15. This provocative move raised fears that the Allies favored permanent territorial annexations by the ancient enemy of Turkey. Led by Mustapha Kemal, a Nationalist movement arose that denounced Damad Ferid and pledged resistance to inequitable peace terms. Eventually, it organized a separate rebel government at Angora to oppose the sultan's appeasement of the Allies.[43] The Smyrna occupation particularly discredited the idea of war crimes trials. Upon landing at Smyrna, Greek forces committed atrocities that for the most part went unpunished, thus making the Allies appear hypocritical in holding Turkey to a double standard of conduct.[44] Immediately following the incidents at Smyrna, some prison authorities, influenced by nationalistic protests, freed forty-one alleged war criminals. Fearing the release of all such prisoners, the British took many of them into custody. Despite French opposition, British authorities replaced Turkish officials with British soldiers to guard sixty-seven persons held at Seras-Kierak prison in Constantinople. This large group, which contained several of the former leaders then on trial, was deported to Malta on May 28, because the British had little faith in Turkish justice.[45]

Damad Ferid's policy lay in shambles, and Allied leaders at Paris did not accept his claims of success. When he was called to present Turkey's case before the Council of Ten on June 17, the grand vizier pointed with pride to the truncated but continuing trial of Young Turk leaders as proof of the "rehabilitation of the Ottoman nation." The Armenian massacres, he said, would "make the conscience of mankind shudder with horror forever," but "the great trial of the Unionists at Constantinople has proved the responsibility of the leaders of the Committee." Turkey, having purged itself, should be readmitted to the international community without penalty for the tragedies of the past.[46] Damad Ferid asked the Allies a short time later to force the reluctant Germans to extradite Enver, Talaat, and Djemal to Turkey. The Allies rebuffed his appeals. Turkey had to pay for the Young Turk crimes in the peace settlement.[47]

Despite this rebuke, the trials continued, but they produced meager results. The convictions of former Young Turk leaders that were handed down on July 5 had more symbolic than practical value. Only Musa Kiazim was actually present to receive fifteen years at hard labor. The court had to sentence other persons *in absentia* and pronounced the death penalty against Talaat, Enver, Djemal, Dr. Nazim (and Dr. Behaeddin Shakir in a separate prosecution on January 13, 1920). Everyone knew, however, that these judgments were not likely to be carried out. The court acquitted several former officials. It handed down no verdicts for many of the accused, such as Prince Said Halim Pasha, for the British had taken them to Malta.[48] The court-martial of lesser figures went on sporadically for another year, but, with the exception of Avni Bey who was hanged on July 29, 1920, few men were punished.[49]

Distrusted by the skeptical British and strongly opposed by rebellious Nationalists, Turkey's war crimes trials satisfied no one. After Damad Ferid left office for the last time, his successors abandoned his policy and engaged in recriminations against him and other Turkish officials. A new government at Constantinople, then seeking compromise with the Nationalists at Angora, arrested four members of the principal military tribunal in October 1920 on charges of contravening judicial procedure.[50] Evaluating the trials after their collapse, Sir Horace Rumbold, the new British commissioner, said the proceedings had "always been dilatory and nearly always insincere." As proof, he pointed to the record which showed that "only two persons, and these men of quite subordinate standing," had "paid the extreme penalty."[51] The British never seriously considered accepting these disappointing results as final and made plans for Allied prosecutions.

4

The Allies were even less successful than the sultan's government in trying Turkish war criminals. A lack of legal precedent posed serious difficulties. At the Paris Peace Conference, the Commission on Responsibility unanimously concluded that more than two hundred thousand Armenians had been massacred.[52] Some members of the commission did not believe, however, that this horror constituted a war crime that the Allies could legitimately punish. Not until 1948 would genocide (racial extermination) be clearly defined by treaty as an international crime, and in 1919 adherence to time-honored notions of sovereignty placed limitations upon the scope of the traditional laws and customs of war. The Hague conventions dealt with acts committed during war by soldiers of one nation against those of another country, not with a state's treatment of its own citizens. From this perspective, Turkish action against Armenians was an internal matter, not subject to the jurisdiction of another government.

Nicolas Politis urged the Commission on Responsibility to adopt a new category of war crimes. "Technically these acts [Armenian massacres] did not come within the provisions of the penal code," he said, but surely they were such an affront to civilization as to offend "what might be called the law of humanity or the moral law." Robert Lansing and James Brown Scott objected to the ex post facto character of this standard and to its unfixed content, which might vary according to conscience and circumstance. Most members of the commission hesitantly agreed with Politis, relying for justification upon the Hague conventions' declaration that, where its written regulations did not suffice, persons, nonetheless, were protected by the law of nations resulting "from the usages established among civilized peoples, from the laws of humanity, and the dictates of the public conscience."[53] The proposal of Politis foreshadowed the category of "crimes against humanity" set forth in the charter of the Nuremberg Tribunal after the Second World War to deal with the Nazi slaughter of European Jews, but in 1919 such a new departure in international law proved impossible.[54]

The war crimes clauses of the treaty of Sèvres (August 10, 1920) did not resolve the problem with certainty. Articles 226 to 229 followed the pattern of the Versailles treaty for cases involving the mistreatment of prisoners of war and similar incidents. These articles repudiated the Turkish trials and provided for surrender to Allied national or mixed military tribunals of all persons charged with offenses against the laws and customs of war. Article 230 made special provisions for dealing with individuals who perpetrated the Armenian massacres. It called for their surrender but specified neither the law nor the court by which they would be tried. Rather, it reserved to the Allies "the right to designate the tribunal which shall try the persons so accused."

The Allies hoped to relinquish this problem to the League of Nations, for article 230 bound Turkey to recognize its jurisdiction if the League "created in sufficient time a tribunal competent to deal with the said massacres."[55] The Advisory Commission of Jurists, which met at The Hague during the summer of 1920 to frame the statute of the Permanent Court of International Justice, recommended establishment of a High Court of International Justice "to try crimes constituting a breach of international public order or against the universal law of nations." The League ignored this suggestion, for neutral states did not want to become embroiled in controversy over the trial of war criminals.[56]

Delays in making peace also undermined the war crimes project. During the two years between the armistice of Mudros and the signing of the treaty of Sèvres, the Turkish Nationalist movement grew into a major force, and the Allied coalition virtually dissolved. By 1920 most of the victors no longer included among their aims the punishment of Turkish war criminals. The United States had repudiated the Versailles treaty and was retreating into isolationism. The Senate turned down a mandate for Armenia, and the American government, which had never declared war on the Ottoman Empire, took no part in drawing up the treaty of Sèvres. The French were not eager to prosecute Turks. The French made no provision for war crimes trials in an initial draft treaty with Turkey.[57] Jules Cambon blocked British efforts to get the Conference of Ambassadors to demand the surrender of Enver and others from Germany in March 1920.[58] At the same time, the Italians evaded a British request for the arrest of former Young Turk leaders then reported as meeting within their territory.[59] The French and the Italians hoped to secure concessions in Asia Minor and did not want to antagonize powerful factions in Turkey unnecessarily, particularly the rising Nationalists.[60]

Only the British government continued to pursue Turkish war criminals. The British public would not willingly forgo retribution against persons who had mistreated British prisoners of war. A sizable and very vocal segment of opinion also remained concerned about the suffering of Christian Armenia. Moreover, the Foreign Office believed that the Young Turks posed a revolutionary threat to Britain's Moslem possessions. British diplomats tracked the movements across Europe of former Young Turk leaders and tried to have them arrested.[61] Preserving integrity of the empire was, then, a factor in British concern about Turkish war criminals.

The British government's use of its war crimes policy for political purposes, however, helped discredit the whole scheme. Assured by the law officers that deportation to Malta was an act of state that could not be questioned in any court,[62] British military forces at Constantinople continued to arrest Turkish citizens during the last half of 1919 and throughout 1920. The high commissioner's staff drew up a list of 142 persons whose surrender would be demanded from the sultan once the peace treaty went into effect. Eight were charged with breaches of the armistice, 18 with mistreating prisoners of war, and 130 with massacring Armenians. From time to time, the British arrested men whose names appeared on the "black list" and took them to Malta.[63] Often the British deported individuals as "Nationalist undesirables" or for "having troubled public security," although invariably they also officially charged such persons with having massacred Christians. By December 1920 it was clear that 39 of the approximately 120 Turks held at Malta were political prisoners.[64] Sir Horace Rumbold pointed out problems caused by lumping all the prisoners together. He said that "it was unfortunate that so many of the deportees were held on grounds which would not justify eventual criminal prosecution," because "this fact helped to intensify the bitter feeling aroused." Many Turks came to regard all the prisoners, irrespective of the reasons for their arrest, "as victims of British injustice."[65]

The most flagrant instance of political arrests occurred during the occupation of Constantinople in March 1920. The Allies were in the process of preparing peace terms, but events in Turkey gave no promise of easy acceptance. Nationalists' victories in recent elections for a new Chamber of Deputies and their military successes against French forces in Cilicia, where thousands of Armenians had also been massacred at Marash, seemed likely to encourage additional resistance to Allied authority. The Allies decided to take dramatic action. Allied troops took full control of Constantinople on March 16 and took into custody prominent anti-Allied politicians and intellectuals.[66] Allied soldiers detained the most important Nationalist members of the Chamber of Deputies, including Hussein Reouf Bey, Mustapha Kemal's closest associate. These men were taken to Malta to share quarters with the accused war criminals.[67]

The Nationalists struck back. At Angora on the night of March 16, the Turks arrested Lieutenant-Colonel Alfred Rawlinson, brother of Lord Henry Rawlinson, commander-in-chief in India, and four subordinates in retaliation for the seizure of Hussein Reouf Bey.[68] Subsequently, some twenty-five other British soldiers and nationals were taken hostage for the Turks on Malta.[69] Protesting vigorously against the deportations, Mustapha Kemal told Curzon that, henceforth, the Grand National Assembly at Angora would assume all power in Turkey since the Allies had made the government at Constantinople their puppet.[70] When the rigorous terms of the treaty of Sèvres became known in May, the Nationalists launched an attack against British positions on the Ismid Peninsula. The Allies compelled the sultan to sign the treaty anyway, but many people doubted that the Nationalists could ever be reconciled to it.[71]

Faced with this resistance in Turkey, the British Cabinet could not agree on an appropriate response. The India Office and the War Office had always questioned the desirability of a harsh Turkish peace settlement, but the Foreign Office had vigorously supported such a policy. Churchill began to press for moderation in the spring of 1920.[72] He urged release of some of the Turks held at Malta as a gesture of goodwill and the use of more discrimination in deportations to Malta. Despite opposition from the Foreign Office, he took the matter to the Cabinet in July. He pointed out that failure to free some of the "less guilty and less hostile" immediately might result later in the necessity of liberating "in the first instance the most guilty and the most hostile in exchange for British officers and men captured by the Nationalist forces."[73] The Cabinet adopted Churchill's proposal on August 4 and directed the attorney-general to review the cases to determine which should be prosecuted so that all other Turks at Malta could be "released at first convenient opportunity."[74]

This directive of the Cabinet revealed additional divisions within the British government. The law officers, who had the primary responsibility for war crimes trials, recommended holding only six individuals whom the Committee of Enquiry had accused of brutalities against British prisoners of war. The law officers had no intention of trying persons charged with the Armenian massacres.[75] The high commissioner's office in Constantinople, on the other hand, proposed in November the trial of fifty-nine Turks and release of thirty-five.[76] Clearly, the British government had no coordinated policy on war crimes.

The confusion in the British government was reflected in the treatment of the Turks on Malta. Their status was that of prisoners, yet hardly that of war criminals. They were lodged at Polverista in apartments originally built for noncommissioned officers and their families. Although surrounded by barbed wire and guarded by detachments of the Essex and Lancashire regiments, they enjoyed much freedom of movement. The papacy had urged "special privileges consonant with their rank" for some personages, such as Prince Said Halim Pasha,[77] and the British paroled the Turks to walk about town twice weekly and to attend the opera. The sympathetic attitudes of some British officers raised their hope of release. They spent much of their time sending letters and petitions to London, claiming that their imprisonment without indictment or trial violated every canon of English common law.[78] Two individuals took advantage of the lax supervision and on December 6 fled by boat to Italy. They were two of the most notorious members of the group: Tahir Djevdet Bey, Enver's brother-in-law, who as governor of Van in 1915 had bloodily crushed an Armenian uprising, an event that some people believed was contrived as a pretext for launching the general policy of deporting and massacring Armenians; and Mustapha Kirzade (Adjente Mustapha), an alleged executioner at Trebizond who reportedly carried Armenians out to sea and dumped them overboard as the most efficient means of extermination in 1915.[79] Their escape symbolized the paradoxical character that the war crimes problem had assumed. Those who should have been released remained prisoners, and those who should have been prosecuted gained their freedom. Understandably, Sir Horace Rumbold concluded that "the whole matter had drifted by the end of 1920 into a hopelessly involved and unsatisfactory state."[80]

5

Believing reconciliation with the Nationalists necessary, the British government in early 1921 dropped much of its policy on war crimes. During the abortive London Conference, which sought to revise the treaty of Sèvres, Curzon and Bekir Sami, the foreign minister of the Angora government, signed an agreement on March 16 for the release of all British prisoners held by the Nationalists and all Turks on Malta, except those accused of massacres or violations of the laws and customs of war. The exchange involved approximately sixty-four Turks and twenty-two British soldiers and nationals.[81]

Neither side, however, trusted the other, and negotiations collapsed. The Nationalists must have suspected that the Greek military offensive launched against them on March 24 to compel acceptance of the treaty of Sèvres had the support of Great Britain. The British rightly believed that the treaties recently concluded by the Nationalists with the Soviet Union, France, and Italy would encourage chauvinistic elements at Angora, particularly in view of the rapid defeat of the Greek attack.[82] The British freed forty Turkish prisoners, including Prince Said Halim Pasha, who landed in Italy on April 29-30, but detained the others, including Hussein Reouf Bey, to await a Nationalist response.[83] In May, Bekir Sami resigned, and more uncompromising leaders took power at Angora.[84] The new foreign minister, Yusuf Kemal, informed Curzon on June 28 that the Grand National Assembly would not ratify the pact made by Bekir Sami because it infringed upon Turkey's sovereignty over its own citizens. He pointed out that the Allies had conceded the right of Germany's jurisdiction over Germans accused of war crimes. Turkey's national pride required the equal treatment due a sovereign nation. He proposed, therefore, an exchange of all Turkish prisoners for all British prisoners.[85] The Nationalists sent eight persons to Constantinople in July but kept the most important captives, including Colonel Rawlinson. A member of Rumbold's staff concluded that the Nationalists kept Rawlinson "as a means of pressure on His Majesty's Government to release all Turkish prisoners in Malta including the worst war criminals."[86]

The British made further concessions, for many officials believed that prosecution of individuals responsible for the Armenian massacres had become impossible. The law officers in a final recommendation to the Cabinet in January 1921 called for the trial of eight men accused of cruelty to British prisoners of war, but the law officers asserted that no proceedings could take place until the treaty of Sèvres had come into force, an unlikely event. They warned of serious difficulties in trying those accused of massacring Armenians. The case had fatal flaws, they said, because "it seems more than probable that the great majority of those who could appear as witnesses against the accused are dead or have been irretrievably dispersed."[87] After discovering that the Foreign Office possessed "practically no *legal* evidence" and that the American State Department would not cooperate in supplying the scanty information it had regarding the massacre of Armenians,[88] several officials in the Foreign Office concluded on August 3 that "the chances of obtaining convictions are almost nil." There was also "the extreme unlikelihood that the French & Italians would agree to participate in constituting the court provided for in art. 230 of the treaty." Rumbold's staff generally concurred. Rumbold strongly urged the prosecution of the eight men charged with ill-treating British prisoners of war and mildly recommended trying four individuals "gravely implicated" in massacres.[89] On September 6, however, three of the four escaped from Malta, along with thirteen other Turks who broke parole by merely stepping aboard a boat and sailing for Italy.[90] With them went all reason for detaining the Turks believed responsible for the Armenian massacres.

The fate of Colonel Rawlinson came to outweigh even the desire to try the eight accused of mistreating British prisoners of war. The Army Council informed the Foreign Office on September 16 that the release of all hostages held by Angora was "a matter of urgent necessity," because another harsh winter in captivity might result in their deaths. It was "vastly more important to save the lives of these British subjects than to bind ourselves by the strict letter of the law as regards the Turkish prisoners in Malta." Accordingly, the Army Council urged freeing all internees at Malta in exchange for all British prisoners in Anatolia.[91] Rumbold and Admiral John de Robeck, commander of the Mediterranean fleet, opposed freeing the eight accused of cruelty to British prisoners,[92] but Curzon reluctantly authorized an "all for all" exchange since the Nationalists would settle for nothing less. Rawlinson and his compatriots were exchanged for the remaining Turks on Malta on November 1.[93]

After the Nationalists triumphed over the Greeks and British on the battlefield a year later, they achieved what no other previously vanquished nation of the First World War had managed—the complete renunciation of war crimes trials by the Allies. Ending the conflict, the treaty of Lausanne, which replaced the treaty of Sèvres, omitted all mention of war crimes. It also resulted in the release of the last alleged war criminal, Lieutenant Mohammed Rafki, who was sent home from an Indian prison in November 1923.[94]

This capitulation was a bitter disappointment to some people in Britain. Several members of Parliament asked a question for which there was no satisfactory answer: why had the British government failed to try Turkish prisoners whom it had actually held for more than two years?[95] The *Times* denounced the "extraordinary negligence" of the government whose "dawdling, hesitating, ambiguous Near Eastern policy had involved us in no greater humiliation than this."[96] Later, Curzon had regrets and wrote: "I think we made a great mistake in ever letting these people out. I had to yield at the time to a pressure which I always felt to be mistaken."[97]

Private vengeance now took over. Several young Armenian fanatics decided to inflict the retribution that the Allies had not exacted. They assassinated former Turkish leaders one after another in 1921-1922: Talaat Pasha in Berlin, March 15, 1921; Prince Said Halim Pasha in Rome, December 6, 1921; Dr. Behaeddin Shakir and Djemal Azmi in Berlin, April 17, 1922; and Djemal Pasha in Tiflis, July 25, 1922. Enver Pasha died in battle in Central Asia on August 4, 1922, killed, many have suspected or hoped, by an Armenian.[98] Such action was, of course, no proper substitute for impartial judgment, but the Armenians had no other recourse. The Allies had abandoned war crimes trials, and they merely looked on as the Turkish Nationalists and the Russian Bolsheviks destroyed the newly founded Armenian Republic.

This first tentative step toward defining and punishing genocide failed because of Turkish nationalism and Allied indifference. The Armenians, victims and survivors, had been virtually unrepresented in Allied councils. They were too easily ignored and forgotten. The League of Nations might have established an international tribunal to bring to justice men whose policies and actions had led to the deaths of hundreds of thousands of Armenians, an act of genocidal magnitude. But the League ignored this effort, and the British mishandled and then abandoned it. Of all failures to punish the war criminals of the First World War, this one was, perhaps, most regrettable, and it would have terrible consequences.

10

TO NUREMBERG

Subsequent developments in international law and the punishment of war criminals, particularly those associated with the establishment of the International Military Tribunal at Nuremberg at the end of the Second World War, are far too large and complex to treat in detail here; yet a study of the punishment of war criminals of the First World War would not be complete without noting the connections between that episode and those later developments. The first major international effort to bring war criminals to justice failed. But the idea of an international criminal court and code, which Baron d'Estournelles, Hugh H. Bellot, and its other supporters had unsuccessfully urged upon the Allies, continued to exercise an influence in the quest for means to curb international violence.

1

President Wilson and other statesmen believed that their work at the Paris Peace Conference marked the beginning of a new world order. They expected that the League of Nations would eventually bring an end to the anarchy of international politics, substituting cooperation and law in place of competition and war. They recognized, however, that new methods of limiting and controlling violence in international relations were likely to evolve slowly through gradual accommodation with the nationalistic fears and ambitions of leaders and peoples concerned primarily with the interests of their own countries. Consequently, they either ignored or left to later resolution many potentially divisive questions and propositions relating to the League and other possible international reforms.

One such measure was the development of institutions to deal with future war crimes. In the discussions at the peace conference regarding the prosecution of the war criminals of the First World War, some delegates revealed a readiness to consider new solutions. Members of the Commission on Responsibility not only proposed setting up an international tribunal and numerous other innovations to punish their enemies but also recommended future efforts to provide individual penal responsibility for the crime of aggression. Several members of the commission and other individuals involved in Allied planning for war crimes trials envisioned creation of a permanent international criminal court and code with jurisdiction over all war crimes. Wilson, Lloyd George, and other leaders clearly believed that the principles of the new international order must include the obligation of individuals as well as states to observe international law when waging war. Although they held differing views about other aspects of the effort, they did agree that the precedent of trying the war criminals of the First World War could help establish that principle. They did not, however, discuss other means of implementing it. If they had considered the French proposal to set up an international criminal court associated with the League, they would have had to confront vexing questions that undoubtedly would have provoked disagreeable disputes. It was troublesome enough for negotiators at Paris to arrive at a compromise regarding trials of their enemies; it would have been far more difficult, if not impossible, to reach agreement regarding a tribunal of the League before which they themselves or their fellow citizens might be arraigned on some future occasion. It is clear that throughout the effort to punish enemy war criminals political and diplomatic pressures of the moment influenced Allied leaders and other officials much more than thoughts of creating a permanent international criminal jurisdiction. Most of them understood the need to relate their plans for retribution to such a larger purpose in order fully to justify them, but they were not prepared to act immediately on that perception.

As people forgot the shock and horror of the war crimes of the First World War in the years following the return to peace, new leaders proved even less willing than those at Paris to consider such a reform. Many international conferences did attempt to revise and strengthen the laws of war and to adopt new prohibitions of weapons that had so outraged people during the war. Numerous agreements were drafted to forbid unrestricted use of submarines, poisonous gases and bacteriological warfare, and aerial bombardment of civilian populations. The Geneva conventions were thoroughly revised and updated.[1] Yet several of the treaties to bring the conduct of war under the rule of law went unratified when their humanitarian concerns appeared likely to interfere with possible military advantage. Moreover, agreements that were adopted did not go beyond the system of enforcement of the Hague conventions and declarations of 1899 and 1907, which events of the First World War and the peace settlement had proved so unsatisfactory.

When a new solution to the problem of enforcement was included in a treaty of the Washington Naval Conference of 1921-1922, it led to rejection of the agreement. At that conference, the elder American statesman Elihu Root, a strong believer in the development of international law who thought the peace conference had "missed a great opportunity" to initiate an international criminal code, suggested an innovative approach to repress unrestricted submarine warfare. Some acts, such as piracy, he argued had long been treated as international crimes, subject to universal jurisdiction of the criminal courts of all nations, regardless of the nationality of the victim or the location of the crime. Unrestricted submarine warfare could be dealt with in a similar manner, he declared. He proposed that any individual who participated in sinking merchant vessels without warning or provision for safety of crew and passengers, even upon orders of governmental superiors, should be subject to trial and punishment by the courts of any nation into whose hands he fell "as if for an act of piracy."[2]

Other delegates to the conference, particularly military representatives, strongly objected. They warned that such an undertaking might undermine national loyalties and military discipline and, thus, threaten the ability of a government to devise defense policies appropriate to its needs. Ironically, in view of the Admiralty's attitude toward U-boat crews during the war, one British naval expert complained that a submarine commander might "have to decide between being shot by his own country for disobedience or shot by another for breaking international law. It was rather the heads of States," he declared, "than their tools who should be tried and punished."[3] Such reasoning, of course, was really an argument against restraints in war, except for limitations individual governments chose to accept in particular strategic or tactical situations. By sheer force of prestige and personality, Root overcame resistance, and the conference included his proposal as article three of a treaty banning unrestricted submarine warfare. But small naval powers, seeking means to offset surface superiority of British and American fleets, determined to give the submarine a prominent role in their naval defenses and remained wary of weakening the potential of that weapon. Consequently, the French declined to ratify the treaty largely because of article three, and the agreement became a nullity.[4]

Proposals to establish an international criminal court and code also met opposition. The Advisory Committee of Jurists, meeting at The Hague in 1920 to draft a statute for the Permanent Court of International Justice, discussed a resolution to recommend that the League sponsor creation of an international criminal court. Several jurists had participated in Allied plans for war crimes trials, and they pointed out that only an international tribunal could avoid the kinds of difficulties that had stymied the Allied undertaking. There was, moreover, said Albert de Lapradelle, the need to provide for an institution that could impartially "take action against those guilty of crimes against international justice, no matter what nation they belonged to." Lord Phillimore, who had prepared the first official British plan for a League of Nations, favored such a court, believing it would contribute to the League's ability to repress international violence. Raoul Fernandes of Brazil, pointing out "serious technical and political difficulties," declared that such a tribunal, unless properly limited, might actually be "a menace to peace." He no doubt envisioned a possible confrontation if a large and powerful nation refused to surrender citizens to judgment. Elihu Root opposed giving the League or its judicial institutions the attributes of a "super-State," but he suggested that an approach that did not at first require governments to surrender too much sovereignty might prove feasible. He thought the gradual suppression of the slave trade provided an example of how concerted action against outlawed activities might evolve. Governments could reach agreement to disown and to extradite for international trial individuals charged with certain especially reprehensible crimes. As confidence grew in the new system, the jurisdiction of this tribunal and a code of offenses could be progressively expanded. Jurists from nations that had remained neutral during the war generally opposed even the discussion of an international court, for they feared it was intended to support Allied efforts to punish former enemies. Despite this concern and a recognition of the many barriers facing creation of such an institution, the Advisory Committee concluded that the idea should be pursued, and they recommended to the League the establishment of a High Court of International Justice to try crimes against international law.[5]

The Assembly of the League paid little attention. Delegates to the Assembly accepted without debate a report of a committee that rejected the idea as "premature." Representatives of some governments no doubt feared that such a project might embroil the League and them in the conflicts, still occurring, over Allied efforts to prosecute war criminals. Moreover, the Assembly considered this recommendation at its first meeting, and it is not surprising that it did not want to deal with a measure having such far-reaching implications before the League itself had barely begun to function.[6]

Subsequently, during the 1920s, discussion of an international criminal jurisdiction occurred not in League debates or governmental negotiations but in meetings of private organizations devoted to the study of international law. A small group of international lawyers, including Hugh H. Bellot, Vespasien V. Pella, Nicolas Politis, Henri Donnedieu de Vabres, Megalos Caloyanni, and Quintiliano Saldaña, drafted statutes for an international criminal court and code, wrote articles and books analyzing the subject, and urged adoption of such measures. The Interparliamentary Union approved one of Pella's early proposals in 1925, and the International Law Association expressed support of Bellot's draft statute in 1926. That same year, several of these scholars helped to found the Association internationale de droit pénale, which became one of the principal forums to advance study of the question.[7]

These scholars were generally men of wide experience in government, diplomacy, and law, and they fully recognized the legal and political constraints to realization of their ideas. The most prominent governmental figure in their ranks, Politis, who had become Greece's ambassador to France as well as his country's representative at meetings of the League, told an audience at Columbia University in 1926 that "there was no use blinking the fact that any innovation in this direction tends to upset the ingrained habit of centuries." One major obstacle standing in their way resulted from the tendency of these scholars to focus their attention upon the most vexing of all problems—aggression—rather than pursue the piecemeal approach suggested by Elihu Root.

But for Politis and other advocates of this reform, aggression was the greatest evil, from which other war crimes were likely to flow. It was, declared Politis, "the real domain of international criminality." The idea that leaders might escape legal responsibility for decisions resulting in this most terrible of crimes, said Politis, was the "greatest spectacle of immorality offered by the international community."[8] Supporters of an international criminal jurisdiction knew that if resistance to providing for the judicial repression of aggression could be overcome, then dealing with other war crimes would be easy. Politis viewed efforts of the League to devise a definition of aggression as a promising step forward, and he made significant contributions to that work.

The purpose of these endeavors to define aggression was not intended, at least not directly, to establish an international criminal code but to strengthen collective security by filling so-called gaps in the Covenant of the League. At the heart of collective security was article ten of the Covenant, which required member states of the League "to respect and preserve as against external aggression the territorial integrity and existing political independence of all Members of the League." Wilson and other founders of the League hoped that collective security, an international method of preserving peace and protecting nations from aggression, would replace traditional means by which states sought safety, such as contraction of military alliances and pursuit of a balance of power. But in drawing up the Covenant, they had not resolved many questions regarding the actual functioning of collective security. They had not, for example, attempted to define aggression. It seemed to delegates of the Assembly during the 1920s that a definition was necessary to reduce the possibility of disagreements among League members in determining who was at fault in any particular conflict and in taking joint action against the guilty party. It became clear that devising a definition of aggression acceptable to governments and peoples of widely varying character and needs was a complex undertaking and that a definition could not be developed in isolation from other matters such as arbitration and disarmament. Simply defining aggression as the first military attack across an international boundary, although valuable, might not cover all possible means by which the territorial integrity and political independence of a nation could be threatened. Quite apart from questions regarding an aggressive use of subversion or economic domination, a mere imbalance in possession of armaments might allow the government of one country to engage in military coercion of another without ever actually launching an attack. Finally, any ban on resort to force in international relations might be used to prevent changes in the status quo, even to perpetuate unjust conditions, unless there was also a positive and compulsory obligation to use peaceful methods to redress grievances, inequities, and injuries.

The most comprehensive effort of the League to resolve such interrelated issues was the Protocol for the Peaceful Settlement of International Disputes, in whose drafting Politis had an important role. This agreement, whose preamble condemned a war of aggression as an international crime, advanced a relatively simple formula: any state that went to war rather than accept compulsory arbitration of a dispute would be considered an aggressor against whom members of the League would be required to impose sanctions, unless the Council of the League unanimously decided otherwise. Linked to disarmament efforts, this treaty was scheduled to take effect once the Council determined that reduction in armaments provided a margin of security safe enough for nations to assume these obligations. The Assembly of the League unanimously approved this protocol in 1924. But, shortly afterwards, the new Conservative government in Britain, doubting the scheme's practicability and disliking its obligations, rejected the plan, effectively killing any chance of its adoption.[9] Other efforts to define aggression at League-sponsored negotiations, including a detailed listing of aggressive acts that a committee headed by Politis urged upon the World Disarmament Conference, also failed to win acceptance. Several Conventions for the Definition of Aggression were signed by the Soviet Union and East European and Near Eastern governments in 1933, but these regional pacts remained anomalies, not least because subsequently some signatories, particularly the Soviet Union, blatantly violated them.[10]

Rather than persist in trying to devise a definition, the Assembly of the

League contented itself with the adoption of resolutions in 1925 and 1927 denouncing aggression as an international crime. Other governmental, as well as private, organizations during this era took similar action. The Pan American Conference, meeting at Havana in 1928, for example, affirmed that a "war of aggression constitutes an international crime against the human species." Although indicative of a moral aversion to war, one of the positive results of the First World War, these rhetorical resolutions had no immediate political or legal effect upon the concepts of collective security or international criminality.[11]

The most notable of such condemnations of war occurred in the Treaty for the Renunciation of War of 1928, an agreement for the "outlawry" of war, originally linked to the idea of individual criminality. Samuel O. Levinson, a Chicago lawyer, sparked an informal movement for the outlawry of war that gained considerable political strength in the United States. The most powerful supporter of the idea was Senator Borah, an isolationist who wanted a substitute for American participation in the League. Levinson included in several of his early plans a provision for international sanctions against aggressor states and criminal penalties against their leaders, but in deference to Borah's anxiety about preserving American sovereignty Levinson eventually decided that each nation should be obliged to impose individual penalties upon its own culprits. Borah sponsored Levinson's proposal in a Senate resolution in 1923. The resolution declared that war should be "outlawed" as a means of settling disputes "by making it a public crime under the law of nations and that every nation should by solemn agreement . . . bind itself to indict and punish its own international war breeders or instigators and war profiteers. . . ."[12] When official circles took up the idea to outlaw war some years later, provisions for penalties against individuals and other inconvenient ideas were dropped. Seeking a means of avoiding conflict between the United States and France, Premier Briand proposed that the two nations agree to outlaw resort to war in their disputes. Under strong pressure from an enthusiastic American press and public, Secretary of State Frank B. Kellogg reluctantly decided, instead, to sponsor a multilateral agreement.

In the end, signatories of the Peace Pact of Paris or the Kellogg-Briand treaty, which included most governments in the world, simply pledged to "renounce war as an instrument of national policy." Because the treaty made no provision for any kind of sanction or enforcement and because all signatories explicitly reserved the right of self-defense, which remained undefined, it was not clear what this renunciation meant.[13] Some participants at a meeting of the International Law Association in 1934 argued that the pact had created a "norm of international penal law" whose violation must be "considered as an international crime."[14] But most scholars did not think so, for the statesmen who signed the document had not indicated any such intention.

Ignoring the elaborate draft statutes and codes of scholars, few officials paid serious attention to proposals for an international criminal law and court until the mid-1930s. The difficulties and dangers of such a scheme seemed all too obvious and too large to overcome. The immediate advantages appeared too small to matter. Then as a result of the assassination by Croatian nationalists of King Alexander I of Yugoslavia and the French foreign minister at Marseilles in 1934, revulsion against terrorism and fears of a repetition of Sarajevo prompted new consideration of the value of an international criminal jurisdiction. To help resolve a diplomatic crisis arising from the incident, the Council of the League, at the request of the French government, initiated study of this means of dealing with international terrorism. Of the members of the committee that carried out this task, the most important contributor was Vespasien V. Pella, Rumania's representative to the League, who was one of the most prolific writers on the subject of an international criminal court and code. He had been advocating this reform since 1919 when the controversies surrounding the work of the Commission on Responsibility had inspired him to prepare a paper on the subject during his legal studies at the University of Paris. Pella was primarily responsible for drafting a Convention for the Prevention and Punishment of Terrorism and a Convention for the Creation of an International Criminal Court, both of which the League Council submitted to an international conference in 1937. Pella and other supporters of an international criminal jurisdiction had long since recognized that a full-fledged judicial system to deal with all forms of international violence, including aggression, was not yet feasible. But they now hoped that this minimal design for repressing terrorism represented a first step toward achievement of the larger reform.

Representatives from thirty-six nations gave their approval to these two conventions at a Special Conference on the Repression of Terrorism, but there was much opposition to the agreements. The conventions made attacks against governmental officials and other forms of political terrorism international crimes and bound all signatories to prosecute individuals accused of such acts or to extradite them for trial elsewhere. An international criminal court was also to be established to assume jurisdiction in instances in which governments felt a need for an alternative method of handling controversial cases. Critics feared that this scheme might be used to suppress revolutions against tyrannies or to interfere with asylum for political dissidents and refugees. In the end, few governments ratified the conventions, and the proposed international criminal court was never set up.[15] Had such a court existed in 1914, of course, it would have provided one means of punishing the assassin of Franz Ferdinand and might have averted the First World War. An international tribunal to deal with terrorists would not, of course, have stopped the outbreak of the Second World War.

The international order established after the First World War came under increasing challenge during the 1930s. Ideologically hostile to the democratic states and liberal values that underpinned that order, the governments of Japan, Italy, Germany, and the Soviet Union resorted to threats and the use of force to attain national objectives in ways that defied the League of Nations and violated international law. Support of collective security in defense of that order was tested and found wanting. The cost of maintaining peace through collective political, economic, and military sanctions against aggressors was more than most nations were prepared to pay. People in the interwar years, as in other eras, longed for peace without sacrifice, and many leaders, when faced with the choice, placed avoidance of the risk of war in situations where national interests were not immediately imperiled ahead of any obligation to oppose aggression wherever and whenever it occurred. This reaction was particularly true of the major powers of the League—Britain and France—and of the United States, standing outside the League, without whose military strength and commitment action against aggression was impossible. During the Manchurian Crisis in 1931 and the Italian-Ethiopian War in 1935, these great powers refused to adopt strong and effective sanctions against the aggressors. In the midst of the worldwide depression and the nationalistic, inward-looking political climate it engendered within these nations, this weak response was understandable. Perhaps, it would have occurred regardless of other events and influences. It was clearly fatal to the future of world peace, for it helped convince Adolf Hitler that he could repudiate the Versailles peace settlement, embark upon a program of expansionism, and ultimately launch a war of conquest and annihilation.[16]

Hitler might have pursued exactly the same course he in fact followed in beginning the Second World War and in then exterminating millions of people, particularly the European Jews, regardless of international law and its judicial institutions. Since the Kellogg-Briand Peace Pact and the League of Nations did not daunt Hitler, the mere existence of an international criminal court and code almost certainly would have had no effect on him. Even if the war criminals of the First World War, particularly those responsible for the Armenian massacres, had been brought to judgment, the mass murderers of Auschwitz and the other death camps might have remained undeterred. But surely Hitler, then, would not have been able to infer the negative lesson that he did in fact draw from the tragic fate of the Armenians. Shortly before Hitler sent his armies to crush Poland in 1939, he told a group of German officers and Nazi officials:

Our strength lies in our quickness and in our brutality; Genghis Khan has sent millions of women and children into death knowingly and with a light heart. History sees in him only the great founder of States. . . . And so for the present only in the East I have put my death-head formations in place with the command relentlessly and without compassion to send into death many women and children of Polish origin and language. Only thus we can gain the living space that we need. Who after all is today speaking about the destruction of the Armenians?[17]

At the end of the Second World War one of Hitler's ministers, Albert Speer, following conviction of war crimes for his role in the Nazi slave-labor program, an operation far more brutal but similar to the deportation of Belgians to work in German factories in 1916, expressed regret that Allied efforts to punish war criminals of the First World War had not succeeded. He thought such prosecutions might have made some difference. He declared that "it would have encouraged a sense of responsibility on the part of leading political figures if after the First World War the Allies had actually held the trials they had threatened for the Germans involved in the forced-labor program of that era."[18] It is, of course, impossible to know to what extent such trials would have influenced subsequent events. But one cannot help wondering whether their failure and the failure of later efforts to create some sort of international criminal jurisdiction did not contribute in some measure to the barbarous character of the Second World War, a conflict in which almost every belligerent government adopted military strategies that violated international law to one degree or another.

2

Many complex factors affected decisions of the victorious governments of the United States, Britain, the Soviet Union, France, and their smaller allies to bring defeated German and Japanese leaders and other enemy individuals before war crimes tribunals at the end of the Second World War; this book must limit itself to noting the influences that efforts to provide for punishment of war criminals after the First World War had on those decisions.[19]

Individuals concerned with punishing the war criminals of the Second World War looked to that earlier experience for legal precedents and historical lessons. Scholars and journalists closely studied that first episode of war crimes punishment and wrote numerous articles suggesting what should be learned from it.[20] The international lawyers and governmental representatives who sat on the United Nations War Crimes Commission, which gathered evidence of atrocities and discussed means of punishing the guilty, drew heavily on the work of the Commission on Responsibility in their deliberations. The United Nations War Crimes Commission was set up in 1943 especially to avoid the lack of previous agreement and preparation that was thought to have been a fundamental mistake of the Allies during the First World War.

Everyone concerned, as the chairman of that organization said, was determined not to repeat the "fiasco of the Leipzig Trials."[21] British leaders, particularly Prime Minister Winston Churchill, who was, of course, personally familiar with events after the First World War, believed the best way to avoid those difficulties again would be to forgo efforts to hold international war crimes trials. Citing the "experience of that ill-starred enterprise at the end of the last War," British Foreign Minister Anthony Eden told the War Cabinet: "I am convinced that we should avoid commitments to 'try the war criminals' and to 'hang the Kaiser (alias Hitler)'."[22] The British, instead, argued in favor of summary executions of captured enemy leaders and speedy court-martial by national tribunals of ordinary offenders immediately upon the conclusion of the war.[23]

President Franklin D. Roosevelt and other American leaders disagreed with the British. Strongly supported by representatives of countries that had suffered conquest and occupation, they decided near the end of the war on the necessity of international trials. The Americans believed their country's refusal to join the League and later to take vigorous measures against aggression had contributed to the catastrophe of the Second World War. They now determined to abandon isolationism in favor of a strongly internationalist foreign policy and led the way in establishing a new international organization, the United Nations, to preserve world peace against future aggressors. American officials, particularly Secretary of War Henry L. Stimson, a former protégé of Elihu Root, believed that the earlier failure to make much advance in international criminal law had also been a mistake and that the United States should now assume leadership of international war crimes trials, especially to establish as a deterrent to future rulers the principle that aggression was an international crime.[24]

The strong American commitment to this policy prevailed in plans to punish the war criminals of the Second World War. During negotiations regarding the establishment of an International Military Tribunal to try German leaders at Nuremberg, the American representative, Supreme Court Justice Robert H. Jackson, argued for provisions to charge those men with aggression and explained that "sentiment in the United States and the better world opinion have greatly changed since Mr. James Brown Scott and Secretary Lansing announced their views on matters of war and peace."[25] The new American position, which prevailed in the negotiations, was that aggression had become a customary, uncodified war crime by virtue of a progressive chain of events stretching from the proposed trial of the kaiser, through the approval of resolutions by the League and other organizations denouncing aggression as an international crime, to the adoption of the Kellogg-Briand treaty outlawing war.

The trial of the major German war criminals at Nuremberg, the Japanese leaders at Tokyo, and the other prosecutions of lesser figures after the Second World War revived and brought to fruition many ideas that had initially appeared during the First World War. Those proceedings in fact produced few fundamentally new concepts or methods of war crimes punishment that had not been the subject of deliberations by either the British Committee of Enquiry Into Breaches of the Laws of War or the Commission on Responsibility. Because the Second World War was waged to a total victory, the victors were, however, able to carry out their plans virtually unopposed, achieving results that the earlier effort did not. Consequently, to a far greater degree than the decisions and actions after the First World War, the decisions of the war crimes tribunals at the end of the Second World War established firm legal precedents in international law.

The judgment at Nuremberg—the first and most important of these decisions—made clear that international law applied to all individuals waging war, even to the highest governmental leaders. It placed strict limits on the scope of many defenses against war crimes punishment, including superior orders, act of state, and military necessity. It affirmed the existence of a new category of offenses—crimes against humanity— to condemn individuals responsible for carrying out Hitler's inhuman policy of exterminating six million Jews and other people deemed racially unfit. Most importantly, it declared that aggression (now termed "crimes against peace") was indeed a violation of international law for which guilty individual leaders must bear legal responsibility. These judicial decisions laid the foundation for a new legal order in international relations. They repudiated decisively the international anarchy of absolute sovereign states in which leaders and their followers could use force according to the "law of the jungle." Henceforth, all men were to be legally obliged not to use force in the service of their nation in war except in compliance with the requirements of international law.[26]

Although the judgment at Nuremberg had moral and legal flaws, which critics have examined at length,[27] it also appeared at the time as a large step toward the new international order initially envisioned during the First World War. Most contemporaries hailed it as a turning point in world history. Walter Lippmann, the famous American intellectual and journalist, declared that the judgment at Nuremberg ultimately would find a place alongside epochal documents such as the Magna Charta, the habeas corpus, and the Bill of Rights.[28]

Supporters of an international criminal court and code expected that adoption of these institutions would soon follow. In the immediate postwar era, the General Assembly of the United Nations expressed approval of the legal principles announced at the Nuremberg trials and sponsored a Convention on the Prevention and Punishment of the Crime of Genocide.[29] The Geneva conventions were revised in 1949, and subsequently other international conferences made additional changes in the laws of the war. The United Nations devoted considerable attention to a Draft Code of Offenses Against the Peace and Security of Mankind and a Draft Statute for an International Criminal Court. After an initial failure that caused these projects to be set aside for several years, the General Assembly took them up once more, approving a Consensus Definition of Aggression in 1974 and subsequently renewing consideration of a permanent international criminal jurisdiction.[30]

The possibility of adopting and implementing such reforms, however, still seems remote. Such measures face not only many of the same kinds of difficulties that blocked acceptance of similar plans after the First World War; they also confront new scientific and political developments— particularly the proliferation of nuclear weapons with their capacity to kill hundreds of millions of innocent people and the spread of nationalist and ideological movements further dividing mankind—that have substantially altered for the worst the prospect of devising international solutions to the problems of war and war crimes.[31]

Consequently, whatever lasting significance the effort to punish the war criminals of the First World War may have remains uncertain. That endeavor did mark the appearance of a new design for a world order. It was the prologue of a revolutionary development in international law, and like other revolutions it emerged from varied influences and motives, some noble, others base. During violent upheavals, such is often the character of change that challenges an established order. Imperfectly conceived and implemented, marred by vengeful politics and expedient diplomacy, it represented nonetheless in its ideals a desire to establish a world community. If the failure of the effort illustrates in certain respects the magnitude of the obstacles to creation of a new world order, the sad history of the wars and war crimes of the twentieth century attests to the necessity of its realization.

APPENDIX

WAR CRIMES CLAUSES OF PEACE TREATIES OF THE FIRST WORLD WAR

TREATY OF VERSAILLES, JUNE 28, 1919

Article 227

The Allied and Associated Powers publicly arraign William II of Hohenzollern, formerly German Emperor, for a supreme offence against international morality and the sanctity of treaties.

A special tribunal will be constituted to try the accused, thereby assuring him the guarantees essential to the right of defence. It will be composed of five judges, one appointed by each of the following Powers: namely, the United States of America, Great Britain, France, Italy and Japan.

In its decision the tribunal will be guided by the highest motives of international policy, with a view to vindicating the solemn obligations of international under-takings and the validity of international morality. It will be its duty to fix the punishment which it considers should be imposed.

The Allied and Associated Powers will address a request to the Government of the Netherlands for the surrender to them of the ex-Emperor in order that he may be put on trial.

Article 228

The German Government recognises the right of the Allied and Associated Powers to bring before military tribunals persons accused of having committed acts in violation of the laws and customs of war. Such persons shall, if found guilty, be sentenced to punishments laid down by law. This provision will apply notwith-standing any proceedings or prosecution before a tribunal in Germany or in the territory of her allies.

The German Government shall hand over to the Allied and Associated Powers, or to such one of them as shall so request, all persons accused of having committed

SOURCE: Carnegie Endowment for International Peace, *The Treaties of Peace, 1919-1923*, 2 vols. (New York: Carnegie Endowment for International Peace, 1924). Used with the permission of the Carnegie Endowment for International Peace.

an act in violation of the laws and customs of war, who are specified either by name or by the rank, office or employment which they held under the German authorities.

Article 229

Persons guilty of criminal acts against the nationals of one of the Allied and Associated Powers will be brought before the military tribunals of that Power.

Persons guilty of criminal acts against the nationals of more than one of the Allied and Associated Powers will be brought before military tribunals composed of members of the military tribunals of the Powers concerned.

In every case the accused will be entitled to name his own counsel.

Article 230

The German Government undertakes to furnish all documents and information of every kind, the production of which may be considered necessary to ensure the full knowledge of the incriminating acts, the discovery of offenders and the just appreciation of responsibility.

TREATY OF SAINT-GERMAIN-EN-LAYE, SEPTEMBER 10, 1919

Article 173

The Austrian Government recognises the right of the Allied and Associated Powers to bring before military tribunals persons accused of having committed acts in violation of the laws and customs of war. Such persons shall, if found guilty, be sentenced to punishments laid down by law. This provision will apply notwithstanding any proceedings or prosecutions before a tribunal in Austria or in the territory of her allies.

The Austrian Government shall hand over to the Allied and Associated Powers, or to such one of them as shall so request, all persons accused of having committed an act in violation of the laws and customs of war, who are specified either by name or by the rank, office or employment which they held under the Austrian authorities.

Article 174

Persons guilty of criminal acts against the nationals of one of the Allied and Associated Powers will be brought before the military tribunals of that Power.

Persons guilty of criminal acts against the nationals of more than one of the Allied and Associated Powers will be brought before military tribunals composed of members of the military tribunals of the Powers concerned.

In every case the accused will be entitled to name his own counsel.

Article 175

The Austrian Government undertakes to furnish all documents and information of every kind, the production of which may be considered necessary to ensure the full knowledge of the incriminating acts, the discovery of offenders and the just appreciation of responsibility.

Article 176

The provisions of Articles 173 to 175 apply similarly to the Governments of the States to which territory belonging to the former Austro-Hungarian Monarchy has been assigned, in so far as concerns persons accused of having committed acts contrary to the laws and customs of war who are in the territory or at the disposal of the said States.

If the persons in question have acquired the nationality of one of the said States, the Government of such State undertakes to take, at the request of the Power concerned and in agreement with it, all the measures necessary to ensure the prosecution and punishment of such persons.

TREATY OF NEUILLY-SUR-SEINE, NOVEMBER 27, 1919

Article 118

The Bulgarian Government recognises the right of the Allied and Associated Powers to bring before military tribunals persons accused of having committed acts in violation of the laws and customs of war. Such persons shall, if found guilty, be sentenced to punishments laid down by law. This provision will apply notwithstanding any proceedings or prosecution before a tribunal in Bulgaria or in the territory of her allies.

The Bulgarian Government shall hand over to the Allied and Associated Powers or to such one of them as shall so request, all persons accused of having committed an act in violation of the laws and customs of war, who are specified either by name or by the rank, office or employment which they held under the Bulgarian authorities.

Article 119

Persons guilty of criminal acts against the nationals of one of the Allied and Associated Powers will be brought before the military tribunals of that Power.

Persons guilty of criminal acts against the nationals of more than one of the Allied and Associated Powers will be brought before military tribunals composed of members of the military tribunals of the Powers concerned.

In every case the accused will be entitled to name his own counsel.

Article 120

The Bulgarian Government undertakes to furnish all documents and information of every kind, the production of which may be considered necessary to ensure the full knowledge of the incriminating acts, the discovery of offenders and the just appreciation of responsibility.

TREATY OF TRIANON, JUNE 4, 1920

Article 157

The Hungarian Government recognises the right of the Allied and Associated Powers to bring before military tribunals persons accused of having committed acts in violation of the laws and customs of war. Such persons shall, if found guilty, be sentenced to punishments laid down by law. This provision will apply notwithstanding any proceedings or prosecutions before a tribunal in Hungary or in the territory of her allies.

The Hungarian Government shall hand over to the Allied and Associated Powers, or to such one of them as shall so request, all persons accused of having committed an act in violation of the laws and customs of war, who are specified either by name or by the rank, office or employment which they held under the Hungarian authorities.

Article 158

Persons guilty of criminal acts against the nationals of one of the Allied and Associated Powers will be brought before the military tribunals of that Power.

Persons guilty of criminal acts against the nationals of more than one of the Allied and Associated Powers will be brought before military tribunals composed of members of the military tribunals of the Powers concerned.

In every case the accused will be entitled to name his own counsel.

Article 159

The Hungarian Government undertakes to furnish all documents and information of every kind, the production of which may be considered necessary to ensure the full knowledge of the incriminating acts, the discovery of offenders and the just appreciation of responsibility.

Article 160

The provisions of Articles 157 to 159 apply similarly to the Governments of the States to which territory belonging to the former Austro-Hungarian Monarchy has been assigned, in so far as concerns persons accused of having committed acts contrary to the laws and customs of war who are in the territory or at the disposal of the said States.

If the persons in question have acquired the nationality of one of the said States, the Government of such State undertakes to take, at the request of the Power concerned and in agreement with it, all the measures necessary to ensure the prosecution and punishment of such persons.

TREATY OF SÈVRES, AUGUST 10, 1920

Article 226

The Turkish Government recognises the right of the Allied Powers to bring before military tribunals persons accused of having committed acts in violation of the laws and customs of war. Such persons shall, if found guilty, be sentenced to punishments laid down by law. This provision will apply notwithstanding any proceedings or prosecution before a tribunal in Turkey or in the territory of her allies.

The Turkish Government shall hand over to the Allied Powers or to such one of them as shall so request all persons accused of having committed an act in violation of the laws and customs of war, who are specified either by name or by the rank, office or employment which they held under the Turkish authorities.

Article 227

Persons guilty of criminal acts against the nationals of one of the Allied Powers shall be brought before the military tribunals of that Power.

Persons guilty of criminal acts against the nationals of more than one of the Allied Powers shall be brought before military tribunals composed of members of the military tribunals of the Powers concerned.

In every case the accused shall be entitled to name his own counsel.

Article 228

The Turkish Government undertakes to furnish all documents and information of every kind, the production of which may be considered necessary to ensure the full knowledge of the incriminating acts, the prosecution of offenders and the just appreciation of responsibility.

Article 229

The provisions of Articles 226 to 228 apply similarly to the Governments of the States to which territory belonging to the former Turkish Empire has been or may be assigned, in so far as concerns persons accused of having committed acts contrary to the laws and customs of war who are in the territory or at the disposal of such States.

If the persons in question have acquired the nationality of one of the said States, the Government of such State undertakes to take, at the request of the Power concerned and in agreement with it, or upon the joint request of all the Allied Powers, all the measures necessary to ensure the prosecution and punishment of such persons.

Article 230

The Turkish Government undertakes to hand over to the Allied Powers the persons whose surrender may be required by the latter as being responsible for the massacres committed during the continuance of the state of war on territory which formed part of the Turkish Empire on August 1, 1914.

The Allied Powers reserve to themselves the right to designate the tribunal which shall try the persons so accused, and the Turkish Government undertakes to recognise such tribunal.

In the event of the League of Nations having created in sufficient time a tribunal competent to deal with the said massacres, the Allied Powers reserve to themselves the right to bring the accused persons mentioned above before such tribunal, and the Turkish Government undertakes equally to recognise such tribunal.

The provisions of Article 228 apply to the cases dealt with in this Article.

NOTES

PREFACE

1. Michael Walzer, *Just and Unjust Wars: A Moral Argument With Historical Illustrations* (New York: Basic Books, 1977), pp. 61-63, 113-21.

CHAPTER 1

1. Roger Chickering, *Imperial Germany and a World Without War: The Peace Movement and German Society, 1892-1914* (Princeton, N.J.: Princeton University Press, 1975); David S. Patterson, *Toward a Warless World: The Travail of the American Peace Movement, 1887-1914* (Bloomington, Ind.: Indiana University Press, 1976).

2. For the Hague Conferences, see Calvin D. Davis, *The United States and the First Hague Peace Conference* (Ithaca, N.Y.: Cornell University Press, 1962); idem, *The United States and the Second Hague Peace Conference: American Diplomacy and International Organization, 1899-1914* (Durham N.C.: Duke University Press, 1975). For the historical development of the laws of war, see Coleman Phillipson, *The International Law and Customs of Ancient Greece and Rome*, 2 vols. (London: Macmillan & Co., 1911), 2:166-384; Maurice H. Keen, *The Laws of War in the Late Middle Ages* (London: Routledge & Kegan Paul, 1965); Robert R. Wilson, "Standards of Humanitarianism in War," *American Journal of International Law* 34 (April 1940):320-24; Frank Freidel, *Francis Lieber: Nineteenth Century Liberal* (Baton Rouge, La.: Louisiana University Press, 1947), pp. 317-41; Morris Greenspan, *The Modern Law of Land Warfare* (Berkeley and Los Angeles, Calif.: University of California Press, 1959); Geoffrey Best, *Humanity in Warfare* (New York: Columbia University Press, 1980). For the text of the Hague conventions, see Leon Friedman, ed., *The Law of War: A Documentary History*, 2 vols. (New York: Random House, 1972), 1:221-50, 270-369.

3. George W. Egerton, *Great Britain and the Creation of the League of Nations: Strategy, Politics, and International Organization, 1914-1919* (Chapel Hill, N.C.: University of North Carolina Press, 1978); Keith Robbins, *The Abolition of War:*

The "Peace Movement" in Britain, 1914-1919 (Cardiff, Wales: University of Wales, 1976).

4. Michael Howard, War and the Liberal Conscience (New Brunswick, N.J.: Rutgers University Press, 1978), pp. 77-83.

5. Fritz Fischer, War of Illusions: German Policies from 1911 to 1914, trans. Marian Jackson (New York: W. W. Norton & Co., 1975). The debate over German war guilt was rekindled in the 1960s by the work of this German historian and his students. For a discussion of this controversy, see Walter Laqueur and George L. Mosse, eds., 1914: The Coming of the First World War (New York: Harper & Row, Harper Torchbooks, 1966). See also Volker Rolf Berghahn, Germany and the Approach of War in 1914 (London: Macmillan Press, 1973); Imanuel Geiss, German Foreign Policy, 1871-1914 (London and Boston: Routledge & Kegan Paul, 1976); Zara S. Steiner, Britain and the Origins of the First World War (New York: St. Martin's Press, 1977).

6. France, Chambre des Députés, Annales de Chambre des Députés Débats Parlementaires 2 (1 June-23 December 1914):907.

7. For the full text of Bethmann Hollweg's remarks, see Ralph H. Lutz, ed., The Fall of the German Empire, 1914-1918, 2 vols. (Stanford, Calif.: Stanford University Press, 1932), 1:12-13. For the strategy of invading Belgium and the moral dilemma of German leaders, see Konrad H. Jarausch, The Enigmatic Chancellor: Bethmann Hollweg and the Hubris of Imperial Germany (New Haven, Conn., and London: Yale University Press, 1973); Gerhard Ritter, The Schlieffen Plan: Critique of a Myth, trans. Andrew and Eva Wilson (London: Oswald Wolff Publishers, 1958).

8. Fritz Fischer, Germany's Aims in the First World War (New York: W. W. Norton & Co., 1967), pp. 111-17.

9. A fully satisfactory biography of Wilhelm II has yet to be written. Two of the most recent efforts are Alan Palmer, The Kaiser: Warlord of the Second Reich (New York: Charles Scribner's Sons, 1978); and Tyler Whittle, The Last Kaiser: A Biography of Wilhelm II, German Emperor and King of Prussia (New York: New York Times Books, 1977).

10. Fischer, War of Illusions, pp. 161-64.

11. William L. Langer, The Diplomacy of Imperialism, 1890-1902, 2nd ed. (New York: Alfred A. Knopf, 1968), p. 699.

12. Franz Petri and Peter Schöller, "Zur Bereinigung des Franktireurproblems vom August 1914," Vierteljahrshefte für Zeitgeschichte 9 (1961):234-48; Henri Pirenne, La Belgique et la guerre mondiale (Paris: Carnegie pour la Paix Internationale, 1928), pp. 63-64; James M. Read, Atrocity Propaganda: 1914-1919 (New Haven, Conn.: Yale University Press, 1941), pp. 83-84. The most complete analysis of violations of the laws of war during the war is James Garner, International Law and the World War, 2 vols. (London: Longmans, Green & Co., 1920). For German views of reprisal and military necessity, see James Garner, The German War Code (Urbana, Ill.: University of Illinois Press, 1918).

13. Peter Schöller, Le Cas de Louvain et le Livre Blanc allemand: Étude critique de la documentation allemande relative aux événements qui se sont déroulés à Louvain du 25 au 28 août 1914, trans. E. Nieuwborg (Louvain, Belgium: Éditions E. Nauwelaerts, 1958).

14. *Times* (London), 5 September 1914, p. 10.

15. Walter Görlitz, ed., *The Kaiser and His Court: The Diaries, Note Books, and Letters of Admiral Georg Alexander von Müller, Chief of the Naval Cabinet, 1914-1918* (London: Macdonald & Co., 1961), pp. 36, 38.

16. Barbara Tuchman, *The Guns of August* (New York: Dell Publishing Co., 1963), p. 297.

17. *Times*, 31 August 1914, p. 9. For an indication about how widespread was this demand, see "The Kaiser," *The Spectator* 113 (10 October 1914):486-87.

18. Michel Corday, *The Paris Front: An Unpublished Diary 1914-1918* (New York: E. P. Dutton & Co., 1934), pp. 10-11, 19.

19. Hugh H. L. Bellot, "The Detention of Napoleon Buonaparte," *Law Quarterly Review* 39 (April 1923): 170-92.

20. "Germany and the Laws of War," *The Edinburgh Review* 220 (October 1914):278-97.

21. Arthur Nussbaum, *A Concise History of the Law of Nations* (New York: Macmillan Co., 1947), pp. 17, 40, 106. For a recent analysis of this idea, see Frederick H. Russell, *The Just War in the Middle Ages* (London: Cambridge University Press, 1975).

22. *Times*, 16 September 1914, p. 9.

23. Lady Algernon Gordon Lennox, ed., *The Diary of Lord Bertie of Thame: 1914-1918*, 2 vols. (London: George H. Doran Co., 1924), 1:36. For a letter of A. Pearce Higgins, a prominent international lawyer, see *Times*, 14 September 1914, p. 13. See also Read, *Atrocity Propaganda*, p. 241; Irene Cooper Willis, *England's Holy War: A Study of English Liberal Idealism During the Great War* (1928; reprint ed., New York: Garland Publishing, 1972), p. 187; Stephen Koss, *Fleet Street Radical: A. G. Gardiner and the Daily News* (Hamden, Conn.: Archon Books, 1973), pp. 156-57.

24. *Times*, 17 September 1914, p. 9.

25. On Allied war aims, see A. J. P. Taylor, "The War Aims of the Allies in the First World War," in *Politics in Wartime and Other Essays* (London: Hamish Hamilton, 1964), pp. 93-122; Pierre Renouvin, "Les Buts de guerre du gouvernement français, 1914-1918," *Revue Historique* 235 (January-March 1966):1-38; V. H. Rothwell, *British War Aims and Peace Diplomacy, 1914-1918* (Oxford: Oxford University, 1971); Barry Hunt and Adrian Preston, eds., *War Aims and Strategic Policy in the Great War, 1914-1918* (Totawa, N.J.: Rowman & Littlefield, 1977).

26. For military developments, see John Buchan, *A History of the Great War*, 4 vols. (Boston and New York: Houghton Mifflin Co., 1923); Cyril Falls, The *Great War* (New York: Capricorn Books, 1961); Sir Llewellyn Woodward, *Great Britain and the War of 1914-1918* (Boston: Beacon Press, 1970).

27. Among the many works on propaganda, the most authoritative is Read, *Atrocity Propaganda*.

28. Colonel A. S. Rezanoff, *Les Atrocités allemandes du côté russe*, trans. René Marchand (Petrograd: W. Kirschbaum, 1915), p. 3.

29. *Le Matin* (Paris), 21 September 1914, p. 2.

30. Julian Symons, *Horatio Bottomley* (London: Cresset Press, 1955), p. 164.

31. Albert Marrin, *The Last Crusade: The Church of England in the First World War* (Durham, N.C.: Duke University Press, 1974), pp. 125-35, 184-85, 232-34; Arthur Marwick, *The Deluge: British Society and the First World War* (New York: W. W. Norton & Co., 1970), pp. 48-50.

32. Radhabinod Pal, *Crimes in International Relations* (Calcutta, India: Calcutta University Press, 1955), p. 426; H. Lauterpacht, "The Law of Nations and the Punishment of War Crimes," *The British Year Book of International Law* 21 (1944):61-62.

33. German soldiers, for example, did continue to shoot hostages in France. See Patrick Fridenson, *1914-1918: L'Autre front* (Paris: Éditions Ouvrières, 1977), pp. 35-48.

34. Görlitz, *Kaiser and His Court*, pp. 36, 38.

35. *Le Matin*, 3 October 1914, p. 2.

36. Ibid., 6 October 1914, p. 1. See also ibid., 5 November 1914, p. 2; 22 November 1914, p. 2; *L'Echo de Paris*, 29 September 1914, p. 1; 6 October 1914, p. 2; 13 October 1914, p. 4.

37. *Chambre des Députés Débats* 1 (12 January-30 July 1915):6.

38. Ebba Dahlin, *French and German Public Opinion on Declared War Aims, 1914-1918* (Stanford, Calif.: Stanford University Press, 1933), p. 39.

39. See letters of Andre Weiss, a professor of law at the University of Paris, and William Loubat, a legal official in Lyons, in *Le Temps* (Paris), 28 April 1915, p. 1; 2 May 1915, p. 1; 13 May 1915, p. 1.

40. James Garner, "Punishment of Offenders Against the Laws and Customs of War," *American Journal of International Law* 14 (January 1920):71.

41. Herman J. Wittgens, "The German Foreign Office Campaign Against the Versailles Treaty: An Examination of the Activities of the Kriegsschuldreferat in the United States" (Ph. D. diss., University of Washington, 1970), pp. 166-67.

42. Louis Renault, "De l'Application du droit pénal aux faits de guerre," *Journal du Droit International* 40 (1915):313-44.

43. *Le Temps*, 15 May 1915, p. 1.

44. Albrecht von Stosch, *Die Kriegsbeschuldigtenfrage: Ihre Bedeutung für Deutschland und den Feindbund* (Hannover, Ger., and Leipzig, Ger.: Ernst Letsch Verlag, 1924), pp. 244-45.

45. Hans-Heinrich Jescheck, *Die Verantwortlichkeit der Staatsorgane nach Völkerstrafrecht: Eine Studie zu den Nürnberger Prozessen* (Bonn, W. Ger.: Ludwig Röhrscheid Verlag, 1952), pp. 49-50; Hermann Schild, ed., *Professor Dr. Friedrich Grimm, mit Offenem Visier: Aus den Lebenserinnerungen eines Deutschen Rechtsanwalt* (Leoni am Starnberger See, W. Ger.: Druffel-Verlag, 1961), pp. 16-17.

46. Georges Cahen-Salvador, *Les Prisonniers de guerre (1914-1919)* (Paris: Payot, 1929), pp. 50-51; Raymond Poincaré, *Au Service de la France*, 10 vols. (Paris: Librairie Plon, 1926-33), 6:145-46; Georges Louis, *Les Carnets de Georges Louis, 1908-1917*, 4th ed., 2 vols. (Paris: F. Rieder et Cie, 1926), 2:203-5; Abel Ferry, *Les Carnets secrets (1914-1918)* (Paris: Bernard Grasset, 1957), p. 95.

47. Édouard Herriot, *Jadis*, 2 vols. (Paris: Flammarion, 1952), 2:29.

48. George Bernard Shaw, "Common Sense About the War," *New York Times Current History* 1 (December 1914): 38.

49. Gordon A. Craig, "The Revolution in War and Diplomacy," in *World War I: A Turning Point in Modern History*, ed. Jack J. Roth (New York: Alfred A. Knopf, Borzoi Books, 1967), pp. 7-24.

50. Fischer, *Germany's Aims.*

51. Christopher Martin, *English Life in the First World War* (London: Wayland, 1974), pp. 27-31, 94; Woodward, *Great Britain and the War*, pp. 370-71.

52. Arthur J. Marder, *From the Dreadnought to Scapa Flow: The Royal Navy in the Fisher Era, 1904-1919*, vol. 2: *The War Years to the Eve of Jutland* (London: Oxford University Press, 1965), pp. 150-51.

53. Sir Arthur Conan Doyle, "A Policy of Murder," *New York Times Current History* 2 (June 1915):547; "The 'Zeppelin' Raid Into England," *Literary Digest* 50 (6 February 1915):235.

54. Andrew Boyle, *Trenchard* (New York: W. W. Norton & Co., 1962); Neville Jones, *The Origins of Strategic Bombing: A Study of the Development of British Air Strategic Thought and Practice up to 1918* (London: William Kimber, 1973).

55. Meeting of the War Council, 24 February 1915, Papers of the Cabinet of Great Britain 42/1, Public Record Office, London (hereafter cited as CAB). "Proposed Devastation of the Enemy's Crops: Report of a Conference, September 28, 1915," Committee of Imperial Defense Paper 226-B, CAB 42/3; Edward David, ed., *Inside Asquith's Cabinet: From the Diaries of Charles Hobhouse* (New York: St. Martin's Press, 1977), p. 188; John W. Coogan, "The End of Neutrality: The United States, Britain, and Neutral Rights, 1899-1915" (Ph. D. diss., Yale University, 1976), p. 220 n. 2.

56. Marion C. Siney, *The Allied Blockade of Germany, 1914-1916* (Ann Arbor, Mich.: University of Michigan Press, 1957), pp. 256-57.

57. For military aspects of the U-boat campaign, see Arno Spindler, *La Guerre sous-marine*, trans. René Jouan, 3 vols. (Paris: Payot, 1933-35); R. H. Gibson and Maurice Prendergast, *The German Submarine War, 1914-1918* (New York: Richard R. Smith, 1931).

58. Arthur J. Marder, *From the Dreadnought to Scapa Flow: The Royal Navy in the Fisher Era, 1904-1919*, vol. 1: *The Road to War, 1904-1914* (London: Oxford University Press, 1961), pp. 332, 363-64; Winston Churchill, *The World Crisis*, 4 vols. (New York: Charles Scribner's Sons, 1923-27), 2:288.

59. *Times*, 9 March 1915, p. 8; 6 March 1915, p. 8; 11 March 1915, p. 8. For details of the imprisonment, see Admiralty Memorandum on Imprisoned Germans, Winston Churchill to Lord Stamfordham, 14 April 1915, the Papers of Herbert Asquith, Earl of Oxford and Asquith (4), Bodleian Library, Oxford University, Oxford (hereafter cited as Asquith Papers). See also Report of Grafton Minot on Imprisoned Submarine Officers at Chatham, 24 May 1915, enclosure in letter from Mrs. Graham Watson to Andrew Bonar Law, the Papers of Andrew Bonar Law (50/3/45), Beaverbrook Library, London (hereafter cited as Bonar Law Papers).

60. *Times*, 7 April 1915, p. 9; "The Treatment of Submarine Crews," *The Nation* (London) 16 (20 March 1915):789-90.

61. *Times*, 15 March 1915, p. 9; 23 March 1915, p. 9. See also letters of A. F. Pollard, a history professor at the University of London, in *Times*, 20 March 1915, p. 8; and letters of Frederic Harrison in *Times*, 10 March 1915, p. 11; 12 March 1915, p. 9; 16 March 1915, p. 7; 18 March 1915, p. 8.

62. *Times*, 13 March 1915, p. 9.

63. See letters of Sir Herbert Stephen in *Times*, 11 March 1915, p. 9; 19 March 1915, p. 10; and a letter of Sir Harry Poland in *Times*, 17 March 1915, p. 9.

64. Sir Graham Bower, "The Laws of War: Prisoners of War and Reprisal," *Transactions of the Grotius Society* 1 (1915):29. See also Bower's letters in *Times*, 16 March 1915, p. 7; 19 March 1915, p. 10. The great jurist Lasa Oppenheim, Whewell professor of international law at Cambridge University, was apparently responsible for this new addition on superior orders, which had little support in Anglo-American traditions before 1914. See the analysis in Dr. Hugh H. L. Bellot, "War Crimes and War Criminals," *The Canadian Law Times* 36 (October 1916):763-64.

65. Walter Hines Page to Sir Edward Grey, 20 March 1915, Papers of the Foreign Office of Great Britain 383/32 (32842/263/1218A), Public Record Office, London (hereafter cited as FO).

66. Admiralty to Foreign Office, 29 March 1915, FO 383/32 (36804/263/1218A); Minutes of Grey and Sir Horace Rumbold, 30 March 1915, FO 383/32 (36804/263/1218A).

67. Grey to Page, 1 April 1915, FO 383/32 (36804/263/1218A). This correspondence between Britain and Germany was published in *Times*, 3 April 1915, p. 8.

68. For a complete list of the officers and their family background, see *Times*, 26 April 1915, p. 6.

69. Stamfordham to Sir Maurice Bonham-Carter, 3 May 1915, with enclosure of letter from Captain Ronald Stewart-Menzies, 17 April 1915, Asquith Papers (4).

70. Princess Blücher, *An English Wife in Berlin* (New York: E. P. Dutton & Co., 1920), pp. 63-64.

71. Stamfordham to Churchill, 14 April 1915, Asquith Papers (4); Churchill to Stamfordham, 14 April 1915, Asquith Papers. On the king's attitude toward Churchill in general, see Martin Gilbert, *Winston Churchill*, vol. 3: *The Challenge of War, 1914-1916* (Boston: Houghton Mifflin Co., 1971), pp. 87-88.

72. Minute of Rumbold, 14 April 1915, FO 383/32 (45699/263/1218A).

73. Stamfordham to Herbert Asquith, 16 April 1915, Asquith Papers (4). This letter is partially quoted in Sir Harold Nicolson, *King George the Fifth: His Life and Reign* (London: Constable & Co., 1952), pp. 272-73.

74. Asquith to King George V, 27 April 1915, CAB 41/36. On the agreement to permit American inspections, see Grey to Page, 19 April 1915, FO 383/32 (45699/263/1218A). See also comments of American ambassador in Germany, James W. Gerard, in *My First Eighty-Three Years in America* (Garden City, N.Y.: Doubleday & Co., 1951), p. 202.

75. A. J. P. Taylor, ed., *Lloyd George: A Diary by Frances Stevenson* (New York: Harper & Row, 1971), p. 46; David, ed., *Inside Asquith's Cabinet*, p. 238. There is no official record of Kitchener's proposal. Sir Maurice Hankey had not completed his organization of the secretariat that would later provide a complete account of Cabinet meetings. The only record kept during this era was a brief letter after each meeting from the prime minister to the king. Asquith's letter to King George of 23 April 1915 merely noted a discussion of the treatment of prisoners. See CAB 41/36. For the war crimes punishment of the Boers, see Cecil Headlam, ed., *The Milner Papers: South Africa, 1899-1905*, 2 vols. (London: Cassell & Co., 1933), 2:250-59, 327-32; Sir George Arthur, *Life of Lord Kitchener*, 3 vols.

(New York: Macmillan Co., 1920), 2:20-26, 93, 102; Dr. Hugh H. L. Bellot, "A Permanent International Criminal Court," *International Law Association* 1 (1922):71. Scholarly research after the Second World War revealed the existence of precedents for war crimes prosecutions that were unknown in 1914. See Robert K. Woetzel, *The Nuremberg Trials in International Law* (London: Stevens & Sons, 1962), pp. 17-19.

76. A. J. P. Taylor, *English History, 1914-1945* (New York and Oxford: Oxford University Press, 1965), p. 17.

77. Great Britain, Parliament, House of Commons, *Parliamentary Debates*, 5th series, 70 (1915):1525. See also *Times*, 15 May 1915, p. 7; "Pampered Prisoners," *Literary Digest* 50 (10 April 1915):799; Great Britain, Parliament, House of Lords, *Parliamentary Debates* 18 (1915):745-50.

78. *Parliamentary Debates*, Lords, 18 (1915): 852-81. See also "Criminal Warfare and Retaliation," *The Spectator* 114 (24 April 1915):579-80.

79. *Parliamentary Debates*, Commons, 71 (1915): 651-64.

80. Ibid., cols. 1201-8.

81. *Times*, 28 April 1915, p. 9.

82. "The German Treatment of Prisoners," *The New Statesman* 5 (1 May 1915):76-77.

83. *Parliamentary Debates*, Commons, 71 (1915):679.

84. Austin Harrison, "Our Duty to the Prisoners," *The English Review* 20 (May 1915):237-40. See his similar demand made earlier in "Clearness and Pertinacity," *The English Review* 20 (April 1915):104-13.

85. Thomas A. Bailey and Paul B. Ryan, *The Lusitania Disaster: An Episode in Modern Warfare and Diplomacy* (New York: The Free Press, 1975).

86. *Times*, 15 May 1915, p. 5.

87. The most complete study of wartime politics is Cameron Hazlehurst, *Politicians at War, July 1914 to May 1915: A Prologue to the Triumph of Lloyd George* (New York: Alfred A. Knopf, 1971).

88. Asquith to King George V, 6 June 1915, CAB 41/36; Asquith to King George V, 9 June 1915, CAB 41/36.

89. *Parliamentary Debates*, Commons, 72 (1915):267-68; *Times*, 10 June 1915, p. 8. For details of the release of submariners and the British officers, see Grey to Page, 12 June 1915, FO 383/61 (76338/48319/1218); *Times*, 14 June 1915, p. 5; 16 June 1915, p. 8.

90. Memorandum by Cecil, 8 June 1915, FO 383/61 (74605/48319/1218); Lord Robert Cecil to Sir John Simon and Lieutenant-General Sir Herbert Belfield, 14 August 1915, FO 383/62 (113103/57534/1218); Dame Adelaide Livingston to Cecil, 5 October 1915, FO 383/62 (145806/57534/1218). Curiously, neither the memoirs nor the principal biographies of Cecil, Asquith, Churchill, Grey, King George V, and most other British leaders mention special detention of U-boat crews or threats of war crimes punishment.

CHAPTER 2

1. William L. Langer, *The Diplomacy of Imperialism, 1890-1902*, 2nd ed. (New York: Alfred A. Knopf, 1968), pp. 152-63, 195-210, 321-51; Richard G. Hovannisian, *Armenia on the Road to Independence, 1918* (Berkeley and Los

190   Notes

Angeles, Calif.: University of California Press, 1967), pp. 1-28; James B. Gidney, *A Mandate for Armenia* (Kent, Ohio: Kent State University Press, 1967), pp. 1-36.

2. Hovannisian, *Armenia on the Road to Independence*, pp. 37-39. On the "Young Turks," see Feroz Ahmad, *The Young Turks: The Committee of Union and Progress in Turkish Politics, 1908-1914* (Oxford: Oxford University Press, 1969).

3. Ulrich Trumpener, *Germany and the Ottoman Empire, 1914-1918* (Princeton, N.J.: Princeton University Press, 1968), pp. 202-3, 268; Hovannisian, *Armenia on the Road to Independence*, pp. 41-54. See also "Turkish Foreign Minister's Defense of Armenian Massacres," *New York Times Current History* 5 (December 1916): 544-45.

4. On the continuing debate about the total number of Armenians who died and who was responsible, see Gwynne Dyer, "Turkish 'Falsifiers' and Armenian 'Deceivers': Historiography and the Armenian Massacres," *Middle Eastern Studies* 12 (1976):99-107; Sarkis J. Karajian, "An Inquiry into the Statistics of the Turkish Genocide of the Armenians, 1915-1918," *The Armenian Review* 25 (Winter 1972):3-44; Stanford J. Shaw and Ezel Kural Shaw, *History of the Ottoman Empire and Modern Turkey*, vol. 2: *Reform, Revolution, and Republic: The Rise of Modern Turkey, 1808-1975* (London: Cambridge University Press, 1977), pp. 314-17. See also Helen Fein, *Accounting for Genocide: National Responses and Jewish Victimization During the Holocaust* (New York: The Free Press, 1979), pp. 9-30; Jean-Marie Carzou, *Un Génocide exemplaire: Arménie, 1915* (Paris: Flammarion, 1975).

5. Viscount Bryce and Arnold Toynbee, *The Treatment of Armenians in the Ottoman Empire, 1915-1916* (London: His Majesty's Stationery Office, 1916). Other contemporary works highly critical of the Turks include: Herbert Adams Gibbons, *The Blackest Page of Modern History: Events in Armenia in 1915; The Facts and the Responsibilities* (New York and London: Putnam's Sons, 1916); Dr. Johannes Lepsius, *Deutschland und Armenien, 1914-1918, Sammlung Diplomatischer Aktenstücke* (Potsdam, Ger.: Tempel Verlag, 1919); Henry Morgenthau, *Ambassador Morgenthau's Story* (Garden City, N.Y.: Doubleday, Page & Co., 1918).

6. Arnold J. Toynbee, *Acquaintances* (London: Oxford University Press, 1967), p. 242.

7. "German Guilt for Armenian Blood," *Literary Digest* 55 (27 October 1917): 29-30; James M. Read, *Atrocity Propaganda: 1914-1919* (New Haven, Conn.: Yale University Press, 1941), p. 216.

8. Trumpener, *Germany and the Ottoman Empire*, pp. 204-19, 229-33, 244-45, 269-70.

9. On Allied plans to divide Turkey, see Harry N. Howard, *The Partition of Turkey: A Diplomatic History, 1913-1923* (Norman, Okla.: University of Oklahoma Press, 1931).

10. No. 609, Sergei Sazanov to Alexander Izvolski and Count Alexander Benckendorff, 25/12 April 1915, Russia, *Die Internationalen Beziehungen im Zeitalter des Imperialismus. Dokumente aus den Archiven der Zarischen und der Provisorischen Regierung. . .* , ed. M. N. Pokrowski, 2d series (Berlin: Verlag Reimar Hobbing G.M.B.H., 1935), 7:602. Sazanov said nothing about this episode in his autobiography.

11. *Times*, 2 February 1915, p. 8.

12. No. 768, Sazanov to Benckendorff, 15/2 May 1915, *Internationalen Beziehungen im Zeitalter des Imperialismus*, 7:750-51.

13. See C. Jay Smith, Jr., *The Russian Struggle for Power, 1914-1917: A Study of Russian Foreign Policy During the First World War* (New York: Philosophical Library, 1956), which does not, however, deal with the threat to punish Turkish leaders.

14. Toynbee, *Acquaintances*, pp. 149-50. The French ambassador to Russia described this brutality toward Jews, claiming that more than eight hundred thousand were violently expelled from war zones in Poland and Lithuania, but he did not mention the threat to punish Turks. See Maurice Paléologue, *An Ambassador's Memoirs*, trans. F. A. Holt, 3 vols. (New York: George H. Doran Co., n.d.), 1:315, 2:41-42.

15. No. 609, n. 3, Izvolski to Sazanov, 27/14 April 1915, *Internationalen Beziehungen im Zeitalter des Imperialismus*, 7:602. Studies of French foreign policy and of Delcassé do not deal with the threat against the Turks.

16. Norman Stone, *The Eastern Front, 1914-1917* (New York: Charles Scribner's Sons, 1975).

17. No. 609, n. 3, Sir Edward Grey to Sir George Buchanan, 30/17 April 1915, *Internationalen Beziehungen im Zeitalter des Imperialismus*, 7:602. The British ambassador to Russia, Sir George Buchanan, did not mention the threat against the Turks in his memoirs.

18. No. 740, Benckendorff to Sazanov, 12 May/29 April 1915, ibid., 7:721.

19. No. 799, Benckendorff to Sazanov, 20/7 May 1915, ibid., pp. 773-74.

20. *Times*, 14 May 1915, p. 9; 15 May 1915, p. 8; Henry Morgenthau to William J. Bryan, 2 May 1915; 6 May 1915; James W. Gerard to Bryan, 14 May 1915; Morgenthau to Bryan, 15 May 1915, United States, Department of State, *Papers Relating to the Foreign Relations of the United States, 1915, Supplement, The World War* (Washington, D.C.: United States Government Printing Office, 1928), pp. 969-71.

21. For this tradition, see R. T. Shannon, *Gladstone and the Bulgarian Agitation, 1876* (London: Thomas Nelson & Sons, 1963); David Harris, *Britain and the Bulgarian Horrors of 1876* (Chicago: University of Chicago Press, 1939).

22. No. 724, n. 1, Sazanov to Izvolski, 20/7 May 1915, *Internationalen Beziehungen im Zeitalter des Imperialismus*, 7:772. Grey said nothing in his memoirs about the threat against the Turks. For his attitude toward international law, see F. H. Hinsley, ed., *British Foreign Policy Under Sir Edward Grey* (London: Cambridge University Press, 1977), pp. 89-110.

23. For the official text of the note, see William G. Sharp to Bryan, 28 May 1915, *Foreign Relations of the United States, 1915, The World War*, p. 981. See a slightly different version in *Times*, 24 May 1915, p. 5.

24. Morgenthau, *Ambassador Morgenthau's Story*, p. 359.

25. Morgenthau to Robert Lansing, 18 June 1915, *Foreign Relations of the United States, 1915, The World War*, p. 982; Trumpener, *Germany and the Ottoman Empire*, p. 210.

26. Great Britain, Parliament, House of Lords, *Parliamentary Debates* 19 (1915): 776-78, 1000-1002.

27. H. C. Peterson, *Propaganda for War: The Campaign Against American Neutrality, 1914-1917* (Norman, Okla.: University of Oklahoma Press, 1939), p. 62.

28. For American intervention, see the despatches in United States, Department of State, *Papers Relating to the Foreign Relations of the United States: The Lansing Papers, 1914-1920*, 2 vols. (Washington, D.C.: United States Government Printing Office, 1939-40), 1:48-66. See also A. A. Hoehling, *A Whisper of Eternity: The Mystery of Edith Cavell* (New York: Thomas Yoseloff, 1957).

29. Walter Görlitz, ed., *The Kaiser and His Court: The Diaries, Note Books, and Letters of Admiral Georg Alexander von Müller, Chief of the Naval Cabinet, 1914-1918* (London:Macdonald & Co., 1961), p. 115; Franklin D. Scott, "Gustav V and Swedish Attitudes Toward Germany, 1915," *Journal of Modern History* 39 (June 1967):118.

30. "Edith Cavell," *Literary Digest* 51 (6 November 1915):1001.

31. *Times*, 18 October 1915, pp. 6, 9.

32. Ibid., 21 October 1915, p. 7.

33. Rodney O. Davis, "British Policy and Opinion on War Aims and Peace Proposals, 1914-1918" (Ph.D. diss., Duke University, 1958), p. 117. Von Bissing was absent from Brussels on the day of Cavell's execution. Responsibility for the refusal to postpone it lay with the military governor of Brussels, General von Sauerzweig, and with his chief political adviser, Baron von der Lancken. See Read, *Atrocity Propaganda*, p. 214.

34. Sir John Macdonell, "Modern Treaties of Peace," *Contemporary Review* 108 (September 1915):273-83.

35. Great Britain, Parliament, House of Commons, *Parliamentary Debates* 75 (1915):173.

36. *Times*, 2 November 1915, p. 7.

37. Sir Julian Corbett, *Official History of the War: Naval Operations*, 5 vols. (London: Longmans, Green & Co., 1921-31), 3:131-33.

38. Charles J. Vopicka, *Secrets of the Balkans, Seven Years of a Diplomatist's Life in the Storm Centre of Europe* (Chicago: Rand McNally, 1921), pp. 51-52.

39. Jan Karl Tanenbaum, *General Maurice Sarrail, 1856-1929: The French Army and Left-Wing Politics* (Chapel Hill, N.C.: University of North Carolina Press, 1974), pp. 66-68, 102-19. See also George B. Leon, *Greece and the Great Powers, 1914-1917* (Thessaloniki, Greece: Institute for Balkan Studies, 1974), who argued that Allied violations of international law were merely technical, caused more by the internal political struggle for power in Greece than by deliberate Allied policy.

40. *Parliamentary Debates*, Lords, 22 (1916):264, 980. See similar refusals by Lord Robert Cecil in *Parliamentary Debates*, Commons, 82 (1916):875, 1812.

41. Letter of Lord Robert Cecil, 1 July 1916, circulated to the Cabinet with enclosure of report from Government Committee on the Treatment by the Enemy of British Prisoners of War, 30 June 1916, CAB 37/151.

42. Lord Robert Vansittart, *The Mist Procession: The Autobiography of Lord Vansittart* (London: Hutchinson, 1958), p. 157.

43. Cyril Falls, *The Great War* (New York: Capricorn Books, 1961), pp. 103-16, 186-94.

44. Lord Thomas Newton, *Retrospection* (London: John Murray, 1941), pp. 228-29.

45. W. B. Fest, "British War Aims and German Peace Feelers During the First World War (December 1916-November 1918)," *The Historical Journal* 15 (June 1972):285-308.

46. Sir Llewellyn Woodward, *Great Britain and the War of 1914-1918* (Boston: Beacon Press, 1970), pp. 215-16.

47. Michael G. Fry, *Lloyd George and Foreign Policy*, vol. 1: *The Education of a Statesman: 1890-1916* (Montreal: McGill-Queen's University Press, 1977), pp. 231-33, 245-47.

48. Sir Archibald Hurd, *Official History of the War: The Merchant Navy*, 3 vols. (London: Longmans, Green & Co., 1921-29), 2:308-36.

49. For legal aspects of the armed ship controversy, see James Garner, *International Law and the World War*, 2 vols. (London: Longmans, Green & Co., 1920), 2:384-413. For diplomatic aspects, see Arthur S. Link, *Wilson*, vol. 4: *Confusions and Crises, 1915-1916* (Princeton, N.J.: Princeton University Press, 1964), pp. 153-63.

50. News clipping from London *Observer*, 30 July 1916, enclosed in Turnstall Smith to James Brown Scott, 11 August 1916, the Papers of James Brown Scott, Georgetown University Library, Washington, D.C.

51. Petition from Shipmaster's and Sailor's Protection Society, 1 August 1916, FO 383/195 (1499938/123628/1218); J. Pinkerton to Grey, 30 July 1916, and minute of Sir Horace Rumbold, 3 August 1916, FO 383/195 (150473/123628/1218).

52. *Parliamentary Debates*, Commons, 84 (1916): 2080-81.

53. See extracts of British press in *New York Times*, 1 August 1916, p. 2; *Times*, 1 August 1916, p. 9; "The Latest German Barbarism," *The Spectator* 117 (5 August 1916):148-49.

54. "Events of the Week," *The Nation* (London), 19 (5 August 1916):551.

55. Dr. Hugh H. L. Bellot, "War Crimes: Their Prevention and Punishment," *The Nineteenth Century and After* 80 (September 1916):636-60. See an expanded version of this article in "War Crimes and War Criminals," *The Canadian Law Times* 36 (October 1916):754-68; (November 1916):876-86; 37 (January 1917): 9-22. See also letters by the Reverend William Boyd Carpenter, subdean of Westminster, in *Times*, 3 August 1916, p. 7; 8 August 1916, p. 7; 14 August 1916, p. 8; 22 August 1916, p. 7; and a letter by J. A. Stewart, professor of moral philosophy at Oxford University, *Times*, 16 August 1916, p. 5.

56. War Committee meeting, 1 August 1916, CAB 42/17. See also Rumbold, "Memo of Prisoner's Department Relative to Reprisals, 31 July 1916," FO 383/195 (151547/123628/1218).

57. Grey to Buchanan and Lord Bertie, 2 August 1916, FO 412/113, Confidential Print No. 234 (151547).

58. Minute of Cecil, 14 August 1916, FO 383/195 (157823/123628/1218). See also the public statements of Cecil and Sir Edward Carson in *Times*, 5 August 1916, p. 8; 14 August 1916, p. 5.

59. Read, *Atrocity Propaganda*, pp. 169-70.

60. Grey to Carson, 13 August 1916, FO 383/195 (162979/123628/1218); Earl Grandville to Grey, 9 August 1916, FO 412/113, Confidential Print No. 248

(157823); Buchanan to Grey, 7 August 1916, FO 383/195 (156595/123628/1218); Paul Cambon to Grey, 6 September 1916, FO 383/195 (177588/123628/1218); Grey to Cambon, 2 October 1916, FO 383/195 (177588/123628/1218).

61. Georges Cahen-Salvador, *Les Prisonniers de guerre (1914-1919)* (Paris: Payot, 1929), pp. 70, 82-83.

62. France, Sénat, *Annales du Sénat Débats Parlementaires* 87 (11 January-31 December 1916): 548-50; Fernand Engerand, "Les Sanctions des crimes de guerre," *L'Echo de Paris,* 15 September 1916, quoted in "Des Sanctions à établir pour la répression des crimes commis par les allemands en violation du droit des gens et des traités internationaux," *Journal du Droit International* 44(1917):134-38.

63. All of these individuals are quoted in Jacques Dumas, *Les Sanctions pénales des crimes allemands* (Paris: Librairie Arthur Rousseau, 1916). See also Charles Benoist, "Chronique de la quinzaine," *Revue des Deux Mondes* 34 (15 August 1916):958; Joseph Reinach, "He Is the Master Assassin," *New York Times Current History* 4 (September 1916):1103-4.

64. Paul Pic, "Violations systématique des lois de la guerre par les austro-allemands: Les Sanctions nécessaires," *Revue Générale de Droit International Public* 23 (1916):243-68.

65. See Leo Bouyssou's public letter to Aristide Briand in "Des Sanctions . . . et des traites internationaux," *Journal du Droit International* 44 (1917):125-26. Bouyssou also confronted Briand in the Chamber of Deputies. See *Annales de la Chambre des Députés* 105 (14 April-22 September 1916):1699-1700.

66. *Annales de la Chambre des Députés* 105 (14 April-22 September 1916):1706-7. See the analysis of this speech in Robert E. Cleveland, "French Attitudes Toward the 'German Problem,' 1914-1919" (Ph.D. diss., University of Nebraska, 1957), pp. 107-11.

67. Paul Morand, *Journal d'un attaché d'ambassade, 1916-1917* (Paris: Gallimard, 1963), pp. 20-21.

68. Georges Suarez, *Briand, sa vie-son oeuvre,* 6 vols. (Paris: Librairie Plon, 1938-52), 3:412-21.

69. *Times,* 24 August 1916, p. 5.

70. A. J. P. Taylor, *English History, 1914-1945* (New York and Oxford: Oxford University Press, 1965), pp. 62-63; Falls, *Great War,* pp. 195-208.

71. Ernst Stenzel, *Die Kriegführung des Deutschen Imperialismus und das Völkerrecht zur Planung und Vorbereitung des Deutschen Imperialismus auf die Barbarische Kriegführung im Ersten und Zweiten Weltkrieg* (Berlin, E. Ger.: Militärverlag der Deutschen Demokratischen Republik, 1973), p. 50; Michael F. Palo, "The Diplomacy of Belgian War Aims During the First World War" (Ph.D. diss., University of Illinois, 1978), pp. 461-62; Martin Kitchen, *The Silent Dictatorship: The Politics of the German High Command under Hindenburg and Ludendorff, 1916-1918* (New York: Holmes & Meier, 1976), pp. 97-98; Gerald Feldman, *Army, Industry, and Labor in Germany, 1914-1918* (Princeton, N.J.: Princeton University Press, 1966), pp. 197, 308, 386.

72. Hurd, *Merchant Navy,* 3:309-39.

73. War Cabinet meeting No. 50(5), January 31, 1917, CAB 23/1.

74. Newton, *Retrospection,* pp. 237-40.

75. Read, *Atrocity Propaganda*, p. 245. For a description of Martel's book, *Comment finiront Guillaume II et ses complices?*, see Francis Gribble, "Peace Without Amnesties," *The Nineteenth Century and After* 84 (October 1918):607-11.

76. *Annales du Sénat Débats* 88 (9 January-31 December 1917):433-39.

77. A. J. P. Taylor, *The First World War* (1963; reprint ed., New York: Capricorn Books, 1972), pp. 165-209.

CHAPTER 3

1. "Why Europe Is at War," *Literary Digest* 49 (15 August 1914):253-54; "Blaming Germany for the War," *Literary Digest* (22 August 1914):293-94. See also Robert J. Menner, "The Kaiser and Germany in Popular Opinion," *South Atlantic Quarterly* 15 (April 1916):101-12; Edwin Costrell, *How Maine Viewed the War, 1914-1917* (Orono, Maine: University of Maine Press, 1940), p. 34; Cedric C. Cummins, *Indiana Public Opinion and the World War, 1914-1917* (Indianapolis, Ind.: Indiana Historical Bureau, 1945), p. 10.

2. Henry F. Pringle, *The Life and Times of William Howard Taft*, 2 vols. (New York: Farrar & Rinehart, 1939), 2:872.

3. Joseph Hodges Choate to Henry White, 9 September 1914, the Papers of Henry White (General Correspondence, Box 20), Library of Congress, Washington, D.C. (hereafter cited as White Papers). See similar remarks in Philip C. Jessup, *Elihu Root*, 2 vols. (New York: Dodd, Mead & Co., 1938), 2:313-15. See also James Ford Rhodes to Viscount James Bryce, 28 September 1916, the Papers of Viscount James Bryce, Bodleian Library, Oxford University, Oxford (hereafter cited as Bryce Papers).

4. Arthur S. Link, *Wilson*, vol. 3: *The Struggle for Neutrality, 1914-1915* (Princeton, N.J.: Princeton University Press, 1960), pp. 1-56; Ernest R. May, *The World War and American Isolation, 1914-1917* (1959; reprint ed., Chicago: Quadrangle Books, 1966), pp. 34-36.

5. Ray Stannard Baker, *Woodrow Wilson: Life and Letters*, 8 vols. (New York: Doubleday, Doran & Co., 1927-39), 5:166; "America's Duty and the Rules of War," *The Outlook* 109 (3 February 1915):252-55; William Harbaugh, *The Life and Times of Theodore Roosevelt*, rev. ed. (New York: Collier Books, 1963), pp. 440-47; A. Russell Buchanan, "Theodore Roosevelt and American Neutrality, 1914-1917," *American Historical Review* 43 (July 1938):775-90. For a typical reaction by an American who was not pro-Ally, see Mary Bryan, ed., *The Memoirs of William Jennings Bryan* (Chicago: John C. Winston Co., 1925), pp. 415-16.

6. Robert Lansing to President Wilson, 23 November 1914, United States, Department of State, *Papers Relating to the Foreign Relations of the United States: The Lansing Papers, 1914-1920*, 2 vols. (Washington, D.C.: United States Government Printing Office, 1939-40), 1:35-37 (hereafter cited as *Lansing Papers*); Wilson to Lansing, 26 November 1914, *Lansing Papers*, p. 37. See also the memorandum by Lansing on criticisms of failure to protest violations of the Hague conventions, 9 February 1915, *Lansing Papers*, pp. 201-10.

7. "Two Ex-Presidents' Views," *New York Times Current History* 2 (June

1915):444. For similar comments, see "The Law of the Lusitania Case," *New York Times*, 9 May 1915, sec. 3 and 4, p. 2; "The 'Lusitania' Torpedoed," *Literary Digest* 50 (15 May 1915):1133-34; "The Lusitania Massacre: What Should America Do," *The Outlook* 110 (19 May 1915):103-5.

8. "The Bryce Report on German Atrocities," *Literary Digest* 50 (29 May 1915):1257-59.

9. Theodore S. Woolsey, "Retaliation and Punishment," *Proceedings of the American Society of International Law, 1915*, pp. 62-69.

10. Link, *Wilson*, 3:321-455. For instances in which Wilson requested individual punishment of U-boat captains, see Lansing to Frederick C. Penfield, 6 December 1915, United States, Department of State, *Papers Relating to the Foreign Relations of the United States, 1915, Supplement, The World War* (Washington, D.C.: United States Government Printing Office, 1928), pp. 623-25; Memorandum by the Secretary of State of a conversation with the Austro-Hungarian *Chargé*, 21 December 1915, *Lansing Papers*, 1:503-4, Draft note from Secretary of State to German Ambassador, 26 January 1916, *Lansing Papers*, 1: 527-29.

11. Link, *Wilson*, 4:273.

12. The Diary of Edward M. House, Yale University Library, New Haven, Conn. (hereafter cited as House Diary), 27 January 1916. See Link, *Wilson*, 4:121, for an evaluation.

13. Lansing to Joseph C. Grew, 29 November 1916, United States, Department of State, *Papers Relating to the Foreign Relations of the United States, 1916, Supplement, The World War* (Washington, D.C.: United States Government Printing Office, 1929), p. 71; House Diary, 15 November 1916; 27 November 1916.

14. Arthur S. Link, *Wilson*, vol. 5: *Campaigns for Progressivism and Peace, 1916-1917* (Princeton, N.J.: Princeton University Press, 1965), pp. 220-431; May, *World War and American Isolation*, pp. 345-437.

15. A. Russell Buchanan, "American Editors Examine American War Aims and Plans in April, 1917," *Pacific Historical Review* 9 (September 1940):253-65; Baker, *Wilson*, 5:492-501.

16. James R. Mock and Cedric Larson, *Words That Won the War: The Story of the Committee on Public Information, 1917-1919* (Princeton, N.J.: Princeton University Press, 1939), p. 12, passim. Atrocity stories were a topic of conversation at all levels of society, including table talk at dinners of Cabinet officers in Washington. See E. David Cronon, ed., *The Cabinet Diaries of Josephus Daniels: 1913-1921* (Lincoln, Nebr.: University of Nebraska Press, 1963), pp. 134, 148, 166.

17. *Life* cartoon of 27 January 1918 reproduced in Mark Sullivan, *Our Times, 1900-1925*, vol. 5: *Over Here, 1914-1918* (New York: Charles Scribner's Sons, 1933), p. 433.

18. *New York Times*, 8 September 1918, p. 7; 9 October 1918, p. 7.

19. Contemporary photograph reproduced in Sullivan, *Our Times*, 5:349.

20. Carl Sandburg, *Complete Poems* (New York: Harcourt, Brace & Co., 1950), pp. 143-44. From "The Four Brothers: Notes for War Songs (November, 1917)," in *Cornhuskers*, by Carl Sandburg, copyright © 1918, by Holt, Rinehart and Winston, Inc.; copyright © 1946, by Carl Sandburg. Reprinted by permission of Harcourt Brace Jovanovich, Inc. For another poem see Harry A. Kemp, "A Song

of St. Helena and the Two Emperors," *The Century Magazine* (New York) 97 (November 1918):114-15.

21. Ray H. Abrams, *Preachers Present Arms: The Role of the American Churches and Clergy in World Wars I and II, With Some Observations on the War in Vietnam,* rev. ed. (Scottsdale, Pa.: Herald Press, 1969), pp. 28, 103-5, 230. See also James D. Squires, *British Propaganda at Home and in the United States from 1914 to 1917* (Cambridge, Mass.: Harvard University Press, 1935), p. 68.

22. *New York Times,* 3 December 1917, p. 11. I have a copy of the sheet music: Kendis and Brockman, "We're Going to Hang the Kaiser Under the Linden Tree" (New York: Kendis & Brockman Music Co., 1917).

23. *The New York Times Film Reviews, 1913-1968,* 6 vols. (New York: New York Times, Arno Press, 1970), 1:33; George Sylvester Viereck, *Spreading Germs of Hate* (New York: Liveright, 1930), p. 307; Mock and Larson, *Words That Won the War,* pp. 151-52.

24. "Essentials in Making Peace With Germany," handed by Professor C. G. Reisce to Lansing, 15 August 1917, the Papers of Robert Lansing (File VIIa, German Matters), Princeton University Library (hereafter cited as Lansing Papers, Princeton). See also remarks of Everett P. Wheeler, 27 April 1917, *Proceedings of the American Society of International Law, 1917,* pp. 36-37.

25. Walter Lippmann to Colonel Edward M. House, 28 December 1917, United States, Department of State, *Papers Relating to the Foreign Relations of the United States: The Paris Peace Conference, 1919,* 13 vols. (Washington, D.C.: United States Government Printing Office, 1942-47), 1:54 (hereafter cited as *FRUS: Paris Peace Conference, 1919*).

26. David Hunter Miller, James Brown Scott, and L. H. Woolsey to Lansing, 10 July 1918, ibid., pp. 99-101.

27. The Diary of Robert Lansing, Library of Congress, Washington, D.C., 25 May 1915 (hereafter cited as Lansing Diary). See also Lansing's comments in his "Sketch of Jules Jusserand," Lansing Diary, May 1916.

28. House Diary, 24 July 1915.

29. Elihu Root to Lansing, 23 October 1918; Lansing to Root, 28 October 1918; Charles L. Pauwley to Lansing, 11 November 1918; Lansing to Edward N. Smith, 14 November 1918, the Papers of Robert Lansing, Library of Congress, Washington, D.C. (hereafter cited as Lansing Papers, Library of Congress).

30. Charles Seymour, ed., *The Intimate Papers of Colonel House,* 4 vols. (Boston and New York: Houghton Mifflin Co., 1926-28), 3:56; W. B. Fowler, *British-American Relations, 1917-1918: The Role of Sir William Wiseman* (Princeton, N.J.: Princeton University Press, 1969), pp. 25-31.

31. Sterling J. Kernek, *Distractions of Peace During War: The Lloyd George Government's Reactions to Woodrow Wilson, December 1916-November 1918* (Philadelphia: Transactions of the American Philosophical Society, 1975), pp. 50-51.

32. Fowler, *British-American Relations,* pp. 118-23; Seth P. Tillman, *Anglo-American Relations at the Paris Peace Conference of 1919* (Princeton, N.J.: Princeton University Press, 1961), pp. 24-32.

33. Baker, *Wilson,* 7:213; Allan Nevins, ed., *The Letters and Journal of Brand Whitlock,* 2 vols. (New York: D. Appleton-Century Co., 1936), 1:506.

34. N. Gordon Levin, Jr., *Woodrow Wilson and World Politics: America's Response to War and Revolution* (New York: Oxford University Press Paperback, 1970), pp. 37-41, 53-54, 83-85.

35. See Wilson's speeches of 2 April 1917, 14 June 1917, 6 April 1918, 4 July 1918, in Ray Stannard Baker and William E. Dodd, eds., *The Public Papers of Woodrow Wilson, War and Peace*, 2 vols. (New York: Harper & Bros., 1927), 1:6-16, 60-67, 198-202, 231-35. See also John L. Snell, "Wilsonian Rhetoric Goes to War," *The Historian* 14 (Spring 1952):191-208.

36. "Emperor William Must Go, Says Morgenthau," *New York Times*, 30 September 1917, sec. 7, p. 2.

37. Walter Görlitz, ed., *The Kaiser and His Court: The Diaries, Note Books, and Letters of Admiral Georg Alexander von Müller, Chief of the Naval Cabinet, 1914-1918* (London: Macdonald & Co., 1961), pp. 333-34.

38. Hans Peter Hanssen, *Diary of a Dying Empire*, trans. Oscar O. Winther (Bloomington, Ind.: Indiana University Press, 1955), p. 308.

39. Fowler, *British-American Relations*, p. 283.

40. John L. Snell, "Die Republic aus Versäumnissen Unterlassungen Führen 1918 aum Zusammenbruch der Monarchie," *Die Welt als Geschichte* 15 (1955):198; Victor S. Mamatey, *The United States and East Central Europe, 1914-1918: A Study in Wilsonian Diplomacy and Propaganda* (Princeton, N.J.: Princeton University Press, 1957), p. 294.

41. *New York Times*, 18 August 1918, sec. 2, p. 2.

42. See the following letters in the *New York Times:* 1 September 1918, sec. 4, p. 1; 15 September 1918, sec. 3, p. 3; 14 October 1918, p. 16; 20 October 1918, sec. 3, pp. 1-2; 3 November 1918, sec. 3, p. 7. See also the description of YMCA units in France who spent enjoyable hours thinking up punishments for the kaiser in Margaret Deland, *Small Things* (New York: D. Appleton & Co., 1919), pp. 312-16. One Minnesota lawyer sent his proposal on war crimes trials to the British Embassy in Washington. See James M. Witherow to Colville Barclay, 18 September 1918, the Papers of Sir William Wiseman (Drawer 91, no. 94), Yale University Library, New Haven, Conn. (hereafter cited as Wiseman Papers).

43. "Passing Sentence on the Kaiser and on His People," *Literary Digest* 59 (26 October 1918):14-16; *New York Times*, 7 October 1918, p. 12; 12 October 1918, p. 12; 14 October 1918, p. 3; 16 October 1918, p. 14.

44. *New York Times*, 14 October 1918, p. 16. See also Cronon, *Diaries of Josephus Daniels*, p. 340.

45. *New York Times*, 8 October 1918, p. 1; 10 October 1918, p. 7.

46. Ibid., 13 October 1918, sec. 8, p. 1.

47. "The Punishment of the Kaiser," *The Outlook* 119 (28 August 1918):648-49; "With Whom and for What Are We at War," *The Outlook* 120 (9 October 1918):216-18; "Justice to Germany," *The Outlook* 120 (23 October 1918):283-84.

48. *New York Times*, 22 October 1918, p. 2.

49. Cronon, *Diaries of Josephus Daniels*, pp. 344, 346.

50. Charles Seymour, *American Diplomacy During the World War* (Baltimore: The Johns Hopkins Press, 1934), p. 359. Seymour doubted that Wilson's actions in the armistice negotiations could be explained by election politics.

51. Lansing to Wilson, 4 October 1918, *Lansing Papers*, 2:156; "More U-Boat Savagery," *Literary Digest* 59 (26 October 1918):16. In reality, 176 persons died in the sinking of the *Leinster*. See R. H. Gibson and Maurice Prendergast, *The German Submarine War, 1914-1918* (New York: Richard R. Smith, 1931), pp. 322-23.

52. Sir Eric Geddes to Lloyd George, 13 October 1918, the Papers of David Lloyd George (F/18/2/23), Beaverbrook Library, London (hereafter cited as Lloyd George Papers).

53. Lansing to Frederick Oederlin, Swiss *Chargé*, 14 October 1918, United States, Department of State, *Papers Relating to the Foreign Relations of the United States, 1918, Supplement 1, The World War*, 2 vols. (Washington, D.C.: United States Government Printing Office, 1933), 1:358-59.

54. Lansing to Oederlin, 23 October 1918, ibid., pp. 381-83.

55. Harry R. Rudin, *Armistice 1918* (New Haven, Conn.: Yale University Press, 1944), p. 133.

56. Cronon, *Diaries of Josephus Daniels*, p. 343; Anne W. Lane and Louise H. Wall, eds., *The Letters of Franklin K. Lane, Personal and Political* (Boston: Houghton Mifflin & Co., 1922), pp. 295-96.

57. Memorandum of Dr. Wilhelm Solf, 31 October 1918, Ralph H. Lutz, ed., *The Fall of the German Empire, 1914-1918*, 2 vols. (Stanford, Calif.: Stanford University Press, 1932), 2:498-500; Alma Luckau, *The German Delegation at the Paris Peace Conference* (New York: Columbia University Press, 1941), pp. 18-23; Maurice Baumont, *The Fall of the Kaiser*, trans. E. Ibbetson James (New York: Alfred A. Knopf, 1931).

58. Baumont, *Fall of the Kaiser*, passim.

59. *New York Times*, 12 November 1918, pp. 4-5. Similar demonstrations had occurred on November 7-8 when false reports of the signing of the armistice led to early celebrations. See *New York Times*, 8 November 1918, p. 3; 9 November 1918, p. 8.

60. "Wilhelm to the Bar of Justice," *Literary Digest* 59 (30 November 1918):12-13. Among these groups were the Sons of the Revolution of the District of Columbia, the Cleveland, Ohio, Presbytery of the United Presbyterian Church, and an American Trade Journalist group touring western Europe. See *New York Times*, 21 November 1918, p. 13; 11 December 1918, p. 2; *Times*, 21 December 1918, p. 10. "The Peace Conference." *Banker's Magazine* (New York), 97 (December 1918):715. See also U.S., Congress, House, "Joint Resolution on the Trial of the Kaiser," H.J.R. 371, 65th Cong., 3rd sess., 18 December 1918, *Congressional Record* 57:647. For the statements of the governors, see *New York Times*, 23 November 1918, p. 4; *Times*, 13 November 1918, p. 8.

61. *New York Times*, 25 November 1918, p. 12; *Times*, 15 November 1918, p. 6; 6 December 1918, p. 12; 11 December 1918, p. 9.

62. *New York Times*, 8 December 1918, sec. 4, pp. 1, 14.

63. U.S. Congress, House, *Letter of Secretary of War on Trial of Captain Henry Wirz*, Executive Document No. 23, 40th Cong., 2nd sess., 1868.

64. Jessup, *Elihu Root*, 2:454; Theodore Roosevelt to Rudyard Kipling, 23 November 1918, Elting E. Morison, ed., *The Letters of Theodore Roosevelt*, 8 vols.

(Cambridge, Mass.: Harvard University Press, 1951-54), 8:1403-6. Frank L. Polk to George Wharton Pepper, 5 November and 20 November 1918, the Diary and Papers of Frank L. Polk (Drawer 74, no. 115), Yale University Library, New Haven, Conn.

65. "Editorials," *The Dial* 66 (8 February 1919): 143-44.

66. British Embassy to State Department, 3 December 1918, United States, Department of State, *Papers Relating to the Foreign Relations of the United States, 1919*, 2 vols. (Washington, D.C.: United States Government Printing Office, 1934), 2:653-54.

67. Sir George Grahame to Arthur Balfour, 3 December 1918, FO 371/3227 (199367/187616/18).

68. Arthur Walworth, *America's Moment: 1918 American Diplomacy at the End of World War I* (New York: W. W. Norton & Co., 1977), pp. 106-7.

69. Manuscript of a book about Wilson by Charles L. Swem, Chapter 21, "Journey to the Peace Conference," p. 9, Woodrow Wilson Manuscripts Collected by Charles L. Swem (Box 12), Princeton University Library, Princeton, N.J. Swem was one of Wilson's secretaries, a shorthand specialist who often took down the president's words verbatim.

70. Wilson to House, 21 November 1918, *Foreign Relations of the United States, 1919*, 2:653.

71. *New York Times*, 15 December 1918, p. 1. The official text of Wilson's speech is in Lansing to William G. Sharp, 11 December 1918, *FRUS: Paris Peace Conference, 1919*, 1:147-48.

72. Joseph P. Tumulty, *Woodrow Wilson as I Know Him* (Garden City, N.Y.: Doubleday, Page & Co., 1921), p. 515.

73. Arthur S. Link, *Woodrow Wilson, Revolution, War, and Peace* (Arlington Heights, Ill.: AHM Publishing Corp., 1979), p. 13.

CHAPTER 4

1. During the war, Germany had punished or threatened to punish for violating the laws of war British aviators who dispersed propaganda pamphlets, captains of neutral armed ships, and American soldiers who used shotguns. See James Garner, *International Law and the World War*, 2 vols. (London: Longmans, Green & Co., 1920), 1:495; United States, Department of State, *Papers Relating to the Foreign Relations of the United States, 1917, Supplement 1, The World War* (Washington, D.C.: United States Government Printing Office, 1931), pp. 91-92; United States, Department of State, *Papers Relating to the Foreign Relations of the United States, 1918, Supplement 2, The World War* (Washington, D.C.: United States Government Printing Office, 1933), p. 785.

2. Erich Ludendorff, *Ludendorff's Own Story, August 1914-November 1918*, 2 vols. (New York and London: Harper & Bros., 1919), 2:194-95; Count Ottokar Czernin, *In the World War* (London: Cassell & Co., 1919), pp. 260-61. Kaiser Wilhelm II said he would not lift a finger to save the Rumanian dynasty. See Kurt de Grünau to Foreign Office, No. 283, 23 February 1918, André Schere

and Jacques Grunewald, eds., *L'Allemagne et les problèms de la paix pendant la Première Guerre Mondiale*, vol. 3: *De la Revolution Sovietique à la paix de Brest-Litovsk (9 novembre 1917-3 mars 1918)* (Paris: Publications de la Sorbonne, 1976), p. 413.

3. Czernin, *In the World War*, p. 265; Gr. Antipa, *L'Occupation ennemie de la Roumanie et ses conséquences économiques et sociales* (New Haven, Conn.: Yale University Press, 1929), pp. 37-44, 61-65.

4. See article thirty-three of the supplementary political and legal treaty between Rumania and Germany of May 7, 1918, in the *Frankfurter Zeitung*, no. 130 (second morning edition), 11 May 1918, p. 3; Ludendorff, *Ludendorff's Own Story*, 2:198; Mirceau Djuvara, *La Guerre Roumanie, 1916-1918* (Nancy, Paris, Strasbourg, France: Berger-Levrault Éditeurs, 1919), pp. 197-98.

5. A. Joseph Berlau, *The German Social Democratic Party, 1914-1921* (New York: Columbia University Press, 1949), p. 153.

6. Cyril Falls, *The Great War* (New York: Capricorn Books, 1961), pp. 331-51, 372-82, 407-17.

7. *Le Temps* (Paris), 25 August 1918, p. 1. See also Abel Ferry, *Les Carnets secrets (1914-1918)* (Paris: Bernard Grasset, 1957), p. 240.

8. *Journal du Droit International* 45 (1918): 1619-20; *New York Times*, 4 October 1918, p. 8.

9. Ray Stannard Baker, *Woodrow Wilson: Life and Letters*, 8 vols. (New York: Doubleday, Doran & Co., 1927-39), 8:392-93.

10. War Cabinet meeting, 20 September 1918, CAB 23/7.

11. Quoted in James M. Read, *Atrocity Propaganda: 1914-1919* (New Haven, Conn.: Yale University Press, 1941), p. 246.

12. *New York Times*, 12 January 1918, p. 3. For the full text of this speech, see "Law, War, and the Future," Lord Birkenhead, *The Speeches of Lord Birkenhead* (London: Cassell & Co., 1929), pp. 93-115. See the analysis in William Camp, *The Glittering Prizes: A Biographical Study of F. E. Smith, First Earl of Birkenhead* (London: MacGibbon & Kee, 1960), pp. 108-9. See also the preface to Smith's treatise on international law, written on 18 September 1918, reprinted in Lord Birkenhead, *International Law*, 6th ed. (London and Toronto: J. M. Dent & Sons, 1927), p. viii.

13. Trevor Wilson, *The Downfall of the Liberal Party, 1914-1935* (Ithaca, N.Y.: Cornell University Press, 1966), p. 135; *Times*, 24 July 1918, p. 6, indicated an election was planned for November.

14. *Times*, 19 September 1918, p. 3.

15. Sir F. E. Smith and Gordon Hewart to Lloyd George, 30 September 1918, CAB 24/66 (G.T. 5956).

16. *Times*, 7 October 1918, p. 6; *New York Times*, 5 October 1918, p. 1.

17. *Annales du Sénat Débats* 89 (8 January-31 December 1918):779-80; *Le Matin*, 16 October 1918, p. 1; *Journai du Droit International* 45 (1918):1624-30.

18. Francis Gribble, "Peace Without Amnesties," *The Nineteenth Century and After* 84 (October 1918):600-613. For similar views, see the comments of Sir Joseph Cook, minister for the Australian navy, in *Times*, 21 September 1918, p. 8· the minister of marine for New Zealand in *Times*, 14 October 1918, p. 10.

Numerous persons, including Lord Morris, former prime minister of Newfoundland; Kennedy Jones, a Conservative back-bencher; and Dr. Christopher Addison, the minister of reconstruction, called for punishment of guilty individuals. See *Times,* 8 October 1918, p. 10; 11 October 1918, p. 10; 15 October 1918, p. 8. See also Caroline E. Playne, *Britain Holds On, 1917, 1918* (London: George Allen & Unwin, 1933), pp. 361-77.

19. Lord Thomas Newton, *Retrospection* (London: John Murray, 1941), pp. 255-61; Sir Charles Mallet, *Lord Cave: A Memoir* (London: John Murray, 1931), pp. 207-12.

20. "A British View of German Prison-Camps," *Literary Digest* 58 (28 September 1918):53-56. See reports of the Younger Committee in *Times,* 15 October 1918, p.4.

21. Pemberton Billing charged in his scandal sheet, the *Vigilante,* that the Germans held a Black Book containing the names of forty-seven thousand British citizens, among them prominent leaders, guilty of homosexuality and consequently blackmailed into helping Germany. An actress sued Billing for libel, but a jury acquitted him, after a ludicrous trial in which he claimed the sitting judge's name appeared in the Black Book. See Robert Blake, *The Unknown Prime Minister: The Life and Times of Andrew Bonar Law, 1858-1923* (London: Eyre & Spottiswoode, 1955), pp. 378-79, 388-90. Lord Newton and Sir George Cave successfully sued the *Daily Mail* for libelous attacks. See Newton, *Retrospection,* pp. 264-72; Mallet, *Lord Cave,* pp. 220-21.

22. *Times,* 2 October 1918, p. 9; 5 October 1918, p. 7.

23. *Daily Mail,* 7 October 1918, quoted in *New York Times,* 8 October 1918, p. 2.

24. *Times,* 8 October 1918, p. 9; 9 October 1918, p. 7; 10 October 1918, p. 9; 12 October 1918, p. 8; 14 October 1918, pp. 4, 6; 15 October 1918, p. 8; 18 October 1918, p. 8.

25. Ibid., 4 October 1918, p. 6; 5 October 1918, p. 7.

26. Revised minutes of the Inter-Departmental Committee on Prisoners, 9 October 1918, FO 383/474 (115112/114592/1250). For references to German war crimes punishment in Rumania, see also comments of Lord Newton on 16 October 1918, Great Britain, House of Lords, *Parliamentary Debates* 31 (1918):718; "Prisoners of War," *The Spectator* 121 (2 November 1918):478; "The Kaiser," *The Spectator* 121 (16 November 1918):542.

27. War Cabinet-Imperial War Cabinet meeting No. 484 (6), October 11, 1918, CAB 23/8.

28. *Times,* 14 October 1918, p. 9.

29. *Parliamentary Debates,* Lords, 31 (1918):709-29.

30. War Cabinet meeting No. 488 (6), October 17, 1918, CAB 23/8.

31. David Lloyd George, *War Memoirs,* 6 vols. (London: Ivor Nicholson & Watson, 1933-36), 6:3291.

32. Tom Jones, *Whitehall Diary,* ed. Keith Middlemas, 3 vols. (London: Oxford University Press, 1969-71), 1:69-70.

33. *Evening Standard,* 17 October 1918, in Newspaper Cuttings, 13 August-19 December 1918, the Papers of Lord Milner (320), Bodleian Library, Oxford University, Oxford. The Milner papers do not reveal additional information on war crimes punishment. For analyses of Milner's comments, see Alfred M. Gollin, *Proconsul in Politics: A Study of Lord Milner in Opposition and in Power*

(London: Anthony Bond, 1964), p. 571; John Evelyn Wrench, *Alfred Lord Milner: The Man of No Illusions, 1854-1925* (London: Eyre & Spottiswoode, 1958), pp. 348-49.

34. *Times,* 26 October 1918, p. 8. See also the lord chancellor's remarks in *Times,* 11 November 1918, p. 4.

35. *Times,* 30 October 1918, p. 7; *New York Times,* 31 October 1918, p. 2.

36. *Times,* 23 October 1918, p. 6; 26 October 1918, p. 7.

37. Great Britain, House of Commons, *Parliamentary Debates* 110 (1918): 1311-90.

38. *Times,* 31 October 1918, p. 7; "Prisoners of War," *The Spectator* 121 (2 November 1918):478-79; Carl F. Ahlstrom, "British Public Opinion and the Versailles Conference, October, 1918-January, 1919" (M.A. thesis, Duke University, 1944), p. 110.

39. War Cabinet meeting No. 494A (3), October 31, 1918, CAB 23/14.

40. House Diary, 31 October 1918.

41. War Cabinet-Imperial War Cabinet meeting No. 497 (6), November 5, 1918, CAB 23/8.

42. Northcliffe was director of propaganda in enemy countries, a division of Lord Beaverbrook's Ministry of Information, and the set of war aims he published had the approval of Balfour. Bonar Law, however, denied in answer to a question in the Commons that Northcliffe's set of war aims were official. See War Cabinet meeting No. 486 (7), October 15, 1918, CAB 23/8; Arthur Balfour to E. S. Montagu, 31 October 1918, FO 800/207 (Private Foreign Office Papers of A. J. Balfour); Henry Wickham Steed, *Through Thirty Years, 1892-1922: A Personal Narrative,* 2 vols. (Garden City, N.Y.: Doubleday, Page & Co., 1924), 2:242-44; Sir Campbell Stuart, *Secrets of Crewe House* (London, New York, and Toronto: Hodder & Stoughton, 1920), pp. 218-30; *The History of the Times,* 4 vols. (New York: Macmillan Co., 1935-52), 4:387-91; *Parliamentary Debates,* Commons, 110 (1918):1799-1800.

43. *Times,* 6 November 1918, p. 6.

44. Ibid., 8 November 1918, p. 7.

45. "Interim Reports from the Committee of Enquiry into Breaches of the Laws of War, with Appendices, Presented to the Attorney-General, 13 January 1919," pp. 3-4, CAB 24/72 (G.T. 6550).

46. "Interim Reports from the Committee of Enquiry . . . 13 January 1919," pp. 6-11, CAB 24/72 (G.T. 6550),

47. Sir Almeric Fitzroy, *Memoirs,* 2 vols. (New York: George H. Doran Co., 1925), 2:686; James G. Harbord, *Leaves from a War Diary* (New York: Dodd, Mead & Co., 1925), p. 391.

48. *Times,* 12 November 1918, pp. 6, 8; 18 November 1918, p. 5; 20 November 1918, p. 6; 25 November 1918, pp. 5, 7.

49. "Punishing the Criminals," *The New Statesman* 12 (16 November 1918):129-31.

50. "The Kaiser," *The Spectator* 121 (16 November 1918):542; "How Ought We to Deal With the Kaiser?" *The Spectator* 121 (7 December 1918):644-45.

51. Sir C. E. Callwell, *Field-Marshal Sir Henry Wilson: His Life and Diaries,* 2 vols. (London: Cassell & Co., 1927), 2:149.

52. Lord Curzon to David Lloyd George, 13 November 1918, Lord Beaverbrook, *Men and Power, 1917-1918* (London: Hutchinson, 1956), pp. 385-87.

53. David Lloyd George, "A Real League of Nations," *New York Times Current History* 8 (August 1918):351.

54. Dudley Sommer, *Haldane of Cloan: His Life and Times, 1856-1928* (London: George Allen & Unwin, 1960), p. 360.

55. Lloyd George's biographers provided little information about the reasons for his attitude. Without access to the minutes of the Imperial War Cabinet, they failed to emphasize the role of Lloyd George and, instead, stressed the role of Smith and Curzon too much. See Malcolm Thomson, *David Lloyd George: The Official Biography* (London: Hutchinson & Co., 1948), pp. 301-2; Thomas Jones, *Lloyd George* (Cambridge, Mass.: Harvard University Press, 1951), pp. 160-63; Frank Owen, *Tempestuous Journey: Lloyd George, His Life and Times* (London: Hutchinson & Co., 1954), pp. 498-502. Donald McCormick unfairly charged that Lloyd George sought a trial of the kaiser solely because of the election. See *The Mask of Merlin: A Critical Study of David Lloyd George* (London: Macdonald, 1963).

56. Winston Churchill, *The World Crisis, 1918-1928: The Aftermath* (New York: Charles Scribner's Sons, 1929), p. 30. Curzon's biographers found his attitude toward a trial of the kaiser inexplicable. Leonard Mosley, *The Glorious Fault: The Life of Lord Curzon* (New York: Harcourt, Brace & Co., 1960), was critical of Curzon. Earl of Ronaldshay, *The Life of Lord Curzon*, 3 vols. (London: Ernest Benn, 1928), said nothing at all about the subject.

57. Imperial War Cabinet meeting No. 37, November 20, 1918, CAB 23/43. Lloyd George's memoirs are seriously misleading about his role in this meeting. Every statement used in this paragraph is omitted from the otherwise extensively quoted minutes of this meeting in his memoirs. See *Memoirs of the Peace Conference*, 2 vols. (New Haven, Conn.: Yale University Press, 1939), 1:56-58.

58. Imperial War Cabinet meeting No. 37, November 20, 1918, CAB 23/43.

59. Beaverbrook, *Men and Power, 1917-1918*, p. 306; Stephen W. Roskill, *Hankey, Man of Secrets, 1919-1931* (London: Collins Press, 1972), p. 20.

60. Clive Wigram to Theo Russell, 10 January 1919, Lloyd George Papers (F/29/3/3).

61. Henry Borden, ed., *Robert Laird Borden: His Memoirs*, 2 vols. (New York: Macmillan Co., 1938), 2:869; Harold Nicolson, *King George the Fifth: His Life and Reign* (London: Constable & Co., 1952), p. 337.

62. Lord Maurice Hankey, *The Supreme Control at the Paris Peace Conference of 1919* (London: George Allen & Unwin, 1963), p. 13. See also Borden, *Robert Laird Borden*, 2:868.

63. Imperial War Cabinet meeting No. 37, November 20, 1918, CAB 23/43.

64. J. H. Morgan, the chairman of the Sub-Committee on Law, said that the attorney-general made clear that "the taking of proceedings *was* 'desirable.'" Morgan's recollection is wrong on several other points. See *Times*, 24 March 1932, p. 13.

65. Report of Special Sub-Committee on Law to law officers of the crown, 28 November 1918, "Interim Reports from the Committee of Enquiry into Breaches of Laws of War . . . 13 January 1919," pp. 95-99, CAB 24/72 (G.T. 6550).

66. Lloyd George, *Memoirs of Peace Conference*, 1:65. The official biography of Smith gives the false impression that his participation in this matter was limited to extricating the British from difficulty when the Netherlands refused to surrender the kaiser in early 1920. See Second Earl of Birkenhead, *The Life of F. E. Smith: First Earl of Birkenhead* (London: Eyre & Spottiswoode, 1960), pp. 340-42. Camp's *Glittering Prizes* is more complete.

67. Lloyd George misstated the facts in claiming as "worthy of note that those who expressed doubts at the first discussion were all present on this occasion and all now concurred in the Attorney-General's recommendation." See Lloyd George, *Memoirs of Peace Conference*, 1:65.

68. Imperial War Cabinet meeting No. 39, November 28, 1918, CAB 23/43.

69. War Office to Foreign Office, 27 December 1918, FO 371/3227 (213745/ 187616/18).

70. *Times*, 28 November 1918, p. 8.

71. Ibid., 29 November 1918, p. 9. See similar assessments in ibid., 2 December 1918, p. 9; 6 December 1918, p. 10.

72. Trevor Wilson, "The Coupon and the British General Election of 1918," *Journal of Modern History* 36 (March 1964):40.

73. "On Hanging the Kaiser," *The Nation* (London), 24 (7 December 1918):274- 75. *The Nation* (New York), 108 (11 January 1919):76-77, agreed.

74. "Bernard Shaw on Retaliation: A Plea Against Letting Clamor for the Personal Punishment of Germans Distract Attention from the Settlement of Europe," *Manchester Guardian*, reprinted in *Springfield Republican*, 7 December 1918, clipping sent by Joseph P. Tumulty to Woodrow Wilson, 10 December 1918, the Papers of Woodrow Wilson (5[B], Box 1, Peace Conference), Library of Congress, Washington, D.C. (hereafter cited as Wilson Papers); Margaret Cole, ed., *Beatrice Webb's Diaries, 1912-1924*, 2 vols. (London: Longmans, Green & Co., 1952), 1:139.

75. Ahlstrom, "British Public Opinion and the Versailles Conference," p. 118.

76. Kenneth O. Morgan, *Consensus and Disunity: The Lloyd George Coalition Government, 1918-1922* (Oxford: Clarendon Press, 1979), pp. 38-43. For comments of Arthur Henderson, Ramsay MacDonald, J. R. Clynes, Violet Markam, William S. Royce, Walter Runciman, and Sir John Simon, see Ahlstrom, "British Public Opinion and the Versailles Conference," p. 112; *Times*, 9 December 1918, p. 10; 11 December 1918, pp. 10, 12; 14 December 1918, p. 12; 30 November 1918, p. 10; 6 December 1918, p. 12.

77. *Times*, 9 December 1918, p. 12.

78. Ibid., 11 December 1918, p. 12.

79. Ibid., 14 December 1918, p. 12.

80. Ibid., 11 December 1918, p. 5.

81. Ibid., 2 December 1918, p. 10. Barnes was more moderate in later speeches. See ibid., 7 December 1918, p. 12.

82. Ibid., 5 December 1918, p. 12.

83. Statements of Dr. Christopher Addison, William Fisher, Sir Edward Carson, Sir Eric Geddes, Walter Long, Sir Alfred Mond, Lord Robert Cecil, and others in the *Times*, 29 November 1918, p. 10; 3 December, p. 10; 6 December, pp. 10, 12; 7 December, p. 12; 10 December, p. 10; 12 December, p. 10. For Cecil's numer-

ous speeches, see ibid., 26 November 1918, p. 8; 5 December, p. 5; 6 December, p. 12; 9 December, p. 10; 12 December, p. 12; 14 December, p. 12.

84. Ibid., 10 December 1918, p. 10; Stanley Salvidge, *Salvidge of Liverpool: Behind the Political Scene, 1890-1928* (London: Hodder & Stoughton, 1934), p. 169.

85. *Times*, 27 November 1918, p. 10; Churchill, *World Crisis: Aftermath*, pp. 28-29; Donald G. Boadle, *Winston Churchill and the German Question in British Foreign Policy, 1918-1922* (The Hague: Martinus Nijhoff, 1973), pp. 13, 16-18.

86. See Lloyd George's denials in the *Times*, 23 March 1932, p. 15; 24 March 1932, p. 13.

87. Ibid., 30 November 1918, p. 6.

88. Lord Bryce to Albert V. Dicey, 6 December 1918; Bryce to Dicey, 13 December 1918; Dicey to Bryce, 15 December 1918; Dicey to Bryce, 19 December 1918; Dicey to Bryce, 31 December 1918, Bryce Papers (4); Bryce to Theodore Roosevelt, 30 October 1918, Herbert A. L. Fisher, *James Bryce*, 2 vols. (New York: Macmillan Co., 1927), 2:196.

89. *Times*, 18 December 1918, p. 10; 30 November 1918, p. 6; 23 December 1918, p. 6.

90. Ibid., 3 December 1918, p. 3. See similar letters in ibid.: Lord Channing, 30 November, p. 6; A. H. Hastie, 2 December, p. 9; E. Ray Lankestor, 11 December, p. 9; J. S. Phillpotts, 14 December, p. 9; George Hamilton, 23 December, p. 6; J. Holland Rose, 17 December, p. 6; December 20, p. 3; December 27, p. 7.

91. Colonel Edward M. House to Wilson, 30 November 1918, Wilson Papers (5[C]).

92. House Diary, 5 December 1918, quoted in Charles Seymour, ed., *The Intimate Papers of Colonel House*, 4 vols. (Boston and New York: Houghton Mifflin Co., 1926-28), 4:242. For a similar description of Clemenceau's attitude, see Général Jean Mordacq, *Le Ministère Clemenceau: Journal d'un témoin*, 4 vols. (Paris: Librairie Plon, 1930-31), 3:28-29. Neither Clemenceau's memoirs nor the several biographies of him contain anything of value on this subject.

93. *Times*, 16 November 1918, p. 6.

94. Frank L. Polk to Wilson, 2 December 1918, with enclosure of French proposals for organization of peace conference, Wilson Papers (Letterbooks, Box 189). The printed version of this revised proposal is incomplete. See House to Robert Lansing, 21 November 1918, *FRUS: Paris Peace Conference, 1919*, 1:354.

95. *Le Matin*, 26 November 1918, p. 1; *Times*, 22 November 1918, p. 8.

96. *New York Times*, 20 November 1918, p. 3; *Times*, 11 November 1918, p. 7.

97. *Le Matin*, 1 December 1918, p. 2.

98. Ibid., 14 November 1918, p. 1.

99. *Times*, 19 November 1918, p. 5; 23 November 1918, p. 6.

100. Read, *Atrocity Propaganda*, p. 249; *Times*, 2 December 1918, p. 8.

101. Inter-Allied Conference meeting (I.C. 98), December 2, 1918, at 11 a.m., CAB 28/5.

102. Maxime Weygand, *Mémoires*, 3 vols. (Paris: Flammarion, 1950-57), 2:33.

103. Inter-Allied Conference meeting (I.C. 98), December 2, 1918, at 11 a.m., CAB 28/5. Orlando's memoirs are misleading. He claimed to have opposed a trial

of the kaiser. See Vittorio Orlando, *Memorie (1915-1919)*, ed. Rodolfo Mosca (Milan: Rizzoli, 1960), pp. 487-97.

104. Inter-Allied Conference meetings (I.C. 98 and 99), December 2, 1918, at 11 a.m. and 4 p.m., CAB 28/5.

105. British Embassy to State Department, 3 December 1918, United States, Department of State, *Papers Relating to the Foreign Relations of the United States, 1919*, 2 vols. (Washington, D.C.: United States Government Printing Office, 1934), 2:653-54.

CHAPTER 5

1. H. J. Scheffer, *November 1918: Journaal van een Revolutie die niet Doorging* (Amsterdam: Uitgeverij de Arbeiderspers, 1968), pp. 60-63; No. 194, Friedrich Rosen to Friedrich Ebert, 17 November 1918, The Netherlands, Commissee voor Rijks Geschiedkundige Publicatiën, *Bescheiden Betreffende de Buitenlandse Politiek van Nederland, 1848-1919 . . . Achtste Deel, Buitenlandse Bronnen, 1917-1919*, ed. C. Smit (The Hague: Martinus Nijhoff, 1973), 145:214-15 (hereafter cited as *Buitenlandse Politiek van Nederland, Buitenlandse Bronnen, 1917-1919*). See also Alan Palmer, *The Kaiser: Warlord of the Second Reich* (New York: Charles Scribner's Sons, 1978), pp. 212-13. Queen Wilhelmina revealed little in her memoirs.

2. Klaus W. Jonas, *The Life of Crown Prince William*, trans. Charles W. Bangert (London: Routledge & Kegan Paul, 1961), pp. 124-31.

3. Whether the kaiser was invited to the Netherlands is a question that persists. Scheffer's *November 1918*, pp. 266-76, made a circumstantial case that Queen Wilhelmina and van Karnebeek, without the knowledge of other Dutch leaders, did secretly invite him.

4. Henri Allizé to Stephen Pinchon, No. 716, November 11, 1918, La Série Europe, 1918-1929, Allemagne, vol. 25, "Guillaume II—Le Kronprinz, septembre 1918-mai 1919," Archives des Affaires Étrangères, Ministère des Affaires Étrangères, Quai d'Orsay, Paris (hereafter cited as MAE). See also in the above collection numerous other despatches during November and December from the French ambassador at The Hague. For British reports, see No. 564, De Fleuriau to Arthur Balfour, 25 November 1918, and No. 568, Sir Walter Townley to Balfour, 1 December 1918, *Buitenlandse Politiek van Nederland, Buitenlandse Bronnen, 1917-1919*, 145:627, 629.

5. No. 775, René de Marees van Swinderen to Herman A. van Karnebeek, 27 November 1918, The Netherlands, Commissee voor Rijks Geschiedkundige Publicatiën, *Bescheiden Betreffende de Buitenlandse Politiek van Nederland, 1848-1919 . . . Vijfde Deel, 1917-1919*, ed. C. Smit (The Hague: Martinus Nijhoff, 1964), 117:729 (hereafter cited as *Buitenlandse Politiek van Nederland, 1917-1919*). See also in the above volume: No. 747, pp. 761-62; No. 746, pp. 741-42; No. 748, pp. 743-44; No. 782, pp. 768-69; No. 784, p. 770; No. 796, p. 782; No. 820, pp. 800-801; No. 755, pp. 748-49.

6. Townley to Balfour, 22 November 1918, FO 371/3256 (265/197010/W29); No. 787, van Karnebeek Diary, 3 December 1918, *Buitenlandse Politiek van Nederland, 1917-1919*, 117:771-72.

7. No. 795, Heldring Diary, 8 December 1918, *Buitenlandse Politiek van Nederland, 1917-1919*, 117:780-81.

8. For this speech, see "Holland and the Refugee Ex-Kaiser," *New York Times Current History* 9 (January 1919):58; Townley to Balfour, 11 December 1918, 13 December 1918, FO 371/3227 (204162/187616/18).

9. Balfour to Townley, 14 December 1918, FO 371/3227 (207705/187616/18).

10. Memorandum by Sir L. Worthington-Evans of a conversation with Hendrikus Colijn, 18 December 1918, CAB 24/72 (G.T. 6523).

11. No. 827, Heldring Diary, 19 December 1918, *Buitenlandse Politiek van Nederland, 1917-1919*, 117: 809-10.

12. No. 869, Ernst Heldring to van Karnebeek, 5 January 1919, ibid., pp. 861-62.

13. No. 791, Minutes of the Council of Ministers, 6 December 1918, ibid., p. 777; No. 793, Minutes of an Extraordinary Council of Ministers, 7 December 1918, ibid., p. 778.

14. No. 801, Heldring Diary, 10 December 1918, ibid., p. 786.

15. No. 824, de Marees van Swinderen to van Karnebeek, 17 December 1918, ibid., pp. 805-6.

16. No. 826, de Marees van Swinderen to van Karnebeek, 18 December 1918, ibid., p. 808.

17. No. 1041, de Marees van Swinderen to van Karnebeek, 8 May 1919, ibid., pp. 1052-53.

18. Council of Ten meeting, 13 January 1919, at 4 p.m., *FRUS: Paris Peace Conference, 1919*, 3:536.

19. Council of Ten meeting, 17 January 1919, at 3 p.m., ibid., pp. 606-7; Preliminary Peace Conference, Protocol No. 1, Session of 18 January 1919, ibid., p. 169.

20. Council of Ten meeting, 23 January 1919, at 10:30 a.m., ibid., pp. 699-703; Preliminary Peace Conference, Protocol No. 2, Plenary Session of 25 January 1919, ibid., pp. 177-93, 202.

21. Mineitero Adatci and Édouard Rolin-Jaequemyns.

22. Rolin-Jaequemyns, James Brown Scott, and Albert de Lapradelle, who was the commission's secretary-general.

23. Rolin-Jaequemyns—*Revue de Droit International et de Législation Comparée;* Lapradelle—*Revue de Droit International;* and Scott—*American Journal of International Law.*

24. Daniel M. Smith, *Robert Lansing and American Neutrality, 1914-1917* (Berkeley and Los Angeles, Calif.: University of California Press, 1958), pp. 1-2.

25. George A. Finch, "James Brown Scott, 1866-1943," *American Journal of International Law* 38 (April 1944):183-217.

26. "Baron Édouard Rolin-Jaequemyns," *The British Year Book of International Law* 18 (1937):156-57.

27. Rudolf Holsti, "Nicolas Politis," *American Journal of International Law* 36 (July 1942):475-79.

28. James Brown Scott, "The Trial of the Kaiser," in *What Really Happened at Paris*, ed. Colonel E. M. House and Charles Seymour (New York: Charles Scribner's Sons, 1921), p. 480.

29. Lansing to Polk, 14 March 1919, Lansing Papers, Princeton (File VII, Personal Correspondence, 1916-1919).

30. American Peace Commission meeting, 5 March 1919, *FRUS: Paris Peace Conference, 1919*, 11:94.

31. American Peace Commission meeting, 4 March 1919, *FRUS: Paris Peace Conference, 1919*, 11:92. See also Henry White to John Campbell White, 26 June 1919, White Papers (Family Correspondence, Box 10); Tasker Bliss to Mrs. Bliss, 19 March 1919, the Papers of Tasker H. Bliss (Personal File, Box 66), Library of Congress, Washington, D.C. (hereafter cited as Bliss Papers).

32. Robert Lansing to Frank L. Polk, 14 March 1919, Lansing Papers, Princeton (File VII, Personal Correspondence, 1916-1919).

33. This group made three reports totaling 472 pages. See the first report of 13 January 1919, CAB 24/72 (G.T. 6550); the second report of 3 June 1919, CAB 24/85 (G.T. 7806); the third report of 26 February 1920, CAB 24/111 (G.P. 1813). The Americans hurriedly prepared four short memoranda on war crimes punishment. See Document 212 by David Hunter Miller and James Brown Scott; Document 213 by George A. Finch; Document 214 by Manley O. Hudson; Document 216 by James T. Shotwell, in David Hunter Miller, *My Diary at the Conference of Paris With Documents*, 21 vols. (New York: Privately Printed by Appeal Printing Co., 1924), 3:456-526, 4:1-3.

34. Minutes of the first meeting, 3 February 1919, at 3 p.m., "Commission on the Responsibility of the Authors of the War and on the Enforcement of Penalties: Minutes of Meetings of the Commission," pp. 1-4. This document is found in the Papers of Frank L. Polk (Drawer 76), Yale University Library, New Haven, Conn. (hereafter cited as "Commission on Responsibility Minutes," Polk Papers). This document contains only the minutes of plenary sessions, not the minutes of subcommittees. A French documentary series contains both sets of minutes. I have used both sets where necessary.

35. Sir Ernest Pollock to Lloyd George, 7 February 1919, Lloyd George Papers (F/27/1/1).

36. Minutes of the second meeting, 8 February 1919, at 11:30 a.m., "Commission on Responsibility Minutes," pp. 19-24, Polk Papers.

37. Pollock to Balfour, 8 February 1919, the Papers of Lord Hanworth (Sir Ernest Pollock), Bodleian Library, Oxford University, Oxford (hereafter cited as Hanworth Papers). Council of Ten meeting, 10 February 1919, at 3 p.m., *FRUS: Paris Peace Conference, 1919*, 3:953-54.

38. Commission on the League of Nations meeting, 10 February 1919, David Hunter Miller, *The Drafting of the Covenant*, 2 vols. (New York and London: G. P. Putnam's Sons, 1928), 2:282; Commission on the League of Nations meeting, 13 February 1919, in Miller, *The Drafting of the Covenant*, 2:298-99. The French draft for an international court is on p. 406.

39. Recent scholarship on the peace conference suggests that British and American leaders did not appreciate the magnitude of the "German problem" and should have been more supportive of French plans to constrain German expansionism. See Lloyd

E. Ambrosius, "Wilson, Clemenceau and the German Problem at the Paris Peace Conference of 1919," *Rocky Mountain Social Science Journal* 12 (April 1975):69-80; Walter A. McDougall, "Political Economy versus National Sovereignty: French Structures for German Economic Integration after Versailles," *Journal of Modern History* 51 (March 1979): 4-23.

40. Ernst Fraenkel, *Military Occupation and the Rule of Law: Occupation Government in the Rhineland, 1918-1923* (New York: Oxford University Press, 1944), pp. 55-62.

41. R. H. Gibson and Maurice Prendergast, *The German Submarine War, 1914-1918* (New York: Richard R. Smith, 1931), pp. 288-89, 305; *New York Times*, 11 May 1919, p. 20.

42. See chapter 9 for the Turks and the Bulgarian. At least five Germans were imprisoned at Malta. See Admiral John de Robeck to Lord Curzon, 11 March 1920, FO 371/5089 (E2293/37/44).

43. Friedrich Grimm, *Politische Justiz, die Krankheit unserer Zeit: 40 Jahre Dienst am Recht* (Bonn, W. Ger.: Verlag Bonner Universitäts-Buchdruckerai, 1953), pp. 38-41; Fraenkel, *Military Occupation and the Rule of Law*, pp. 59-60.

44. William Bishop et al., "Judicial Decisions: The Case Against Hermann Roechling and Others," *American Journal of International Law* 43 (January 1949):191-93.

45. For the minutes of this subcommittee, see La Documentation Internationale, *La Paix de Versailles*, vol. 3: *Responsabilités des auteurs de la guerre et sanctions*, ed. Albert de Lapradelle, 12 vols. (Paris: Les Éditions Internationales, 1929-39), pp. 235-60 (hereafter cited as *La Paix de Versailles*).

46. For the report of the subcommittee as incorporated in the final report of the commission, see Carnegie Endowment for International Peace, *Violations of the Laws and Customs of War: Report of the Majority and Dissenting Reports of the American and Japanese Members of the Commission on Responsibilities at the Conference of Paris, 1919*, Pamphlet No. 32 (Oxford: At the Clarendon Press, 1919), pp. 18-21, 28-57 (hereafter cited as *Violations of the Laws and Customs of War*).

47. Hajo Holborn, "Diplomats and Diplomacy in the Early Weimar Republic," in *The Diplomats, 1919-1939*, ed. Gordon A. Craig and Felix Gilbert, 2 vols. (1953; reprint ed., New York: Atheneum, 1965), 1:142-45; Philip Mason Burnett, *Reparations at the Paris Peace Conference*, 2 vols. (New York: Columbia University Press, 1940), 1:x. For the most complete study of the connection between articles 227 and 231 and the concept of aggression, see Fritz Dickmann, "Die Kriegsschuldfrage auf der Friedenskonferenz von Paris, 1919," *Historische Zeitschrift* 197 (August 1963):1-101.

48. For minutes of this subcommittee's meetings, see *La Paix de Versailles*, 3:263-79.

49. Fernand Larnaude and Albert de Lapradelle, "Examen de la responsabilité pénale de l'empereur Guillaume II d'Allemagne," *Journal du Droit International* 46 (1919):131-59. A copy of this study was given to all delegations at the first plenary session of the peace conference. See 18 January 1919, *FRUS: Paris Peace Conference, 1919*, 3:169.

50. First meeting of the subcommittee on the responsibility for the war, 17 February 1919, *La Paix de Versailles*, 3:263-66.

51. Philip Kerr to David Lloyd George, 28 February 1919, Lloyd George Papers

(F/89/2/34); Kerr to Lloyd George, 1 March 1919, Lloyd George Papers (F/89/2/36); Kerr to Lloyd George, 3 March 1919, Lloyd George Papers (F/89/2/38).

52. Council of Four meeting, 2 April 1919, at 4 p.m., Paul Mantoux, *Paris Peace Conference, 1919: Proceedings of the Council of Four (March 24-April 18)*, trans. John Boardman Whitton (Geneva: Institut universitaire de hautes études inter- nationales, 1964), p. 90 (hereafter cited as *Proceedings of the Council of Four*).

53. *Violations of the Laws and Customs of War*, pp. 22-23.

54. For minutes of this subcommittee's meetings, see *La Paix de Versailles*, 3:295-324.

55. 18 February 1919, ibid., pp. 295-302.

56. 21 February 1919, ibid., pp. 303-9.

57. 25 February 1919, ibid., pp. 312-24.

58. Minutes of the third meeting, 12 March 1919, at 11 a.m., "Commission on Responsibility Minutes," pp. 37-39, Polk Papers; Minutes of the fourth meeting, 13 March 1919, at 10:30 a.m., "Commission on Responsibility Minutes," pp. 57-61, Polk Papers.

59. Minutes of the fourth meeting, 13 March 1919, at 10:30 a.m., "Commission on Responsibility Minutes," p. 38, Polk Papers.

60. Smith, *Robert Lansing*, pp. 6-8.

61. "Commission on Responsibility Minutes," pp. 59-60, Polk Papers.

62. Ibid., pp. 67-68.

63. Lansing Desk Diary, 15 March 1919.

64. "Commission on Responsibility Minutes," pp. 69-72, Polk Papers. For the dissenting Japanese memorandum on immunity of heads of state, see *Violations of the Laws and Customs of War*, p. 65.

65. *Violations of the Laws and Customs of War*, pp. 4-27. For the dissenting report, see pp. 58-79.

66. Ibid.

67. Quincy Wright, "The Legal Liability of the Kaiser," *The American Political Science Review* 13 (February 1919):120-28; James W. Garner, "Punishment of Offenders Against the Laws and Customs of War," *American Journal of International Law* 14 (January 1920):70-94. See also R. Floyd Clarke, "The Status of William Hohenzollern, Kaiser of Germany, Under International Law," *American Law Review* 53 (May-June 1919):401-26.

68. Pollock to Lloyd George, 29 March 1919, Lloyd George Papers (F/27/1/2).

69. Lansing to Wilson, 4 April 1919, United States, Department of State, Papers of the American Commission to Negotiate Peace, Record Group 256, vol. 116 (F.W. 181.1202/7), National Archives, Washington, D.C.

70. The Department of State provided Wilson with a summary of American public reaction to the report of the Commission on Responsibility. See Polk to American Peace Commission, 10 April 1919, Wilson Papers (Series 5[B], Box 27). See also "How America Would Punish Wilhelm," *Literary Digest* 61 (26 April 1919): 13. For Wilson's regular reading of *Springfield Republican*, see Arthur S. Link, *Woodrow Wilson and the Progressive Era: 1910-1917* (New York: Harper & Row, Harper Torchbooks, 1954), p. 288.

71. Paul Birdsall, *Versailles Twenty Years After* (New York: Reynal & Hitch-

cock, 1941), p. 167; Thomas A. Bailey, *Woodrow Wilson and the Lost Peace* (1944; reprint ed., Chicago: Quadrangle Books, 1963), pp. 222-23.

72. For the clearest explanation of Wilson's role in peacemaking and his ambivalence about punishing Germany, see N. Gordon Levin, Jr., *Woodrow Wilson and World Politics: America's Response to War and Revolution* (New York: Oxford University Press Paperback, 1970), pp. 123-82.

73. Council of Four meeting, 1 April 1919, at 4 p.m., *Proceedings of the Council of Four*, p. 83.

74. Council of Four meeting, 2 April 1919, at 4 p.m., ibid., pp. 90-93.

75. Lloyd George received a telegram on April 8, 1919, from 370 members of Parliament asking assurances that he would fulfill his election pledges. See Henry Wickham Steed, *Through Thirty Years, 1892-1922: A Personal Narrative*, 2 vols. (Garden City, N.Y.: Doubleday, Page & Co., 1924), 2:320-21.

76. Seth P. Tillman, *Anglo-American Relations at the Paris Peace Conference of 1919* (Princeton, N.J.: Princeton University Press, 1961), pp. 184-89, 287-97.

77. Tillman did not directly link these decisions but did conclude that without Wilson's compromise the differences over the kaiser's trial "might have generated a serious Anglo-American controversy." See ibid., pp. 311-14. For a different perspective arguing that Wilson's compromises were to placate the French, see Inga Floto, *Colonel House in Paris: A Study of American Policy at the Paris Peace Conference, 1919* (Aarhus, Denmark: Universitetsforlaget, 1973), pp. 205-8.

78. Council of Four meeting, 8 April 1919, at 3 p.m., *Proceedings of the Council of Four*, pp. 144-51.

79. Pierre Miquel, *La Paix de Versailles et l'opinion publique française* (Paris: Flammarion, 1972), pp. 236-38.

80. Council of Four meeting, 8 April 1919, at 3 p.m., *Proceedings of the Council of Four*, pp. 144-51.

81. Lansing Desk Diary, 8 April 1919; Lansing to Wilson, 8 April 1919, Wilson Papers (Series 5[B], Box 26); Ephraim K. Smith, Jr., "Robert Lansing and the Paris Peace Conference (Ph.D. diss., The Johns Hopkins University, 1972), pp. 488-89.

82. Council of Four meeting, 9 April 1919, at 11 a.m., *Proceedings of the Council of Four*, pp. 153-54.

83. Arthur S. Link, *Woodrow Wilson, Revolution, War, and Peace* (Arlington Heights, Ill.: AHM Publishing Corp., 1979), p. 89.

84. Council of Ten meeting, 16 April 1919, at 4 p.m., *FRUS: Paris Peace Conference, 1919*, 4:482.

85. Minutes of the British Empire Delegation at Paris, 28 April 1919, at 11 a.m., CAB 29/28. Smuts bombarded Lloyd George with protests on this issue throughout the conference. See Jan Smuts to Lloyd George, 26 March 1919; 5 May 1919; 22 May 1919, in William Hancock and Jean van der Poel, eds., *Selections from the Smuts Papers, November 1918-August 1919* (London: Cambridge University Press, 1966), 4:83-87, 149, 186-87. Sir Maurice Hankey, secretary to the Cabinet, also warned Lloyd George against making impossible demands for war crimes punishment. See Sir Maurice Hankey to Lloyd George, 19 March 1919, Lloyd George Papers (F/23/4/39). George Barnes also indicated his opposition. See George Barnes to Lloyd George, 6 May 1919, Lloyd George Papers (F/4/3/14).

86. Lansing Desk Diary, 28 April 1919; Council of Four meeting, 5 May 1919, at 11 a.m., *FRUS: Paris Peace Conference, 1919*, 5:470-71.

87. Howard Elcock, *Portrait of a Decision: The Council of Four and the Treaty of Versailles* (London: Eyre Methuen, 1972), p. 247.

88. Council of Four meeting, 1 May 1919, at 11 a.m., *FRUS: Paris Peace Conference, 1919*, 5:389-90.

89. Council of Four meeting, 28 June 1919, at 5 p.m., ibid., 6:755-56; Appendix I to Council of Four meeting, 25 June 1919, at 4 p.m., ibid., p. 679. The British and French on several occasions advanced proposals to use hostages. See Council of Five meeting, 26 April 1919, at 3 p.m., ibid., 4:635-37; Council of Four meeting, 29 April 1919, at 4 p.m., ibid., 5:338.

90. Knowlton L. Ames, Jr., *Berlin After the Armistice* (Privately Printed, 1919), pp. 81-82, 93. See also German press extracts and comments of radical leaders reprinted in *New York Times*, 27 November 1918, p. 1; 28 November 1918, p. 1; 4 December 1918, p. 4; 15 May 1919, p. 3; *Times*, 5 March 1919, p. 6; 8 March 1919, p. 3.

91. S. William Halperin, *Germany Tried Democracy: A Political History of the Reich from 1918 to 1933* (1946; reprint ed., New York: W. W. Norton & Co., 1965), pp. 95-106; William H. Maehl, "The German Socialists and the Foreign Policy of the Reich, 1917-1922" (Ph.D. diss., University of Chicago, 1947), pp. 190-91.

92. Hans Sulzer to Lansing, 2 December 1918, *FRUS: Paris Peace Conference, 1919*, 2:71-72; William Phillips to Sulzer, 1 February 1919, *FRUS: Paris Peace Conference, 1919*, 2:73-74.

93. Germany, Nationalversammlung, *Verhandlungen der Verfassunggebenden Deutsche Nationalversammlung* 327 (13 March-9 July 1919):809-10, 836-62, 924, 936-42.

94. No. 20, Cabinet meeting, 22 March 1919, at 11:30 a.m., Hagen Schulze, ed., *Akten der Reichskanzlei Weimarer Republik: Das Kabinett Scheidemann 13. Februar bis 20. Juni 1919* (Boppard, W. Ger.: Harald Boldt Verlag, 1971), pp. 85-91. See also in Schulze, ed., *Akten der Reichskanzlei Weimarer Republik:* No. 10a, Cabinet meeting, 12 March 1919, at 4 p.m., p. 40; No. 22, Cabinet meeting, 25 March 1919, at 5 p.m., pp. 99-100; No. 38, Cabinet meeting, 8 April 1919, at 8 p.m., pp. 146-49; No. 39, Cabinet meeting, 10 April 1919, at 6 p.m., p. 152; No. 40, Cabinet meeting, 11 April 1919, at 4:30 p.m., p. 155; No. 49, Instructions for German peace delegation, 21 April 1919, pp. 203-4; No. 102, Cabinet meeting, 6 June 1919, at 11 a.m., pp. 426-27. Udo Wengst, *Graf Brockdorff-Rantzau und die Aussenpolitischen Anfänge der Weimarer Republick* (Bern, Switz.: Herbert Lang; Frankfurt, W. Ger.: Peter Lang, 1973), pp. 57, 70-71.

95. Langwerth von Simmern to German Peace Delegation, 30 April 1919, Germany, Auswärtiges Amt, United States National Archives Microfilm Publication of German Foreign Ministry Archives, Washington, D.C., T-120, roll 2404, frames E213223-24 (hereafter cited as AA [microfilm publication number/roll number/ frame number]). See also Langwerth to German Peace Delegation, 1 May 1919, T-120/2404/E213221-22; Wedel to Langwerth, 18 June 1919, T-120/2404/E213424-25.

96. Document 15, Memorandum on the destruction of industry in occupied France, 11 March 1919, Alma Luckau, *The German Delegation at the Paris Peace Conference* (New York: Columbia University Press, 1941), pp. 177-81.

97. *Times,* 16 December 1918, p. 7; General Neill Malcolm to Lord Kilmarnock, 26 May 1920, Great Britain, Foreign Office, *Documents on British Foreign Policy, 1919-1939,* first series, ed. E. L. Woodward et al., 18 vols. (London: His Majesty's Stationery Office, 1947-72), 9:740. The reports of this commission and similar material can be found in Germany, Reichstag, *Das Völkerrecht im Weltkreig,* ed. Eugen Fischer, 5 vols. (Berlin: Deutsche Verlangsgesellschafts für Politik und Geschichte, 1927).

98. Luckau, *German Delegation at Paris,* pp. 220-23.

99. Ibid., pp. 94-100.

100. Document 36, German note of 10 May 1919 on repatriation of prisoners of war and interned civilians, ibid., p. 240.

101. Document 43, Allied note of 20 May 1919 on prisoners of war, ibid., pp. 252-53.

102. Document 54, German note of 28 May 1919 on prisoners of war and interned civilians, ibid., pp. 300-301.

103. Ibid., pp. 81-84.

104. Document 53, German note of 28 May 1919 on the responsibility of the authors of the war, ibid., pp. 288-99.

105. Document 57, German counterproposals of 29 May 1919, ibid., pp. 369-71.

106. Council of Four meeting, 12 June 1919, at 11 a.m., *FRUS: Paris Peace Conference, 1919,* 6:326-27.

107. Document 60, Allied reply to German counterproposals, 16 June 1919, Luckau, *German Delegation at Paris,* pp. 411-14.

108. Marianne Weber, *Max Weber: Ein Lebensbild* (Heidelberg, W. Ger.: Verlag Lambert Schneider, 1950), pp. 700-703; Wolfgang J. Mommsen, *Max Weber und die Deutsche Politik, 1890-1920* (Tübingen, W. Ger.: J. C. B. Mohr, 1959), pp. 315-18.

109. Margarethe Ludendorff, *My Married Life With Ludendorff,* trans. Raglan Somerset (London: Hutchinson & Co., 1930), pp. 176-78; Donald Goodspeed, *Ludendorff: Genius of World War I* (Boston: Houghton Mifflin Co., 1966), pp. 276-79.

110. Weber, *Max Weber,* pp. 700-703; Mommsen, *Max Weber,* pp. 315-18.

111. For a full account of this crisis, see Luckau, *German Delegation at Paris,* pp. 104-12; Alma Luckau, "Unconditional Acceptance of the Treaty of Versailles By the German Government, June 22-28, 1919," *Journal of Modern History* 18 (September 1945):215-20.

112. Klaus Epstein, *Matthias Erzberger and the Dilemma of German Democracy* (Princeton, N.J.: Princeton University Press, 1959), pp. 314-23.

113. Philip Scheidemann, *Memoirs of a Social Democrat,* trans. J. E. Mitchell, 2 vols. (London: Hodder & Stoughton, 1929), 2:631.

114. Gustav Noske, *Von Kiel bis Kapp; zur Geschichte der Deutschen Revolution* (Berlin, Ger.: Verlag für Politik und Wirtschaft, 1920), pp. 151-55; John W. Wheeler-Bennett, *The Nemesis of Power: The German Army in Politics, 1918-1945* (New York: St. Martin's Press, 1954), pp. 54-56; Gordon A. Craig, *The Politics of the Prussian Army, 1640-1945* (New York: Oxford University Press, 1955), pp. 370-73; F. L. Carsten, *The Reichswehr and Politics, 1918 to 1933* (London:

Oxford University Press, 1966), pp. 40-42. See also the warning of the chief of the German navy, Admiral von Trotha, to President Ebert in No. 115, Admiral von Trotha to Ebert, 19 June 1919, Schulze, *Akten der Reichskanzlei: Das Kabinett Scheidemann*, pp. 492-93.

115. Epstein, *Matthias Erzberger*, pp. 318-19.

116. Document 63, German note of 22 June 1919, Luckau, *German Delegation at Paris*, pp. 480-81.

117. Hugh Gaisford to Lord Curzon, 23 June 1919, with enclosure of letter from Cardinal Gasparri, 22 June 1919, FO 371/4271 (95832/9019/W39).

118. Notebook (Diary), 22 June 1919, the Papers of Ray Stannard Baker (Box 125), Library of Congress, Washington, D.C.

119. Council of Four meeting, 22 June 1919, at 7:15 p.m., *FRUS: Paris Peace Conference, 1919*, 6:605-6.

120. Wheeler-Bennett, *Nemesis of Power*, pp. 57-59; Document 66, German note of 23 June 1919, Luckau, *German Delegation at Paris*, p. 482.

CHAPTER 6

1. Joachim von Kürenberg, *The Kaiser: A Life of Wilhelm II, Last Emperor of Germany*, trans. H. T. Russell and Herta Hagen (New York: Simon & Schuster, 1955),pp. 379-82.

2. Sigurd von Ilsemann, *Der Kaiser in Holland: Aufzeichnungen des Letzten Flügeladjutanten Kaiser Wilhelms II*, ed. Harald von Koenigswald, 2 vols. (Munich, W. Ger.: Biederstein Verlag, 1967), 1:68-70; No. 814, Minutes of a Council of Ministers, 13 December 1918, *Buitenlandse Politiek van Nederland, 1917-1919*, 117:796; Tyler Whittle, *The Last Kaiser: A Biography of Wilhelm II, German Emperor and King of Prussia* (New York: New York Times Books, 1977), pp. 311-12.

3. Von Ilsemann, *Kaiser*, 1:70-71. Friedrich Rosen's memoirs do not reveal much about his activities in helping the kaiser.

4. Ibid., pp. 70-72.

5. Ibid., pp. 72-76.

6. *New York Times*, 1 February 1919, p. 3; 4 June 1919, p. 1.

7. Von Ilsemann, *Kaiser*, 1:74, 77-78.

8. Ibid., p. 69; von Kürenberg, *Kaiser*, p. 381.

9. Von Ilsemann, *Kaiser*, 1:99-100. See also the kaiser's comments on a proposed tribunal in Kaiser Wilhelm II, *The Kaiser's Memoirs*, trans. Thomas R. Ybarra (New York and London: Harper & Bros., 1922), pp. 292-95.

10. Von Ilsemann, *Kaiser*, 1:91, 101; No. 932, Van Lijnden van Sandenburg to Herman A. van Karnebeek, 14 February 1919, *Buitenlandse Politiek van Nederland, 1917-1919*, 117:935-37; *New York Times*, 25 February 1919, p. 3.

11. Von Ilsemann, *Kaiser*, 1:77-79. For reports of the kaiser's illness, see *New York Times* on the following dates: 3 January 1919, p. 1; 5 January, p. 3; 6 January, p. 3; 10 January, p. 7; 15 January, p. 3; 17 January, p. 5; 19 January, p. 3; 20 January, p. 1; 20 February, p. 1; 28 February, p. 3. See also reports in *Times:* 6 January 1919, p. 8; 28 February, p. 9; 27 March, p. 12.

12. William T. Alderson, ed., "The Attempt to Capture the Kaiser By Luke

Lea," *Tennessee Historical Quarterly* 20 (September 1961):222-61; T. H. Alexander, "They Tried to Kidnap the Kaiser and Brought Back an Ash Tray," *The Saturday Evening Post* 210 (23 October 1937):5-7, 84-89; *New York Times*, 12 January 1919, p. 3; John W. Garrett to Acting Secretary of State, *FRUS: Paris Peace Conference, 1919*, 2:85-87; von Kürenberg, *Kaiser*, pp. 387-90; von Ilsemann, *Kaiser*, 1:85-86.

13. Council of Four meeting, 8 April 1919, at 3 p.m., *Proceedings of the Council of Four*, p. 150. For a legal analysis of the kaiser's crime and extradition, see Bernabe Africa, *Political Offences in Extradition* (Manila, Philippines: Benipay Press, 1926), pp. 136-47.

14. Council of Four meeting, 25 June 1919, at 4 p.m., *FRUS: Paris Peace Conference, 1919*, 6:677.

15. For reports of the expected attempt of the kaiser to escape, see Sir Walter Townley to Lord Curzon, 27 June 1919, FO 371/4271 (94780/9019/W39); American Military Attaché at The Hague to American Peace Commission, 25-26 June 1919, Bliss Papers (Office File, Peace Conference, Box 259); Fernand Prevost to Stephen Pinchon, Nos. 278, 279, and 280, June 27, 1919, La Série Europe, 1918-1929, Allemagne, vol. 26, "Guillaume II—Le Kronprinz, juin 1919-janvier 1921," MAE.

16. Council of Four meeting, 26 June 1919, at 11 a.m., *FRUS: Paris Peace Conference, 1919*, 6:699-700;26 June 1919, at 4 p. m., p. 710; 27 June 1919, at 12 noon, p. 721; 28 June 1919, at 11 a.m., p. 740; Great Britain, Foreign Office, *Documents on British Foreign Policy, 1919-1939*, first series, ed. E. L. Woodward et al., 18 vols. (London: His Majesty's Stationery Office, 1947-72), 5:8-9.

17. Arnold Robertson to Arthur Balfour, 10 July 1919, *Documents on British Foreign Policy*, first series, 5:22-23.

18. Robertson to Theophilus Russell, 3 July 1919, ibid., pp. 12-13; Frank Gunther to Acting Secretary of State at Paris, 1 July 1919, United States, Department of State, *Papers Relating to the Foreign Relations of the United States, 1919*, 2 vols. (Washington, D.C.: United States Government Printing Office, 1934), 2:645-55.

19. Frank Gunther to Henry White, 21 July 1919, White Papers (Peace Conference File, Box 44). See also Gunther to Acting Secretary of State at Paris, 21 July 1919, *Foreign Relations of the United States, 1919*, 2:656.

20. James Brown Scott, "The Trial of the Kaiser," in *What Really Happened at Paris*, ed. Colonel E. M. House and Charles Seymour (New York: Charles Scribner's Sons, 1921), pp. 240-41; Arnold J. Toynbee, "The Main Features in the Landscape," in Lord Riddell et al., *The Treaty of Versailles and After* (New York: Oxford University Press, 1935), pp. 54-55.

21. Council of Four meeting, 25 June 1919, at 4 p.m., *FRUS: Paris Peace Conference, 1919*, 6:670-71; 26 June 1919, at 11 a.m., p. 701.

22. Great Britain, House of Commons, *Parliamentary Debates* 117 (1919): 1216-17.

23. *New York Times*, 4 July 1919, p. 1; *Times*, 4 July 1919, p. 15; 9 July 1919, p. 13.

24. *Times*, 9 July 1919, p. 13. There were letters to the editor on this subject almost every day from July 7 to 15, and a majority of them opposed a trial of the kaiser.

25. "Politics and Affairs: The Kaiser 'Stunt,' " *The Nation* (London), 25 (12 July 1919):436. See also "The Trial of the Kaiser," *The New Statesman* 13 (12 July 1919):360-61.

26. "The Arraignment of the Kaiser," *The Spectator* 123 (12 July 1919):41-42; "The No-Martyr Argument," *The Spectator* 123 (12 July 1919):42-43; "The Trial of the Kaiser," *Times*, 16 July 1919, p. 13. Some letters in the *Times* approved Lloyd George's plans. See especially the letter of the poet Alfred Noyes, 17 July 1919, p. 8.

27. See quotations from the *Daily Mail* reprinted in *New York Times*, 4 July 1919, p. 1.

28. *Parliamentary Debates*, Commons, 118 (1919):955-1051; Great Britain Parliament, House of Lords, *Parliamentary Debates* 35 (1919):1010-11, 1021-22.

29. Quoted in *New York Times*, 6 July 1919, p. 5.

30. Stephen W. Roskill, *Hankey, Man of Secrets, 1919-1931*, 2 vols. (London: Collins Press, 1972), 2:99, 110. The official biography, Harold Nicolson's *King George the Fifth: His Life and Reign* (London: Constable & Co., 1952), pp. 336-38, does not reveal much about the king's influence.

31. Lord Beaverbrook, *Men and Power, 1917-1918* (London: Hutchinson, 1956), p. 307. See also Leonard Mosley, *The Glorious Fault: The Life of Lord Curzon* (New York: Harcourt, Brace & Co., 1960), pp. 214-16.

32. The reason why few British officials knew of the plan to hold the trial at London was because Lloyd George secured Clemenceau's approval of the idea through a hurried telephone call to Paris, shortly before Lloyd George spoke to the Commons. See Roskill, *Hankey*, 2:99.

33. The full text of the letter is in Beaverbrook, *Men and Power, 1917-1918*, pp. 387-92.

34. Ibid., p. 309.

35. David Lloyd George to Lord Curzon, 8 July 1919, Lloyd George Papers (F/12/1/22). Beaverbrook, *Men and Power, 1917-1918*, pp. 308-9, quoted extensively from this letter, but he omitted several points, particularly, Lloyd George's accusation that King George V had prompted Curzon's call for reconsideration by the Cabinet of a trial of the kaiser.

36. War Cabinet meeting No. 598 (3), July 23, 1919, CAB 23/11.

37. Lord Maurice Hankey, *Politics, Trials, and Errors* (Chicago: Henry Regnery Co., 1950), p. 3; Anglo-French conference, 13 December 1919, at 3:30 p.m., *Documents on British Foreign Policy*, first series, 2:774.

38. Memorandum by Sir Maurice Hankey on trial of Kaiser, 29 July 1919, CAB 24/85 (G.T. 7874). Raymond W. Woods was the clerk who worked on article 227. He spent most of his time preparing cases against lesser Germans, not the kaiser. See the two volumes of his correspondence in Treasury Solicitor Miscellaneous 3/43-44, Public Record Office, London (hereafter cited as TS). For his work relating to the trial of the kaiser, see Raymond W. Woods to Foreign Office, 23 October 1919, TS 3/43; Woods to Gordon Hewart, 5 December 1919, TS 3/43. Journalists erroneously reported on several occasions the impending appointment of judges to try the kaiser. Among the men named as likely appointees were Lord Sumner or Lord Reading for Britain; Chief Justice of the Supreme Court Edward Douglass White, Charles Evans Hughes, or ex-President William Howard Taft for the United States, and Leon Bourgeois for France. See *New York Times*,

5 July 1919, p. 1; 6 July 1919, p. 1; "Dutch View of Giving Up the Kaiser," *Literary Digest* 61 (21 June 1919):22; "William Hohenzollern, to the Bar!" *Literary Digest* 62 (19 July 1919):17.

39. Winston Churchill, *The World Crisis, 1918-1929: The Aftermath* (New York: Charles Scribner's Sons, 1929), p. 160.

40. Paul Hymans, *Mémoires*, 2 vols. (Brussels: Université libre de Bruxelles, 1958), 1:479.

41. Robertson to Curzon, 8 August 1919, *Documents on British Foreign Policy*, first series, 5:178; Robertson to Curzon, 24 September 1919, *Documents on British Foreign Policy*, first series, 5:571.

42. Robert Lansing to Gunther, 21 July 1919, *Foreign Relations of the United States, 1919*, 2:657.

43. Heads of Delegations meeting, 15 September 1919, at 10:30 a.m., *Documents on British Foreign Policy*, first series, 1:698; Heads of Delegations meeting, 11 August 1919, at 3:30 p.m., *Documents on British Foreign Policy*, first series, 1:391; *Times*, 12 September 1919, p. 9.

44. Van Karnebeek to Queen Wilhelmina, 18 July 1919, Kabinetsarchief 1871-1940, Inventarisnummer 174, Rubriek A^n, Uitlevering ex-Keizer Wilhelm II, Archieven van het Ministerie van Buitenlandse Zaken, The Hague (hereafter cited as MBZ).

45. *Chambre des Députés Débats* 108 (1 July-17 September 1919):3661-67.

46. Paul Cambon to Jules Cambon, 5 July 1919, Henri Cambon, ed., *Paul Cambon, Correspondance, 1870-1924*, 3 vols. (Paris: Éditions Bernard Grasset, 1940-46), 3:342-43. See also Cambon's interview with Curzon reported in Curzon to Earl of Derby, 4 July 1919, FO 371/4292 (98689/52517/W39). See also remarks attributed to General Maxime Weygang in *New York Times*, 1 August 1919, p.2.

47. Curzon to Robertson, 17 July 1919, *Documents on British Foreign Policy*, first series, 5:37.

48. Eyre Crowe to Curzon, 3 October 1919, ibid., p. 610. See also Gunther to Lansing, 15 December 1919, *Foreign Relations of the United States, 1919*, 2:658. Clemenceau and an aide in their memoirs admitted no weakening of determination to secure the kaiser, and they blamed the British for the failure. See Georges Clemenceau, *Grandeur and Misery of Victory*, trans. F. M. Atkinson (New York: Harcourt, Brace & Co., 1930), p. 400; Général Jean Mordacq, *Le Ministère Clemenceau: Journal d'un témoin*, 4 vols. (Paris: Librairie Plon, 1930-31), 4:8, 43-44, 227-29, 292-93.

49. *Times*, 21 July 1919, p. 11; 2 August 1919, p. 11; Lord Acton to Curzon, 28 January 1920, FO 371/4272 (176975/9019/W39); Patrick Ramsay to Curzon, 15 July 1919, FO 371/4271 (106589/9019/W39).

50. Van Royen to van Karnebeek, 7 December 1919, Particulier Collectie van Karnebeek (I-R), MBZ; Sir Esme W. Howard to Curzon, 31 January 1920, *Documents on British Foreign Policy*, first series, 9:624-26. See also King Alfonso's remarks to the American diplomat in Frank L. Polk Confidential Diary, 7 November 1919, Polk Papers (Drawer 88, No. 18). For King Gustav's remarks, see Sweerts De Landas Wybourgh to van Karnebeek, 5 December 1919, Particulier Collectie van Karnebeek (I-S), MBZ.

51. Cardinal Gasparri to Balfour, 4 July 1919, *Documents on British Foreign*

Policy, first series, 5:17; Benedict XV to President Wilson, 1 July 1919, Wilson Papers (Letterbooks, Box 190); Wilson to Benedict XV, 15 August 1919, Wilson Papers (Letterbooks, Box 191); Count de Salis to Curzon, 26 January 1920, *Documents on British Foreign Policy*, first series, 9:619-20.

52. Van Karnebeek Diary, 15 July 1919, Collectie van Karnebeek No. 2, MBZ; van Karnebeek to Queen Wilhelmina, 18 July 1919, Kabt. Inv. 174 A^n, MBZ.

53. Von Ilsemann, *Kaiser*, 1:318-19.

54. Van Karnebeek to Queen Wilhelmina, 18 July 1919, Kabt. Inv. 174, A^n, MBZ. The queen said little in her autobiography about the formulation of Dutch policy.

55. Notes by Thiel of a Conversation with Dr. Togo, 23 November 1919, AA (T-149/383/00218-21).

56. Carl-Ludwig von Bergen to German Foreign Ministry, 19 January 1920, AA (T-149/383/00273).

57. "Germany Debates Trying the Kaiser," *Neue Zürcher Zeitung*, reprinted in *The Living Age* 304 (13 March 1920):626-30; "Preparations for the Trial of the Former Kaiser," *New York Times Current History* 10 (August 1919):223; *New York Times*, 13 January 1920, p. 19; General Neill Malcolm to Curzon, 6 July 1919, *Documents on British Foreign Policy*, first series, 6:29-31. The archives of the Dutch Foreign Office contain no record of any intervention on the kaiser's behalf by the new German government.

58. Eduard Heilfron, "Die Auslieferung Kaiser Wilhelms," *Deutsche Allgemeine Zeitung*, no. 336 (morning ed.), 16 July 1919; no. 35 (morning ed.), 20 January 1920; Dr. Richard Petong, "Die Auslieferung des Kaisers und Deutschen Heerführer," *Preussische Jahrbücher* 179 (January-March 1920):185-200.

59. Von Ilsemann, *Kaiser*, 1:144.

60. Walter H. Kaufmann, *Monarchism in the Weimar Republic* (New York: Bookman Associates, 1953), pp. 78-79; Dorothea Groener-Geyer, *General Groener, Soldat und Staatsmann* (Frankfurt, W. Ger.: Societäts-Verlag, 1955), p. 175; Adolf Mueller to German Foreign Ministry, 17 July 1919, AA (T-149/383/00176).

61. More than three hundred German women sent a petition to Lloyd George in August 1919 offering themselves as scapegoats for Wilhelm II. See German women to Lloyd George, August 1919, FO 371/4271 (118611/9019/W39). See also Prince Eitel Friedrich to King George, 21 July 1919, FO 371/4271 (105444/9019/W39); Nicolson, *King George*, pp. 337-38; *Times*, 10 July 1919, p. 12.

62. Konrad H. Jarausch, *Enigmatic Chancellor: Bethmann Hollweg and the Hubris of Imperial Germany* (New Haven, Conn., and London: Yale University Press, 1973), pp. 1-3, 425 n.1; Theobald von Bethmann Hollweg, *Reflections on the World War*, trans. George Young, 2 vols. (London: Thornton Butterworth, 1920), 1:129-30, 162-63; Council of Four meeting, 28 June 1919, at 5 p.m., *FRUS: Paris Peace Conference, 1919*, 6:751-52; Heads of Delegations meeting, 29 July 1919, at 3:30 p.m., *Documents on British Foreign Policy*, first series, 1:240.

63. Henry Fournier-Foch, "Lettre inédite du Maréchal Hindenburg au Maréchal Foch du 3 juillet 1919," *Revue Historique de l'Armée* 29, no. 2. (1973):70-75; Erich von Falkenhayn to Friedrich Ebert, 5 July 1919, and Kurt von Lersner to Georges Clemenceau, 5 August 1919, AA (T-149/383/00181-84, 00190).

64. Curzon to Robertson, 17 July 1919, *Documents on British Foreign Policy*, first series, 5:36-38.

65. René de Marees van Swinderen to van Karnebeek, 31 July 1919, Collectie Van Karnebeek (I-S), MBZ.

66. Prevost to Pinchon, No. 388, October 15, 1919, La Série Europe, 1918-1929, Allemagne, vol. 26, "Guillaume II-Le Kronprinz, juin 1919-janvier 1921," MAE; Robertson to Curzon, 1 August 1919, *Documents on British Foreign Policy*, first series, 5:83-85; Robertson to Curzon, 21 October 1919, *Documents on British Foreign Policy*, first series, pp. 739-40.

67. Robertson to Curzon, 20 August 1919, *Documents on British Foreign Policy*, first series, 5:230.

68. Sir Ronald Graham to Curzon, 17 December 1919, ibid., pp. 924-29.

69. Heads of Delegations meeting, 15 January 1920, at 3 p.m., *Documents on British Foreign Policy*, first series, 2:884-85, 890-92; Second Earl of Birkenhead, *The Life of F. E. Smith: First Earl of Birkenhead* (London: Eyre & Spottiswoode, 1960), pp. 340-42.

70. Heads of Delegations meeting, 16 January 1919, at 4 p.m., *Documents on British Foreign Policy*, first series, 2:910-13; Roger H. Beadon, *Some Memories of the Peace Conference* (London: Lincoln Williams, 1933), pp. 264-65. For the first note to the Dutch, see Clemenceau to van Karnebeek, 15 January 1920, Netherlands Orange Book, *Mededeelingen van den Minister van Buitenlandsche Zaken aan de Staten-Generaal, Juni 1919-April 1920*, p. 12 (hereafter cited as *Netherlands Orange Book*). This volume contains copies of all notes between the Allies and the Dutch concerning the kaiser.

71. John Loudon to van Karnebeek, 19 January 1920, No. 210/86, zeer vertrouwelijk, B.Z., Kabtdoss., Uitlevering Keizer (A-1), Exh. 2 februari, Kabt. No. 1, MBZ.

72. Loudon to van Karnebeek, 23 January 1920, No. 280/116, B.Z., Kabtdoss., Uitlevering Keizer (A-1), Exh. 24 januari, Kabt. No. 11, MBZ.

73. Micheliels van Verduynen to van Karnebeek, 19 January 1920, No. 3, B.Z., Kabtdoss., Uitlevering Keizer (A-1), Exh. 23 januari, Kabt. No. 7, MBZ.

74. Van Karnebeek to Alexandre Millerand, 23 January 1920, *Netherlands Orange Book*, pp. 12-13.

75. Lord Birkenhead to Lloyd George, 27 January 1920, Lloyd George Papers (F/4/7/14); Birkenhead to Lloyd George, 28 January 1920, Lloyd George Papers (F/4/7/15); Foreign Office memorandum on possible reprisals, undated, *Documents on British Foreign Policy*, first series, 9:629-30. The editors stated in footnote 1 that Lord Hardinge asked on 30 January 1920 that this memorandum be prepared for Lloyd George.

76. For the relationship between Hardinge and Graham, see Roberta M. Warman, "The Erosion of Foreign Office Influence in the Making of Foreign Policy, 1916-1918," *Historical Journal* 15 (March 1972):156. For Hardinge's attitude, see Lord Hardinge of Penshurst, *Old Diplomacy: The Reminiscences of Lord Hardinge of Penshurst* (London: John Murray, 1947), pp. 247-48.

77. Lord Hardinge to Graham, 28 January 1920, *Documents on British Foreign Policy*, first series, 9:620; 31 January 1920, p. 624; 3 February 1920, p. 633.

78. Graham to Curzon, 1 February 1920, ibid., pp. 627-28.

79. Graham to Curzon, 4 February 1920, ibid., pp. 646-49. Van Karnebeek confirmed Graham's account of this meeting. See van Karnebeek Diary, 2 February 1920, MBZ.

80. Charles Benoist, "Guillaume II en Hollande," *Revue des Deux Mondes* 19 (15 January 1934):393.

81. Cabinet meeting No. 9 (20), February 5, 1920, at 12 noon, CAB 23/20.

82. Graham to Curzon, 6 February 1920, *Documents on British Foreign Policy*, first series, 9:652-53.

83. Van Karnebeek to Loudon, 10 February 1920, D (geheim archief), No. 13/109, B.Z., Kabtdoss., Uitlevering Keizer (A-1), MBZ.

84. Millerand to Charles Benoist, No. 92, February 1, 1920, La Série à paix, 1914-1920, vol. 71, "Demande de pourscrites contre Guillaume II, 1 février-31 décembre 1920," MAE.

85. Van Royen to van Karnebeek, 19 February 1920, No. 307/35, B.Z., Kabtdoss., Uitlevering Keizer (A-1), Exh. 17 februari, Kabt. No. 5, MBZ. See also van Royen to van Karnebeek, 11 February 1920, No. 17, B.Z., Kabtdoss., Uitlevering Keizer (A-1), Exh. 14 februari, Kabt. No. 8, MBZ; van Nispen to van Karnebeek, 7 February 1920, No. 6, Kabt. Inv. 174 A^n, Exh. 7 februari, Kabt. No. 5, MBZ.

86. Confidential aide-memoire, Legation of the Netherlands to Lansing, 11 February 1920, Lansing Papers, Library of Congress (Correspondence, vol. 52); Lansing to Wilson, 11 February 1920, Lansing Papers, Library of Congress (Correspondence, vol. 52); Dutch Minister at Washington to van Karnebeek, 12 February 1920, No. 36, Kabt. Inv. 174 A^n, Exh. 14 februari, Kabt. No. 9, MBZ.

87. Minutes of the Council of Ministers, 5 February 1920, No. 11, MBZ.

88. Graham to Curzon, 6 February 1920, *Documents on British Foreign Policy*, first series, 9:662-63; Graham to Curzon, 7 February 1920, *Documents on British Foreign Policy*, first series, 9:671; Graham to Curzon, 22 January 1921, "Netherlands: Annual Report, 1920," Confidential Print 11666, FO 371/7090 (W885/W855/29); van Karnebeek Diary, 6 February 1920, MBZ.

89. Allied conference, 12 February 1920, at 3:30 p.m., *Documents on British Foreign Policy*, first series, 7:21. See also 13 February 1920, at 11:30 a.m., pp. 24-26; 13 February 1920, at 4 p.m., pp. 31, 37; 14 February 1920, at 10:30 a.m., p. 42; Lloyd George to van Karnebeek, 14 February 1920, *Netherlands Orange Book*, pp. 13-14.

90. Curzon to Graham, 14 February 1920, *Documents on British Foreign Policy*, first series, 9:681-82.

91. Graham to Curzon, 16 February 1920, ibid., pp. 682-84.

92. Graham to Curzon, 20 March 1920, ibid., p. 721.

93. Allied conference, 24 February 1920, at 11 a.m., ibid., 7:220-25.

94. Curzon to Graham, 25 February 1920, ibid., 9:687.

95. Graham to Curzon, 26 February 1920, ibid., p. 689; 27 February 1920, ibid., pp. 690-91.

96. Van Karnebeek to Lloyd George, 2 March 1920, *Netherlands Orange Book*, pp. 14-15.

97. De Marees van Swinderen to van Karnebeek, 5 March 1920, No. 445/190, Kabinet der Koningen (1), MBZ.

98. Conference of Ambassadors and Foreign Ministers, 5 March 1920, at 3 p.m., *Documents on British Foreign Policy,* first series, 7:423-28, 431.

99. Curzon to Graham, 6 March 1920, ibid., 9: 698-99.

100. Graham to Curzon, 8 March 1920, ibid., p. 700; 9 March 1920, ibid., pp. 702-5.

101. Graham to Curzon, 9 March 1920, ibid., pp. 700-701.

102. Millerand to Prevost, No. 201, March 10, 1920, La Série à paix, 1914-1920, vol. 71, "Demande de pourscrites contre Guillaume II, 1 février-31 décembre 1920," MAE; Prevost to Millerand, No. 140, March 13, 1920, La Série à paix, 1914-1920, vol. 71, "Demande de pourscrites contre Guillaume II, 1 février-31 décembre 1920," MAE.

103. Graham to Curzon, 12 March 1920, *Documents on British Foreign Policy,* first series, 9:706-10.

104. Minute by Curzon, 16 March 1920, on the despatch from Graham to Curzon, 12 March 1920, ibid., p. 710 n. 3.

105. Millerand to Prevost, No. 210, March 14, 1920, La Série à paix, 1914-1920, vol. 71, "Demande de pourscrites contre Guillaume II, 1 février-31 décembre 1920," MAE.

106. Graham to Curzon, 17 March 1920, *Documents on British Foreign Policy,* first series, 9:716-17. For the text of the decree of internment, see *Documents on British Foreign Policy,* first series, 7:552.

107. Curzon to Graham, 14 March 1920, ibid., 9:711, Graham to Curzon, 15 March 1920, ibid., 9:711-12; Graham to Curzon, 16 March 1920, ibid., 9:712; Allied conference, 15 March 1920, at 12 noon, ibid., 7:493.

108. Allied conference, 18 March 1920, at 4 p.m., ibid., 7:547-50. Dignified retreat was also the advice of Sir Eyre Crowe. See his memorandum, 17 March 1920, ibid., 9:713-15.

109. Conference of Ambassadors and Foreign Ministers, 23 March 1920, at 4 p.m., ibid., 7:591-92; Conference of Ambassadors and Foreign Ministers, 24 March 1920, at 4 p.m., ibid., 7:606, 617; Conference of Ambassadors and Foreign Ministers, 26 March 1920, at 3:30 p.m., ibid., 7:657-58. The last Allied note to the Netherlands was delivered on 29 March 1920. See Graham to Curzon, 29 March 1920, ibid., 9:728. For the text of the last note, see Lloyd George to van Karnebeek, 24 March 1920, *Netherlands Orange Book,* p. 15.

110. "Why William Ought to Be Tried," *Literary Digest* 64 (31 January 1920):20; "Article 227," *The Nation* (London), 26 (24 January 1920):565-67; "The Reign of Public Law," *The Nation* (London), 26 (31 January 1920): 590-92; "Shall the Kaiser Be Tried?" *The Spectator* 124 (31 January 1920):133-34. The *Times* during this period contained virtually no letters or editorials on the subject. For French opinion, see *Times,* 26 January 1920, p. 12; and A. Merignhac, "De Responsabilité pénale des actes criminels commis au cours de la guerre de 1914-1918," *Revue de Droit International et de Législation Comparée,* 3rd series, 1 (1920):35-70. A small group of back-benchers criticized Lloyd George for months after the failure to extradite the kaiser. See *Parliamentary Debates,* Commons, 127 (1920):873-74, 1380-81, 1857; 128 (1920):16-18, 1490, 2218-19; 129 (1920):637-38; 130 (1920):1431-32; 131 (1920):19-20, 1635-36, 1953; 133 (1920):792-93; 150 (1922):626.

111. "American Jurists Sentence the Kaiser," *Literary Digest* 64 (7 February

1920):47-59. Of 328 lawyers polled, 298 disapproved of Lansing's attitude at the peace conference toward a trial of the kaiser and wanted a trial. A death sentence for the kaiser was favored by 106, imprisonment or internment by 137. These lawyers included scholars in the major American law schools and state supreme court, district, circuit, and county judges.

112. Paul Cambon to Millerand, No. 192, March 9, 1920, La Série à paix, 1914-1920, vol. 71, "Demande de pourscrites contre Guillaume II, 1 février-31 décembre 1920," MAE.

113. *Parliamentary Debates*, Commons, 127 (1920): 873-74.

114. Curzon to Graham, 20 January 1921, *Documents on British Foreign Policy*, first series, 16:620; also in *Documents on British Foreign Policy*, first series, Graham to Curzon, 21 January 1921, 16:621-22; 21 January 1921, 16:622; Hardinge to Curzon, 21 January 1921, 16:623; Graham to Curzon, 26 January 1921, 16:625-26; Curzon to Graham, 1 February 1921, 16:628-29; Lord Kilmarnock to Curzon, 2 February 1921, 16:629.

115. David Lloyd George, *War Memoirs*, 6 vols. (London:Ivor Nicholson & Watson, 1933-36), 6:3347-48.

116. For the kaiser's postwar life, the best source is von Kürenberg, *Kaiser*, pp. 382-419. See also Michael Balfour, *The Kaiser and His Times* (Boston: Houghton Mifflin Co., 1964), pp. 411-20; Virginia Cowles, *The Kaiser* (New York and Evanston, Ill.: Harper & Row, 1963), pp. 415-30. The works of Balfour and Cowles, however, contain numerous errors on the war crimes issue.

117. George Sylvester Viereck, *The Kaiser on Trial* (Richmond, Va.: William Byrd Press, 1937). Viereck, a German-American journalist, was a friend and strong supporter of Wilhelm II. His study, cast in the form of a trial, complete with all witnesses, living and dead, used some verifiable evidence and considerable literary license to exonerate the kaiser.

118. Alan Palmer, *The Kaiser: Warlord of the Second Reich* (New York: Charles Scribner's Sons, 1978), pp. 224-25.

CHAPTER 7

1. Dr. Paul Eckardt to War Minister and Chief of the Admiralty, 14 July 1919, AA (T-149/383/00171-73); Wedding to the Chancellor, 8 December 1919, AA (T-149/383/00232-33); Wedding to Editor of *Deutsche Allgemeine Zeitung*, 2 January 1920, AA (T-149/383/00243-48); Wedding to Foreign Minister, 27 February 1920, AA (T-149/383/00320-21).

2. Wedding to War Minister and Chief of the Admiralty, 17 July 1919, AA (T-149/383/00174-75); Friedrich Rosen to Foreign Ministry, 1 July 1919, AA (T-149/383/00159).

3. Erich Raeder, *My Life*, trans. Henry W. Drexel (Annapolis, Md.: United States Naval Institute, 1960), p. 109.

4. German Consul in Zurich to Foreign Ministry, 18 November 1919, AA (T-149/383/00216).

5. Eyre Crowe to Lord Curzon, 27 November 1919, with enclosure of letter from General Sauberzweig to Hoffmann, 30 July 1919, Great Britain, Foreign

Office, *Documents on British Foreign Policy, 1919-1939*, first series, ed. E. L. Woodward et al., 18 vols. (London: His Majesty's Stationery Office, 1947-72), 5:862-64; Director of Military Intelligence to Foreign Office, 26 August 1919, FO 371/4271 (121235/9019/W39).

6. Oskar Freiherr von der Lancken Wakenitz, *Meine Dreissig Dienstjahre, 1888-1918: Potsdam-Paris-Brussels* (Berlin: Verlag für Kulturpolitik, 1931), pp. 238-50; Hugh Gaisford to Curzon, 22 August 1919, with enclosure of Cardinal Gasparri to Gaisford, 18 August 1919, FO 371/4271 (122372/9019/W39).

7. Walther Rathenau to Colonel House, 11 July 1919, House Papers (Correspondence with Walther Rathenau, 1918-22); Count Harry Kessler, *Walther Rathenau: His Life and Work*, trans. W. D. Robson-Scott and Lawrence Hyde (New York: Harcourt, Brace & Co., 1930), pp. 263-64, 268-69. For reports of other Germans who worried about their extradition, see idem, *In the Twenties: The Diaries of Harry Kessler*, trans. Charles Kessler (New York: Holt, Rinehart & Winston, 1971), pp. 102-3; Sir Ralph S. Paget to Curzon, 5 February 1920, FO 371/4272 (176892/9019/W39).

8. John W. Wheeler-Bennett, *Wooden Titan: Hindenburg in Twenty Years of German History, 1914-1934* (New York: William Morrow & Co., 1936), p. 230; *New York Times*, 3 July 1919, p. 3.

9. Prince Rupprecht to Ritter von Brettreich, President of Bavarian Red Cross, 9 December 1919, AA (T-149/383/00235-36).

10. F. L. Carsten, *The Reichswehr and Politics, 1918 to 1933* (London: Oxford University Press, 1966), p. 62; John W. Wheeler-Bennett, *The Nemesis of Power, The German Army in Politics, 1918-1945* (New York: St. Martin's Press, 1954), pp. 64-65; Professor Haguenin to Georges Clemenceau, 1 July 1919, La Série à paix, 1914-1920, vol. 70, "Demande de pourscrites contre Guillaume II, 8 décembre 1918-31 janvier 1920," MAE.

11. Johannes Erger, *Der Kapp-Lüttwitz-Putsch: Ein Beitrag zur Deutschen Innenpolitik, 1919/1920* (Düsseldorf, W. Ger.: Droste Verlag, 1967), pp. 26, 43, 108-9.

12. *Verhandlungen der Deutsche Nationalversammlung*, 327 (13 March-9 July 1919):1407-20; "Germany's Ratification of the Treaty," *New York Times Current History* 10 (August 1919):218.

13. Erich Eyck, *A History of the Weimar Republic*, trans. Harlan P. Hanson and Robert G. L. Waite, 2 vols. (Cambridge, Mass.: Harvard University Press, 1962), 1:122-60.

14. Haguenin to Clemenceau, 29 June 1919, La Série Europe, 1918-1929, Allemagne, vol. 325, "Responsabilité de la guerre, juin 1918-octobre 1919," MAE.

15. Klaus Epstein, *Matthias Erzberger and the Dilemma of German Democracy* (Princeton, N.J.: Princeton University Press, 1959), pp. 328-30.

16. John G. Williamson, *Karl Helfferich, 1872-1924: Economist, Financier, Politician* (Princeton, N.J.: Princeton University Press, 1971), pp. 301-2.

17. Arthur Rosenberg, *A History of the German Republic*, trans. Ian F. D. Morrow and L. Marie Sieveking (London: Methuen & Co., 1936), pp. 130-31.

18. *New York Times*, 30 July 1919, p. 2.

19. Eyck, *Weimar Republic*, 1:134-39.

20. General Nudant to Marshal Foch, 1 August 1919, *FRUS: Paris Peace Conference, 1919,* 7:462.

21. Heads of Delegations meeting, 1 August 1919, at 3:30 p.m., *Documents on British Foreign Policy,* first series, 1:271-73, 284.

22. Philip Kerr to David Lloyd George, 2 August 1919, Lloyd George Papers (F/89/3/18); Heads of Delegations meeting, 6 August 1919, at 3:30 p.m., *Documents on British Foreign Policy,* first series, 1:336, 352.

23. Epstein, *Erzberger,* p. 349 n. 2.

24. Manfred J. Enssle, "Germany and Belgium, 1919-1929: A Study of German Foreign Policy" (Ph.D. diss., University of Colorado, 1970), pp. 69-72.

25. General Charles Joseph Dupont to Foch, 4 August 1919, *FRUS: Paris Peace Conference, 1919,* 7:660-61.

26. General Neill Malcolm to Arthur Balfour, 5 August 1919, *Documents on British Foreign Policy,* first series, 6:124-25; Malcolm to Colonel Twiss, 7 August 1919, *Documents on British Foreign Policy,* first series, 6:135-36.

27. Heads of Delegations meeting, 11 August 1919, at 3:30 p.m., ibid., 1:387-91, 397-98; Balfour to Curzon, 11 August 1919, ibid., 6:144-45; 12 August 1919, 6:145-46.

28. Curzon to Balfour, 13 August 1920, ibid., 6:146; Lloyd George to Balfour, 13 August 1919, Lloyd George Papers (F/3/4/29).

29. Robert Lansing to Frank L. Polk, 16 August 1919, Lansing Papers, Library of Congress (Correspondence, vol. 45).

30. Heads of Delegations meeting, 15 September 1919, at 10:30 a.m., *Documents on British Foreign Policy,* first series, 1:685, 699.

31. Jean-Jacques Boisvert, *Les Relations franco-allemandes en 1920* (Montreal: Les Presses de l'université du Québec, 1977), pp. 46-47.

32. Crowe to Curzon, 3 October 1919, *Documents on British Foreign Policy,* first series, 5:609-10.

33. Polk to Tasker H. Bliss, 21 October 1919, Bliss Papers (Personal File, Box 69, Correspondence with American Peace Commissioners). Clemenceau received a steady stream of petitions insisting upon punishment. For the file containing these petitions, see "Cabinet du sous-secrétarie d'état office interministeriel," No. 2415, December 9, 1918, La Série à paix, 1914-1920, vol. 70, "Demande de pourscrites contre Guillaume II, 8 décembre 1918-31 janvier 1920," MAE.

34. Heads of Delegations meeting, 7 November 1919, at 10:30 a.m., *Documents on British Foreign Policy,* first series, 2:217-18; Heads of Delegations meeting, 11 November 1919, at 10:30 a.m., *Documents on British Foreign Policy,* first series, 2:275, 279; Commission on the Organization of Mixed Tribunals meeting, 19 November 1919, *Documents on British Foreign Policy,* first series, 2:809-22.

35. Anglo-French conference, 13 December 1919, at 11 a.m., ibid., 2:753, 756-60; 13 December 1919, at 3:30 p.m., ibid., 2:772, 774.

36. Baron Kurt von Lersner, "Die Auslieferung der Deutschen Kriegsverbrecher," in *Zehn Jahre Versailles,* ed. Heinrich Schnee and Hans Draeger, 3 vols. (Berlin, Ger.: Bruckenverlag, 1929-30), 1:15-27.

37. Crowe to Curzon, 6 November 1919, *Documents on British Foreign Policy,* first series, 6:332-34; 7 November 1919, 6:353-54; Heads of Delegations meeting,

21 November 1919, at 10:30 a.m., *FRUS: Paris Peace Conference, 1919*, 9:289–90; Baron Kurt von Lersner to Clemenceau, 25 January 1920, Great Britain, Parliament, *Parliamentary Papers* (Commons), *1921*, vol. 43, Cmnd. 1325, "Protocols and Correspondence between the Supreme Council and the Conference of Ambassadors and the German Government and the German Peace Delegation between January 10, 1920, and July 17, 1920, respecting the execution of the Treaty of Versailles of June 28, 1919," pp. 19–20 (hereafter cited as Cmnd. 1325).

38. Von Lersner to Clemenceau, 25 January 1920, with enclosure of German law of 13 December 1919, Cmnd. 1325, p. 22.

39. Heads of Delegations meeting, 9 September 1919, at 11 a.m., *Documents on British Foreign Policy*, first series, 1:653–61; 10 September 1919, at 11:15 a.m., 1:644–66; 11 September 1919, at 11 a.m., 1:672–73; 22 September 1919, at 11 a.m., 1:755, 762.

40. Polk Confidential Diary, 5 November 1919, Polk Papers (Drawer 88, no. 18); von Lersner to Polk, 6 November 1919, White Papers (Peace Conference File, Box 54); Bliss to Polk, 14 October 1919, Bliss Papers (Personal File, Box 69, Correspondence with American Peace Commissioners); Otto Meissner, *Staatssekretär unter Ebert-Hindenburg-Hitler: Der Schicksalsweg des Deutschen Volkes von 1918-1945, wei ich ihn erlebte* (Hamburg, W. Ger.: Hoffmann & Campe Verlag, 1950), p. 82.

41. Carl-Ludwig von Bergen to Foreign Ministry, 2 February 1920, AA (T-149/383/00286); 18 February 1920, AA (T-149/383/00313).

42. Sir Almeric Fitzroy, *Memoirs*, 2 vols. (New York: George H. Doran Co., 1925), 2:716–20; William Stewart Roddie, *Peace Patrol* (New York: G. P. Putnam's Sons, 1933), pp. 128–30.

43. Cabinet meeting, 23 December 1919, CAB 23/18.

44. Heads of Delegations meeting, 20 December 1919, at 3 p.m., *Documents on British Foreign Policy*, first series, 2:576–80.

45. Commission on the Organization of Mixed Tribunals meeting, 9 January 1920, ibid., 5:968–77.

46. Commission on the Organization of Mixed Tribunals meeting, 13 January 1920, ibid., 9:602–11.

47. Heads of Delegations meeting, 15 January 1920, at 3 p.m., ibid., 2:884, 886–87.

48. Heads of Delegations meeting, 16 January 1920, at 10:30 a.m., ibid., pp. 893–94.

49. Meeting in Stephen Pinchon's room, 20 January 1920, at 10:30 a.m., ibid., pp. 927–28.

50. Haguenin to Clemenceau, No. 20383, December 16, 1919, La Série à paix, 1914-1920, vol. 70, "Demande de pourscrites contre Guillaume II, 8 décembre 1918-31 janvier 1920," MAE.

51. De Marcilly to Alexandre Millerand, No. 12, January 27, 1920, ibid.

52. Lord Stamfordham to Lloyd George, 6 February 1920, with enclosure of letter from Lieutenant Colonel William Stewart Roddie to Sir Almeric Fitzroy, 30 January 1920, Lloyd George Papers (F/29/4/3).

53. Lord Kilmarnock to Curzon, 26 January 1920, *Documents on British Foreign Policy*, first series, 9:618–19. See also Kilmarnock to Curzon, 24 January 1920,

Documents on British Foreign Policy, first series, 10:1-2, 26 January 1920, 9:616-17; 31 January 1920, 9:25-28.

54. Epstein, *Erzberger*, pp. 355-59.

55. Earl of Derby to Curzon, 31 January 1920, *Documents on British Foreign Policy*, first series, 9:626.

56. Lord Hardinge to Derby, 30 January 1920, ibid., p. 626.

57. Derby to Lloyd George, 31 January 1920, Lloyd George Papers (F/53/1/14).

58. Derby to Curzon, 4 February 1920, *Documents on British Foreign Policy*, first series, 9:642-43.

59. Edwin L. James, "7 Nations Demand 890 War Culprits," *New York Times*, 4 February 1920, p. 1.

60. Joseph Borkin, *The Crime and Punishment of I. G. Farben* (New York: The Free Press, 1978), pp. 34-35.

61. For the official list of the accused, see Lloyd George Papers (F/157). Incomplete versions of the list are in *New York Times*, 4 February 1920, p. 1; 5 February 1920, p. 1; *Times*, 2 February 1920, p. 11; 9 February 1920, p. 16.

62. Kilmarnock to Curzon, 5 February 1920, *Documents on British Foreign Policy*, first series, 9:651; 6 February 1920, p. 652; 10 February 1920, pp. 56-57.

63. Kilmarnock to Curzon, 7 February 1920, ibid., p. 675.

64. Meeting of the Reichsrat Committee on Foreign Affairs, 2 February 1920, AA (T-149/383/00287-88).

65. Quoted in *New York Times*, 12 February 1920, p. 15.

66. No. 812, Declaration in Berlin of Generals and Admirals on 6 February 1920 on the Extradition Demand of the Entente, Herbert Michaelis and Ernst Schraepler, eds., *Ursachen und Folgen vom Deutsche Zusammenbruch 1918 bis 1945 zur Staatlichen Neuordnung Deutschlands in der Gegenwart; Eine Urkunden—und Dokumentensammlang zur Zeitgeschichte*, vol. 4: *Die Weimarer Republik Vertragserfüllung und innere Bedrohung, 1919-1922* (Berlin, W. Ger.: Dokumenten—Verlag Dr. Herbert Wendler, 1960), pp. 24-25.

67. Haguenin to Millerand, No. 483, February 9, 1920, La Série Europe, 1918-1929, Allemagne, vol. 17, "Rapports de M. Haguenin de février-mars 1920," MAE.

68. *New York Times*, 10 February 1920, p. 3.

69. Thomas E. Boyle, "France, Great Britain, and German Disarmament, 1919-1927" (Ph.D. diss., State University of New York at Stony Brook, 1972), p. 45.

70. Erger, *Kapp-Lüttwitz-Putsch*, pp. 108-11.

71. Wheeler-Bennett, *Nemesis of Power*, p. 71.

72. Hardinge to Derby, 4 February 1920, *Documents on British Foreign Policy*, first series, 9:639; Derby to Curzon, 4 February 1920, *Documents on British Foreign Policy*, first series, 9:645-46.

73. Cabinet meeting, No. 9(20), February 5, 1920, 12 noon, CAB 23/20.

74. Cabinet: War Crimes Committee meeting, 5 February 1920, at 2:45 p.m., CAB 24/98 (C.P. 607).

75. Lansing to Ellis Loring Dresel, 5 February 1920, Lansing Papers, Library of Congress (Correspondence, vol. 51).

76. Lansing to Woodrow Wilson, 7 February 1920, Wilson Papers (Letterbooks, Box 195).

77. Wilson to Lansing, 12 February 1920, Lansing Papers, Library of Congress (Correspondence, vol. 52).

78. Derby to Curzon, 6 February 1920, *Documents on British Foreign Policy*, first series, 9:661; Conference of Ambassadors meeting, 6 February 1920, at 6:30 p.m., *Documents on British Foreign Policy*, first series, 9:654-60.

79. Conference of Ambassadors meeting, 7 February 1920, at 10:30 a.m., ibid., pp. 663-69; Derby to Curzon, 7 February 1920, ibid., pp. 670-71; Derby to Kilmarnock, 7 February 1920, ibid., pp. 671-72; Millerand to Gustav Bauer, 8 February 1920, Cmnd. 1325, pp. 28-29.

80. Sir George Grahame to Curzon, 8 February 1920, *Documents on British Foreign Policy*, first series, 9:676-77.

81. Conference of Ministers, 9 February 1920, at 12 noon, CAB 23/20.

82. Allied conference, 12 February 1920, at 11 a.m., *Documents on British Foreign Policy*, first series, 7:1, 8-12; 12 February 1920, at 3:30 p.m., pp. 12-21.

83. Allied conference, 13 February 1920, at 11:30 a.m., ibid., pp. 22-29.

84. Lloyd George to Bauer, 13 February 1920, Cmnd. 1325, p. 32; Kilmarnock to Curzon, 17 February 1920, *Documents on British Foreign Policy*, first series, 9:684-85.

85. *Chambre des Députés Débats* 110 (13 January-31 March 1920):556-63; Édouard Bonnefous, *Histoire politique de la troisième république*, vol. 3: *L'Après-Guerre, 1919-1924* (Paris: Presses universitaires de France, 1959), pp. 134-35, 140-41.

86. Great Britain, Parliament, House of Commons, *Parliamentary Debates* 125 (1920):270-356; *New York Times*, 6 February 1920, p. 2; *Times*, 16 February 1920, p. 15; "The Problem of War Criminals," *The Spectator* 124 (14 February 1920):201-2; "The Crowning Ineptitude," *The New Statesman* 14 (7 February 1920):512-13; "The Danger of the German Trials," *The Nation* (London), 26 (7 February 1920): 629-30; "The Blunder and the Way Out," *The Nation* (London), 26 (14 February 1920):661-62.

87. Austin Harrison, "The Punishment of War Guilt," *The English Review* 30 (February 1920):163-69. At Amritsar, India, in April 1919 British troops opened fire on a peaceful protest demonstration, killing 379 persons. To combat the Irish Republican Army in 1919, the British set up counterterror squads, and both sides engaged in terrorism and murder of innocent people. See A. J. P. Taylor, *English History, 1914-1945* (New York and Oxford: Oxford University Press, 1965), pp. 152-55.

88. "Germany's Elusive War-Criminals," *Literary Digest* 64 (21 February 1920):16-17; "Germany to Try Her Own War-Criminals," *Literary Digest* 64 (28 February 1920):19.

89. *New York Times*, 9 February 1920, p. 8.

90. See the provocative psychological analysis in Richard M. Hunt, "Myths, Guilt, and Shame in Pre-Nazi Germany," *Virginia Quarterly Review* 34 (Summer 1958): 355-71.

CHAPTER 8

1. Lord Kilmarnock to Lord Curzon, 24 February 1920, Great Britain, Foreign Office, *Documents on British Foreign Policy, 1919-1939*, first series, ed. E. L.

Woodward et al., 18 vols. (London: His Majesty's Stationery Office, 1947-72), 9:686; Notes of Chancellor Hermann Müller, 24 February 1920, AA (T-149/ 383/00318).

2. Johannes Erger, *Der Kapp-Lüttwitz Putsch: Ein Beitrag zur Deutschen Innenpolitik, 1919/1920* (Düsseldorf, W. Ger.: Droste Verlag, 1967), pp. 108-11.

3. No. 46, Otto Gessler to Müller, 16 April 1920, and No. 97, Cabinet meeting, 14 May 1920, Martin Vogt, ed., *Akten der Reichskanzlei Weimarer Republik: Das Kabinett Müller I 27. März bis 21. Juni 1920* (Boppard, W. Ger.: Harald Boldt Verlag, 1971), pp. 115-17, 243.

4. Kilmarnock to Curzon, 2 March 1920, FO 371/4273 (183400/9019/W39); *Times*, 16 February 1920, p. 13; *New York Times*, 8 March 1920, p. 9.

5. *Verhandlungen der Deutsche Nationalversammlung*, 332 (16 January-30 March 1920):4659-73, 4694-4702.

6. Walter H. Kaufmann, *Monarchism in the Weimar Republic* (New York: Bookman Associates, 1953), p. 72.

7. Gordon A. Craig, *Germany, 1866-1945* (New York: Oxford University Press, 1978), pp. 432-33; Erich Eyck, *A History of the Weimar Republic*, trans. Harlan P. Hanson and Robert G. L. Waite, 2 vols. (Cambridge, Mass.: Harvard University Press, 1962), 1:161-65.

8. Otto von Stülpnagel, *Die Wahrheit über die Deutschen Kriegsverbrechen* (Berlin, Ger.: Staatspolitischer Verlag, 1921).

9. Germany, Reichstag, *Verhandlungen des Reichstags*, 345 (4 August-25 November 1920):872; Gustav Stresemann to Foreign Minister, 25 October 1920, AA (T-120/1567/D684985-86); Gustav Stresemann, *Schriften*, ed. Arnold Harttung (Berlin, W. Ger.: Berlin Verlag, 1976), pp. 273-76.

10. André Fribourg, *Les Semeurs de haine: Leur Oeuvre en Allemagne avant et depuis la guerre* (Paris: Berger-Levrault, 1922), pp. 177-85; Jean-Jacques Boisvert, *Les Relations franco-allemandes en 1920* (Montreal: Les Presses de l'université du Québec, 1977), p. 49.

11. Prince Max of Baden to Major von Stülpnagel, 3 November 1920, AA (T-120/1567/D684984).

12. Sir Eric Drummond to Gerald Spicer, 23 February 1920, FO 371/4273 (180777/9019/W39); Sir Horace Rumbold to Curzon, 25 February 1920, *Documents on British Foreign Policy*, first series, 11:229; 5 March 1920, pp. 238-39; Curzon to Rumbold, 3 April 1920, *Documents on British Foreign Policy*, first series, 11:275.

13. Conference of Ministers, 25 February 1920, at 5 p.m., CAB 23/20.

14. "Third Interim Report from the Committee of Enquiry into Breaches of the Laws of War . . . 26 February 1920," pp. 419-28, CAB 24/111 (C.P. 1813).

15. "Breaches of the Laws of War by the Enemy; Observations by the Air Council Upon the Recommendations of the Attorney-General's Committee," 26 September 1919, CAB 24/89 (G.T. 8258); Winston Churchill, "Breaches of the Laws of War by the Enemy," 6 October 1919, CAB 24/89 (G.T. 8280); "Demand for Surrender of German Airmen for Trial: Memorandum from the Air Council," 16 February 1920, CAB 24/98; War Cabinet meeting, No. 631(5), October 16, 1919, CAB 23/12.

16. For the report of this committee and the select list of forty-five names, see *Documents on British Foreign Policy*, first series, 8:234-52.

17. Lord Hardinge to Curzon, 23 April 1920, *Documents on British Foreign Policy*, first series, 9:732-35; Conversation of David Lloyd George and Alexandre Millerand, 18 April 1920, at 9:30 a.m., *Documents on British Foreign Policy*, first series, 8:5-9; Notes of meeting at San Remo, 18 April 1920, at 5 p.m., *Documents on British Foreign Policy*, first series, 8:10-19; Notes of conversation at San Remo, 24 April 1920, at 10:30 a.m., *Documents on British Foreign Policy*, first series, 8:144, 154-55; Supreme Council meeting at San Remo, 26 April 1920, at 5 p.m., *Documents on British Foreign Policy*, first series, 8:215, 226-29.

18. Millerand to Dr. Otto Göppert, 7 May 1920, Cmnd. 1325, pp. 110-11.

19. Inter-Allied Rhineland High Commission meeting, 23-24 March 1920, *Documents on British Foreign Policy*, first series, 9:726-27.

20. Conversation of Sir Eyre Crowe with German Chargé, 14 April 1920, ibid., pp. 730-31; Count August de Saint-Aulaire to Curzon, 31 March 1920, FO 371/4274 (192627/9019/W39).

21. Minister of War to Aristide Briand, No. 3684, January 15, 1921, and No. 4143, January 17, 1921, La Série Europe, 1918-1929, Allemagne, vol. 571, "Sanctions aux violations du droit des gens: Punition des coupables, juin 1920-mars 1921," MAE; *New York Times*, 16 August 1919, p. 1; 21 November 1919, p. 1; 2 June 1920, p. 1.

22. Müller to Millerand, 7 March 1920, Cmnd. 1325, pp. 50-51; Göppert to Millerand, 13 March 1920, FO 371/4273 (189796/9019/W39); 19 July 1920, FO 371/4796 (C2660/726/18).

23. German Chargé to Curzon, 18 March 1920, *Documents on British Foreign Policy*, first series, 9:717-18; Conversation of Crowe and Dr. Karl von Schubert, 8 May 1920, *Documents on British Foreign Policy*, first series, 9:736-38; Admiralty to Foreign Office, 5 July 1920, FO 371/4731 (C564/13/18); Count de Salis to Curzon, 11 September 1920, with enclosure of Cardinal Gasparri to Curzon, FO 371/4731 (C6905/13/18); Curzon to Army Council and Admiralty, 21 September 1920, FO 371/4731 (C6612/13/18).

24. Albert Dufour-Feronce to Miles W. Lampson, 7 May 1926, FO 371/11325 (C5606/5606/18); Foreign Office to Lord Chancellor, 28 December 1926, FO 371/11325 (C12551/5606/18).

25. No. 77, Cabinet meeting, 3 May 1920, Vogt, ed., *Akten der Reichskanzlei Weimarer Republik: Das Kabinett Müller I*, p. 183.

26. Conference at Spa, 9 July 1920, at 12 noon, *Documents on British Foreign Policy*, first series, 8:496-500.

27. Minutes of sub-conference at Spa, 9 July 1920, at 3 p.m., ibid., pp. 500-502.

28. Conference at Spa, 9 July 1920, at 4:30 p.m., ibid., pp. 507, 512; Protocol of Spa Conference respecting war criminals, 9 July 1920, Cmnd. 1325, p. 171.

29. Lord D'Abernon to Curzon, 24 October 1920, *Documents on British Foreign Policy*, first series, 10:322; Earl of Derby to Curzon, 27 October 1920, *Documents on British Foreign Policy*, first series, 10:323-24; Attorney-General to Foreign Office, 13 December 1920, *Documents on British Foreign Policy*, first series, 10:346-48.

30. For the statements of these witnesses, see 21 October 1920, FO 371/4732 (C9811/13/18).

31. Kilmarnock to Curzon, 26 January 1921, FO 371/5860 (C2149/29/18); Allied conference, 12 August 1921, at 11 a.m., *Documents on British Foreign*

Policy, first series, 15:708; Hardinge to Curzon, 25 April 1921, FO 371/5861 (C8546/29/18).

32. Friedrich Sthamer to Curzon, 8 February 1921, FO 371/5860 (C2850/29/18); Raymond W. Woods to Gordon Hewart, 24 February 1921, TS 3/43; Woods to Foreign Office, 2 March 1921, TS 3/43.

33. Interrogatory hearings were held in London at the Bow Street Police Court from April 26 to 29. See *Times,* 26 April 1921, p. 7; 27 April 1921, p. 6; 28 April 1921, p. 8; 29 April 1921, p. 7; 30 April 1921, p. 6; Woods to Hewart, 29 April 1921, TS 3/43.

34. Minute by Crowe, 17 December 1920, on a letter from Attorney-General to Foreign Office, 13 December 1920, *Documents on British Foreign Policy,* first series, 10:348.

35. No. 161, Cabinet meeting, 26 January 1921, at 5 p.m., Peter Wulf, ed., *Akten der Reichskanzlei Weimarer Republik: Das Kabinett Fehrenbach 25. Juni 1920 bis 4. Mai 1921* (Boppard, W. Ger.: Harald Boldt Verlag, 1972), pp. 425-26.

36. Friedrich Karl Kaul, "Die Vorfolgung Deutscher Kriegsverbrecher nach dem Ersten Weltkrieg," *Zeitschrift für Geschichtswissenschaft* (Berlin, E. Ger.) 14 (1966):31; Kilmarnock to Curzon, 11 January 1921, FO 371/5860 (C1186/29/18); *Times,* 12 January 1921, p. 10.

37. Allied conference, 3 March 1921, at 12 noon, *Documents on British Foreign Policy,* first series, 15:258-65.

38. Allied conference, 4 May 1921, at 9:30 p.m., ibid., pp. 579-80; Ludwig Zimmermann, *Deutsche Aussenpolitik in der Ära der Weimarer Republik* (Göttingen, W. Ger.: Musterschmidt-Verlag, 1958), pp. 101-3.

39. *New York Times,* 5 June 1921, p. 1.

40. Max Quarck, "Das unpolitische Leipzig," *Vörwarts,* no. 328 (evening ed.), 14 July 1921; Rudolf Breitscheid, "The Punishment of the War Criminals," *The Nation* (New York), 113 (12 October 1921):397; Herman Wendel, "National Martyrs and Matters of Opinion," *Die Glocke,* 11 July 1921, reprinted in *The Living Age* 311 (1 October 1921):35-37.

41. Albrecht von Stosch, *Die Kriegbeschuldigtenfrage: Ihre Bedeutung für Deutschland und den Feindbund* (Hanover, Ger.; Leipzig, Ger.: Ernst Letsch Verlag, 1924), pp. 160-61; *Times,* 27 June 1921, p. 9; 2 June 1921, p. 9; 28 May 1921, p. 9; 21 May 1921, p. 10.

42. Vice-Admiral a. D. Hollweg, "Die Kriegsverbrecher Prozess," *Deutsche Allgemeine Zeitung,* no. 221 (evening ed.), 13 May 1921; Count Max Montgelas, "Zu den Bevorstehenden Verhandlungen Wegen Kriegsvergehen," *Berliner Tageblatt,* no. 234 (morning ed.), 21 May 1921; Colonel B. Schwertfeger, "Leipzig— das Brandmal des Eigenes Landes," *Militär-Wochenblatt* 106 (3 September 1921):202-4.

43. Karl Böttner, "Etwas von Kriegsverbrechern—in Frankreich," *Tägliche Rundschau,* no. 193 (evening ed.), 20 August 1921; "Englische Kriegsverbrecher," *Tägliche Rundschau,* no. 181 (morning ed.), 20 April 1921; "Französische Kriegsverbrecher," *Tägliche Rundschau,* no. 303 (morning ed.), 2 July 1921.

44. Boisvert, *Les Relations franco-allemandes,* p. 49; August Gallinger, *The Countercharge: The Matter of War Criminals from the German Side,* trans. from the *Süddeutsche Monatshefte* (Munich, Ger.: Knorr & Hirth, 1922).

45. Cabinet meeting, 30 May 1921, AA (T-120/1567/D684993).

46. Ludwig Ebermayer, *Fünfzig Jahre Dienst am Recht: Erinnerungen eines Juristen* (Leipzig, Ger.; Zürich, Switz.: Grethlein, 1930), pp. 189-93.

47. "Senatspräsident Dr. Schmidt über die Abberufung," *Berliner Tageblatt*, no. 319 (evening ed.), 9 July 1921.

48. "Die Kriegsbeschuldigten vor dem Reichsgericht," *Berliner Tageblatt*, no. 237 (evening ed.), 23 May 1921.

49. Claud Mullins, "The War Criminals' Trials," *Fortnightly Review* 116 (September 1921):417-30; *Times*, 1 June 1921, p. 11; *New York Times*, 24 May 1921, p. 19.

50. Woods to Foreign Office 11 May 1921, FO 371/5861 (C9747/29/18); Curzon to D'Abernon, 13 May 1921, FO 371/5861 (C9628/29/18); Sir Ernest Pollock to Curzon, 9 May 1921, FO 371/5861 (C9853/29/18); Woods to Foreign Office, 22 May 1921, FO 371/5862 (C10928/29/18).

51. Great Britain, Parliament, *Parliamentary Papers* (Commons), 15 February 1921-November 1921 (Reports, vol. 12), Cmnd. 1450, "German War Trials: Report of Proceedings before the Supreme Court in Leipzig," pp. 4-5 (hereafter cited as Cmnd. 1450).

52. For details of these cases, see the daily reports in *Vossische Zeitung*, nos. 238-55, 24 May-2 June 1921; Claud Mullins, *The Leipzig Trials* (London: H. F. G. Witherby, 1921), pp. 51-97; Cmnd. 1450, pp. 8-12, 18-42.

53. Cmnd. 1450, p. 35.

54. Woods to Foreign Office, 30 May 1921, FO 371/5862 (C11680/29/18).

55. "Die Versenkung der 'Dover Castle,' " *Vossische Zeitung*, no. 260 (Sunday ed.), 5 June 1921; Mullins, *Leipzig Trials*, pp. 99-107; Cmnd. 1450, pp. 12-13, 42-45.

56. Cmnd. 1450, pp. 6, 13-15.

57. Claud Mullins, "Notes of a Conversation with Herr von Tippelskirch at Leipzig on Belgian & French War Trials," Hanworth Papers.

58. *Times*, 7 July 1921, p. 9; 13 June 1921, p. 9.

59. "Der 5. Leipziger Prozess," *Vossische Zeitung*, no. 265 (evening ed.), 8 June 1921. See also *Vossische Zeitung*, nos. 266-72, 9 June-12 June 1921; Mullins, *Leipzig Trials*, pp. 136-51; *Times*, 13 June 1921, p. 9.

60. Sir George Grahame to Curzon, 18 June 1921, FO 371/5862 (C12579/29/18); Eric Phipps to Curzon, 7 July 1921, FO 371/5863 (C14111/29/18); "Belgique—criminels de guerre Allemagne—Jugements de la cour de Leipzig—Protestations," *Journal du Droit International* 48 (1921):772-73.

61. *New York Times*, 2 July 1921, p. 3.

62. "Die Plädoyers im Prozess Stenger," *Vossische Zeitung*, no. 310 (morning ed.), 5 July 1921.

63. For details of the Stenger case, see reports in *Vossische Zeitung*, nos. 301-14, 29 June-7 July 1921; Paul Matter, Eugène Leroux, and de Manneville to Briand, No. 7, July 6, 1921, La Série Europe, 1918-1929, Allemagne, vol. 574, "Sanctions aux violations du droit des gens: Punition des coupables, 21 juin-10 juillet 1921," MAE; Mullins, *Leipzig Trials*, pp. 151-73; George Gordon Battle, "The Trials Before the Leipsic Supreme Court of Germans Accused of War Crimes," *Virginia Law Review* 8 (November 1921):12.

64. "Oberleutnant Laule Freigesprochen," *Vossische Zeitung*, no. 316 (morning ed.), 8 July 1921; Mullins, *Leipzig Trials*, pp. 169-73.

65. Charles Laurent to Matter, No. 11, July 8, 1921, La Série Europe, 1918-1929, Allemagne, vol. 589, "Archives des mission de l'avocat Matter de Leipzig," MAE.

66. "Die Generale v. Schack und v. Kruska Freigesprochen," *Berliner Tageblatt*, no. 320 (morning ed.), 10 July 1921. For details of this case, see daily reports in *Vossische Zeitung*, nos. 317-20, 8 July-10 July 1921; Mullins, *Leipzig Trials*, pp. 173-89.

67. Georges Suarez, *Briand, sa vie-son oeuvre*, 6 vols. (Paris: Librairie Plon, 1938-52), 5:201-30.

68. *Chambre des Députés Débats* 114 (19 May-12 July 1921):988; "Les Criminels de guerre devant le Reichsgericht à Leipzig," *Journal du Droit International* 48 (1921): 442-46 .

69. Report of Matter, Leroux, de Manneville, 12 July 1921, La Série Europe, 1918-1929, Allemagne, vol. 589, "Archives des mission de l'avocat Matter de Leipzig," MAE.

70. Briand to Saint-Aulaire, 13 July 1921, La Série Europe, 1918-1929, Allemagne, vol. 575, "Sanctions aux violations du droit des gens: Punition des coupables, 11 juillet-15 août 1921," MAE; French Chargé to Foreign Office, 8 July 1921, FO 371/7529 (C16860/555/18), Confidential Print 11990.

71. M. van Slooten, "Betrachtungen aus Anlass des Prozesses Stenger-Crusius," *Zeitschrift für Völkerrecht* 12 (1922-23):174-81. See interview of van Slooten in *Nieuwe Rotterdamsche Courant*, 14 July 1921, in Sir Ronald Graham to Curzon, 18 July 1921, FO 371/5863 (C14868/29/18).

72. Saint-Aulaire to Briand, No. 645, July 15, 1921, La Série Europe, 1918-1929, Allemagne, vol. 575, "Sanctions aux violations du droit des gens: Punition des coupables, 11 juillet-15 août 1921," MAE.

73. Gabriele Krüger, *Die Brigade Ehrhardt* (Hamburg, W. Ger.: Leibniz Verlag, 1971), p. 91.

74. Stosch, *Die Kriegsbeschuldigtenfrage*, pp. 160-61.

75. "Der Ubootkrieg vor dem Reichsgericht," *Vossische Zeitung*, no. 327 (evening ed.), 14 July 1921; "Das Grosse Gutachten im Leipziger Prozess," *Vossiche Zeitung*, no. 328 (morning ed.), 15 July 1921.

76. "Beginn der Plädoyers in Leipzig," ibid., no. 329 (evening ed.), 15 July 1921.

77. For details of the *Llandovery Castle* case, see reports in *Vossische Zeitung*, nos. 323-32, 12 July-17 July 1921; Mullins, *Leipzig Trials*, pp. 107-34; Cmnd. 1450, pp. 13-15, 45-57.

78. Cmnd. 1450, p. 55. For an analysis of this case as a precedent, see United Nations War Crimes Commission, *History of the United Nations War Crimes Commission and the Development of the Laws of War* (London: His Majesty's Stationery Office, 1948), pp. 286-87. The case served as a precedent, for example, in the *Peleus* case after the Second World War. See Sir David Maxwell Fyfe, ed., *The Peleus Trial* (London: William Hodge & Co., 1948).

79. Dr. Erich Eyck, "Leipziger Urteil," *Vossische Zeitung*, no. 386 (morning ed.), 18 August 1921.

80. Vice-Admiral Andreas D. Michelsen, ed., *Das Urteil im Leipziger Uboots—*

Prozess ein Fehlspruch? Juristische und Mititärischen Gutachen (Berlin, Ger.: Staatspolitischen Verlag, 1922).

81. No. 53, n. 2, Cabinet meeting, 22 July 1921, at 5:30 p.m., Ingrid Schulze-Bidlingmaier, ed., *Akten der Reichskanzlei Weimarer Republik: Die Kabinette Wirth I und II, 10. Mai 1921 bis 22. November 1922*, 2 vols. (Boppard, W. Ger.: Harald Boldt Verlag, 1973), 1:148.

82. *Times*, 27 May 1921, p. 11; "Justice in Leipsic," *The New Statesman* 17 (4 June 1921):232-33. See reprints of British press comments in *New York Times*, 7 June 1921, p. 19; 27 May 1921, p. 1; 3 May 1921, p. 17.

83. Great Britain, Parliament, House of Commons, *Parliamentary Debates* 144 (1921):2420-22.

84. Memorandum by the Solicitor-General, 2 June 1921, CAB 24/125 (C.P. 3008); *Parliamentary Debates*, Commons, 146 (1921):1535-36.

85. Saint-Aulaire to Briand, No. 645, July 15, 1921, La Série Europe, 1918-1929, Allemagne, vol. 575, "Sanctions aux violations du droit des gens: Punition des coupables, 11 juillet-15 août 1921,"MAE.

86. Anne Orde, *Great Britain and International Security, 1920-1926* (London: Royal Historical Society, 1978), pp. 9-16.

87. *Times*, 31 August 1921, p. 7.

88. Minute by R. F. Wigram on despatch from Captain Woolcombe to C. H. Tufton, 14 October 1921, FO 371/5864 (C20103/29/18).

89. Gustav Radbruch, *Der Innere Weg: Aufrisz meines Lebens* (Göttingen, W. Ger.: Vandenhoeck & Ruprecht, 1961), pp. 110-11.

90. No. 53, Cabinet meeting, 22 July 1921, at 5:30 p.m., Schulz-Bidlingmaier, ed., *Akten der Reichskanzlei Weimarer Republik: Das Kabinette Wirth I und II*, 1:148-49; No. 192, Meeting of the Prime Ministers of the Länder, 20 January 1922, at 11 a.m., Schulz-Bidlingmaier, ed., *Akten der Reichskanzlei Weimarer Republik: Das Kabinette Wirth I und II*, 1:522-25.

91. Allied conference, 12 August 1921, at 11 a.m., *Documents on British Foreign Policy*, first series, 15:700-710; 13 August 1921, at 10:30 a.m., pp. 711-12, 725.

92. La Ligue pour perpétuer le souvenir des crimes allemands to Briand, 9 December 1921, La Série Europe, 1918-1929, Allemagne, vol. 576, "Sanctions aux violations du droit des gens: Punition des coupables, 11 août-31 décembre 1921," MAE; Briand to Saint-Aulaire, No. 2806, November 18, 1921, and Briand to Barrere, No. 2155, November 18, 1921, La Série Europe, 1918-1929, Allemagne, vol. 576, "Sanctions aux violations du droit des gens: Punition des coupables, 11 août-31 décembre 1921," MAE.

93. Resolutions on the Leipzig trials, 7 January 1922, FO 371/7529 (C16860/555/18); "Commission Des Coupables De Guerre: Process-Verbal," 6 and 7 January 1922, FO 371/7470 (C1310/38/18); *New York Times*, 15 January 1922, p. 19.

94. Commander Karl Tillesson was convicted on July 10, 1923, for trying to free Boldt and Dithmar. During his trial, he revealed that in one escape effort he was aided by Lieutenant Erwin Kern who later murdered Walther Rathenau. See Kohan to Curzon, 11 July 1923, FO 371/8809 (C12390/3355/18). For the O.C., see Robert G. L. Waite, *Vanguard of Nazism: The Free Corps Movement in Postwar Germany, 1918-1923* (Cambridge, Mass.: Harvard University Press, 1952),

pp. 213-27. See also Ernst von Salomon, *The Answers of Ernst von Salomon to the 131 Questions in the Allied Military Government "Fragebogen,"* trans. Constantine Fitzgibbon (London: Putnam, 1954), pp. 59-67.

95. Laurent to Walther Rathenau, 10 February 1922, AA (T-120/1567/D685017); D'Abernon to Curzon, 18 October 1921, FO 371/5864 (C20371/29/18); 6 January 1922, FO 371/7528 (C555/555/18); Woods to Foreign Office, 31 January 1922, FO 371/7528 (C1521/555/18); Sthamer to Curzon, 2 June 1922, FO 371/7529 (C8289/555/18); D'Abernon to Curzon, 8 April 1922, FO 371/7529 (C5457/555/18).

96. Raymond Poincaré to Saint-Aulaire, No. 666, March 24, 1922, La Série Europe, 1918-1929, Allemagne, vol. 577, "Sanctions aux violations du droit des gens: Punition des coupables, 1 janvier-31 mars 1922," MAE; Pierre Miquel, *Poincaré* (Paris: Librairie Arthème Fayard, 1961), pp. 421-22.

97. *Verhandlungen des Reichstags,* 352 (16 December 1921-17 February 1922): 5560.

98. Dr. Lucien Graux, *Histoire des violations du traité de paix,* 4 vols. (Paris: Crès, 1921-27), 3:329.

99. Great Britain, *The Trial of German Major War Criminals: Proceedings of the International Military Tribunal Sitting at Nuremberg, Germany,* 13 parts (London: His Majesty's Stationery Office, 1946-47), 9:63-64.

100. Reichskanzlei to German Ambassadors in London, Paris, Rome, and Brussels, n.d. January 1922, AA (T-120/1567/D685014-16).

101. Stosch, *Die Kriegsbeschuldigtenfrage,* pp. 3-14, 209-12; *Times,* 4 July 1922, p. 9.

102. La Ligue pour perpétuer le souvenir des crimes allemands to Poincaré, 11 July 1922, La Série Europe, 1918-1929, Allemagne, vol. 579, "Sanctions aux violations du droit des gens: Punition des coupables, 1-31 juillet 1922," MAE.

103. Saint-Aulaire to Curzon, 17 May 1922, FO 371/7529 (C16860/555/18), Confidential Print No. 11990; Curzon to Hardinge, 19 May 1922, FO 371/7529 (C7164/555/18); Unsigned memorandum, 6 July 1922, La Série Europe, 1918-1929, Allemagne, vol. 579, "Sanctions aux violations du droit des gens: Punition des coupables, 1-31 juillet 1922," MAE.

104. Conference of Ambassadors to German Embassy in Paris, 23 August 1922, FO 371/7529 (C16860/555/18), Confidential Print 11990; Woods to Foreign Office, 16 August 1922, FO 371/7529 (C11741/555/18).

105. Note for the President of the Council, 24 June 1922, La Série Europe, 1918-1929, Allemagne, vol. 578, "Sanctions aux violations du droit des gens: Punition des coupables, 1 avril-30 juin 1922," MAE; Unsigned memorandum on prosecution of Germans, 20 December 1924, La Série Europe, 1918-1929, Allemagne, vol. 584, "Sanctions aux violations du droit des gens: Punition des coupables, 1 décembre 1924-31 mars 1925," MAE.

106. Poincaré to Ministry of Justice, No. 148, March 24, 1922, La Série Europe, 1918-1929, Allemagne, vol. 577, "Sanctions aux violations du droit des gens: Punition des coupables, 1 janvier-31 mars 1922," MAE; Ministry of War to Poincaré, No. 1386, October 9, 1924, La Série Europe, 1918-1929, Allemagne, vol. 583. "Sanctions aux violations du droit des gens: Punition des coupables, 1 avril-30

novembre 1924," MAE. Copies of the judgments can be found scattered through these files. See also press reports in *New York Times*, 28 March 1923, p. 21; 15 October 1924, p. 25; 24 July 1925, p. 15.

107. Poincaré to Ministry of War, No. 1578, July 20, 1922, La Série Europe, 1918-1929, Allemagne, vol. 579, "Sanctions aux violations du droit des gens: Punition des coupables, 1-31 juillet 1922," MAE; Ministry of War to Poincaré, 25 August 1922, La Série Europe, 1918-1929, Allemagne, vol. 580, "Sanctions aux violations du droit des gens: Punition des coupables, 1 août-31 décembre 1922," MAE.

108. George Carlier, Minister of Belgium in Washington, D.C., to Peter Guenther, 26 January 1959, cited in Peter W. Guenther, "A History of Articles 227, 228, 229, and 230 of the Treaty of Versailles" (M.A. thesis, University of Texas at Austin, 1960), p. 180.

109. Arnold Wolfers, *Britain and France between Two Wars: Conflicting Strategies of Peace Since Versailles* (New York: Harcourt, Brace & Co., 1940), pp. 57-59; Frederick L. Schuman, *War and Diplomacy in the French Republic* (New York and London: McGraw-Hill Book Co., 1931), pp. 253-301.

110. No. 30, Cabinet meeting, 17 December 1923, at 5 p.m., Günter Abramowski, ed., *Akten der Reichskanzlei Weimarer Republik: Die Kabinette Marx I und II 30. November 1923 bis 15. Januar 1925*, 2 vols. (Boppard, W. Ger.: Harald Boldt Verlag, 1973), 1:125-26.

111. Henry L. Bretton, *Stresemann and the Revision of Versailles: A Fight for Reason* (Stanford, Calif.: Stanford University Press, 1953), p. 75; Gustav Stresemann, *Gustav Stresemann: His Diaries, Letters, and Papers*, ed. and trans. Eric Sutton, 3 vols. (New York: Macmillan Co., 1935-40), 1:211-21; Curzon to Marling, 8 November 1923, FO 371/8755 (A9136/347/18); Curzon to D'Abernon, 14 November 1923, FO 371/8782 (C19749/1083/18).

112. Cabinet meeting, No. 55(23), November 14, 1923, CAB 23/46.

113. Curzon to Marquess of Crewe, 17 November 1923, FO 371/8782 (C19910/1083/18); Lord D'Abernon, *Ambassador of Peace: Lord D'Abernon's Diary*, 3 vols. (London: Hodder & Stoughton, 1929-30), 2:267-72, 277-78; Walter A. McDougall, *France's Rhineland Diplomacy, 1914-1924: The Last Bid for a Balance of Power in Europe* (Princeton, N.J.: Princeton University Press, 1978), p. 336.

114. Jacques Néré, *The Foreign Policy of France from 1914 to 1945* (London and Boston: Routledge & Kegan Paul, 1975), pp. 63-68.

115. Édouard Herriot to Ministeries of War and Justice, 13 June 1924, La Série Europe, 1918-1929, Allemagne, vol. 583, "Sanctions aux violations du droit des gens: Punition des coupables, 1 avril-30 novembre 1924," MAE.

116. Stephen A. Schuker, *The End of French Predominance in Europe: The Financial Crisis of 1924 and the Adoption of the Dawes Plan* (Chapel Hill, N.C.: University of North Carolina Press, 1976).

117. Leopold von Hoesch to Foreign Ministry, No. 708, November 21, 1924, AA (T-120/1567/D685043); Baron Ago von Maltzan to Hoesch, No. 977, November 24, 1924, AA (T-120/1567/D685072-74); Arnold J. Toynbee, *Survey of International Affairs, 1924* (London: Oxford University Press for the Institute of International Affairs, 1926), pp. 401-3.

118. Maltzan to Hoesch, No. 993, November 26, 1924, AA (T-120/1567/ D685087); Memorandum of conversation between Counselor of German Embassy and Seydoux, 28 November 1924, La Série Europe, 1918-1929, Allemagne, vol. 583, "Sanctions aux violations du droit des gens: Punition des coupables, 1 avril-30 novembre 1924," MAE; Herriot to Minister of War, No. 3093, and to Minister of Justice, No. 855, December 8, 1924, La Série Europe, 1918-1929, Allemagne, vol. 584, "Sanctions aux violations du droit des gens: Punition des coupables, 1 décembre 1924-31 mars 1925"; Herriot to Bruno Jacquin de Margerie, Nos. 860, 861, 862, December 12, 1924, La Série Europe, 1918-1929, Allemagne, vol. 584, "Sanctions aux violations du droit des gens: Punition des coupables, 1 décembre 1924-31 mars 1925."

119. Collective letter to French Consuls in Germany, 8 April 1925, La Série Europe, 1918-1929, Allemagne, vol. 585, "Sanctions aux violations du droit des gens: Punition des coupables, 1 avril-31 juillet 1925," MAE; Baligand to Hoesch, No. 1014, September 3, 1925, AA (T-120/1567/D685125-26).

120. Generalleutnant a. O. Ernst Kabisch, "Wie ich 'Kriegsverbrecher' Wurde," *Berliner Tageblatt*, no. 495 (evening ed.), 19 October 1925.

121. Suarez, *Briand*, 6:82.

122. Sally Marks, *The Illusion of Peace: International Relations in Europe, 1918-1933* (New York: St. Martin's Press, 1976), pp. 71-74; Jon Jacobson, *Locarno Diplomacy: Germany and the West, 1925-1929* (Princeton, N.J.: Princeton University Press, 1972).

123. Friedrich von Keller to Foreign Ministry, No. 177, October 29, 1925, AA (T-120/1567/D685128).

124. Unsigned memorandum on the guilty of the war, No. G.D./16, April 8, 1926, La Série Europe, 1918-1929, Allemagne, vol. 588, "Sanctions aux violations du droit des gens: Punition des coupables, 1 janvier 1926-31 décembre 1929," MAE.

125. De Margerie to Briand, No. 229, March 19, 1927, ibid.; Briand to De Margerie, No. 21, January 3, 1928, ibid.; Briand to French Chargé at Berlin, No. 242, March 29, 1928, ibid.; Briand to De Margerie, No. 1799, October 17, 1928, ibid.; Collective letter to French Consuls in Germany, 10 April 1929, ibid.; De Margerie to Briand, No. 431, May 27, 1929, ibid.

126. Briand to Minister of Interior, No. BC/19, October 28, 1929, ibid.; Memorandum of a conversation between German Ambassador and Philippe Berthelot, 13 November 1929, ibid.

127. Bretton, *Stresemann*, pp. 46-53, 79-83, 117; Phipps to Austen Chamberlain, 23 September 1926, Great Britain, Foreign Office, *Documents on British Foreign Policy, 1919-1939*, series 1A, ed. E. L. Woodward et al., 5 vols. (London: His Majesty's Stationery Office, 1966-73), 2:396; Ingram to Chamberlain, 19 September 1927, *Documents on British Foreign Policy, 1919-1939*, series 1A, 4:29-30.

128. Herman J. Wittgens, "The German Foreign Office Campaign Against the Versailles Treaty: An Examination of the Activities of the Kriegsschuldreferat in the United States" (Ph.D. diss., University of Washington, 1970), pp. 166-67.

129. Postscript by Stresemann, 20 October 1926, AA (T-120/1567/D685139); Stresemann to German Embassy at London, No. 559, November 25, 1926, AA (T-120/1567/D685134).

130. Germany, Reichstag, *Das Völkerrecht in Weltkrieg,* ed. Eugen Fischer, 5 vols. (Berlin, Ger.: Deutsche Verlangsgesellschaft für Politik und Geschichte, 1927); Wittgens, "The German Foreign Office Campaign Against the Versailles Treaty," pp. 90-110.

131. Manfred J. Enssle, "Germany and Belgium, 1919-1929, A Study of German Foreign Policy" (Ph.D. diss., University of Colorado, 1970), pp. 243-47.

132. Germany, Reichstag, *Das Völkerrecht im Weltkrieg,* 3:57-58.

133. Memorandum regarding Captain von Forstner, 6 January 1933, AA (T-120/1567/D685257-59); Kaul, "Die Verfolgung deutscher Kriegsverbrecher nach dem ersten Weltkrieg," pp. 31-32.

134. Fritz Dickmann, "Die Kriegsschuldfrage auf der Friedenskonferenz von Paris, 1919," *Historische Zeitschrift* 197 (August 1963): 94-95.

CHAPTER 9

1. Council of Ten meeting, 12 March 1919, at 3 p.m., *FRUS: Paris Peace Conference, 1919,* 4:332-34; Council of Four meeting, 9 May 1919, at 4 p.m., *FRUS: Paris Peace Conference, 1919,* 5:530.

2. Gordon Brook-Shepherd, *The Last Habsburg* (New York: Weybright & Talley, 1968), pp. 222-46.

3. "Annex I: Summary of Examples of Offences . . . by Central Empires . . . Against the Laws and Customs of War. . . ," "Commission on Responsibility: Minutes," pp. 129-61, Polk Papers.

4. Council of Four meeting, 8 May 1919, at 11 a.m., *FRUS: Paris Peace Conference 1919,* 5:517.

5. Ibid.; Heads of Delegations meeting, 12 August 1919, at 3:30 p.m., ibid., 8:673.

6. Council of Four meeting, 14 May 1919, at 12:15 p.m., ibid., 5:605.

7. Austrian observation on the peace treaty, 12 July and 16 July 1919, Austria, Constituierende Nationalversammulung, *Bericht Über die Tatigkeit der Deutschöster-reichischen Friedensdelegation in St. Germain-en-Laye,* 2 vols. (Vienna: Deutschösterreichischen Staatsdruckerei, 1919), 1:138-39.

8. Carnegie Endowment for International Peace, *The Treaties of Peace, 1919-1923,* 2 vols. (New York: Carnegie Endowment for International Peace, 1924), 1:326-27, 517-18.

9. *Times,* 14 April 1920, p. 13; 20 April 1920, p. 13; 7 June 1920, p. 11; 16 September 1920, p. 9.

10. Earl of Derby to Lord Curzon, 1 May 1920, Great Britain, Foreign Office, *Documents on British Foreign Policy, 1919-1939,* first series, ed. E. L. Woodward et al., 18 vols. (London: His Majesty's Stationery Office, 1947-72), 12:181; Sir George Grahame to Curzon, 6 August 1920, *Documents on British Foreign Policy,* first series, 12:248-49; Gordon Hewart to Foreign Office, 24 December 1920, FO 371/4858 (C14768/141/21); Lord Hardinge to Curzon, 16 September 1921, with enclosure of lists of Hungarians to be surrendered to Rumania, Yugoslavia, and Italy, FO 371/6141 (C18217/15382/21).

11. Nikola Paschitch, Eleutherios Venizelos, and Ion Bratianu to Georges Clemenceau, 19 May 1919, in Bulletin 309, May 27, 1919, David Hunter Miller, *My Diary at the Conference of Paris With Documents*, 21 vols. (New York: Privately Printed by Appeal Printing Co., 1924), 18:406-9.

12. Commission on Responsibility meeting, 15 July 1919, "Commission on Responsibility: Minutes," pp. 177-82, Polk Papers; 17 July 1919, pp. 185-88; 22 July 1919, pp. 191-97; "Conditions of Peace with Bulgaria: Report Presented by the Commission on the Responsibility of the Authors of the War and on the Enforcement of Penalties," 22 July 1919, *FRUS: Paris Peace Conference 1919*, 7:282-87.

13. Heads of Delegations meeting, 25 July 1919, at 3:30 p.m., *Documents on British Foreign Policy*, first series, 1:181-84.

14. Edson James Drake, "Bulgaria at the Paris Peace Conference: A Diplomatic History of the Treaty of Neuilly-sur-Seine" (Ph.D. diss., Georgetown University, 1967), pp. 192-94, 213-15, 228-29.

15. Grahame to Curzon, 6 August 1920, with enclosure of minutes of War Criminals Committee meeting, 5 August 1920, FO 371/4715 (C3398/2915/62); Derby to Curzon, 21 August 1920, FO 371/4715 (C4544/2915/62); V. R. Gattie to Foreign Office, 27 August 1920, FO 371/4673 (C5181/328/19); Derby to Curzon, 7 September 1920, FO 371/4715 (C6161/2915/62).

16. "Third Interim Report from the Committee of Enquiry into Breaches of the Laws of War . . . 26 February 1920," CAB 24/111 (G.P. 1813).

17. Swedish Legation to Curzon, 10 July 1920, with enclosure of letter from Georges Nicoloff to War Office, 21 June 1920, FO 371/4664 (C1203/236/19); Sir Herbert G. Dering to Curzon, 5 July 1920, with enclosure of note from Alexander Stamboliski to Dering, 3 July 1920, FO 371/4664 (C1790/236/19); Army Council to Foreign Office, 23 July 1920, FO 371/4664 (C2078/236/19); Derby to Curzon, 11 August 1920, FO 371/4664 (C3637/236/19).

18. Curzon to Hewart, 18 October 1920, FO 371/4671 (C8608/326/19); Law Officers to Curzon, 20 October 1920, FO 371/4671 (C9192/326/19); Curzon to Dering, 21 October 1920, *Documents on British Foreign Policy*, first series, 12:495-96.

19. Inter-Allied Committee meeting, 10 November 1920, FO 371/4732 (C12778/13/18); Sir Arthur Peel to Curzon, 24 October 1920, FO 371/4671 (C10362/326/19); *New York Times*, 25 October 1920, p. 14; Conversation between David Lloyd George and Stamboliski, 27 October 1920, *Documents on British Foreign Policy*, first series, 8:803-4.

20. Two of his associates claimed Stamboliski was not motivated by political revenge. See Nadejda Muir, *Dimitri Stancioff:Patriot and Cosmopolitan, 1864-1940* (London: John Murray, 1957), p. 259; Kosta Todorov, *Balkan Firebrand: The Autobiography of a Rebel, Soldier, and Statesman* (Chicago and New York: Ziff-Davis Co., 1943), pp. 130-40, 171. After both world wars, it seems clear that the Bulgarians used war crimes trials to eliminate political enemies. After the Second World War the Bulgarian government executed 101 ministers and legislators and punished more than 9,000 other persons. See *Encyclopaedia Britannica*, 1972 ed., s.v. "Bulgaria."

21. Dering to Curzon, 8 August 1920, FO 371/4673 (C4155/328/19).

22. Peel to Curzon, 24 March 1921, FO 371/5799 (C6439/440/7); 31 March 1921, FO371/5799 (C7002/440/7); Sir William Erskine to Curzon, 28 January 1922, FO 371/7376 (C2196/2196/7); John D. Bell, *Peasants in Power: Alexander Stamboliski and the Bulgarian Agrarian National Union, 1899-1923* (Princeton, N.J.: Princeton University Press, 1977), pp. 146-47.

23. Elmer Davis, "Bulgar War Cabinet Placed on Trial," *New York Times*, 14 October 1921, p. 19.

24. Erskine to Curzon, 11 October 1921, FO 371/5800 (C19894/440/7); *Times*, 24 October 1921, p. 9; *New York Times*, 23 August 1922, p. 17; Walter Littlefield, "A People to Be Judge and Jury," *New York Times*, 29 October 1922, sec. 2, p. 7; *New York Times*, 2 April 1923, p. 2; Erskine to Curzon, 1 April 1923, FO 371/8559 (C6363/484/7).

25. Dering to Curzon, 18 August 1920, FO 371/4673 (C4155/328/19).

26. Hugh Seton-Watson, *Eastern Europe Between the Wars, 1918-1941*, 3rd rev. ed. (New York: Harper & Row, Harper Torchbooks, 1967), pp. 242-44.

27. Peel to Curzon, 23 March 1921, "Bulgaria: Annual Report, 1920," FO 371/5813 (C6438/6438/7), Confidential Print 11701. For reports of these court-martials, see *New York Times*, 23 July 1919, p. 2.

28. Dimitri Stancioff to Curzon, 12 February 1921, FO 371/5807 (C3300/1821/7); Hardinge to Curzon, 14 February 1921, FO 371/5807 (C3261/1821/7); Stancioff to Curzon, 17 January 1921, FO 371/5798 (C1396/377/7); Sir Albans Young to Curzon, 31 December 1920, FO 371/5798 (C377/377/7).

29. Peel to Curzon, 26 May 1921, FO 371/5815 (C11280/11280/7); Todorov, *Balkan Firebrand*, p. 141.

30. Bell, *Peasants in Power*, pp. 210-44; Erskine to Curzon, 3 October 1922, FO 371/7374 (C14005/769/7); 30 January 1923, FO 371/8559 (C2606/484/7); *Times*, 13 March 1923, p. 13; 7 June 1923, p. 13.

31. Vice Admiral Sir Somerset Calthorpe to Arthur Balfour, 29 November 1918, FO 406/40, Confidential Print 55 (210534); Richard G. Hovannisian, *The Republic of Armenia*, vol. 1: *The First Years, 1918-1919* (Berkeley, Los Angeles, and London: University of California Press, 1971), 1:419-20; *Times*, 22 April 1919, p. 9; Ahmed Emin, *Turkey in the World War* (New Haven, Conn.: Yale University Press, 1930), pp. 272-75.

32. "The Treatment of British and Indo-British Prisoners of War in Asia Minor and Constantinople," pp. 163-69, and "Turkish and Turko-German Offenders Against the Laws of War," pp. 169-235, in "Second Interim Report from the Committee of Enquiry into Breaches of the Laws of War . . . 3 June 1919, With an Appendix," CAB 24/85 (G.T. 7806).

33. Foreign Office to Law Officers, 10 July 1919, FO 371/5091 (E15109/37/44).

34. War Cabinet meeting, No. 516(1), January 15, 1919, CAB 23/9.

35. Sir Horace Rumbold to Curzon, 20 November 1920, FO 371/5091 (E14893/37/44); *Times*, 24 February 1919, p. 9.

36. Clive Wigram to Theo Russell, 10 January 1919, Lloyd George Papers (F/29/3/3).

37. Otto Liman von Sanders, *Five Years in Turkey* (Baltimore, Md.: Williams & Wilkins Co. for the United States Naval Institute, 1928), pp. 324-25; Frank G.

Weber, *Eagles on the Crescent: Germany, Austria, and the Diplomacy of the Turkish Alliance, 1914-1918* (Ithaca, N.Y.: Cornell University Press, 1970), p. 255.

38. Details of the arrest of General Ali Ihsan Pasha and all other Turks at Malta are found in "Negotiations With the Turkish Nationalists for the Mutual Release of Prisoners of War, Memorandum by the Secretary of State for War, 29 August 1921, Appendix C. Nominal Roll of Turkish Political Internees, Malta," FO 371/6504 (E10117/132/44).

39. Stanford J. Shaw and Ezel Kural Shaw, *History of the Ottoman Empire and Modern Turkey*, vol. 2: *Reform, Revolution, and Republic: The Rise of Modern Turkey, 1801-1975* (London: Cambridge University Press, 1977), 2:332-34.

40. Haigazn K. Kazarian, "A Turkish Military Court Tries the Principal Genocidists of the District of Yozgat," *The Armenian Review* 25 (Summer 1972):34-39; *Times*, 14 April 1919, p. 11; *New York Times*, 14 April 1919, p. 1; Jean-Marie Carzou, *Un Génocide exemplaire: Arménie, 1915* (Paris: Flammarion, 1975), pp. 233-46.

41. Foreign Office to Law Officers, 10 July 1919, FO 371/5091 (E15109/37/44).

42. Haigazn K. Kazarian, "Turkey Tries Its Chief Criminals: Indictment and Sentence Passed Down by Military Court of 1919," *The Armenian Review* 24 (Winter 1971):3-26; *Times*, 3 May 1919, p. 11; A. A. Cruickshank, "The Young Turk Challenge in Postwar Turkey," *Middle East Journal* 22 (Winter 1968):17.

43. On the Nationalists and Mustapha Kemal, see Lord Kinross, *Ataturk: A Biography of Mustafa Kemal, Father of Modern Turkey* (New York: William Morris & Co., 1965). For the significance of the Smyrna landing, see Paul C. Helmreich, *From Paris to Sèvres: The Partition of the Ottoman Empire at the Peace Conference of 1919-1920* (Columbus, Ohio: Ohio State University Press, 1974), pp. 98-99.

44. Laurence Evans, *United States Policy and the Partition of Turkey, 1914-1924* (Baltimore, Md.: The Johns Hopkins Press, 1965), pp. 180-81.

45. W. S. Edmonds, "Malta Internees," 8 November 1920, FO 371/5091 (E15109/37/44); Rumbold to Curzon, 12 March 1921, FO 371/6500 (E3553/132/44).

46. Council of Ten meeting, 17 June 1919, *FRUS: Paris Peace Conference 1919*, 4:508-12.

47. Damad Ferid to Clemenceau, 30 June 1919, FO 371/4174 (98910/1270/44); *New York Times*, 16 July 1919, p. 1; Helmreich, *From Paris to Sèvres*, pp. 109-10.

48. Kazarian, "Turkey Tries Its Chief Criminals," pp. 3-26; "Turkey and the Levant," *New York Times Current History* 10 (August 1919):247; *New York Times*, 13 July 1919, p. 1; Haigazn K. Kazarian, "The Genocide of Kharpert's Armenians: A Turkish Judicial Document and Cipher Telegrams Pertaining to Kharpert," *The Armenian Review* 19 (Spring 1966):16-23; *New York Times*, 21 January 1920, p. 1; Admiral John de Robeck to Curzon, 18 February 1920, FO 371/5089 (E949/37/44).

49. *Times*, 3 August 1920, p. 9; Haigazn K. Kazarian, "The Massacres and Deportations at Papert: Findings of a Turkish Military Court," *The Armenian Review* 25 (Autumn 1972):59-67.

50. Rumbold to Curzon, 31 December 1920, *Documents on British Foreign Policy*, first series, 13:213-14.

51. Rumbold to Curzon, 27 April 1921, "Turkey: Annual Report, 1920," FO 371/6469 (E5233/1/44), Confidential Print 11705.

52. "Summary of Examples of Offences Committed by the Authorities or Forces of the Central Empires and Their Allies . . ." in "Commission on Responsibility: Minutes," p. 131, Polk Papers.

53. Meeting of 7 February 1919, ibid., p. 19; Meeting of 8 February 1919, ibid., pp. 81-82.

54. For a brief history of the development of this kind of war crime, see Egon Schwelb, "Crimes Against Humanity," *The British Year Book of International Law* 23 (1946):178-226.

55. For articles 226-230 of the treaty of Sèvres, see Carnegie Endowment for International Peace, *Treaties of Peace*, 2:862-63. For discussions of article 230, see Allied Conference, 21 February 1920, at 11 a.m., *Documents on British Foreign Policy*, first series, 7:173, 191; Conference of Ambassadors and Foreign Ministers meeting, 23 March 1920, at 4 p.m., *Documents on British Foreign Policy*, first series, 7:593-96.

56. Manley O. Hudson, "The Proposed International Criminal Court," *American Journal of International Law* 32 (July 1938):549-54.

57. Robert Vansittart to Curzon, 12 January 1920, *Documents on British Foreign Policy*, first series, 4:1016-25.

58. Earl of Derby to Curzon, 11 March 1920, ibid., 9:127-28.

59. Minute by W. S. Edmonds, 20 April 1920, on the despatch of Sir George Buchanan to Curzon, 22 April 1920, FO 371/5173 (E3712/272/44).

60. Calthorpe to Curzon, 6 May 1919, FO 406/41, Confidential Print 43 (75892). For the lack of Allied unity, see Helmreich, *From Paris to Sèvres*, passim.

61. For the activities of Young Turk leaders, see Cruickshank, "The Young Turk Challenge in Postwar Turkey," pp. 17-28. For British efforts to have them arrested, see Lord Kilmarnock to Curzon, 2 March 1920, *Documents on British Foreign Policy*, first series, 9:115; 4 March 1920, p. 119; also in *Documents on British Foreign Policy*, first series: Curzon to Kilmarnock, 6 March 1920, p. 122; Curzon to Derby, 8 March 1920, pp. 125-26; Curzon to Kilmarnock, 1 May 1920, p. 456; Kilmarnock to Curzon, 25 May 1920, p. 495; Curzon to Grant Watson, 28 May 1920, pp. 500-501.

62. Foreign Office to Law Officers, 10 July 1919, and Law Officers to Foreign Office, 7 August 1919, FO 371/5091 (E15109/37/44).

63. De Robeck to Curzon, 12 February 1920, FO 371/5089 (E1346/37/44); 16 May 1920, FO 371/5090 (E5746/37/44); 15 June 1920, FO 371/5090 (E7334/37/44); 9 September 1920, FO 371/5090 (E11651/37/44); 20 October 1920, FO 371/5091 (E13844/37/44).

64. The most complete listing of Turks held at Malta is found in "Negotiations With the Turkish Nationalists for the Mutual Release of Prisoners of War, Memorandum by the Secretary of State for War, 29 August 1921, Appendix C, Nominal Roll of Turkish Political Internees, Malta," FO 371/6504 (E10117/132/44) (C.P. 3269).

65. Rumbold to Curzon, 27 April 1921, "Turkey: Annual Report 1920," FO 371/6469 (E5233/1/44), Confidential Print 11705.

66. Harold Nicolson, *Curzon: The Last Phase, 1919-1925* (Boston and New York: Houghton Mifflin Co., 1934), pp. 247-49; Helmreich, *From Paris to Sèvres,* pp. 252-53, 277-82; Winston Churchill, *World Crisis, 1918-1929: The Aftermath* (New York: Charles Scribner's Sons, 1929), pp. 397-98.

67. De Robeck to Curzon, 20 March 1920, FO 371/5089 (E1997/37/44); 25 March 1920, FO 371/5089 (E2805/37/44).

68. Alfred Rawlinson, *Adventures in the Near East, 1918-1922* (New York: Dodd, Mead & Co., 1924), pp. 271-74.

69. "Negotiations With the Turkish Nationalists for the Mutual Release of Prisoners of War, Memorandum by the Secretary of State for War, 29 August 1921, Appendix A," FO 371/6504 (E10117/132/44) (C.P. 3269).

70. Mustapha Kemal to Curzon, 30 April 1920, *Documents on British Foreign Policy,* first series, 13:67-68.

71. Helmreich, *From Paris to Sèvres,* pp. 315-21.

72. Churchill, *World Crisis: Aftermath,* pp. 395-401.

73. Sir Archibald Sinclair to R. H. Campbell, 29 May 1920, FO 371/5090 (E5815/37/44); Campbell to Sinclair, 11 June 1920, FO 371/5090 (E5815/37/44); Sinclair to Campbell, 17 June 1920, FO 371/5090 (E6825/37/44); "Position of Turkish Political Prisoners Interned at Malta: Memorandum by the Secretary of State for War," 19 July 1920, CAB 24/109 (C.P. 1649).

74. Cabinet meeting No. 45(5), August 4, 1920, CAB 23/22.

75. Memorandum by Law Officers, 4 August 1920, CAB 24/110 (C.P. 1770); Curzon to de Robeck, 20 August 1920, *Documents on British Foreign Policy,* first series, 13:124-25.

76. Rumbold to Curzon, 24 November 1920, FO 371/5091 (E15116/37/44).

77. Cardinal Gasparri to Count de Salis, 17 February 1920, and de Salis to Curzon, 25 February 1920, FO 371/5089 (E1114/37/44).

78. Ahmed Emin Yalman, *Turkey in My Time* (Norman, Okla.: University of Oklahoma Press, 1956), pp. 96-104; War Office to Foreign Office, 4 November 1920, FO 371/5091 (E13668/37/44), and 19 December 1921, FO 371/6505 (E13968/132/44).

79. Rumbold to Curzon, 21 December 1920, FO 371/5091 (E16080/37/44); *Times,* 4 October 1921, p. 10.

80. Rumbold to Curzon, 27 April 1921, "Turkey: Annual Report, 1920," FO 371/6469 (E5233/1/44), Confidential Print 11705.

81. "Negotiations With the Turkish Nationalists for the Mutual Release of Prisoners of War, Memorandum by the Secretary of State for War, 29 August 1921, Appendix D: Agreement for the Immediate Release of Prisoners," FO 371/6504 (E10117/132/44) (C.P. 3269); Rumbold to Curzon, 23 March 1921, *Documents on British Foreign Policy,* first series, 17:84-85.

82. Martin Gilbert, *Sir Horace Rumbold: Portrait of a Diplomat, 1869-1941* (London: Heinemann, 1973), pp. 233-40.

83. Curzon to Buchanan, 2 April 1921, *Documents on British Foreign Policy,* first series, 17:102; 6 April 1921, p. 113; Curzon to Rumbold, 9 May 1921, *Documents on British Foreign Policy,* first series, 17:175-76; Buchanan to Curzon, 10 May 1921, *Documents on British Foreign Policy,* first series, 17:177-78.

84. Rumbold to Curzon, 17 May 1921, ibid., pp. 181-82.

85. Frank Rattigan to Curzon with enclosure from Youssuf Kemal, 12 July 1921, FO 371/6503 (E8225/132/44); Salahi Ramsdan Sonyel, *Turkish Diplomacy, 1918-1923: Mustafa Kemal and the Turkish National Movement* (London and Beverly Hills, Calif.: Sage Publications, 1975), pp. 104-5, 115.

86. Rattigan to Curzon, 3 July 1921, *Documents on British Foreign Policy*, first series, 17:292-93; *Times*, 6 July 1921, p. 12.

87. "Cabinet: Trial of Turkish Subjects Accused of Breaches of the Laws of War: Memorandum by the Attorney-General and the Solicitor-General," 18 January 1921, CAB 24/118 (C.P. 2464); Raymond W. Woods to Foreign Office, 20 May 1921, FO 371/6502 (E5845/132/44); Woods to Lancelot Oliphant, 29 July 1921, FO371/6504 (E8745/132/44).

88. Minute by Edmonds, 24 May 1921, on the letter of Woods to Foreign Office, 20 May 1921, FO 371/6502 (E5845/132/44); Sir Eric Geddes to Curzon, 13 July 1921, FO 371/6504 (E8319/132/44).

89. Minute by Edmonds and Malkins, 3 August 1921, on a letter of Woods to Oliphant, 29 July 1921, FO 371/6504 (E8745/132/44); Rumbold to Curzon, 30 August 1921, FO 371/6504 (E10023/132/44).

90. Army Council to Foreign Office, 2 November 1921, FO 371/6505 (E12118/132/44); Rumbold to Curzon, 13 August 1921, *Documents on British Foreign Policy*, first series, 17:355.

91. Sir Andrew Ryan, *The Last of the Dragomans* (London: Geoffrey Bles, 1951), p. 156; Army Council to Foreign Office, 16 September 1921, FO 371/6504 (E10411/132/44); Rumbold to Curzon, 13 August 1921, *Documents on British Foreign Policy*, first series, 17:355.

92. See footnote to despatch of Curzon to Rumbold, 27 September 1921, *Documents on British Foreign Policy*, first series, 17:403-4; de Robeck to Admiralty, 4 October 1921, FO 371/6505 (E11012/132/44).

93. Curzon to Rumbold, 27 September 1921, *Documents on British Foreign Policy*, first series, 17:403-4; *Times*, 3 November 1921, p. 9.

94. Army Council to Foreign Office, 19 November 1921, and Foreign Office to War Office, 26 November 1921, FO 371/6505 (E12740/132/44); India Office to Foreign Office, 17 December 1923, FO 371/9137 (E11939/497/44).

95. Great Britain, Parliament, House of Lords, *Parliamentary Debates* 47 (1921): 277-85.

96. *Times*, 6 October 1921, p. 11.

97. See footnote to despatch of Rumbold to Curzon, 24 April 1922, *Documents on British Foreign Policy*, first series, 17:791-92.

98. See Hovannisian, *Republic of Armenia*, 1:420 n.11; Arshavir Shiragian, "The Assassination of Dr. Behaeddin Shakir," *The Armenian Review* 19 (Autumn 1966):17-31.

CHAPTER 10

1. Leon Friedman, ed., *The Law of War: A Documentary History*, 2 vols. (New York: Random House, 1972), 1:435-55, 471-522.

2. Philip C. Jessup, *Elihu Root*, 2 vols. (New York: Dodd, Mead & Co., 1938), 2:453-57.

3. British Empire Delegation meeting, 31 December 1921, at 3 p.m., CAB 29/28.

4. Richard Dean Burns, "Regulating Submarine Warfare, 1921-41: A Case Study in Arms Control and Limited War," *Military Affairs* 35 (April 1971):56-63.

5. Benjamin B. Ferencz, *An International Criminal Court: A Step Toward World Peace—A Documentary History and Analysis,* 2 vols. (New York: Oceana Publications, 1980), 1:196-224; United Nations, General Assembly, International Law Commission, *Historical Survey of the Question of International Criminal Jurisdiction* (A/CN. 4/7/Rev. 1) (1949), pp. 8-12; Lord Phillimore, "An International Criminal Court and the Resolutions of the Committee of Jurists," *The British Year Book of International Law* 3 (1922-23):79-86.

6. Ferencz, *International Criminal Court,* 1:226-43.

7. Ibid., pp. 39-46, 252-68; Antoine Sottile, "The Problem of the Creation of a Permanent International Criminal Court," *Revue de Droit International de Sciences Diplomatiques et Politiques* 29 (October-December 1951):267-72.

8. Nicolas Politis, "International Penal Law," in Nicolas Politis, *The New Aspects of International Law* (Washington, D.C.: Carnegie Endowment for International Peace, 1928), pp. 32-48.

9. F. P. Walters, *A History of the League of Nations* (London: Oxford University Press, 1960), pp. 268-89; Benjamin B. Ferencz, *Defining International Aggression: The Search for World Peace, A Documentary History and Analysis,* 2 vols. (Dobbs Ferry, N.Y.: Oceana Publications, 1975), 1:10-18.

10. Ferencz, *Defining International Aggression,* 1:29-34, 260-69.

11. Hans-Heinrich Jescheck, *Die Verantwortlichkeit der Staatsorgane nach Völkerstrafrecht: Eine Studie zu den Nürnberger Prozessen* (Bonn, W. Ger.: Ludwig Röhrscheid Verlag, 1952), pp. 69-89; Ian Brownlie, *International Law and the Use of Force by States* (Oxford: Clarendon Press, 1963), pp. 66-111.

12. John E. Stoner, *S. O. Levinson and the Pact of Paris: A Study in the Techniques of Influence* (Chicago: University of Chicago Press, 1943), pp. 85-89, 345-46; John Chalmers Vinson, *William E. Borah and the Outlawry of War* (Athens, Ga.: University of Georgia Press, 1957).

13. Robert H. Ferrell, *Peace in Their Time, The Origins of the Kellogg-Briand Pact* (New Haven, Conn.: Yale University Press, 1952).

14. Jescheck, *Verantwortlichkeit der Staatsorgane nach Völkerstrafrecht,* p. 81.

15. Ferencz, *International Criminal Court,* 1:48-54, 269-398; Manley O. Hudson, *The Permanent Court of International Justice, 1920-1942: A Treatise* (New York: Macmillan Co., 1943), pp. 85-89.

16. Raymond J. Sontag, *A Broken World, 1919-1939* (New York: Harper & Row, Harper Torchbooks, 1971), pp. 236-381; Walters, *History of the League,* pp. 465-810.

17. Sir G. Ogilvie-Forbes to Kirkpatrick, 25 August 1939, with enclosures of Hitler's speech to Chief Commanders and Commanding Generals, 22 August 1939, Great Britain, Foreign Office, *Documents on British Foreign Policy, 1919-1939,* third series, ed. E. L. Woodward et al., 9 vols. (London: His Majesty's Stationery Office, 1949-55), 7:258. For an analysis of the various versions of Hitler's speech, see Winfried Baumgart, "Zur Ansprache Hitlers vor den Führen der Wehrmacht am 22 August 1939: Eine Quellenkritische Untersuchung," *Vierteljahrshefte für Zeitgeschichte* 16 (April 1968):120-49.

18. Albert Speer, *Spandau: The Secret Diaries*, trans. Richard and Clara Winston (New York: Macmillan Co., 1976), p. 43.

19. Among the many studies of the punishment of the war criminals of the Second World War, see Eugene Davidson, *The Trial of the Germans: An Account of the Twenty-two Defendants before the International Military Tribunal at Nuremberg* (New York: Macmillan Co., 1966); William J. Bosch, *Judgment on Nuremberg: American Attitudes Toward the Major German War-Crime Trials* (Chapel Hill, N.C.: University of North Carolina Press, 1970); Bradley F. Smith, *Reaching Judgment At Nuremberg* (New York: Basic Books, 1977); Werner Maser, *Nuremberg: A Nation on Trial*, trans. Richard Barry (New York: Charles Scribner's Sons, 1979); John A. Appleman, *Military Tribunals and International Crimes* (Indianapolis, Ind.: Bobbs-Merrill Co., 1954); Richard H. Minear, *Victor's Justice: The Tokyo War Crimes Trial* (Princeton, N.J.: Princeton University Press, 1971); Philip R. Piccigallo, *The Japanese on Trial: Allied War Crimes Operations in the East, 1945-1951* (Austin, Tex.: University of Texas Press, 1979); Bradley F. Smith, *The Road to Nuremberg* (New York: Basic Books, 1981).

20. See, for example, "The Treatment of War Crimes and Crimes Incidental to the War—The Experience of 1918-1922," *The Bulletin of International News* 22 (February 3, 1945):95-102; C. J. Cadoux, "The Punishing of Germany After the War of 1914-1918," *Hibbert Journal* 43 (January 1945): 107-13; George Creel, *War Criminals and Punishment* (London: Hutchinson & Co., 1945); Sheldon Glueck, *War Criminals: Their Prosecution and Punishment* (New York: Alfred A. Knopf, 1944); Albert G. D. Levy, "The Law and Procedure of War Crime Trials," *American Political Science Review* 37 (December 1943): 1052-81.

21. United Nations War Crimes Commission, *History of the United Nations War Crimes Commission and the Development of the Laws of War* (London: His Majesty's Stationery Office, 1948), pp. 2-3, 10-11, 111, 170-71.

22. "Action of the German Authorities in Occupied Territory: Memorandum by the Secretary of State for Foreign Affairs," 5 October 1941, CAB 66/19 (W.P. [41] 233); War Cabinet meeting, No. 101 (41), October 9, 1941, at 12:15 p.m., CAB 65/19. See also Memorandum by Anthony Eden on treatment of war criminals, 22 June 1942, CAB 66/25 (W.P. [42] 264).

23. Note by Winston Churchill on punishment of war criminals, 9 November 1943, CAB 66/42 (W.P. [43] 496); War Cabinet meeting, No. 152 (43), November 10, 1943, at 6 p.m., CAB 65/36; Eden to Sir Cecil Hurst, 4 January 1945, FO 371/39010 (C17674/14/62); "Aide-Mémoire from the United Kingdom, April 23, 1945," in United States, Department of State, *Report of Robert H. Jackson, United States Representative to the International Conference on Military Trials, London, 1945* (Washington, D.C.: United States Government Printing Office, 1949), pp. 18-20.

24. Smith, *Reaching Judgment at Nuremberg*, pp. 22-45; Smith, *Road to Nuremberg*, pp. 75-151, 207-46.

25. Conference minutes, 25 July 1945, *Report of Robert H. Jackson*, pp. 295, 299.

26. For the best legal analysis of these decisions, see Robert K. Woetzel, *The Nuremberg Trials in International Law* (London: Stevens & Sons, 1962).

27. For criticism, see Wilbourn E. Benton and Georg Grimm, eds., *Nuremberg: German Views of the War Trials* (Dallas, Tex.: Southern Methodist University Press, 1955); Viscount Frederic Maugham, *U.N.O. and War Crimes* (London: John Murray, 1951); George A. Finch. "The Nuremberg Trial and International Law," *American Journal of International Law* 41 (January 1947): 20-37.

28. Bosch, *Judgment on Nuremberg*, pp. 102-3. See also Quincy Wright, "The Law of the Nuremberg Trial," *American Journal of International Law* 41 (January 1947): 38-72.

29. Woetzel, *Nuremberg Trials*, pp. 232-40.

30. Ferencz, *International Criminal Court*, 2:1-100; Ferencz, *Defining International Aggression*, 2:1-53. For contrasting views of efforts to define aggression, see C. A. Pompe, *Aggressive War: An International Crime* (The Hague: Martinus Nijhoff, 1953); Julius Stone, *Aggression and World Order: A Critique of United Nations Theories of Aggression* (Berkeley, Calif.: University of California Press, 1958); Julius Stone, *Conflict Through Consensus: United Nations Approaches to Aggression* (Baltimore and London: The Johns Hopkins University Press, 1977).

31. For an unfavorable analysis of the Nuremberg principles, see Eugene Davidson, *The Nuremberg Fallacy: Wars and War Crimes Since World War II* (New York: Macmillan Co., 1973). For positive appraisals of an international criminal jurisdiction, see the various articles in Julius Stone and Robert K. Woetzel, eds., *Toward a Feasible International Criminal Court* (Geneva: World Peace Through Law Center, 1970); Gerhard O. W. Mueller and Edward M. Wise, eds., *International Criminal Law* (London: Sweet & Maxwell, 1965); M. Cherif Bassiouni and Ved P. Nanda, eds., *A Treatise on International Criminal Law*, 2 vols. (Springfield, Ill.: Charles C. Thomas, 1973).

BIBLIOGRAPHICAL NOTE

The sources for this study are so numerous that a description of each of them would require an essay of prohibitive length. This brief note deals only with unpublished sources and with previous studies of this topic.

Among the principal sources for this study are the diaries and papers of public officials and unpublished governmental records of Britain, France, Germany, the Netherlands, and the United States. The most important documents for this topic are found in the Foreign Office and Cabinet papers at the Public Record Office in London and include especially the files of the Prisoners of War Department and the Committee of Enquiry into Breaches of the Laws of War, which reveal the dominant role of the British government in the origins of the first effort at international war crimes punishment. Foreign Office despatches and Cabinet minutes for the period 1915-1922 are also essential because of the leading role of the British in almost every phase of attempts to implement the war crimes clauses of the peace treaties of the First World War. The records of the French Foreign Ministry at Paris generally cover the same ground as British documents before 1922. For the period from the Leipzig trials to 1929, however, French diplomatic despatches provide information found in no other source. No previous study of this topic has made use of these unpublished materials in British and French archives, which generally remained unavailable to researchers until the late 1960s.

Unpublished records of the governments of Germany, the Netherlands, and the United States, which have been used by the scholars listed below, are important for particular aspects of this topic. The microfilmed records of the German Foreign Ministry found in the National Archives at Washington, D.C., are most useful for tracing developments following the Leipzig trials. The files of the Dutch Foreign Ministry at The Hague are, of course, important for describing efforts to secure surrender of the kaiser, but they are best used in conjunction with British and French sources. The records of the Department of State at the National Archives contain materials relating to the negotiations at the Paris Peace Conference but little else.

The papers of statesmen that were consulted for this study provide some valuable individual items, but none of the collections contains extensive correspondence or memoranda about war crimes trials. The collections of papers containing the most important materials for this topic are those of Herbert Asquith, Lord Hanworth (Sir Ernest Pollock), Edward M. House, Robert Lansing, and David Lloyd George.

Previous studies of this topic include works by the following writers: Gordon W. Bailey, David A. Foltz, Peter W. Guenther, Friedrich K. Kaul, James M. Read, and J. Verseput. Citations of the works of these writers are listed in the bibliography. These studies make significant contributions in their treatment of particular aspects of this topic. This book has benefitted from their bibliographies. But none of these studies deals comprehensively with the effort to punish the war criminals of the First World War, and none of them represents extensive research in the archives of more than one government. It is hoped that this book meets the need for a comprehensive study of this important subject.

BIBLIOGRAPHY

MANUSCRIPTS

The Papers of Herbert Asquith, Earl of Oxford and Asquith, Bodleian Library, Oxford University, Oxford.

The Papers of Ray Stannard Baker, Library of Congress, Washington, D.C.

The Papers of Tasker H. Bliss, Library of Congress, Washington, D.C.

The Papers of Andrew Bonar Law, Beaverbrook Library, London.

The Papers of Viscount James Bryce, Bodleian Library, Oxford University, Oxford.

The Papers of Viscount Cecil of Chelwood (Lord Robert Cecil), British Museum, London.

The Papers of Lord Hanworth (Sir Ernest Pollock), Bodleian Library, Oxford University, Oxford.

The Diary and Papers of Edward M. House, Yale University Library, New Haven, Conn.

The Diary and Papers of Robert Lansing, Library of Congress, Washington, D.C.

The Papers of Robert Lansing, Princeton University Library, Princeton, N.J.

The Papers of David Lloyd George, Beaverbrook Library, London.

The Papers of Lord Milner, Bodleian Library, Oxford University, Oxford.

The Diary and Papers of Frank L. Polk, Yale University Library, New Haven, Conn.

The Papers of James Brown Scott, Georgetown University Library, Washington, D.C.

The Papers of Henry White, Library of Congress, Washington, D.C.

The Papers of Woodrow Wilson, Library of Congress, Washington, D.C.

The Woodrow Wilson Manuscripts Collected by Charles L. Swem, Princeton University Library, Princeton, N.J.

The Papers of Sir William Wiseman, Yale University Library, New Haven, Conn.

UNPUBLISHED GOVERNMENT RECORDS

France, Archives des Affaires Étrangères, Ministère des Affaires Étrangères, Quai d'Orsay, Paris (cited as MAE).

Germany, Auswärtiges Amt, United States National Archives Microfilm Publication of German Foreign Ministry Archives, Washington, D.C. (cited as AA microfilm publication number/roll number/frame number).

Great Britain, Papers of the Cabinet, Public Record Office, London (cited as CAB).

Great Britain, Papers of the Foreign Office, Public Record Office, London (cited as FO).

Great Britain, Papers of the Treasury Solicitor Miscellaneous, Public Record Office, London (cited as TS).

Netherlands, Archieven van het Ministerie van Buitenlandse Zaken, The Hague (cited as MBZ).

United States, Department of State, Papers of the American Commission to Negotiate Peace, Record Group 256, National Archives, Washington, D.C.

PUBLIC DOCUMENTS

Abramowski, Günter, ed. *Akten der Reichskanzlei Weimarer Republik: Die Kabinette Marx I und II 30. November 1923 bis 15. Januar 1925.* 2 vols. Boppard, W. Ger.: Harald Boldt Verlag, 1973.

Austria. Constituierende Nationalversammlung. *Bericht Über die Tatigkeit der Deutschösterreichischen Freidensdelegation in St. Germain-en-Laye.* 2 vols. Vienna: Deutschösterreichischen Staatsdruckerei, 1919.

Carnegie Endowment for International Peace. *The Treaties of Peace, 1919-1923.* 2 vols. New York: Carnegie Endowment for International Peace, 1924.

————. *Violations of the Laws and Customs of War: Report of the Majority and Dissenting Reports of the American and Japanese Members of the Commission on Responsibilities at the Conference of Paris, 1919.* Pamphlet No. 32. Oxford: At the Clarendon Press, 1919.

La Documentation Internationale. *La Paix de Versailles.* Vol. 3: *Responsabilités des auteurs de la guerre et sanctions.* Edited by Albert de Lapradelle. 12 vols. Paris: Les Éditions Internationales, 1929-39.

France. Chambre des Députés. *Annales de la Chambre des Députés Débats Parlementaires.* 1914-30.

————. Sénat. *Annales du Sénat Débats Parlementaires.* 1914-30.

Germany. Nationalversammlung. *Verhandlungen der Verfassunggebenden Deutsche Nationalversammlung. 1919-20.*

————. Reichstag. *Verhandlungen des Reichstags.* 1920-30.

————. *Das Völkerrecht im Weltkrieg.* Edited by Eugen Fischer. 5 vols. Berlin, Ger.: Deutsche Verlangsgesellschafts für Politik und Geschichte, 1927.

Great Britain. Foreign Office. *Documents on British Foreign Policy, 1919-1939.* First Series. Edited by E. L. Woodward et al. 18 vols. London: His Majesty's Stationery Office, 1947-72.

————. *Documents on British Foreign Policy, 1919-1939.* Series IA. Edited by E. L. Woodward et al. 5 vols. London: His Majesty's Stationery Office, 1966-73.

————. *Documents on British Foreign Policy, 1919-1939.* Third Series. Edited by E. L. Woodward et al. 9 vols. London: His Majesty's Stationery Office, 1949-55.

_____. *The Trial of German Major War Criminals: Proceedings of the International Military Tribunal Sitting at Nuremberg, Germany.* 13 parts. London: His Majesty's Stationery Office, 1946-47.

_____. Parliament. House of Commons. *Parliamentary Debates.* 1914-30.

_____. House of Lords. *Parliamentary Debates.* 1914-30.

_____. *Parliamentary Papers* (Commons), *1921.* Vol. 43. Cmnd. 1325, "Protocols and Correspondence between the Supreme Council and the Conference of Ambassadors and the German Government and the German Peace Delegation between January 10, 1920, and July 17, 1920, respecting the execution of the Treaty of Versailles of June 28, 1919."

_____. *Parliamentary Papers* (Commons), *1921.* Vol. 12. Cmnd. 1450, "German War Trials: Report of Proceedings before the Supreme Court in Leipzig."

Lutz, Ralph H., ed. *The Fall of the German Empire 1914-1918.* 2 vols. Stanford, Calif.: Stanford University Press, 1932.

Mantoux, Paul. *Paris Peace Conference 1919: Proceedings of the Council of Four (March 24-April 18).* Translated by John Boardman Whitton. Geneva: Institut universitaire de hautes études internationales, 1964.

Michaelis, Herbert, and Ernst Schraepler, eds. *Ursachen und Folgen vom Deutsche Zusammenbruch 1918 bis 1945 zur Staatlichen Neuordnung Deutschlands in der Gegenwart; Eine Urkunden—und Dokumentensammlang zur Zeitgeschichte.* Vol. 4: *Die Weimarer Republik Vertragserfüllung und innere Bedrohung, 1919-1922.* Berlin, W. Ger.: Dokumenten—Verlag Dr. Herbert Wendler, 1960.

Netherlands. Commissee voor Rijks Geschiedkundige Publicatiën. *Bescheiden Betreffende de Buitenlandse Politiek van Nederland, 1848-1919 . . . Vijfde Deel, 1917-1919.* Edited by C. Smit. The Hague: Martinus Nijhoff, 1964. Vol. 117.

_____. *Bescheiden Betreffende de Buitenlandse Politiek van Nederland, 1848-1919 . . . Achtste Deel, Buitenlandse Bronnen, 1917-1919.* Edited by C. Smit. The Hague: Martinus Nijhoff, 1973. Vol. 145.

Netherlands Orange Book. *Mededeelingen van den Minister van Buitenlandsche Zaken aan de Staten-Generaal, Juni 1919-April 1920.*

Russia. *Die Internationalen Beziehungen im Zeitalter des Imperialismus. Dokumente aus den Archiven der Zarischen und der Provisorischen Regierung. . . .* Edited by M. N. Pokrowski. Series 2. Berlin, Ger.: Verlag Reimar Hobbing G.M.B.H., 1935. Vol. 7.

Scherer, André, and Jacques Grunewald, eds. *L'Allemagne et les problèmes de la paix pendant la Première Guerre Mondiale.* Vol. 3: *De la Revolution Sovietiques à la paix de Brest-Litovsk (9 novembre 1917-3 mars 1918).* Paris: Publications de la Sorbonne, 1976.

Schulze, Hagen, ed. *Akten der Reichskanzlei Weimarer Republik: Das Kabinett Scheidemann 13. Februar bis 20. Juni 1919.* Boppard, W. Ger.: Harald Boldt Verlag, 1971.

Schulze-Bidlingmaier, Ingrid, ed. *Akten der Reichskanzlei Weimarer Republik: Die Kabinette Wirth I und II, 10. Mai 1921 bis 22. November 1922.* 2 vols. Boppard, W. Ger.: Harald Boldt Verlag, 1973.

United States. Congress. House. Joint Resolution on the Trial of the Kaiser. H.J.R.

371, 65th Cong., 3rd sess., 18 December 1918. *Congressional Record,* vol. 57:647.

————. *Letter of Secretary of War on Trial of Captain Henry Wirz.* Executive Document No. 23, 40th Cong., 2nd sess., 1868.

United States. Department of State. *Papers Relating to the Foreign Relations of the United States, 1915, Supplement, The World War.* Washington, D.C.: United States Government Printing Office, 1928.

————. *Papers Relating to the Foreign Relations of the United States, 1916, Supplement, The World War.* Washington, D.C.: United States Government Printing Office, 1929.

————. *Papers Relating to the Foreign Relations of the United States, 1917, Supplement 1, The World War.* Washington, D.C.: United States Government Printing Office, 1931.

————. *Papers Relating to the Foreign Relations of the United States, 1918, Supplement 1, The World War.* 2 vols. Washington, D.C.: United States Government Printing Office, 1933.

————. *Papers Relating to the Foreign Relations of the United States, 1918, Supplement 2, The World War.* Washington, D.C.: United States Government Printing Office, 1933.

————. *Papers Relating to the Foreign Relations of the United States, 1919.* 2 vols. Washington, D.C.: United States Government Printing Office, 1934.

————. *Papers Relating to the Foreign Relations of the United States: The Peace Conference, 1919.* 13 vols. Washington, D.C.: United States Government Printing Office, 1942-47.

————. *Papers Relating to the Foreign Relations of the United States: The Lansing Papers, 1914-1920.* 2 vols. Washington, D.C.: United States Government Printing Office, 1939-40.

————. *Report of Robert H. Jackson, United States Representative to the International Conference on Military Trials, London, 1945.* Washington, D.C.: United States Government Printing Office, 1949.

Vogt, Martin, ed. *Akten der Reichskanzlei Weimarer Republik: Das Kabinett Müller I 27. März bis 21. Juni 1920.* Boppard, W. Ger.: Harald Boldt Verlag, 1971.

Wulf, Peter, ed. *Akten der Reichskanzlei Weimarer Republik: Das Kabinett Fehrenbach 25. Juni 1920 bis 4. Mai 1921.* Boppard, W. Ger.: Harald Boldt Verlag, 1972.

AUTOBIOGRAPHIES, COLLECTED WORKS, DIARIES, LETTERS, AND MEMOIRS

Alderson, William T., ed. "The Attempt to Capture the Kaiser By Luke Lea." *Tennessee Historical Quarterly* 20 (September 1961):222-61.

Ames, Knowlton L., Jr. *Berlin After the Armistice.* Privately printed, 1919.

Asquith, Herbert, Earl of Oxford and Asquith. *Memories and Reflections, 1852-1927.* 2 vols. London: Cassell & Co., 1928.

Baker, Ray Stannard. *Woodrow Wilson: Life and Letters.* 8 vols. New York: Doubleday, Doran & Co., 1927-39.

Baker, Ray Stannard, and William E. Dodd, eds. *The Public Papers of Woodrow Wilson, War and Peace*. 2 vols. New York: Harper & Bros., 1927.

Beadon, Roger H. *Some Memories of the Peace Conference*. London: Lincoln Williams, 1933.

Benoist, Charles. "Guillaume II en Hollande." *Revue des Deux Mondes* 19 (15 January 1934):386-403.

Bethmann Hollweg, Theobald von. *Reflections on the World War*. Translated by George Young. 2 vols. London: Thornton Butterworth, 1920.

Birkenhead, Lord. *The Speeches of Lord Birkenhead*. London: Cassell & Co., 1929.

Blücher, Princess. *An English Wife in Berlin*. New York: E. P. Dutton & Co., 1920.

Borden, Henry, ed. *Robert Laird Borden: His Memoirs*. 2 vols. New York: Macmillan Co., 1938.

Bryan, Mary, ed. *The Memoirs of William Jennings Bryan*. Chicago: John C. Winston Co., 1925.

Callwell, Sir C. E. *Field-Marshal Sir Henry Wilson: His Life and Diaries*. 2 vols. London: Cassell & Co., 1927.

Cambon, Henri, ed. *Paul Cambon, Correspondance, 1870-1924*. 3 vols. Paris: Éditions Bernard Grasset, 1940-46.

Cecil, Lord Robert. *All the Way*. London: Hodder & Stoughton, 1949.

Clemenceau, Georges. *Grandeur and Misery of Victory*. Translated by F. M. Atkinson. New York: Harcourt, Brace & Co., 1930.

Cole, Margaret, ed. *Beatrice Webb's Diaries, 1912-1924*. 2 vols. London: Longmans, Green & Co., 1952.

Corday, Michel. *The Paris Front: An Unpublished Diary, 1914-1918*. New York: E. P. Dutton & Co., 1934.

Cronon, E. David, ed. *The Cabinet Diaries of Josephus Daniels: 1913-1921*. Lincoln, Nebr.: University of Nebraska Press, 1963.

Czernin, Count Ottokar. *In the World War*. London: Cassell & Co., 1919.

D'Abernon, Lord. *An Ambassador of Peace: Lord D'Abernon's Diary*. 3 vols. London: Hodder & Stoughton, 1929-30.

David, Edward, ed. *Inside Asquith's Cabinet: From the Diaries of Charles Hobhouse*. New York: St. Martin's Press, 1977.

Deland, Margaret. *Small Things*. New York: D. Appleton & Co., 1919.

Ebermayer, Ludwig. *Fünfzig Jahre Dienst am Recht: Erinnerungen eines Juristen*. Leipzig, Ger.; Zürich, Switz.: Grethlein & Co., 1930.

Ferry, Abel. *Les Carnets secrets (1914-1918)*. Paris: Bernard Grasset, 1957.

Fitzroy, Sir Almeric. *Memoirs*. 2 vols. New York: George H. Doran Co., 1925.

Fournier-Foch, Henry, ed. "Lettre inedite du Maréchal Hindenburg au Maréchal Foch de 3 juillet 1919." *Revue Historique de l'Armée* 29, No. 2 (1973):70-75.

Gerard, James W. *My First Eighty-Three Years in America*. Garden City, N.Y.: Doubleday & Co., 1951.

Görlitz, Walter, ed. *The Kaiser and His Court: The Diaries, Note Books, and Letters of Admiral Georg Alexander von Müller, Chief of the Naval Cabinet, 1914-1918*. London: Macdonald & Co., 1961.

Grey of Fallodon, Viscount. *Twenty-Five Years, 1892-1916*. 2 vols. New York: Frederick A. Stokes Co., 1925.

Grimm, Friedrich. *Politische Justiz, die Krankheit unserer Zeit: 40 Jahre Dienst am Recht*. Bonn, W. Ger.: Verlag Bonner Universitäts-Buchdruckerai, 1953.

Hancock, William, and Jean van der Poel, eds. *Selections from the Smuts Papers, November 1918-August 1919*. London: Cambridge University Press, 1966.

Hanssen, Hans Peter. *Diary of a Dying Empire*. Translated by Oscar O. Winther. Bloomington, Ind.: Indiana University Press, 1955.

Harbord, James G. *Leaves from a War Diary*. New York: Dodd, Mead & Co., 1925.

Hardinge of Penshurst, Lord. *Old Diplomacy: The Reminiscences of Lord Hardinge of Penshurst*. London: John Murray, 1947.

Headlam, Cecil, ed. *The Milner Papers: South Africa, 1899-1905*. 2 vols. London: Cassell & Co., 1933.

Herriot, Édouard. *Jadis*. 2 vols. Paris: Flammarion, 1952.

Hymans, Paul. *Mémoires*. 2 vols. Brussels:Université libre de Bruxelles, 1958.

Ilsemann, Sigurd von. *Der Kaiser in Holland: Aufzeichnungen des Letzten Flügeladjutanten Kaiser Wilhelms II*. Edited by Harald von Koenigswald. 2 vols. Munich, W. Ger.: Biederstein Verlag, 1967.

Jones, Tom. *Whitehall Diary*. Edited by Keith Middlemas. 3 vols. London: Oxford University Press, 1969-71.

Kessler, Harry. *In the Twenties: The Diaries of Harry Kessler*. Translated by Charles Kessler. New York: Holt, Rinehart & Winston, 1971.

Lancken Wakenitz, Baron Oskar von der. *Meine Dreissig Dienstjahre, 1888-1918: Potsdam-Paris-Brussels*. Berlin, Ger.: Verlag für Kulturpolitik, 1931.

Lane, Anne W., and Louise H. Wall, eds. *The Letters of Franklin K. Lane, Personal and Political*. Boston: Houghton Mifflin & Co., 1922.

Lennox, Lady Algernon Gordon, ed. *The Diary of Lord Bertie of Thame: 1914-1918*. 2 vols. London: George H. Doran, 1924.

Lersner, Baron Kurt von. "Die Auslieferung der Deutschen Kriegsverbrecher." In *Zehn Jahre Versailles*, 1: 15-27. Edited by Heinrich Schnee and Hans Draeger. 3 vols. Berlin, Ger.: Bruckenverlag, 1929-30.

Liman von Sanders, Otto. *Five Years in Turkey*. Baltimore: William & Wilkins Co. for the United States Naval Institute, 1928.

Lloyd George, David. *Memoirs of the Peace Conference*. 2 vols. New Haven, Conn.: Yale University Press, 1939.

————. *War Memoirs*. 6 vols. London: Ivor Nicholson & Watson, 1933-36.

Louis, Georges. *Les Carnets de Georges Louis, 1908-1917*. 2 vols. 4th ed. Paris: F. Rieder et Cie, 1926.

Ludendorff, Erich. *Ludendorff's Own Story, August 1914-November 1918*. 2 vols. New York and London: Harper & Bros., 1919.

Ludendorff, Margarethe. *My Married Life With Ludendorff*. Translated by Raglan Somerset. London: Hutchinson & Co., 1930.

Mallet, Sir Charles. *Lord Cave: A Memoir*. London: John Murray, 1931.

Meissner, Otto. *Staatssekretär unter Ebert-Hindenburg-Hitler: Der Schicksalsweg des Deutschen Volkes von 1918-1945, wei ich ihn erlebte*. Hamburg, W. Ger.: Hoffmann & Campe Verlag, 1950.

Miller, David Hunter. *My Diary at the Conference of Paris With Documents*. 21 vols. New York: Privately Printed by Appeal Printing Co., 1924.

Morand, Paul. *Journal d'un attaché d'ambassade, 1916-1917*. Paris: Gallimard, 1963.

Mordacq, Général Jean. *Le Ministère Clemenceau: Journal d'un témoin.* 4 vols. Paris: Librairie Plon, 1930-31.

Morgenthau, Henry, *Ambassador Morgenthau's Story.* Garden City, N.Y.: Doubleday, Page & Co., 1918.

Morison, Elting E., ed. *The Letters of Theodore Roosevelt.* 8 vols. Cambridge, Mass.: Harvard University Press, 1951-54.

Nevins, Allan, ed. *The Letters and Journal of Brand Whitlock.* 2 vols. New York: D. Appleton-Century Co., 1936.

Newton, Lord Thomas. *Retrospection.* London: John Murray, 1941.

Nicolson, Harold. *Peacemaking.* London: Constable & Co., 1933.

Noske, Gustav. *Von Kiel bis Kapp; zur Geschichte der Deutschen Revolution.* Berlin, Ger.: Verlag für Politik und Wirtschaft, 1920.

Orlando, Vittorio. *Memorie (1915-1919).* Edited by Rodolfo Mosca. Milan: Rizzoli, 1960.

Paléologue, Maurice. *An Ambassador's Memoirs.* Translated by F. A. Holt. 3 vols. New York: George H. Doran Co., n.d.

Poincaré, Raymond. *Au Service de la France.* 10 vols. Paris: Librairie Plon, 1926-33.

Radbruch, Gustav. *Der Innere Weg: Aufrisz meines Lebens.* Göttingen, W. Ger.: Vandenhoeck & Ruprecht, 1961.

Raeder, Erich. *My Life.* Translated by Henry W. Drexel. Annapolis, Md.: United States Naval Institute, 1960.

Rawlinson, Alfred. *Adventures in the Near East, 1918-1922.* New York: Dodd, Mead & Co., 1924.

Roddie, William Stewart. *Peace Patrol.* New York: G. P. Putnam's Sons, 1933.

Rosen, Friedrich. *Aus einem Diplomatischen Wanderleben.* 4 vols. Wiesbaden, W. Ger.: Limes Verlag, 1959.

Ryan, Sir Andrew. *The Last of the Dragomans.* London: Geoffrey Bles, 1951.

Salomon, Ernst von. *The Answers of Ernst von Salomon to the 131 Questions in the Allied Military Government "Fragebogen."* Translated by Constantine Fitzgibbon. London: Putnam, 1954.

Salvidge, Stanley. *Salvidge of Liverpool: Behind the Political Scene, 1890-1928.* London: Hodder & Stoughton, 1934.

Sandburg, Carl. *Complete Poems.* New York: Harcourt, Brace & Co., 1950.

Sazonov, Serge. *Fateful Years, 1909-1916: The Reminiscences of Serge Sazonov.* London: Jonathan Cape, 1928.

Scheidemann, Philip. *Memoirs of a Social Democrat.* Translated by J. E. Mitchell. 2 vols. London: Hodder & Stoughton, 1929.

Schild, Hermann, ed. *Professor Dr. Friedrich Grimm, mit Offenem Visier: Aus den Lebenserinnerungen eines Deutschen Rechtsanwalt.* Leoni am Starnberger See, W. Ger.: Druffel-Verlag, 1961.

Scott, James Brown. "The Trial of the Kaiser." In *What Really Happened at Paris,* pp. 231-58. Edited by Colonel E. M. House and Charles Seymour. New York: Charles Scribner's Sons, 1921.

Seymour, Charles, ed. *The Intimate Papers of Colonel House.* 4 vols. Boston and New York: Houghton Mifflin Co., 1926-28.

Speer, Albert. *Spandau: The Secret Diaries.* Translated by Richard and Clara Winston. New York: Macmillan Co., 1976.

Steed, Henry Wickham. *Through Thirty Years, 1892-1922: A Personal Narrative.* 2 vols. Garden City, N.Y.: Doubleday, Page & Co., 1924.

Stresemann, Gustav. *Gustav Stresemann: His Diaries, Letters, and Papers.* Edited and translated by Eric Sutton. 3 vols. New York: Macmillan Co., 1935-40.

———. *Schriften.* Edited by Arnold Harttung. Berlin, W. Ger.: Berlin Verlag, 1976.

Stuart, Sir Campbell. *Secrets of Crewe House.* London, New York, and Toronto: Hodder & Stoughton, 1920.

Taylor, A. J. P., ed. *Lloyd George: A Diary by Frances Stevenson.* New York: Harper & Row, 1971.

Todorov, Kosta. *Balkan Firebrand: The Autobiography of a Rebel, Soldier, and Statesman.* Chicago and New York: Ziff-Davis Co., 1943.

Toynbee, Arnold J. *Acquaintances.* London: Oxford University Press, 1967.

Tumulty, Joseph P. *Woodrow Wilson as I Know Him.* Garden City, N.Y.: Doubleday, Page & Co., 1921.

Vansittart, Lord Robert. *The Mist Procession: The Autobiography of Lord Vansittart.* London: Hutchinson, 1958.

Vopicka, Charles J. *Secrets of the Balkans, Seven Years of a Diplomatist's Life in the Storm Centre of Europe.* Chicago: Rand McNally, 1921.

Weber, Marianne. *Max Weber: Ein Lebensbild.* Heidelberg, W. Ger.: Verlag Lambert Schneider, 1950.

Weygand, Maxime. *Mémoires.* 3 vols. Paris: Flammarion, 1950-57.

Wilhelm, Crown Prince. *I Seek the Truth: A Book on Responsibility for the War.* Translated by Ralph Butler. London: Faber & Gwyer, 1926.

Wilhelm II, Kaiser. *The Kaiser's Memoirs.* Translated by Thomas R. Ybarra. New York and London: Harper & Bros., 1922.

Wilhelmina, Princess. *Lonely but Not Alone.* Translated by John Peereboom. New York: McGraw-Hill Book Co., 1960.

Yalman, Ahmed Emin. *Turkey in My Time.* Norman, Okla.: University of Oklahoma Press, 1956.

MISCELLANEOUS CONTEMPORARY WORKS

Birkenhead, Lord. *International Law.* 6th ed. London and Toronto: J. M. Dent & Sons, 1927.

Bryce, Viscount, and Arnold Toynbee. *The Treatment of Armenians in the Ottoman Empire, 1915-1916.* London: His Majesty's Stationery Office, 1916.

Creel, George. *War Criminals and Punishment.* London: Hutchinson & Co., 1945.

Dumas, Jacques. *Les Sanctions pénales des crimes allemands.* Paris: Librairie Arthur Rousseau, 1916.

Fribourg, André. *Les Semeurs de haine: Leur Oeuvre en Allemagne avant et depuis la guerre.* Paris: Berger-Levrault, 1922.

Gallinger, August. *The Countercharge: The Matter of War Criminals from the German Side.* Translated from the *Süddeutsche Monatshefte.* Munich, Ger.: Knorr & Hirth, 1922.

Garner, James. *The German War Code.* Urbana, Ill.: University of Illinois Press, 1918.

Gibbons, Herbert Adams. *The Blackest Page of Modern History: Events in Armenia in 1915; The Facts and the Responsibilities.* New York and London: Putnam's Sons, 1916.

Lepsius, Dr. Johannes. *Deutschland und Armenien, 1914-1918, Sammlung Diplomatischer Aktenstücke.* Potsdam, Ger.: Tempel Verlag, 1919.

Michelsen, Vice-Admiral Andreas D., ed. *Das Urteil im Leipziger Uboots—Prozess ein Fehlspruch? Juristische and Militärischen Gutachen.* Berlin, Ger.: Staatspolitischen Verlag, 1922.

Rezanoff, A. S. *Les Atrocités allemandes du côté russe.* Translated by René Marchand. Petrograd: W. Kirschbaoum, 1915.

Stosch, Albrecht von. *Die Kriegsbeschuldigtenfrage: Ihre Bedeutung für Deutschland und den Feindbund.* Hannover, Ger.; Leipzig, Ger.: Ernst Letsch Verlag, 1924.

Stüpnagel, Otto von. *Die Wahrheit über die Deutschen Kriegsverbrechen.* Berlin, Ger.: Staatspolitischer Verlag, 1921.

NEWSPAPERS

Berliner Tageblatt
Deutsche Allgemeine Zeitung
L'Echo de Paris
Frankfurter Zeitung
Le Matin
New York Times
Tägliche Rundschau
Le Temps
Times
Vörwarts
Vossische Zeitung

PERIODICALS

American Journal of International Law
American Law Review
American Political Science Review
The British Year Book of International Law
Bulletin of International News
The Canadian Law Times
The Century Magazine
Contemporary Review
The Dial
The Edinburgh Review
The English Review
Fortnightly Review
Hibbert Journal
Journal du Droit International

Literary Digest
The Living Age
Militär-Wochenblatt
The Nation (London)
The Nation (New York)
The New Republic
The New Statesman
New York Times Current History
The Nineteenth Century and After
The Outlook
Preussische Jahrbücher
Revue de Droit International et de Legislation Comparée
Revue des Deux Mondes
Revue Générale de Droit International Public
The Spectator
Transactions of the Grotius Society
Virginia Law Review
Zeitschrift für Völkerrecht

SHEET MUSIC

Kendis and Brockman. "We're Going to Hang the Kaiser Under the Linden Tree." New York: Kendis & Brockman Music Co., 1917.

SIGNED CONTEMPORARY ARTICLES

Battle, George Gordon. "The Trials Before the Leipsic Supreme Court of Germans Accused of War Crimes." *Virginia Law Review* 8 (November 1921):1-26.

Bellot, Dr. Hugh H. L. "A Permanent International Criminal Court." *International Law Association* 1 (1922). *Report of the Thirty-First Conference Held at the Palace of Justice, Buenos Aires, 24 August-30 August 1922.* London: Sweet & Maxwell, 1923, pp. 63-86.

────. "War Crimes: Their Prevention and Punishment." *The Nineteenth Century and After* 80 (September 1916):636-60.

────. "War Crimes and War Criminals." *The Canadian Law Times* 36 (October 1916):754-68.

────. "War Crimes and War Criminals." *The Canadian Law Times* 36 (November 1916):876-86.

────. "War Crimes and War Criminals." *The Canadian Law Times* 37 (January 1917):9-22.

Bower, Sir Graham. "The Laws of War: Prisoners of War and Reprisals." *Transactions of the Grotius Society* 1 (1915):23-37.

Breitscheid, Rudolf. "The Punishment of the War Criminals." *The Nation* (New York), 113 (12 October 1921):397.

Cadoux, C. J. "The Punishing of Germany After the War of 1914-1918." *Hibbert Journal* 43 (January 1945):107-13.

Clarke, R. Floyd. "The Status of William Hohenzollern, Kaiser of Germany, Under International Law." *American Law Review* 53 (May-June 1919): 401-26.

Doyle, Sir Arthur Conan. "A Policy of Murder." *New York Times Current History* 2 (June 1915):547.

Finch, George A. "The Nuremberg Trial and International Law." *American Journal of International Law* 41 (January 1947):20-37.

Garner, James W. "Punishment of Offenders Against the Laws and Customs of War." *American Journal of International Law* 14 (January 1920):70-94.

Gribble, Francis. "Peace Without Amnesties." *The Nineteenth Century and After* 84 (October 1918): 600-613.

Harrison, Austin. "Clearness and Pertinacity." *The English Review* 20 (April 1915):104-13.

_____. "Our Duty to the Prisoners." *The English Review* 20 (May 1915):237-40.

_____. "The Punishment of War Guilt." *The English Review* 30 (February 1920):163-69.

Kemp, Harry A. "A Song of St. Helena and the Two Emperors." *The Century Magazine* (New York), 97 (November 1918):114-15.

Larnaude, Fernand, and Albert de Lapradelle. "Examen de la responsabilité pénale de l'empereur Guillaume II d'Allemagne." *Journal de Droit International* 46 (1919):131-59.

Levy, Albert G. D. "The Law and Procedure of War Crime Trials." *American Political Science Review* 37 (December 1943):1052-81.

Lloyd George, David. "A Real League of Nations." *New York Times Current History* 8 (August 1918):351.

Macdonell, Sir John. "Modern Treaties of Peace." *Contemporary Review* 108 (September 1915):273-83.

Menner, Robert J. "The Kaiser and Germany in Popular Opinion." *South Atlantic Quarterly* 15 (April 1916):101-12.

Merignhac, A. "De la Responsabilité pénale des actes criminels commis au cours de la guerre de 1914-1918." *Revue de Droit International et de Législation Comparée.* 3rd series. 1 (1920):35-70.

Mullins, Claud. "The War Criminals' Trials." *Fortnightly Review* 116 (September 1921):417-30.

Petong, Dr. Richard. "Die Auslieferung des Kaisers und Deutschen Heerführer." *Preussische Jahrbücher* 179 (January-March 1920):185-200.

Phillimore, Lord. "An International Criminal Court and the Resolutions of the Committee of Jurists." *The British Year Book of International Law* 3 (1922-23):79-86.

Pic, Paul. "Violations systématique des lois de la guerre par les austro-allemands: Les Sanctions nécessaires." *Revue Générale de Droit International Public* 23 (1916):243-68.

Reinach, Joseph. "He Is the Master Assassin." *New York Times Current History* 4 (September 1916):1103-4.

Renault, Louis. "De l'Application du droit pénal aux faits de guerre." *Journal du Droit International* 40 (1915):313-44.

Schwertfeger, Colonel B. "Leipzig—das Brandmal des eigenen Landes." *Militär-Wochenblatt* 106 (3 September 1921):202-4.

Shaw, George Bernard. "Common Sense About the War." *New York Times Current History* 1 (December 1914):11-60.

Slooten, M. van. "Betrachtungen aus Anlass des Prozesses Stenger-Crusius." *Zeitschrift für Völkerrecht* 12 (1922-23):174-81.

Wendel, Herman. "National Martyrs and Matters of Opinion." *Die Glocke*, 11 July 1921. Reprinted in *The Living Age* 311 (1 October 1921):35-37.

Woolsey, Theodore S. "Retaliation and Punishment." *Proceedings of the American Society of International Law, 1915*, pp. 62-69.

Wright, Quincy. "The Law of the Nuremberg Trial." *American Journal of International Law* 41 (January 1947):38-72.

_____. "The Legal Liability of the Kaiser." *The American Political Science Review* 13 (February 1919):120-28.

SECONDARY WORKS

Abrams, Ray H. *Preachers Present Arms: The Role of the American Churches and Clergy in World Wars I and II, With Some Observations on the War in Vietnam*. Rev. ed. Scottsdale, Pa.: Herald Press, 1969.

Africa, Bernabe. *Political Offences in Extradition*. Manila, Philippines: Benipay Press, 1926.

Ahlstrom, Carl F. "British Public Opinion and the Versailles Conference, October, 1918-January, 1919." M.A. thesis, Duke University, 1944.

Ahmad, Feroz. *The Young Turks: The Committee of Union and Progress in Turkish Politics, 1908-1914*. Oxford: Oxford University Press, 1969.

Antipa, Gr. *L'Occupation ennemie de la Roumanie et ses conséquences économiques et sociales*. New Haven, Conn.: Yale University Press, 1929.

Appleman, John A. *Military Tribunals and International Crimes*. Indianapolis, Ind.: Bobbs-Merrill Co., 1954.

Arthur, Sir George. *Life of Lord Kitchener*. 3 vols. New York: Macmillan Co., 1920.

Bailey, Gordon W. "Dry Run for the Hangman: The Versailles-Leipzig Fiasco, 1919-1921, Feeble Foreshadow of Nuremberg." Ph.D. dissertation, University of Maryland, 1971.

Bailey, Thomas A. *Woodrow Wilson and the Lost Peace*. 1944. Reprint. Chicago: Quadrangle Books, 1963.

Bailey, Thomas A., and Paul B. Ryan. *The Lusitania Disaster: An Episode in Modern Warfare and Diplomacy*. New York: The Free Press, 1975.

Balfour, Michael. *The Kaiser and His Times*. Boston: Houghton Mifflin Co., 1964.

Bassiouni, M. Cherif, and Ved P. Nanda, eds. *A Treatise on International Criminal Law*. 2 vols. Springfield, Ill.: Charles C. Thomas, 1973.

Baumont, Maurice. *The Fall of the Kaiser*. Translated by E. Ibbetson James. New York: Alfred A. Knopf, 1931.

Beaverbrook, Lord. *Men and Power, 1917-1918*. London: Hutchinson, 1956.

Bell, John D. *Peasants in Power: Alexander Stamboliski and the Bulgarian Agrarian*

National Union, 1899-1923. Princeton, N.J.: Princeton University Press, 1977.

Benton, Wilbourn E., and Georg Grimm, eds. *Nuremberg: German Views of the War Trials*. Dallas, Tex.: Southern Methodist University Press, 1955.

Berghahn, Volker Rolf. *Germany and the Approach of War in 1914*. London: Macmillan Press, 1973.

Berlau, A. Joseph. *The German Social Democratic Party, 1914-1921*. New York: Columbia University Press, 1949.

Best, Geoffrey. *Humanity in Warfare*. New York: Columbia University Press, 1980.

Birdsall, Paul. *Versailles Twenty Years After*. New York: Reynal & Hitchcock, 1941.

Birkenhead, Second Earl of. *The Life of F. E. Smith: First Earl of Birkenhead*. London: Eyre & Spottiswoode, 1960.

Blake, Robert. *The Unknown Prime Minister: The Life and Times of Andrew Bonar Law, 1858-1923*. London: Eyre & Spottiswoode, 1955.

Boadle, Donald G. *Winston Churchill and the German Question in British Foreign Policy, 1918-1922*. The Hague: Martinus Nijhoff, 1973.

Boisvert, Jean-Jacques. *Les Relations franco-allemandes en 1920*. Montreal: Les Presses de l'université du Québec, 1977.

Bonnefous, Édouard. *Histoire politique de la troisième république*. Vol. 3: *L'Après-Guerre, 1919-1924*. Paris: Presses universitaires de France, 1959.

Borkin, Joseph. *The Crime and Punishment of I. G. Farben*. New York: The Free Press, 1978.

Bosch, William J. *Judgment on Nuremberg: American Attitudes Toward the Major German War-Crime Trials*. Chapel Hill, N.C.: University of North Carolina Press, 1970.

Boyle, Andrew. *Trenchard*. New York: W. W. Norton & Co., 1962.

Boyle, Thomas E. "France, Great Britain, and German Disarmament, 1919-1927." Ph.D. dissertation, State University of New York at Stony Brook, 1972.

Bretton, Henry L. *Stresemann and the Revision of Versailles: A Fight for Reason*. Stanford, Calif.: Stanford University Press, 1953.

Brook-Shepherd, Gordon. *The Last Habsburg*. New York: Weybright & Talley, 1968.

Brownlie, Ian. *International Law and the Use of Force by States*. Oxford: Clarendon Press, 1963.

Buchan, John. *A History of the Great War*. 4 vols. Boston and New York: Houghton Mifflin Co., 1923.

Burnett, Philip Mason. *Reparations at the Paris Peace Conference*. 2 vols. New York: Columbia University Press, 1940.

Cahen-Salvador, Georges. *Les Prisonniers de guerre (1914-1919)*. Paris: Payot, 1929.

Camp, William. *The Glittering Prizes: A Biographical Study of F. E. Smith, First Earl of Birkenhead*. London: MacGibbon & Kee, 1960.

Carsten, F. L. *The Reichswehr and Politics, 1918 to 1933*. London: Oxford University Press, 1966.

Carzou, Jean-Marie. *Un Génocide exemplaire: Arménie, 1915*. Paris: Flammarion, 1975.

Chickering, Roger. *Imperial Germany and a World Without War: The Peace Movement and German Society, 1892-1914*. Princeton, N.J.: Princeton University Press, 1975.

Churchill, Winston. *The World Crisis.* 4 vols. New York: Charles Scribner's Sons, 1923-27.

———. *The World Crisis, 1918-1929: The Aftermath.* New York: Charles Scribner's Sons, 1929.

Cleveland, Robert E. "French Attitudes Toward the 'German Problem,' 1914-1919." Ph.D dissertation, University of Nebraska, 1957.

Coogan, John W. "The End of Neutrality: The United States, Britain, and Neutral Rights, 1899-1915." Ph.D. dissertation, Yale University, 1976.

Corbett, Sir Julian. *Official History of the War: Naval Operations.* 5 vols. London: Longmans, Green & Co., 1921-31.

Costrell, Edwin. *How Maine Viewed the War, 1914-1917.* Orono, Maine: University of Maine Press, 1940.

Cowles, Virginia. *The Kaiser.* New York and Evanston, Ill.: Harper & Row, 1963.

Craig, Gordon A. "The Revolution in War and Diplomacy." In *World War I: A Turning Point in Modern History,* pp. 7-24. Edited by Jack J. Roth. New York: Alfred A. Knopf, Borzoi Books, 1967.

Craig, Gordon A. *Germany, 1866-1945.* New York: Oxford University Press, 1978.

———. *The Politics of the Prussian Army, 1640-1945.* New York: Oxford University Press, 1955.

Cummins, Cedric C. *Indiana Public Opinion and the World War, 1914-1917.* Indianapolis, Ind.: Indiana Historical Bureau, 1945.

Dahlin, Ebba. *French and German Public Opinion on Declared War Aims, 1914-1918.* Stanford, Calif.: Stanford University Press, 1933.

Davidson, Eugene. *The Nuremberg Fallacy: Wars and War Crimes Since World World War II.* New York: Macmillan Co., 1973.

———. *The Trial of the Germans: An Account of the Twenty-two Defendants before the International Military Tribunal at Nuremberg.* New York: Macmillan Co., 1966.

Davis, Calvin D. *The United States and the First Hague Peace Conference.* Ithaca, N.Y.: Cornell University Press, 1962.

———. *The United States and the Second Hague Peace Conference: American Diplomacy and International Organization, 1899-1914.* Durham, N.C.: Duke University Press, 1975.

Davis, Rodney O. "British Policy and Opinion on War Aims and Peace Proposals, 1914-1918." Ph.D. dissertation, Duke University, 1958.

Djuvara, Mirceau. *La Guerre Roumanie, 1916-1918.* Nancy, Paris, Strasbourg, France: Berger-Levrault, Éditeurs, 1919.

Drake, Edson James. "Bulgaria at the Paris Peace Conference: A Diplomatic History of the Treaty of Neuilly-sur-Seine." Ph.D. dissertation, Georgetown University, 1967.

Egerton, George W. *Great Britain and the Creation of the League of Nations: Strategy, Politics, and International Organization, 1914-1919.* Chapel Hill, N.C.: University of North Carolina Press, 1978.

Elcock, Howard. *Portrait of a Decision: The Council of Four and the Treaty of Versailles.* London: Eyre Methuen, 1972.

Emin, Ahmed. *Turkey in the World War*. New Haven, Conn.: Yale University Press, 1930.

Enssle, Manfred J. "Germany and Belgium, 1919-1929: A Study of German Foreign Policy." Ph.D. dissertation, University of Colorado, 1970.

Epstein, Klaus. *Matthias Erzberger and the Dilemma of German Democracy.* Princeton, N.J.: Princeton University Press, 1959.

Erger, Johannes. *Der Kapp-Lüttwitz-Putsch: Ein Beitrag zur Deutschen Innenpolitik, 1919/1920.* Düsseldorf, W. Ger.: Droste Verlag, 1967.

Evans, Laurence. *United States Policy and the Partition of Turkey, 1914-1924.* Baltimore, Md.: The Johns Hopkins Press, 1965.

Eyck, Erich. *A History of the Weimar Republic.* Translated by Harlan P. Hanson and Robert G. L. Waite. 2 vols. Cambridge, Mass.: Harvard University Press, 1962.

Falls, Cyril. *The Great War.* New York: Capricorn Books, 1961.

Fein, Helen. *Accounting for Genocide: National Responses and Jewish Victimization During the Holocaust.* New York: The Free Press, 1979.

Feldman, Gerald. *Army, Industry, and Labor in Germany, 1914-1918.* Princeton, N.J.: Princeton University Press, 1966.

Ferencz, Benjamin B. *Defining International Aggression: The Search for World Peace, A Documentary History and Analysis.* 2 vols. Dobbs Ferry, N.Y.: Oceana Publications, 1975.

_____. *An International Criminal Court: A Step Toward World Peace—A Documentary History and Analysis.* 2 vols. New York: Oceana Publications, 1980.

Ferrell, Robert H. *Peace in Their Time, The Origins of the Kellogg-Briand Pact.* New Haven, Conn.: Yale University Press, 1952.

Fischer, Fritz. *Germany's Aims in the First World War.* New York: W. W. Norton & Co., 1967.

_____. *War of Illusions: German Policies from 1911 to 1914.* Translated by Marian Jackson. New York: W. W. Norton & Co., 1975.

Fisher, Herbert A. L. *James Bryce.* 2 vols. New York: Macmillan Co., 1927.

Floto, Inga. *Colonel House in Paris: A Study of American Policy at the Paris Peace Conference, 1919.* Aarhus, Denmark: Universitetsforlaget, 1973.

Foltz, David A. "The War Crimes Issue at the Paris Peace Conference, 1919-1920." Ph.D. dissertation, The American University, 1978.

Fowler, W. B. *British-American Relations, 1917-1918: The Role of Sir William Wiseman.* Princeton, N.J.: Princeton University Press, 1969.

Fraenkel, Ernst. *Military Occupation and the Rule of Law: Occupation Government in the Rhineland, 1918-1923.* New York: Oxford University Press, 1944.

Freidel, Frank. *Francis Lieber: Nineteenth Century Liberal.* Baton Rouge, La.: Louisiana University Press, 1947.

Fridenson, Patrick. *1914-1918: L'Autre front.* Paris: Éditions Ouvrières, 1977.

Friedman, Leon, ed. *The Law of War: A Documentary History.* 2 vols. New York: Random House, 1972.

Fry, Michael G. *Lloyd George and Foreign Policy.* Vol. 1: *The Education of a Statesman: 1890-1916.* Montreal: McGill-Queen's University Press, 1977.

Garner, James. *International Law and the World War.* 2 vols. London: Longmans, Green & Co., 1920.

Geiss, Imanuel. *German Foreign Policy, 1871-1914.* London and Boston: Routledge & Kegan Paul, 1976.

Gibson, R. H., and Maurice Prendergast. *The German Submarine War, 1914-1918.* New York: Richard R. Smith, 1931.

Gidney, James B. *A Mandate for Armenia.* Kent, Ohio: Kent State University Press, 1967.

Gilbert, Martin. *Churchill.* Vol. 3: *The Challenge of War, 1914-1916.* Boston: Houghton Mifflin Co., 1971.

———. *Sir Horace Rumbold: Portrait of a Diplomat, 1869-1941.* London: Heinemann, 1973.

Glueck, Sheldon. *War Criminals: Their Prosecution and Punishment.* New York: Alfred A. Knopf, 1944.

Gollin, Alfred M. *Proconsul in Politics: A Study of Lord Milner in Opposition and in Power.* London: Anthony Bond, 1964.

Goodspeed, Donald. *Ludendorff: Genius of World War I.* Boston: Houghton Mifflin Co., 1966.

Graux, Dr. Lucien. *Histoire des violations du traité de paix.* 4 vols. Paris: Crès, 1921-27.

Greenspan, Morris. *The Modern Law of Land Warfare.* Berkeley and Los Angeles, Calif.: University of California Press, 1959.

Groener-Geyer, Dorothea. *General Groener, Soldat und Staatsmann.* Frankfurt, W. Ger.: Societäts-Verlag, 1955.

Guenther, Peter W. "A History of Articles 227, 228, 229, and 230 of the Treaty of Versailles." M.A. thesis, University of Texas at Austin, 1960.

Halperin, S. William. *Germany Tried Democracy: A Political History of the Reich from 1918 to 1933.* 1946. Reprint. New York: W. W. Norton & Co., 1965.

Hankey, Lord Maurice. *Politics, Trials, and Errors.* Chicago: Henry Regnery Co., 1950.

———. *The Supreme Control at the Paris Peace Conference of 1919.* London: George Allen & Unwin, 1963.

Harbaugh, William. *The Life and Times of Theodore Roosevelt.* Rev. ed. New York: Collier Books, 1963.

Harris, David. *Britain and the Bulgarian Horrors of 1876.* Chicago: University of Chicago Press, 1939.

Hazlehurst, Cameron. *Politicians at War, July 1914 to May 1915: A Prologue to the Triumph of Lloyd George.* New York: Alfred A. Knopf, 1971.

Helmreich, Paul C. *From Paris to Sèvres: The Partition of the Ottoman Empire at the Peace Conference of 1919-1920.* Columbus, Ohio: Ohio State University Press, 1974.

Hinsley, F. H., ed. *British Foreign Policy Under Sir Edward Grey.* London: Cambridge University Press, 1977.

The History of the Times. 4 vols. New York: Macmillan Co., 1935-52.

Hoehling, A. A. *A Whisper of Eternity: The Mystery of Edith Cavell.* New York: Thomas Yoseloff, 1957.

Holborn, Hajo. "Diplomats and Diplomacy in the Early Weimar Republic." In *The Diplomats, 1919-1939*, 1:123-71. Edited by Gordon A. Craig and Felix Gilbert. 2 vols. 1953. Reprint. New York: Atheneum, 1965.

Hovannisian, Richard G. *Armenia on the Road to Independence, 1918.* Berkeley and Los Angeles, Calif.: University of California Press, 1967.

_____. *The Republic of Armenia.* Vol. 1: *The First Years, 1918-1919.* Berkeley and Los Angeles, Calif., and London: University of California Press, 1971.

Howard, Harry N. *The Partition of Turkey: A Diplomatic History, 1913-1923.* Norman, Okla.: University of Oklahoma Press, 1931.

Howard, Michael. *War and the Liberal Conscience.* New Brunswick, N.J.: Rutgers University Press, 1978.

Hudson, Manley O. *The Permanent Court of International Justice, 1920-1942: A Treatise.* New York: Macmillan Co., 1943.

Hunt, Barry, and Adrian Preston, eds. *War Aims and Strategic Policy in the Great War, 1914-1918.* Totowa, N.J.: Rowman & Littlefield, 1977.

Hurd, Sir Archibald. *Official History of the War: The Merchant Navy.* 3 vols. London: Longmans, Green & Co., 1921-29.

Jacobson, Jon. *Locarno Diplomacy: Germany and the West, 1925-1929.* Princeton, N.J.: Princeton University Press, 1972.

Jarausch, Konrad H. *The Enigmatic Chancellor: Bethmann Hollweg and the Hubris of Imperial Germany.* New Haven, Conn., and London: Yale University Press, 1973.

Jenkins, Roy. *Asquith.* London: Collins, 1964.

Jescheck, Hans-Heinrich. *Die Verantwortlichkeit der Staatsorgane nach Völkerstrafrecht: Eine Studie zu den Nürnberger Prozessen.* Bonn, W. Ger.: Ludwig Röhrscheid Verlag, 1952.

Jessup, Philip C. *Elihu Root.* 2 vols. New York: Dodd, Mead & Co., 1938.

Jonas, Klaus W. *The Life of Crown Prince William.* Translated by Charles W. Bangert. London: Routledge & Kegan Paul, 1961.

Jones, Neville. *The Origins of Strategic Bombing: A Study of the Development of British Air Strategic Thought and Practice up to 1918.* London: William Kimber, 1973.

Jones, Thomas. *Lloyd George.* Cambridge, Mass.: Harvard University Press, 1951.

Kaufmann, Walter H. *Monarchism in the Weimar Republic.* New York: Bookman Associates, 1953.

Keen, Maurice H. *The Laws of War in the Late Middle Ages.* London: Routledge & Kegan Paul, 1965.

Kernek, Sterling J. *Distractions of Peace During War: The Lloyd George Government's Reactions to Woodrow Wilson, December 1916-November 1918.* Philadelphia: Transactions of the American Philosophical Society, 1975.

Kessler, Count Harry. *Walther Rathenau: His Life and Work.* Translated by W. D. Robson-Scott and Lawrence Hyde. New York: Harcourt, Brace & Co., 1930.

Kinross, Lord. *Ataturk: A Biography of Mustafa Kemal, Father of Modern Turkey.* New York: William Morris & Co., 1965.

Kitchen, Martin. *The Silent Dictatorship: The Politics of the German High Com-*

mand under Hindenburg and Ludendorff, 1916-1918. New York: Holmes & Meier, 1976.

Koss, Stephen. Asquith. New York: St. Martin's Press, 1976.

_____. Fleet Street Radical: A. G. Gardiner and the Daily News. Hamden, Conn.: Archon Books, 1973.

Krüger, Gabriele. Die Brigade Ehrhardt. Hamburg, W. Ger.: Leibniz Verlag, 1971.

Kürenberg, Joachim von. The Kaiser: A Life of Wilhelm II, Last Emperor of Germany. Translated by H. T. Russell and Herta Hagen. New York: Simon & Schuster, 1955.

Langer, William L. The Diplomacy of Imperialism, 1890-1902. 2nd ed. New York: Alfred A. Knopf, 1968.

Laqueur, Walter, and George L. Mosse, eds. 1914: The Coming of the First World War. New York: Harper & Row, Harper Torchbooks, 1966.

Leon, George B. Greece and the Great Powers, 1914-1917. Thessaloniki, Greece: Institute for Balkan Studies, 1974.

Levin, N. Gordon, Jr. Woodrow Wilson and World Politics: America's Response to War and Revolution. New York: Oxford University Press Paperback, 1970.

Link, Arthur S. Wilson. Vol. 3: The Struggle for Neutrality, 1914-1915. Princeton, N.J.: Princeton University Press, 1960.

_____. Wilson. Vol. 4: Confusions and Crises, 1915-1916. Princeton, N.J.: Princeton University Press, 1964.

_____. Wilson. Vol. 5: Campaigns for Progressivism and Peace, 1916-1917. Princeton, N.J.: Princeton University Press, 1965.

_____. Woodrow Wilson and the Progressive Era: 1910-1917. New York: Harper & Row, Harper Torchbooks. 1954.

_____. Woodrow Wilson, Revolution, War, and Peace. Arlington Heights, Ill.: AHM Publishing Corp., 1979.

Luckau, Alma. The German Delegation at the Paris Peace Conference. New York: Columbia University Press, 1941.

McCormick, Donald. The Mask of Merlin: A Critical Study of David Lloyd George. London: Macdonald, 1963.

McDougall, Walter A. France's Rhineland Diplomacy, 1914-1924: The Last Bid for a Balance of Power in Europe. Princeton, N.J.: Princeton University Press, 1978.

Maehl, William H. "The German Socialists and the Foreign Policy of the Reich, 1917-1922." Ph.D. dissertation, University of Chicago, 1947.

Mamatey, Victor S. The United States and East Central Europe, 1914-1918: A Study in Wilsonian Diplomacy and Propaganda. Princeton, N.J.: Princeton University Press, 1957.

Marder, Arthur J. From the Dreadnought to Scapa Flow: The Royal Navy in the Fisher Era, 1904-1919. Vol. 1: The Road to War, 1904-1914. London: Oxford University Press, 1961.

_____. From the Dreadnought to Scapa Flow: The Royal Navy in the Fisher Era, 1904-1919. Vol. 2: The War Years to the Eve of Jutland. London: Oxford University Press, 1965.

Marks, Sally. The Illusion of Peace: International Relations in Europe, 1918-1933. New York: St. Martin's Press, 1976.

Marrin, Albert. *The Last Crusade: The Church of England in the First World War*. Durham, N.C.: Duke University Press, 1974.

Martin, Christopher. *English Life in the First World War*. London: Wayland, 1974.

Marwick, Arthur. *The Deluge: British Society and the First World War*. New York: W. W. Norton & Co., 1970.

Maser, Werner. *Nuremberg: A Nation on Trial*. Translated by Richard Barry. New York: Charles Scribner's Sons, 1979.

Maugham, Viscount Frederic. *U.N.O. and War Crimes*. London: John Murray, 1951.

Maxwell Fyfe, Sir David, ed. *The Peleus Trial*. London: William Hodge & Co., 1948.

May, Ernest R. *The World War and American Isolation, 1914-1917*. 1959. Reprint. Chicago: Quadrangle Books, 1966.

Miller, David Hunter. *The Drafting of the Covenant*. 2 vols. New York and London: G.P. Putnam's Sons, 1928.

Minear, Richard H. *Victors' Justice: The Tokyo War Crimes Trial*. Princeton, N.J.: Princeton University Press, 1971.

Miquel, Pierre. *La Paix de Versailles et l'opinion publique française*. Paris: Flammarion, 1972.

_____. *Poincaré*. Paris: Librairie Arthème Fayard, 1961.

Mock, James R., and Cedric Larson. *Words That Won the War: The Story of the Committee on Public Information, 1917-1919*. Princeton, N.J.: Princeton University Press, 1939.

Mommsen, Wolfgang J. *Max Weber und die Deutsche Politik, 1890-1920*. Tübingen, W. Ger.: J. C. B. Mohr, 1959.

Morgan, Kenneth O. *Consensus and Disunity: The Lloyd George Coalition Government, 1918-1922*. Oxford: Clarendon Press, 1979.

Mosley, Leonard. *The Glorious Fault: The Life of Lord Curzon*. New York: Harcourt, Brace & Co., 1960.

Mueller, Gerhard O. W., and Edward M. Wise, eds. *International Criminal Law*. London: Sweet & Maxwell, 1965.

Muir, Nadejda. *Dimitri Stancioff: Patriot and Cosmopolitan, 1864-1940*. London: John Murray, 1957.

Mullins, Claud. *The Leipzig Trials*. London: H. F. G. Witherby, 1921.

Néré, Jacques. *The Foreign Policy of France from 1914 to 1945*. London and Boston: Routledge & Kegan Paul, 1975.

Nicolson, Harold. *Curzon: The Last Phase, 1919-1925*. Boston and New York: Houghton Mifflin Co., 1934.

_____. *King George the Fifth: His Life and Reign*. London: Constable & Co., 1952.

Nussbaum, Arthur. *A Concise History of the Law of Nations*. New York: Macmillan Co., 1947.

Orde, Anne. *Great Britain and International Security, 1920-1926*. London: Royal Historical Society, 1978.

Owen, Frank. *Tempestuous Journey: Lloyd George, His Life and Times*. London: Hutchinson & Co., 1954.

Pal, Radhabinod. *Crimes in International Relations*. Calcutta, India: Calcutta University Press, 1955.

Palmer, Alan. *The Kaiser: Warlord of the Second Reich*. New York: Charles Scribner's Sons, 1978.

Palo, Michael F. "The Diplomacy of Belgian War Aims During the First World War." Ph.D. dissertation, University of Illinois, 1978.

Patterson, David S. *Toward a Warless World: The Travail of the American Peace Movement, 1887-1914.* Bloomington, Ind.: Indiana University Press, 1976.

Peterson, H. C. *Propaganda for War: The Campaign Against American Neutrality, 1914-1917.* Norman, Okla.: University of Oklahoma Press, 1939.

Phillipson, Coleman. *The International Law and Customs of Ancient Greece and Rome.* 2 vols. London: Macmillan & Co., 1911.

Piccigallo, Philip R. *The Japanese on Trial: Allied War Crimes Operations in the East, 1945-1951.* Austin, Tex.: University of Texas Press, 1979.

Pingaud, Albert. *Histoire diplomatique de la France pendant le grande guerre.* 3 vols. Paris: Éditions Aesatia, 1938.

Pirenne, Henri. *La Belgique et la Guerre Mondiale.* Paris: Carnegie pour la Paix Internationale, 1928.

Playne, Caroline E. *Britain Holds On, 1917, 1918.* London: George Allen & Unwin, 1933.

Politis, Nicolas. "International Penal Law." In *The New Aspects of International Law,* pp. 32-48. By Nicolas Politis. Washington, D.C.: Carnegie Endowment for International Peace, 1928.

Pompe, C. A. *Aggressive War: An International Crime.* The Hague: Martinus Nijhoff, 1953.

Porter, Charles W. *The Career of Théophile Delcassé.* Philadelphia: University of Pennsylvania Press, 1936.

Pringle, Henry F. *The Life and Times of William Howard Taft.* 2 vols. New York: Farrar & Rinehart, 1939.

Read, James M. *Atrocity Propaganda: 1914-1919.* New Haven, Conn.: Yale University Press, 1941.

Ritter, Gerhard. *The Schlieffen Plan: Critique of a Myth.* Translated by Andrew and Eva Wilson. London: Oswald Wolff Publishers, 1958.

Robbins, Keith. *The Abolition of War: The "Peace Movement" in Britain, 1914-1919.* Cardiff, Wales: University of Wales Press, 1976.

———. *Sir Edward Grey: A Biography of Lord Grey of Fallodon.* London: Cassell & Co., 1971.

Ronaldshay, Earl of. *The Life of Lord Curzon.* 3 vols. London: Ernest Benn, 1928.

Rosenberg, Arthur. *A History of the German Republic.* Translated by Ian F. D. Morrow and L. Marie Sieveking. London: Methuen & Co., 1936.

Roskill, Stephen W. *Churchill and the Admirals.* London: William Collins & Co., 1978.

———. *Hankey, Man of Secrets, 1919-1931.* 2 vols. London: Collins Press, 1972.

Rothwell, V. H. *British War Aims and Peace Diplomacy, 1914-1918.* Oxford: Oxford University Press, 1971.

Rudin, Harry R. *Armistice 1918.* New Haven, Conn.: Yale University Press, 1944.

Russell, Frederick H. *The Just War in the Middle Ages.* London: Cambridge University Press, 1975.

Scheffer, H. J. *November 1918: Journaal van een Revolutie die niet Doorging.* Amsterdam: Uitgeverij de Arbeiderspers, 1968.

Schöller, Peter. *Le Cas de Louvain et le Livre Blanc allemand: Étude critique de la documentation allemande relative aux événement qui se sont déroulés à Louvain du 25 au 28 août 1914.* Translated by E. Nieuwborg. Louvain, Belgium: 'Éditions E. Nauwelaerts, 1958.

Schuker, Stephen A. *The End of French Predominance in Europe: The Financial Crisis of 1924 and the Adoption of the Dawes Plan.* Chapel Hill, N.C.: University of North Carolina Press, 1976.

Schuman, Frederick L. *War and Diplomacy in the French Republic.* New York and London: McGraw-Hill Book Co., 1931.

Seton-Watson, Hugh. *Eastern Europe Between the Wars, 1918-1941.* 3rd rev. ed. New York: Harper & Row, Harper Torchbooks, 1967.

Seymour, Charles. *American Diplomacy During the World War.* Baltimore, Md.: The Johns Hopkins Press, 1934.

Shannon, R. T. *Gladstone and the Bulgarian Agitation, 1876.* London: Thomas Nelson & Sons, 1963.

Shaw, Stanford J., and Ezel Kural Shaw. *History of the Ottoman Empire and Modern Turkey.* Vol. 2: *Reform, Revolution, and Republic: The Rise of Modern Turkey, 1808-1975.* London: Cambridge University Press, 1977.

Siney, Marion C. *The Allied Blockade of Germany, 1914-1916.* Ann Arbor, Mich.: University of Michigan Press, 1957.

Smith, Bradley F. *Reaching Judgment at Nuremberg.* New York: Basic Books, 1977.

_____. *The Road to Nuremberg.* New York: Basic Books, 1981.

Smith, C. Jay, Jr. *The Russian Struggle for Power, 1914-1917: A Study of Russian Foreign Policy During the First World War.* New York: Philosophical Library, 1956.

Smith, Daniel M. *Robert Lansing and American Neutrality, 1914-1917.* Berkeley and Los Angeles, Calif.: University of California Press, 1958.

Smith, Ephraim K., Jr. "Robert Lansing and the Paris Peace Conference." Ph.D. dissertation, The Johns Hopkins University, 1972.

Sommer, Dudley. *Haldane of Cloan: His Life and Times, 1856-1928.* London: George Allen & Unwin, 1960.

Sontag, Raymond J. *A Broken World, 1919-1939.* New York: Harper & Row, Harper Torchbooks, 1971.

Sonyel, Salahi R. *Turkish Diplomacy, 1918-1923: Mustafa Kemal and the Turkish National Movement.* London and Beverly Hills, Calif.: Sage Publications, 1975.

Spender, J. A., and Cyril Asquith. *Life of Herbert Henry Asquith, Lord Oxford and Asquith.* 2 vols. London: Hutchinson & Co., 1932.

Spindler, Arno. *La Guerre sous-marine.* Translated by René Jouan. 3 vols. Paris: Payot, 1933-35.

Squires, James D. *British Propaganda at Home and in the United States from 1914 to 1917.* Cambridge, Mass.: Harvard University Press, 1935.

Steiner, Zara S. *Britain and the Origins of the First World War.* New York: St. Martin's Press, 1977.

Stenzel, Ernst. *Die Kriegführung des Deutschen Imperialismus und das Völkerrecht zur Planung und Vorbereitung des Deutschen Imperialismus auf die Barbarische Kriegführung im Ersten und Zweiten Weltkrieg.* Berlin, E. Ger.: Militärverlag der Deutschen Demokratischen Republik, 1973.

Stone, Julius. *Aggression and World Order: A Critique of United Nations Theories of Aggression.* Berkeley, Calif.: University of California Press, 1958.

_____. *Conflict Through Consensus: United Nations Approaches to Aggression.* Baltimore, Md., and London: The Johns Hopkins University Press, 1977.

Stone, Julius, and Robert K. Woetzel, eds. *Toward a Feasible International Criminal Court.* Geneva: World Peace Through Law Center, 1970.

Stone, Norman. *The Eastern Front, 1914-1917.* New York: Charles Scribner's Sons, 1975.

Stoner, John E. *S. O. Levinson and the Pact of Paris: A Study in the Techniques of Influence.* Chicago: University of Chicago Press, 1943.

Suarez, Georges. *Briand, sa vie-son oeuvre.* 6 vols. Paris: Librairie Plon, 1938-52.

Sullivan, Mark. *Our Times, 1900-1925.* Vol. 5: *Over Here, 1914-1918.* New York: Charles Scribner's Sons, 1933.

Symons, Julian. *Horatio Bottomley.* London: Cresset Press, 1955.

Tanenbaum, Jan Karl. *General Maurice Sarrail, 1856-1929: The French Army and Left-Wing Politics.* Chapel Hill, N.C.: University of North Carolina Press, 1974.

Taylor, A. J. P. *English History, 1914-1945.* New York and Oxford: Oxford University Press, 1965.

_____. *The First World War.* 1963. Reprint. New York: Capricorn Books, 1972.

_____. "The War Aims of the Allies in the First World War." In *Politics in Wartime and Other Essays,* pp. 93-122. By A. J. P. Taylor. London: Hamish Hamilton, 1964.

Thomson, Malcolm. *David Lloyd George: The Official Biography.* London: Hutchinson & Co., 1948.

Tillman, Seth P. *Anglo-American Relations at the Paris Peace Conference of 1919.* Princeton, N.J.: Princeton University Press, 1961.

Toynbee, Arnold J. "The Main Features in the Landscape." In *The Treaty of Versailles and After,* pp. 42-55. By Lord Riddell et al. New York: Oxford University Press, 1935.

_____. *Survey of International Affairs, 1924.* London: Oxford University Press for the British Institute of International Affairs, 1926.

Trumpener, Ulrich. *Germany and the Ottoman Empire, 1914-1918.* Princeton, N.J.: Princeton University Press, 1968.

Tuchman, Barbara. *The Guns of August.* New York: Dell Publishing Co., 1963.

United Nations. General Assembly. International Law Commission. *Historical Survey of the Question of International Criminal Jurisdiction* (A/CN. 4/7/Rev. 1), 1949.

United Nations War Crimes Commission. *History of the United Nations War Crimes Commission and the Development of the Laws of War.* London: His Majesty's Stationery Office, 1948.

Viereck, George Sylvester. *The Kaiser on Trial.* Richmond, Va.: William Byrd Press, 1937.

_____. *Spreading Germs of Hate.* New York: Liveright, 1930.

Vinson, John Chalmers. *William E. Borah and the Outlawry of War.* Athens, Ga.: University of Georgia Press, 1957.

Waite, Robert G. L. *Vanguard of Nazism: The Free Corps Movement in Postwar*

Germany, 1918-1923. Cambridge, Mass.: Harvard University Press, 1952.

Walters, F. P. *A History of the League of Nations*. London: Oxford University Press, 1960.

Walworth, Arthur. *America's Moment: 1918 American Diplomacy at the End of World War I*. New York: W. W. Norton & Co., 1977.

Walzer, Michael. *Just and Unjust Wars: A Moral Argument With Historical Illustrations*. New York: Basic Books, 1977.

Watson, David R. *Georges Clemenceau: A Political Biography*. New York: David McKay, 1974.

Weber, Frank G. *Eagles on the Crescent: Germany, Austria, and the Diplomacy of the Turkish Alliance, 1914-1918*. Ithaca, N.Y.: Cornell University Press, 1970.

Wengst, Udo. *Graf Brockdorff-Rantzau und die Aussenpolitischen Anfänge der Weimarer Republik*. Bern, Switz.: Herbert Lang; Frankfurt, W. Ger.: Peter Lang, 1973.

Wheeler-Bennett, John W. *The Nemesis of Power: The German Army in Politics, 1918-1945*. New York: St. Martin's Press, 1954.

_____. *Wooden Titan: Hindenburg in Twenty Years of German History, 1914-1934*. New York: William Morrow & Co., 1936.

Whittle, Tyler. *The Last Kaiser: A Biography of Wilhelm II, German Emperor and King of Prussia*. New York: New York Times Books, 1977.

Williamson, John G. *Karl Helfferich, 1872-1924: Economist, Financier, Politician*. Princeton, N.J.: Princeton University Press, 1971.

Willis, Irene Cooper. *England's Holy War: A Study of English Liberal Idealism During the Great War*. 1928. Reprint. New York: Garland Publishing, 1972.

Wilson, Trevor. *The Downfall of the Liberal Party, 1914-1935*. Ithaca, N.Y.: Cornell University Press, 1966.

Wittgens, Herman J. "The German Foreign Office Campaign Against the Versailles Treaty: An Examination of the Activities of the Kriegsschuldreferat in the United States." Ph.D. dissertation, University of Washington, 1970.

Woetzel, Robert K. *The Nuremberg Trials in International Law*. London: Stevens & Sons, 1962.

Wolfers, Arnold. *Britain and France between Two Wars: Conflicting Strategies of Peace Since Versailles*. New York: Harcourt, Brace & Co., 1940.

Woodward, Sir Llewellyn. *Great Britain and the War of 1914-1918*. Boston: Beacon Press, 1970.

Wrench, John Evelyn. *Alfred Lord Milner: The Man of No Illusions, 1854-1925*. London: Eyre & Spottiswoode, 1958.

Zimmermann, Ludwig. *Deutsche Aussenpolitik in der Ära der Weimarer Republik*. Göttingen, W. Ger.: Musterschmidt-Verlag, 1958.

SECONDARY ARTICLES

Alexander, T. H. "They Tried to Kidnap the Kaiser and Brought Back an Ash Tray." *The Saturday Evening Post* 210 (23 October 1937):5-7, 84-89.

Ambrosius, Lloyd E. "Wilson, Clemenceau and the German Problem at the Paris

Peace Conference of 1919." *Rocky Mountain Social Science Journal* 12 (April 1975):69-80.

"Baron Édouard Rolin-Jaequemyns." *The British Year Book of International Law* 18 (1937):156-57.

Baumgart, Winfried. "Zur Ansprache Hitlers vor den Führen der Wehrmacht am 22 August 1939: Eine Quellenkritische Untersuchung." *Vierteljahrshefte für Zeitgeschichte* 16 (April 1968):120-49.

Bellot, Hugh H. L. "The Detention of Napoleon Buonaparte." *Law Quarterly Review* 39 (April 1923): 170-92.

Bishop, William et al. "Judicial Decisions: The Case Against Hermann Roechling and Others." *American Journal of International Law* 43 (January 1949): 191-93.

Brügel, J. W. "Das Schicksal der Strafbestimmungen des Versailler Vertrags." *Vierteljahrshefte für Zeitgeschichte* 6 (July 1958):263-70.

Buchanan, A. Russell. "American Editors Examine American War Aims and Plans in April, 1917." *Pacific Historical Review* 9 (September 1940):253-65.

_____. "Theodore Roosevelt and American Neutrality, 1914-1917." *American Historical Review* 43 (July 1938):775-90.

Burns, Richard Dean. "Regulating Submarine Warfare, 1921-41: A Case Study in Arms Control and Limited War." *Military Affairs* 35 (April 1971):56-63.

Cruickshank, A. A. "The Young Turk Challenge in Postwar Turkey." *Middle East Journal* 22 (Winter 1968):17-28.

Dickmann, Fritz. "Die Kriegsschuldfrage auf der Freidenskonferenz von Paris, 1919." *Historische Zeitschrift* 197 (August 1963):1-101.

Dyer, Gwynne. "Turkish 'Falsifiers' and Armenian 'Deceivers': Historiography and the Armenian Massacres." *Middle Eastern Studies* 12 (1976):99-107.

Fest, W. B. "'British War Aims and German Peace Feelers During the First World War (December 1916-November 1918)." *The Historical Journal* 15 (June 1972): 285-308.

Finch, George A. "James Brown Scott, 1866-1943." *American Journal of International Law* 38 (April 1944):183-217.

Holsti, Rudolf. "Nicolas Politis." *American Journal of International Law* 36 (July 1942):475-79.

Hudson, Manley O. "The Proposed International Criminal Court." *American Journal of International Law* 32 (July 1938):549-54.

Hunt, Richard M. "Myths, Guilt, and Shame in Pre-Nazi Germany." *Virginia Quarterly Review* 34 (Summer 1958):355-71.

Karajian, Sarkis J. "An Inquiry into the Statistics of the Turkish Genocide of the Armenians, 1915-1918." *The Armenian Review* 25 (Winter 1972):3-44.

Kaul, Friedrich Karl. "Die Verfolgung Deutscher Kriegsverbrecher nach dem Ersten Weltkrieg." *Zeitschrift für Geschichtswissenschaft* (Berlin, E. Ger.) 14 (1966): 19-32.

Kazarian, Haigazn K. "The Genocide of Kharpert's Armenians: A Turkish Judicial Document and Cipher Telegrams Pertaining to Kharpert." *The Armenian Review* 19 (Spring 1966):16-23.

_____. "The Massacres and Deportations at Papert: Findings of a Turkish Military Court." *The Armenian Review* 25 (Autumn 1972):59-67.

_____. "Turkey Tries Its Chief Criminals: Indictment and Sentence Passed Down by Military Court of 1919." *The Armenian Review* 24 (Winter 1971):3-26.

_____. "A Turkish Military Court Tries the Principal Genocidists of the District of Yozgat." *The Armenian Review* 25 (Summer 1972):34-39.

Lauterpacht, H. "The Law of Nations and the Punishment of War Crimes." *The British Year Book of International Law* 21 (1944):58-95.

Luckau, Alma. "Unconditional Acceptance of the Treaty of Versailles By the German Government, June 22-28, 1919." *Journal of Modern History* 18 (September 1945):215-20.

McDougall, Walter A. "Political Economy versus National Sovereignty: French Structures for German Economic Integration after Versailles." *Journal of Modern History* 51 (March 1979):4-23.

Petri, Franz, and Peter Schöller. "Zur Bereinigung des Franktireurproblems vom August 1914." *Vierteljahrshefte für Zeitgeschichte* 9 (1961):234-48.

Renouvin, Pierre. "Les Buts de guerre du gouvernement français, 1914-1918." *Revue Historique* 235 (January-March 1966):1-38.

_____. "L'Opinion publique en France pendant la guerre 1914-1918." *Revue d'Histoire Diplomatique* 84 (October-December 1970):289-336.

Schwelb, Egon. "Crimes Against Humanity." *The British Year Book of International Law* 23 (1946):178-226.

Scott, Franklin D. "Gustav V. and Swedish Attitudes Toward Germany, 1915." *Journal of Modern History* 39 (June 1967):113-18.

Shiragian, Arshavir. "The Assassination of Dr. Behaeddin Shakir." *The Armenian Review* 19 (Autumn 1966): 17-31.

Snell, John. "Die Republic aus Versäumnissen Unterlassungen Führen 1918 aum Zusammenbruch der Monarchie." *Die Welt als Geschichte* 15 (1955): 196-219.

_____. "Wilsonian Rhetoric Goes to War." *The Historian* 14 (Spring 1952):191-208.

Sottile, Antoine. "The Problem of the Creation of a Permanent International Criminal Court." *Revue de Droit International de Sciences Diplomatiques et Politiques* 29 (October-December 1951):267-359.

Verseput, J. "De Kwestie van de Uitlevering van Ex-Keizer Wilhelm II." *Kleio: Orgaan van de Vereniging van Geschiedenisleraen in Nederland* 4 (November 1963):5-11.

Warman, Roberta M. "The Erosion of Foreign Office Influence in the Making of Foreign Policy, 1916-1918." *Historical Journal* 15 (March 1972):133-59.

Wilson, Robert R. "Standards of Humanitarianism in War." *American Journal of International Law* 34 (April 1940):320-24.

Wilson, Trevor. "The Coupon and the British General Election of 1918." *Journal of Modern History* 36 (March 1964):28-42.

BIBLIOGRAPHICAL AIDS

Higham, Robin, ed. *A Guide to the Sources of British Military History.* Berkeley and Los Angeles, Calif.: University of California Press, 1971.

Lewis, John R., comp. *Uncertain Judgment: A Bibliography of War Crimes Trials.* Santa Barbara, Calif.: American Bibliographical Center-Clio Press, 1979.

Schaffer, Ronald, comp. *The United States in World War I: A Selected Bibliography.* Santa Barbara, Calif.: American Bibliographical Center-Clio Press, 1978.

Stachura, Peter D. *The Weimar Era and Hitler, 1918-1933: A Critical Bibliography.* Oxford: Clio Press, 1977.

Watt, D. C. *Personalities and Policies: Studies in the Formulation of British Foreign Policy in the Twentieth Century.* South Bend, Ind.: University of Notre Dame Press, 1965.

INDEX

About the Author

James F. Willis, Associate Professor of Political Science at Southern Arkansas University in Magnolia, is a former Woodrow Wilson Fellow. His writings have appeared in scholarly journals.